**Discovering Lead**

## Discovering Leadership

This Reader, along with the companion volume *The Principles and Practice of Change* edited by Deborah Price, form part of the Open University course *Making it Happen! Leadership, Influence and Change* (B204), a 60 point level two undergraduate course. The course is a compulsory element of the Foundation Degree in Leadership and Management and the BA (Hons) Leadership and Management, and an optional course in the BA (Hons) Business Studies.

Details of this and other Open University courses can be obtained from the Student Registration and Enquiry Service, The Open University, PO Box 197, Milton Keynes MK7 6BJ, United Kingdom: tel. +44 (0)845 300 6090, e-mail general-enquiries@open.ac.uk

Alternatively, you may visit the Open University website at http://www.open.ac.uk where you can learn more about the wide range of courses and packs offered at all levels by The Open University.

# Discovering Leadership

Edited By

## Jon Billsberry

First published 2009 by
PALGRAVE MACMILLAN

Palgrave Macmillan in the UK is an imprint of Macmillan Publishers Limited, registered in England, company number 785998, of Houndmills, Basingstoke, Hampshire RG21 6XS.

Palgrave Macmillan in the US is a division of St Martin's Press LLC, 175 Fifth Avenue, New York, NY 10010.

Palgrave Macmillan is the global academic imprint of the above companies and has companies and representatives throughout the world.

Palgrave® and Macmillan® are registered trademarks in the United States, the United Kingdom, Europe and other countries.

ISBN-13: 978-0-230-57584-4
ISBN-10: 0-230-57584-6

This book is printed on paper suitable for recycling and made from fully managed and sustained forest sources. Logging, pulping and manufacturing processes are expected to conform to the environmental regulations of the country of origin.

A catalogue record for this book is available from the British Library.

A catalog record for this book is available from the Library of Congress.

10  9  8  7  6  5  4  3  2  1
18  17  16  15  14  13  12  11  10  09

Printed in Great Britain by Creative Print & Design (Wales), Ebbw Vale

# Contents

## Part I   Defining Leadership

## Part II   Effective Leadership

## Part III   Leadership: Image or Substance?

## Part VIII    Ethical Issues in Leadership

# Figures, Tables and Exhibit

## Figures

# Tables

# Exhibit

# Acknowledgements

The author and publishers are grateful to the following for permission to reproduce copyright material: Oxford University Press for extracts from K. Grint (1997) 'Reading Tolstoy's Wave', in K. Grint (ed.), *Leadership: Classical, Contemporary, and Critical Approaches*, pp. 1–10, 17. Harvard Business School Publishing for extracts from J. P. Kotter (1990) 'What Leaders Really Do', *Harvard Business Review*, May–June, pp. 103–11; B. Kellerman (2007) 'What Every Leader Needs to Know about Followership', *Harvard Business Review*, December, pp. 84–91. Elsevier for extracts from G. P. Hollenbeck, M. W. McCall, Jr and R. F. Silzer (2006) 'Leadership Competency Models', *Leadership Quarterly*, vol. 17, pp. 398–413; S. K. Johnson (2008) 'I Second that Emotion: Effects of Emotional Contagion and Affect at Work on Leader and Follower Outcomes', *Leadership Quarterly*, vol. 19, no. 1, pp. 1–19; M. C. Bligh, J. C. Kohles and J. R. Meindl (2004) 'Charisma under Crisis: Presidential Leadership, Rhetoric, and Media Responses before and after the September 11th Terrorist Attacks', *Leadership Quarterly*, vol. 15, pp. 211–39; K. A. Scott and D. J. Brown (2006) 'Female First, Leader Second? Gender Bias in the Encoding of Leadership Behavior', *Organizational Behavior and Human Decision Processes*, vol. 101, pp. 230–42; T. Scandura and P. Dorfman (2004) 'Leadership Research in an International and Cross-Cultural Context', *Leadership Quarterly*, vol. 15, pp. 277–307; J. Sonnenfeld and A. Ward (2008) 'Firing Back: How Great Leaders Rebound after Career Disasters', *Organizational Dynamics*, vol. 37, no. 1, pp. 1–20. John Wiley for extracts from J. M. Kouzes and B. Z. Posner (2007) 'The Five Practices of Exemplary Leadership', in J. M. Kouzes and B. Z. Posner (eds), *The Leadership Challenge*, 4th edn, pp. 3–25, copyright © Wiley. Sage for extracts from A. J. Morris, C. M. Brotheridge and J. C. Urbanski (2005) 'Bringing Humility to Leadership', *Human Relations*, vol. 58, no. 10, pp. 1323–50; D. M. Boje and C. Rhodes (2005) 'The Virtual Leader Construct: The Mass Mediatization and Simulation of Transformational Leadership', *Leadership*, vol. 1, no. 4, pp. 407–28; S. D. Baker (2007) 'Followership: The Theoretical Foundation of a Contemporary Construct', *Journal of Leadership and Organizational Studies*, vol. 14, no. 1, pp. 50–60, copyright © 2007 by *Journal of Leadership and Organizational*

*Studies*; R. Gill (2006) 'Leadership and Influence, Motivation and Inspiration', in R. Gill, *Theory and Practice of Leadership*, pp. 252–64; G. Morgan (1993) 'The Theory Behind the Practice', in G. Morgan, *Imaginization*, pp. 271–94; J. B. Ciulla (2004) 'Ethics and Leadership Effectiveness', in J. Antonakis, A. T. Cianciolo and R. J. Sternberg (eds), *The Nature of Leadership*, pp. 302–27. Cengage for extracts from J. Sandberg (2001) 'The Constructions of Social Constructionism', in S.-E. Sjöstrand, J. Sandberg and M. Tyrstrup (eds), *Invisible Management: The Social Construction of Leadership*, pp. 28–48. Wiley-Blackwell for extracts from F. Westley and H. Mintzberg (1989) 'Visionary Leadership and Strategic Management', *Strategic Management Journal*, vol. 10, pp. 17–32; A. H. Eagly (2007) 'Female Leadership Advantage and Disadvantage: Resolving the Contradictions', *Psychology of Women Quarterly*, vol. 31, pp. 1–12. Academy of Management for extracts from J. P. Doh (2003) 'Can Leadership be Taught? Perspectives from Management Educators', *Academy of Management Learning and Education*, vol. 2, no. 1, pp. 54–67; R. L. Kent and S. E. Moss (1994) 'Effects of Sex and Gender Role on Leader Emergence', *Academy of Management Journal*, vol. 37, no. 5, pp. 1335–46. Olivier Mythodrama Associates for extracts from R. Olivier (2002) *Inspirational Leadership: Henry V and the Muse of Fire*, pp. xxxv–xxxvii, 158–66. Every effort has been made to contact all the copyright-holders, but if any have been inadvertently omitted the publishers will be pleased to make the necessary arrangements at the earliest opportunity.

# A Leadership Curriculum

*Jon Billsberry*

## What is Leadership?

Leadership has attracted the attention of researchers for literally thousands of years. This is quite natural as there is a fascination with people who make a difference and are able to change other people's lives and the planet on which we live. Most of us want to be considered a leader. Fortunately, there is a vast literature to help us. Book shops contain racks full of tomes on leadership with lessons from politicians, generals, business executives, football managers and cartoon characters, all vying for our money. Libraries are storing a rapidly increasing number of journals devoted to the subject. All of which begs two questions: Why do we need another book on leadership? How is this one different?

Perhaps the most interesting feature of this book that sets it apart from others is that it is compiled by someone who does not believe that leadership exists. When I say I do not believe that leadership exists, I am not an agnostic in the sense that I am waiting for someone to convince me that they know what leadership is. Indeed, one of the peculiarities of the leadership literature is that there is no agreed definition of leadership nor any universal guidance on how to improve as a leader, which seems extraordinary given how much has been published on the subject. No, when I say I do not believe that leadership exists, I am an atheist. To my mind, the problem with leadership research is that we have spent all our time studying leaders hoping to establish universal truths about what they do, their characteristics and how situations influence them. But after thousands of years of research these universal truths remain elusive. My explanation is that leadership does not exist in the sense that it is a quality of individual leaders. I do not believe that there are any universals truths about what leaders do, their characteristics, or how they are influenced by events. Instead, I see leadership more like beauty; that is, it resides in the eye of the beholder. Just as every person assesses art, literature, films and performances differently and according to their own values, I believe that leadership is simply an epithet that we confer upon people whom we believe to have done things that we regard as 'leadership'. Everyone is different and has different experiences, so everyone has subtly different assessments of leadership. No wonder that we

1

cannot agree on who is a leader and who is not. So the first unusual element of this leadership book is that it is compiled by a leadership atheist.

Given my views, you might be wondering what this book contains. The articles divide into two types. The first type is a selection of articles that explore leadership from the perspective of the person observing the leader. This perspective is called 'social constructionism'. Although this idea has been around for a very long time, it is only relatively recently that it has been applied to leadership with any vigour. Amongst the articles taking this approach are those that explain the key assumptions and ideas of social constructionism. Others define leadership through this lens and others focus on particular aspects of leadership within this tradition.

The second type of article included in this book provides a grounding in the main leadership subjects. As this book is designed for someone new to the subject, it is vital that the book covers the core ideas in leadership. Also, if you are to appreciate why the social constructionist approach to leadership is important, it is necessary to know the basics of the subject and what the approach is reacting against. This point leads into the second reason for this book to exist: it serves as an introduction to the topic of leadership. But it differs from other leadership texts because it does this through the medium of previously published articles which are widely celebrated as describing leadership in interesting and profound ways.

So, in summary, there are two primary reasons that drove me, a leadership atheist, to produce yet another book on leadership. First, I wanted to give a voice to the social constructionist perspective on leadership. Second, I wanted to provide an exciting and interesting introduction to the topic.

## An Introductory Leadership Curriculum

This book serves as the reader, and the bulk of the course material, for an Open University Business School course looking at leadership, change and influence. The course is written for second year undergraduates and it is the first one that students receive on the subject of leadership. Therefore, no prior knowledge of leadership is assumed and this book has to introduce readers to the main ideas in the subject. Hence, the book begins with parts on defining leadership and leadership effectiveness. The third part offers a critical and contemporary perspective on these views by challenging the notion of leadership. The papers consider issues of celebrity, virtual leaders and provide some underpinning ideas on social constructionism. The fourth part puts the focus squarely on those people who are influenced by leaders. Followership is one of the 'hot' topics in leadership and it is interesting how much we are learning about leaders by observing their followers. The remaining parts of the book look at some key leadership issues. Part V considers at leadership emergence. Part VI examines how leaders inspire others focusing specifically on language and speech. Gender is the subject of Part VII while a consideration of ethical issues in leadership is the subject of the final part.

In each of these parts, the articles represent the very best of contemporary leadership writing by some of the very best people in the field. Almost all of the articles have been previously published, mainly as journal articles or as book chapters, and I have very lucky to have been able to cherry-pick whatever I wanted. In preparing the articles for this book, I have had to edit them. One practical reason was cost; a book that was 50,000 words longer would not have been economic. Regardless, I would have wanted to edit the articles anyway. Some material that is necessary for a journal audience is not necessarily useful for a student audience. Furthermore, I wanted to draw out the main leadership points and remove some of the material that requires some prior knowledge (such as advanced statistics) to understand. In editing the texts, I hope I have not distorted the original authors' intentions. That certainly was not my purpose. Also, I must note that whilst this book has a general social constructionist slant to it, by no means could all of the authors in this book be said to belong to this perspective. Many certainly are not. However, as I chose and edited the articles, I found that even those that adopt a more traditional approach to leadership could be interpreted from a social constructionist perspective.

There are three main elements to the teaching materials in the Open University course that this book accompanies. In addition to this book, students receive a study guide that highlights issues of interest which are debated in online discussion groups. The third element is a set of twelve feature films on DVD. Given that the general approach of the course is to view leadership through the eyes of the observer, students need a common frame of reference to measure how their perceptions differ to other people. In this way, they can discuss leadership meaningfully and discover their own views. The following films are those we included in the first presentation of the course. The first four broadly map onto the first four parts. Thereafter, the films are paired in parts V to VIII.

1. Erin Brockovich *(Steven Soderbergh, 2000)*
2. Lawrence of Arabia *(David Lean, 1962)*
3. Carry On Cleo *(Gerald Thomas, 1963)*
4. Spartacus *(Stanley Kubrick, 1960)*
5. Diarios de Motocicleta *(The Motorcycle Diaries, Walter Salles, 2004)*
6. Aliens *(James Cameron, 1986)*
7. The Chronicle History of King Henry the Fift with His Battell Fought at Agincourt in France *(Henry V, Laurence Olivier, 1944)*
8. Henry V *(Kenneth Branagh, 1989)*
9. The Great Escape *(John Sturges, 1963)*

10. Chicken Run *(Peter Lord and Nick Park, 2000)*
11. Gandhi *(Richard Attenborough, 1982)*
12. Mother India *(Mehboob Khan, 1957)*

Overall, the purpose of this book is to support an introductory course leadership. I hope the articles interest and inspire you to study leadership in more depth. In the rest of this introductory chapter, you will find a more detailed summary of each of the articles included in this book.

# Part I  Defining Leadership

The set of three articles focuses on a definition of leadership. What is leadership? How has it been defined? How is leadership different from management? These are questions that have occupied leadership writers for millennia and although we may not have definitive answers, some agreement is emerging. The first article in this collection was written by Keith Grint. It formed the introduction to his book, *Leadership: Classical, Contemporary, and Critical Approaches.* In this article, he writes about his own frustration in trying to come to terms with the leadership literature. He began reading the leadership literature with the goal of identifying the 'necessary aspects of leadership', but gave up when his list reached 127. He then turned to the binary opposites that he found in the literature (e.g. management vs. leadership, transactional vs. transformational, one best way vs. contingent), but realised that this list was also potentially endless. Instead, he turned his attention to developing a model that allowed him to categorise all of these different approaches to leadership. His simple two-by-two model is particularly successful in capturing the essence of different approaches. Crucially, it highlights a relatively new approach, termed constitutive leadership, which occurs when it is thought impossible to understand the exact nature of the person or the situation in which leadership is recorded. This approach is based on a constructionist view of the world (i.e. reality is created in the mind of the observer; see the Sandberg article for more on this) and it offers an interesting way to conceptualise leadership in our complex world.

The second article was written by me. In it, I have tried to add richness to Grint's model of leadership. In his article, he summarises many of the main leadership theories and plots them on two-by-two grid. I wanted to describe these leadership theories and explore their correct standing. This is important because this book very rapidly disappears down the social constructivist road to leadership and it is important that people new to the subject of leadership have a grounding in the main ideas and theories from which this text departs. In describing these theories, I have attempted to put them into their historical context and show how they evolved as a natural progression.

The article by John Kotter explores the age-old issue of how, if at all, leadership differs from management. He notes that many organisations are run by people who have proven themselves to be effective managers, but they are not necessarily good leaders. Indeed, his definition of management as being about coping with complexity is a crucial survival skill in most organisations. Leadership, he argues, is different. It is about coping with change. These are not mutually exclusive, but neither does one naturally accompany the other.

# Part II  Effective Leadership

James Kouzes and Barry Posner's book on leadership, *The Leadership Challenge*, may be the most successful contemporary book on leadership. Its attraction is that it offers a highly intuitive and appealing model of leadership with sensible guidance for those want to improve their leadership capabilities. They argue that leadership is found everywhere and that everyone can take on leadership roles. For them, leadership is about guiding others along pioneering journeys and they believe that there are five practices of exemplary leadership: Model the way; inspire a shared vision, challenge the process, enable others to act, and encourage the heart. The paper in this volume is taken from the first chapter of their best-selling book and it illustrates these practices beautifully with two in-depth case studies.

One of the recent changes in direction that leadership research has taken is to take the subject of emotions seriously. This important area of psychology has been largely ignored for many years, but its power in shaping leaders and leadership is undeniable. Whether it be the way that leaders' emotions 'infect' their followers with the same emotion, or the way that the leadership messages play to followers' emotions, or the way that leaders' phrasing reflects their own mood, emotions undoubtedly play a major role in defining the success or failure of leaders. One of the leading writers on emotion is Daniel Goleman. His book *Emotional Intelligence*, which was first published in 1995, did much to spark interest in the area. The article in this volume was not taken from this book, but instead is an article that Goleman wrote with Richard Boyatzis and Annie McKee for *Harvard Business Review* in 2001 that specifically focuses on the role of emotion in leadership. The authors conclude by arguing that managing your mood is an essential ingredient for leaders that determines much of their success.

The final paper in this part look at the popularity of competency models of leadership. Broadly speaking, competency models outline a suite of skills and abilities in which leaders must be competent in order to be effective. These are controversial for many reasons, most notably because they are argue that the causes of leadership effectiveness are known, can be developed and are based on a single set of characteristics. To some eyes, competency models of leadership are merely the latest fad in leadership whereas to others they represent an effective way of improving leadership in organisations. This debate was captured in an exchange of letters between George P. Hollenbeck and Morgan W. McCall, Jr. on one side of the debate and Robert Silzer on the other. Unfortunately, space constraints means that the full exchange of letters cannot be captured in this volume, but nevertheless, the first exchange of letters captures the strength of feelings on both sides of the debate and, crucially, the terrain on which the battle is being fought.

## Part III   Leadership: Image or Substance?

The first paper in this part is written by Andrew Morris, Céleste Brotheridge and John Urbanski. Their paper explores the role of humility in leadership. Noting the popular upsurge of celebrity CEOs, the authors argue that effective leadership functioning is most likely to reside in humility, celebrity's antithesis, with humility being defined as 'a personal orientation founded on a willingness to see the self accurately and a propensity to put oneself in perspective'. In defining humility in this way, the authors position leadership close to the concept of servant leadership with the idea that leaders 'serve' rather than 'lead'.

The chapter by Jörgen Sandberg is a little different from the others in this book as it offers a subject introduction rather than a theoretical or empirical development. The subject he introduces is social constructionism. This perspective is important because it offers the underpinning theory to Grint's constitutive approach to leadership and offers a critique of many of the mainstream leadership theories. Sandberg's chapter is impressive in the way it conveys an understanding of some fairly scary-looking words and phrases (e.g. dualistic ontology, individualistic epistemology, objective reality, phenomenological) in a clear and meaningful way without at any point patronising the reader.

David Boje and Carl Rhodes's paper addresses what happens when corporations deliberately create a non-human image of a leader such as Ronald McDonald or Colonel Sanders. Such leaders become fabricated and 'virtualised' through the mass media. Nevertheless, they have considerable influence and the authors argue that such leaders play a powerful transformational leadership role for their corporations. Interestingly, the authors argue that the power of these leaders becomes stronger the more virtualised they become.

## Part IV   Exploring Followership

Over the past twenty years, leadership researchers have shown an increasing interest in followership. Whereas leaders had been studied in isolation from those that they led, the two constituencies are now seen by many as inseparable. As Susan Baker puts it in her paper, there has been a 'transition from the traditional view of a passive, unthinkingly obedient subordinate who was led by a Great Man to a contemporary image of an active, participative, effective follower who must be studied in relation to his or her leader'. Baker's paper tells the history of followership and, in the process, teases out its nature and characteristics.

Barbara Kellerman takes a different perspective on followership. She looks at it from the perspective of the leader and asks how leaders can 'manage' their followers. In doing so, she produces a typology of five different types of followers based on their level of engagement with the leader. The five categories, in order of increasing engagement, are isolates, bystanders, participants, activists and diehards. She defines and describes each form of follower and offers a commentary on some of the issues leaders have working with each type of follower.

The final article in this part focuses on one of the key processes influencing the interaction of leaders and followers, emotional contagion. In her article, Stefanie Johnson looks at how the leader's affect (i.e. the experience of feeling or emotion) influences followers' affect. The results of her empirical study suggest that the emotions of the leader do indeed transfer to others in the organisation and that these relate to performance outcomes. As she says, 'leaders should be advised of the potential effects of their expressed affect' on followers. Emotions, it seems, are catching.

## Part V  Leadership Emergence

Frances Wesley and Henry Mintzberg begin their article powerfully with a metaphor. They fear that the more we try to understand leadership, the more we risk losing its meaning. As they say, 'in attempting to dissect a living phenomenon, the skeleton may be revealed while the specimen dies'. In the body of their paper, the authors focus on visionary leadership as drama, viewing it as dynamic and interactive phenomenon as opposed to a unidirectional one. Then, they define five different types of visionary leaders – the creator, the proselytiser, the idealist, the bricoleur and the diviner – and provide an example of each one.

Many leaders are defined by their rhetoric and oratory. Winston Churchill, John F. Kennedy and Martin Luther King Jr. are leaders who readily spring to mind. George W. Bush is less commonly seen as a great speaker. Indeed, he has been described as having a 'troubled relationship with the English language' (Kornblut, 2001, as cited in the Bligh, Kohles and Meindl paper). It might be thought as strange that his oratory is singled out for analysis by Michelle Bligh, Jeffrey Kohles and James Meindl. However, by analysing his speeches before and after the 9/11 crisis, the researchers were able to demonstrate that his language became more charismatic, that the media's portrayal of him also reflected an increase in charismatic rhetoric, and that there was an increased receptivity to more charismatically based leadership after the crisis.

The third paper in this part moves away from visions and crises and looks at the emergence of leadership through planned efforts. It examines whether leadership can be taught with a particular focus on business leadership. The paper is written by Jonathan Doh who interviewed some of the leading figures in management education noted for teaching leadership. His article relates their views in response to some key questions: Can leadership be taught? How can leadership be taught? To whom can leadership be taught? By whom can leadership be taught? Despite operating in similar situations, it is interesting how much the correspondents' views differ and how much of the discussion is perceptual rather than factual, leading to the inescapable conclusion that we still have a lot to learn about how to teach leadership.

# Part VI   Inspiring Others

The first article in this part has been crafted from Roger Gill's book, *Theory and Practice of Leadership*. The part I have included focuses on inspiration; in particular, on how leaders frame language and can craft their rhetoric. The article offers some practical guidance and echoes two other cases in this book. First, Gill relates and analyses George W. Bush's speech to Congress in September 2001, which embellishes the chapter by Bligh, Kohles and Meindl. Gill supplies a reading of Henry V, which provides a useful overview of the work drawing out leadership matters prior to the focused attention given to the Crispian Day speech in Olivier's chapter.

Few speeches have had the impact of Henry V's rousing speech to his soldiers prior to the Battle of Agincourt. His Crispian's Day speech has served as a model of inspirational speeches for centuries. More than just a model, many have borrowed from or have alluded to it. Winston Churchill, for example, referring back to 'we happy few' and the spirit of the underdog, famously said of the Battle of Britain airmen, 'Never in the field of human conflict was so much owed by so many to so few'. The second article in this part contains Richard Olivier's analysis of the great speech. An interesting aside is that this speech illustrates the notion of the 'powerful voice'. We have no idea whether or not Henry V actually said the words that Shakespeare attributed to him, but it matters not. Shakespeare has made Henry V the great wartime leader who inspires great heroic deeds with his rhetoric.

The third article in this part has been crafted from Gareth Morgan's influential book, *Imaginization*. The word 'imaginization' was coined by Morgan to fuse two concepts, imagination and organisation. It is about 'creative possibility' or, as Morgan puts it, 'it seeks to open the process of organizing to an expansive, creative mode of thinking'. On his website, he describes it as 'an invitation to develop new ways of thinking about organization and management'. Metaphors are a crucial element to imaginization, and in his book Morgan explains both the role of metaphors in helping us understand our environment and also how metaphors work. According to Morgan, 'metaphorical images can provide powerful tools for helping people look at themselves and their situations in new ways and, as a result, see and act in the world somewhat differently'. Given this, their role in leadership is important.

## Part VII  Gender Issues

For many generations, leadership was a study of 'Great Men', as noted in the chapters by Billsberry and Baker. These days, construing leadership as a study of 'Great Men' is not just theoretically incorrect, it is also objectionable. Society has changed and so has business. Women now have the right to be treated as badly as men in the workplace. This is not a flippant turn of phrase, for whilst woman may have the right to be treated as equal as men in the workplace, they are less well represented in senior positions than they should be. Although time lags and career issues may explain some of the difference, there are clearly some important barriers causing the discrepancy. Perceptions are one key factor and it is perceptions that Alice Eagly explores in her paper. She reviews the leadership literature on gender difference and reveals many interesting facts. One of which is the finding that men have an advantage gaining jobs that are seen as male and women have an advantage in gaining jobs that are seen as female, most leadership posts have perceived as male even though women might have better leadership skills than men.

Although predating Eagly's chapter by thirteen years and coming from a different generation of leadership gender research, the paper by Russell Kent and Sherry Moss is particularly interesting. They raise a fundamental question: To what extent can a woman be a 'woman' and still emerge as a leader? This research addresses the commonly heard criticism of female leaders such as Margaret Thatcher who are considered by some to be successful because they behave in a typically 'masculine' fashion. The authors looked at whether possessing male, female or androgynous characteristics are better than actual genders in determining who emerges as a leader. Their data produces a thought-provoking finding: 'the possession of feminine characteristics does not decrease an individual's chances of emerging as a leader *as long as the individual also possesses masculine characteristics*' [emphasis added].

The final paper in this part investigates the process by which we make our assessments of people as leaders. Kristyn Scott and Douglas Brown are interested in gender stereotypes and whether people perceive similar characteristics in leaders when they observe men and women in those roles. Interestingly, they found that when a leader was seen adopting male leadership behaviours, men and women where regarded differently, but when they were adopting female leadership behaviours, there was no difference. Hence, they found an innate gender bias in the ways that people are assessed against leadership stereotypes. The authors conclude by suggesting that this phenomenon may undermine the effectiveness of female leaders.

## Part VIII   Ethical Issues

Was Hitler a leader? You might think this a stupid question: 'Of course he was. His impact may have very been destructive and evil, but there is no denying that he inspired a whole nation to fight a war that at one point created an empire stretching over half of Europe. Only victor's hindsight logic would deny him the epithet of "leader" '. Joanne Ciulla takes a different view. In her paper she considers ethics and leadership effectiveness and specifically looks at the case of Hitler. She argues that according to normative theories of leadership (i.e. those that look at what leaders *should* do), Hitler was not a leader at all. 'He was a bully or tyrant or simply the head of Germany'. In the remainder of her paper, Ciulla looks at different ethical aspects of leadership and concludes by arguing that the responsibility of leaders is to 'create the social and material conditions under which people can and do flourish'.

The second paper in this part is another exchange of letters. This time the correspondents are Terri Scandura and Peter Dorfman. Sadly, space constraints only permit the inclusion of the first exchange of letters. Nevertheless, these contain an excellent overview of international and cross-cultural issues in leadership and, in particular, an overview of the influential GLOBE project, which is occupying 170 researchers in 62 nations in data collection and analysis. The exchange of letters begin with a discussion of *Time* magazine's 'Man of the Year' award in 2001 when the man who might have been thought to have had the most impact on history in that year was Osama bin Laden. This is followed by a discussion of the findings of the GLOBE project including a comparison of the Anglo and Middle East clusters which highlights differences in the ways that leadership is defined in these regions.

The final paper in the book looks at what happens to leaders when they fail or fall from grace. Leadership is a rocky road with its ups and downs. And at some point on that journey, most leaders will suffer setbacks; some minor, some major. Jeffrey Sonnenfeld and Andrew Ward interviewed American business people who had experienced career disasters and drew lessons from the way they rebounded, or didn't. The authors argue that the way that leaders handle adversity is critical to their success and such events often have a silver lining. It helps leaders discover whom they can trust and what they really value. Leaders who can learn from their misfortunes, can return stronger.

# Acknowledgements

Many people have helped me make this project a reality and I want to thank them all. Knowing that I am sure to miss some, for which I genuinely apologise, I must mention Caroline Ramsey, the Course Team Chair of B204 *Making It Happen! Leadership, Influence and Change*, for which course this book is one of the readers. The two Course Managers, Emir Forken and Jo Woods, have helped tremendously in smoothing the way and being supportive of my direction. Without their help, this book would certainly not have seen the light of day in its current form. In the Open University's media department, Gill Gowans has championed this book and been particularly helpful in relations with our publisher, Palgrave Macmillan. And I want to thank Palgrave's Commissioning Editor, Ursula Gavin for her help and accommodation throughout the project. But without diminishing any of the above contributions, I want to make special note of the help of Chris Carter, who helped me find, assess and reference suitable articles.

# Part I
## Defining Leadership

# Reading Tolstoy's Wave

# 1

*Keith Grint*

In whatever direction a ship moves the flow of waves it cuts will always be noticeable ahead of it...When the ship moves in one direction there is one and the same wave ahead of it, when it turns frequently the wave ahead of it also turns frequently. But wherever it may turn there always will be the wave anticipating its movement. Whatever happens it appears that just that event was foreseen and decreed. Wherever the ship may go, the rush of water which neither directs nor increases its movement foams ahead of it, and at a distance seems not merely to move of itself but to govern the ship's movement also.

*(Tolstoy, 1991, p. 1289)*

What is leadership? Tolstoy's bow-wave metaphor for leadership is an extremely fruitful but enigmatic answer: it suggests that leaders are mere figureheads, propelled by events which are beyond their control, even though it appears that events are controlled by them. It also suggests that views about leaders may themselves be subject to fashion and fads – that is, that we may consider certain kinds of leadership more appropriate for certain conditions or that what counts as leadership itself changes across space and time. One thing is clear: leaders are in front of those they lead – but the enigma surrounds the issue of whether they are pulling or being pushed by those behind them. The distinction is not just concerned with what leaders are doing but also with what followers are doing. Can you be a leader without followers? Do followers make leaders by acting as followers? Is the relationship between leading and following a virtuous/vicious circle or is it possible to specify that an action by one of the parties involved must logically precede the other? Bow waves/ leaders may not have anything to do with the direction and speed of the vessel/organization, but does that mean that ships/organizations can move without creating a bow-wave leader? Leaders may not be logically necessary to organizational success, but have we become so accustomed to their exis- tence that we can no longer think them away, even in a thought experiment? Even Dilbert's (Adams, 1996) satirical view on leadership – nature's way of

Grint, K. (1997) 'Reading Tolstoy's Wave', in Grint, K. (ed.) Leadership: Classical, Contemporary, and Critical Approaches, Oxford, Oxford University Press, pp. 1–26.

removing morons from the productive flow – implies that leadership is an essential element of life. Current research certainly suggests that leaders can make a difference to the performance of business organization, perhaps by as much as 10 per cent in annual earnings either way – which also suggests that 90 per cent has little to do with the particular leader in place. However, a 10 per cent change in fortunes for a business, hospital, charity, sports team, or army may be a considerable amount, particularly when the going gets tough (Useem, 1996).

[ ... ] Anyone who has been studying leadership will know that it is an exponentially accelerating arena, though this does not mean we are getting ever nearer understanding what leadership is. In the 1980s there were, very roughly, five articles a day being published on leadership in the English language; by the 1990s this had doubled to ten a day. If this increase persists we shall run out of wood before we can see the tree.

The irony is that so many leaders appear to have led very well without ever reading a book on leadership. One implication of this is that leadership cannot be taught: either you can do it or you cannot. It would be strange if leadership was the only human skill that could not be enhanced through understanding and practice. Perhaps a reflection on musical talent can be considered as an equivalent; are not musical talent and leadership talent both innate gifts? Well, the former is not according to Howe, Davidson, and Sloboda (1996), for, despite the common assumption that some children are naturally talented and others simply incapable of ever learning a note, their research on 200 young musicians suggests that practice, not innate talent, makes perfect. Granted, we are not all going to be turned into professional musicians by a music course, nor world leaders through a leadership course, but this does not mean that one's skill as a leader cannot be improved, notably through practice. Granted some children do seem to be self-evidently better leaders than others from a very early age, though this does not mean they are born leaders, since it may derive from childhood experiences. Nor does it mean that such children grow up to retain whatever leadership skills they appear to have; we simply do not know enough about this to come down on one side of the debate or the other. Indeed, since what counts as leadership appears to change quite radically across time and space, as the waves of fortune and fashion wash across the world, even some kind of systematic and objective research at this point in time and space would not solve Tolstoy's enigmatic wave problem.

An initial reading of leadership material might tend to produce a list of traits, characteristics, and behaviours that leaders are supposed to have – though my preliminary attempt to reproduce the 'ideal' leader ran out of space on one side of paper after I had passed number 127 on the 'necessary-aspects-of-leadership' list. Another approach might be to list the polarities that tend to be generated in such an exercise. For example, such a list might contain any or all of the following binary opposites:

| | | |
|---|---|---|
| management | vs. | leadership |
| leadership | vs. | followership |
| task-oriented | vs. | people-oriented |
| born leaders | vs. | made leaders |
| theory X | vs. | theory Y |
| transactional | vs. | transformational |
| one best way | vs. | contingent |
| how to do it | vs. | what to do |
| doing the right things | vs. | doing the things right |
| essentialist | vs. | non-essentialist |
| taught | vs. | experiential learning |
| charismatic | vs. | ordinary |
| forceful | vs. | enabling |
| people | vs. | people and things |

Such lists are potentially infinite and I make no pretence that this one is either representative or even valid; the point is that we may well tend to perceive leadership in such oppositional terms and this may not be the most appropriate way to analyse or develop leadership. [ ... ]

An alternative to the 'bipolar-shopping-list' approach is to resort to the familiar 2 × 2 in an attempt to keep the variables down to a minimum so that some progress in understanding might be made at the cost of losing a considerable amount of data and complexity. [ ... ] I want to generate yet another model so that the reader may have some grasp of where current research seems to be leading. The most significant divisions at present appear, at least to me, to be twofold. First, around the significance allocated to the individual, as opposed to the situation or context the individual is in. Second, and cross-cutting this division, is one rooted in the traditional split between objective and subjective assumptions about knowledge and data. The resulting model – which is grounded in positions along a continuum rather than opposites – does not encompass all positions nor all the current approaches, but it does represent a useful approach to leadership based on ideal types – heuristic extremes not typical cases. In other words, this is not the *best* way to see leadership, because it seems to me impossible to validate the claim that such a thing exists. Rather, I am suggesting that this model encompasses epistemologically and methodologically different perspectives on leadership that should facilitate a greater understanding of the readings that follow.[1] Since the readings are not based on the model, it would be foolhardy to assume that they fit neatly into any of the quadrants. However, it should be possible to make greater sense of the readings once the model is understood. In this instance the term 'essentialist' implies that we can acquire a definitive/objective account of the phenomenon under investigation; the term 'non-essentialist' implies this is not possible.

In the *trait* approach the 'essence' of the individual leader is critical but the context is not. In short, a leader is a leader under any circumstances, and it is more than likely that such traits are part of the individual's genetic make-up – otherwise the circumstances of the situation that faced the individual at some time in his or her life would have had an influence upon his or her leadership 'traits'. This kind of model implies that organizations should concern themselves with the selection of leaders rather than their development, though traits can, presumably, be honed, just as one's singing can be improved through training or one's athletic ability can be improved. However, since – in this approach – you cannot 'make a silk purse out of a sow's ear', there is no hope for those of us not born with certain gifts or talents for leadership.

In the *contingency* approach both the essence of the individual and the content are knowable and critical. Here one would expect individuals to generate an awareness of their own leadership skills and of the context so that they can compute the degree of alignment between themselves and the context. Where the permutation of the two suggests a high level of alignment – for instance, where a strong leader and a crisis situation coincide – then the leader should step into the breach, only to step out when the situation changes and the context is no

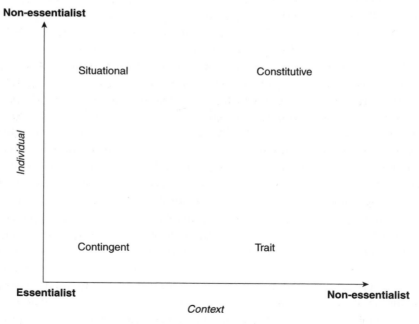

**Figure 1.1** Essentialist and non-essentialist leadership

longer conducive to their vigorous style. Self-awareness and situational analysis are the two developmental areas for such approaches to concentrate upon.

The third variant, the *situational* approach, reproduces the essentialist position with regard to the context – certain contexts demand certain kinds of leadership; however, in this model the leader may be flexible enough to generate a repertoire of styles to suit the particular situation. In effect, the leader's actions and behaviour change to suit the situation. The consequent development work required is both in terms of situational analysis and in terms of expanding the variety or versatility of the leader.

The final, and most recent, model here, the *constitutive* approach, receives most attention because it is the newest and least understood (see Grint, 1995, pp. 124–61). It is derived from constructivist theories in social science and, in its most radical formats, rejects the notion of essences entirely (see Grint and Woolgar, 1997). That is to say, it rejects the idea that we can ever have an objective account of either individual or situation because all such accounts are derived from linguistic reconstructions; they are not, in effect, transparent reproductions of the truth. Instead the approach suggests that what the situation and the leader actually are is a consequence of various accounts and interpretations, all of which vie for domination. Thus we know what a leader or situation is actually like only because some particular version of him, her, or it has secured prominence. The relativism at the heart of the approach does not mean that all interpretations are equal – and that what the leader/context is, is wholly a matter of the whim of the observer – but that some interpretations appear to be more equal than others. For example, my account of a popular individual may be that he or she is an incompetent charlatan, but if the popularity of this person rests upon the support of more powerful 'voices' (including material resources), then my negative voice will carry little or no weight. The critical issue for this approach, then, is not what the leader or the context is 'really' like, but what are the processes by which these phenomena are constituted into successes or failures, crises or periods of calm, and so on. For example, when the chief executive officer (CEO) declares an impending crisis based on information that must remain confidential to prevent the crisis deepening, how are we mere ignorant subordinates to evaluate the claim? When governments declare military 'incidents' to be 'the mother of all victories', how are we to judge? Do we ever really know what happened? When the media represent leaders as villains or heroes, do we really know enough about them to agree or disagree? The point of this approach, therefore, is to suggest that we may never know what the true essence of the leader or the situation actually is and must often base our actions and beliefs on the accounts of others from whom we can (re)constitute our version of events. This does not mean that leaders are simply at the hands of their followers who attribute to their leader whatever they want. It may be that leaders 'fail' to deliver the charismatic performance we expect from them – but what counts as a charismatic performance is still an issue for debate. Nor does it mean that the powerful institutions that control information in our societies can promote and sustain individuals who are blatantly incompetent – though a quick look at the current crop suggests I may be completely wrong here. But it does mean we may only ever achieve an opaque account of 'the truth'. In terms of leadership development, the approach suggests that the ancient study of rhetoric provides one significant element of leadership training since it may be persuasive powers that hold the key to leadership success. Political network-ing, interpersonal skills, material wealth, and negotiating skills are the hallmark of this approach. [ ... ].

However, [ ... ] it is worth reconsidering in a little detail the work of Heifetz, since it is this work that is probably stimulating the most interest today. Heifetz, both in his book *Leadership Without Easy Answers* (1994), and in his leadership courses at Harvard, combines a relatively novel theme – about forcing subordi-nates to reflect upon their influence in the achievement of goals – and a relatively old theme – about the difference between situations that require mechanistic responses (technical issues) and those that require 'adaptive' responses (leader-ship). In so far as Heifetz also distinguishes between the exercise of 'authority' and the exercise of 'leadership' – sometimes labelled power derived from formal role and power derived from informal role – Heifetz also hinges his ideas on a distinction familiar to Weber and many others since. Hence, for Heifetz, the critical issue is whether people have the ability and skill or whatever to intervene in situations that are not routine and in which the answer cannot be derived from previous experience, and where part of the role of the leader is to reflect the problem-solving back into the followers. In sum, the leader must not take on the mantle of magician himself or herself. Heifetz is one of the few leader-ship writers that has made a significant contribution to the debate, and I have no doubt that the refusal of leaders to own the problem is simultaneously the best way to create organizational learning and responsibility, and the best way for leaders to make themselves unpopular with followers whose expectations are premised upon more traditional notions of leadership. Storr (1996), for example, notes how 'gurus' – such as Bhagwan Shree Rajneesh, Jim Jones, and Shoko Asahara – appear to own the problem of purpose and provide meaning for their followers in a way that galvanizes their physical and mental power as well as enervating their critical moral faculties. On the other hand, if we pursue the constitutive model of leadership then it should be apparent that what counts as a situation requiring adaptive or technical work is not something that inheres in the situation itself but is, rather, the consequence of persuasive accounts of the situation. In other words, it may not be that leadership is required when the situation demands it – a derivative of the situational and contingency approaches we have already discussed – but that it is leadership which constitutes the situ-ation as one requiring adaptive or technical work. Hence, the question is less one of being able to analyse the situation and take whatever action is necessary and more one of taking action to provide an analysis of the situation in which adaptive or technical work appears the most appropriate. Let us explore an example to clarify this problem.

Suppose to a tribe that was constantly at war with its neighbour a new invader appeared. Should the response be such that the invader is deemed to have been beaten back by conventional means then we have what Heifetz would call an exercise in authority rather than leadership and in technical rather than adaptive work – the tried-and-tested contingency plan for invaders which has always worked in the past, worked again. Now suppose that the following year the invader reappears and the leader of the tribe fails to respond appropriately – manifest in a successful incursion by the invaders – this is the point at which an exercise of leadership is needed, quite possibly from someone without formal authority, and where adaptive rather than technical work is required. In this scene William Wallace now emerges from an obscure position to lead the Scottish nation against the invading English after the conventional figures of Scottish authority failed. So what was initially a form of technical work moved into a form of adaptive work *when the situation required it*. Thus, in Heifetz's approach, it is the *situation* which deems whether technical or adaptive work is required – though whether the appropriate work is executed depends upon the individuals not upon the situation: there is no situational determinism in here.

Now let us rerun the film to see where the constitutive models offer a different perspective on the scene. In this case we have – to the Scots – the all-too-familiar English invasion. But this time it is not the situation that self-evidently cries out for adaptive work; instead it is the participants who persuade their colleagues that either adaptive work or technical work is necessary. In short, we see William Wallace persuading his Scottish colleagues that the situation is a crisis, and a novel crisis at that, where adaptive not technical work is needed. At this point one hears the all-too-common division between: 'Crisis? What crisis?' and the oppositional cry of 'Run' or 'Fight' and so on. On the one hand, the calmness of the technical approach steadies the fears of the troops as the enemy approaches. On the other hand, the very same calmness instils a degree of misplaced confidence that merely increases the likelihood of defeat. To reiterate, the point here is whether the situation determines what the action should be or whether the rhetorical action of the participants constitutes the situation – from which further action may follow. Thus Dunkirk, during the Second World War, is either a situation of gross incompetence and a humiliating defeat for the British army or it is a miraculous example of true British character in the face of impossible odds. The point is not that the situation of Dunkirk must, objectively, have been one or the other but that what Dunkirk was is a consequence of the way leaders constituted the events. In effect, Churchill's rhetoric, combined with close control over the media – including patriotic self-control-ensured that the Dunkirk 'situation' became the Dunkirk 'miracle' and not the Dunkirk 'humiliation'.

Let us now take an opposite tack and consider a business situation that was 'obviously' one where certain kinds of leadership were appropriate but were not taken. We now travel forward fifty years to 1991 and we have left Churchill's 'Never before have so many owed so much to so few' rhetoric at the nadir of British hopes, to pick up Gerald Ratner, owner and CEO of what was then the largest jewellery chain in the world with 34 per cent of the market. Here is Ratner talking about Ratner's business philosophy at the apex, rather than the nadir, of his organization's fortunes:

> We also do this nice sherry decanter, it's cut glass and it comes complete with six glasses on a silver plated tray that your butler could bring you in and serve you drinks on. And it only costs £4.95. People say to me: 'how can you sell this for such a low price?' I say: 'Because it's total crap' (laughter)...We even sell a pair of earrings for under a pound; gold earrings as well. Some people say: 'that's less than a prawn sandwich at Marks and Spencers', but I have to say that the sandwich will probably last longer!' (laughter) (BBC2, 1995)

Now the point might be that the situation – a speech to business leaders – is not the place to deliver self-mocking humour of this variety; indeed, it seems an act of consummate folly, of appalling leadership, that, in Ratner's words, 'cost the company a few hundred million pounds, £100 million, £200 million? Personally it cost me everything' (ibid.). Assuming this is not the consequence of some kind of commercial death wish, is there anything that the constitutive variant can explain which 'common sense' and situational analysis cannot? Well perhaps. After all, it is the case that Ratner had told these jokes on numerous occasions to similar audiences for the previous four years and they had been printed in the *Financial Times* in December 1987 – over three years before his leadership 'mistake'. It may be, therefore, that what is critical is not what the situation is but what it is made into by those with the power to make it – in this case the popular newspaper writers and editors who deemed it appropriate to splash the jokes on the front of their papers for several days after. Here, then, is a situation that appears to be identical – Ratner has used these jokes before in public but this time it backfires, not because the situation is *actually* different, but because powerful people make the situation different through their actions; in effect, to misquote a current insurance advert, they make a crisis out of a drama.

To sum up, the constitutive approach does not involve doubts about the moral basis of Heifetz's approach – leaders do appear to make unpopular decisions that, often with hindsight, can be justified as necessary. Nor does it deny the importance of leadership. However, it does assert that an epistemological question mark hangs over all of the issues. Thus, whether the situation is a crisis, whether the actions of the authority figure are appropriate actions for the situation, whether acts taken by anyone are acts of 'leadership' or not, and so on are issues that are contingent on the power of persuasive accounts and not contingent on objective or rational analysis. The consequence of this approach is to return us back to the beginning of the debate: it suggests that leadership is essentially interwoven with acts of persuasion; it does not offer a definitive account on the ethical aspects of leadership; indeed, it denies the plausibility of any account that deems itself to be definitive. It suggests we concentrate not just on what leaders do and what the situation is, but on the formative issues that lie behind these phenomena: how do we know what a leader does, and how are we persuaded that a situation is $X$ and that a leader should do $Y$ in such a situation? Finally, let me reaffirm that this does not mean that leadership is whatever anyone wants it to be; it is what certain powerful 'voices' make it. All voices may be equal but some are more equal than others. To resume our ride with Tolstoy, it is not that leaders are those who identify the wave and ride it; rather, leaders are those that persuade us a wave is coming, who go out of their way to appear the most visible surfers to the onlookers, and whose actions are taken by the onlookers as actions appropriate for leaders to take. [ ... ]

## Note

1. Editor's Note: Although Grint's comment refers to a different book, it is equally relevant to this volume.

## References

Adams, S. (1996) *The Dilbert Principle*, New York, Harper Business.

BBC2 (1995) *My Brilliant Career: Ratner, Lord of the Rings*, London: BBC, 4 January.

Grint, K. (1995) *Management: A Sociological Introduction*, Cambridge, Polity Press.

Grint, K. and Woolgar, S. (1997) *The Machine at Work: Technology, Work and Organization*, Cambridge, Polity Press.

Heifetz, R.A. (1994) *Leadership without Easy Answers*, Cambridge, MA, Belknap Press.

Howe, M., Davidson, J. and Sloboda, J. (1996) 'It ain't what you do, it's the way that you do it – that's what gets results', quoted in *Observer*, 13 April.

Storr, A. (1996) *Feet of Clay: A Study of Gurus*, London, HarperCollins.

Tolstoy, L. (1991) *War and Peace*, Oxford, Oxford University Press.

Useem, M. (1996) 'Do leaders make a difference?' *Financial Times*, 8 March.

# Leadership: A Contested Construct 2

*Jon Billsberry*

## Introduction

The purpose of this paper is to provide a summary of leadership theories highlighting current debates. It does not dwell on the difficulty that thinkers have had defining the concept of 'leadership' over the millennia. To do so would be to just repeat the introductions of literally hundreds (possibly thousands) of books on leadership. Instead, this paper tries to categorise the main leadership theories (particularly those that have been commonly used in an organisational context) so that the differences between them may be better understood. It then considers each of the categories of theories and offers a brief explanation of the main theory or theories that it includes. The paper also critically examines each of these theories and describes current issues and debates.

## Grint's Divisions of Leadership Theories

When Grint (1997) looked at the leadership literature, he noted that the enormity of it created difficulties seeing the wood for the trees. His first attempt to make sense of leadership had him writing down characteristics of a good leader as advocated in the literature. He quickly gave up this approach because he 'ran out of space on one side of paper after I had passed number 127 on the 'necessary-aspects-of-leadership' list' (p. 3). He then considered 'polarities' or binary opposites of leadership. For example, 'management' vs. 'leadership', 'task-oriented' vs. 'people-oriented', or 'charismatic' vs. 'ordinary'. Such lists are, of course, potentially infinite. But, more critically, by dividing debates into extremes, there is a danger that subtleties and compromises get lost in the clash of polar opposites.

Following these two abortive attempts to capture 'leadership', Grint took another approach. He noticed that two divisions seemed to appear throughout the literature. The first of these debates concerns the significance attributed to the individual or to the situation or context that the individual is in.

Some leadership theories seem to centre solely on the characteristics of leaders regardless of the situation, whereas others do the opposite. Other theories involve an interaction between these two domains. The second of the divisions lies in the traditional split between objective and subjective assumptions about knowledge and data. That is, to what extent is it possible to understand someone or something? Alternatively, to what extent is knowledge divided between the actual and the perceptual? Or, how essential is it that this dimension is taken into account?

Grint does not claim that these divisions fully capture the methodological and epistemological differences of approach, merely that it is a useful heuristic division that helps him to make sense of the leadership literature. Grint prefers to view the two divisions as continuous axes rather than categorical axes as he believes it inappropriate to view the literature in four separate and distinct quadrants. Some of the reasons that were mentioned above regarding polar opposites are relevant here as well. Grint's model can be produced as a diagram (see Figure 2.1). The four divisions are elaborated in the following pages.

The trait approach encompasses those theories that focus on the individual leader and assume that it is possible to identify and understand the various characteristics that leaders need. In contrast, leadership theories that argue that particular situations and contexts require particular types of leadership action and behaviour are grouped together beneath the situational banner. Both the

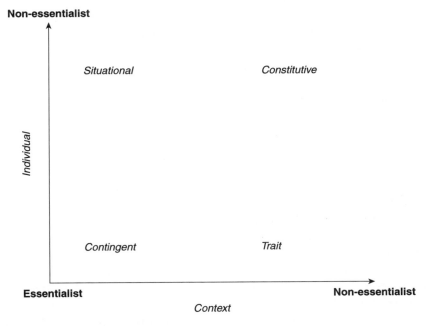

**Figure 2.1**  Grint's divisions of leadership theories

contingent and constitutive approaches contain a focus on both the individual and the context. They differ in that those theories grouped as contingent assume that both of these two domains are knowable, whereas those theories grouped as constitutive do not.

## Trait

Of all approaches to leadership, trait theories probably have the longest history. Conceptually, trait theory is the simplest form of leadership theory as it focuses solely on the leader's characteristics. Traits can be defined as the leader's distinguishing characteristics. These include intelligence, values, confidence, charisma, and appearance. Early trait theories adopted the 'Great Man' approach to understanding leadership and the studies sought to differentiate the characteristics of leaders from those who were not leaders. For example, it was discovered that every American President elected between 1900 and 1968 was taller than his main opponent. It was also found that, generally speaking, leaders were slightly more (but not considerably more) intelligent than their followers (Stogdill, 1974). This approach has the benefit of surfacing the sorts of characteristics that leaders tend to possess, but, as Grint discovered, this list can quickly become unmanageable. Moreover, underpinning this approach is the idea that 'leaders are born, not bred' (Daft, 1999, 2001). Consequently, the trait approach offers little help to people wishing to improve their leadership qualities: you've either got it, or you haven't.

Research on trait theory has dwindled since the early 1950s following literature reviews by Mann (1959) and Stogdill (1948) that concluded 'no traits consistently differentiated leaders from nonleaders across a variety of situations' (Lord, De Vader and Alliger, 1986, p. 402). However, an interesting exception was the meta-analysis of leadership traits conducted by Lord, et al. (1986). These researchers used validity generalisation procedures to re-examine the review of Mann in light of subsequent studies. Their results showed stronger evidence than Mann's results that six traits (intelligence, extroversion–introversion, masculinity–femininity, interpersonal sensitivity, dominance, and conservatism) distinguished leaders from others. Their conclusion was that leaders tend to be more intelligent, extrovert, and 'masculine' than non-leaders. An alternative review by Kirkpatrick and Locke (1991) suggests that six traits distinguish leaders from non-leaders. These traits are drive (achievement, ambition, energy, tenacity, initiative), motivation to be a leader, honesty and integrity, self-confidence (including emotional stability), cognitive ability, and knowledge of the business. Shackleton (1995) concludes thus, 'the trait approach has undergone a revival. Recent research suggests that traits do matter. Yet the research shows that there are only a handful of traits that distinguish leaders from others, and a clear distinction between effective and ineffective leaders has not yet emerged' (p. 10).

Following the dismissive reviews of Stogdill and Mann, emphasis swung away from leadership traits and into leader style or behaviour (the two words were used synonymously). Researchers hoped to identify the types of behaviour that accompanied effective leadership. This approach offered the possibility of helping people develop their leadership style so that they might be able to perform more effectively as leaders.

One of the earliest (conducted just before the Second World War and prior to the reviews by Stogdill and Mann) and most influential series of studies conducted under the style theory banner were those carried out by Lewin and his colleagues (e.g. Lewin, 1939; Lewin and Lippett, 1938; Lewin, Lippett and White, 1939). In experimental conditions, an adult leader was placed in control of a group of children. The adult was instructed to be either autocratic (centralised authority with power emanating from control of rewards and coercion) or democratic (delegates authority, encourages participation, relies on others' knowledge and ability to complete tasks, and influences from follower's respect) in nature. The group of children performed best under the autocratic conditions, so long as the leader was present. But the children did not enjoy the mode of leadership and there was frequent hostility to it. The children performed almost as well under the democratic conditions, and continued to perform well when the leader was not present. Moreover, these conditions were associated with positive feelings, rather than feelings of hostility. Overall, Lewin and his colleagues concluded that the democratic style of leadership was preferable to an autocratic one.

Tannenbaum and Schmidt's much cited work (Tannenbaum and Schmidt, 1958) picked up on Lewin et al.'s conclusion that democratic leadership was preferable and studied participative leadership. These researchers produced a continuum that indicates how different amounts of participation are reflected in leadership behaviours. At one end of the continuum is 'boss-centred leadership', otherwise known as autocratic leadership. And at the other end of the continuum is 'subordinate-centred leadership', otherwise known as democratic leadership. In conditions of 'boss-centred leadership', the leader (interestingly termed a 'manager') makes and announces decisions. With more participation, the leader has to 'sell' a decision. With even more participation, the leader has to present ideas and invite questions. With more, the leader presents a tentative decision that is subject to change. With more, the leader presents the problem, gets suggestions and then makes the decision. With more, the leader defines the limits and asks the group to make the decision. And finally, at the 'subordinate-centred' end of the continuum, the leader permits subordinates to function within limits defined by a superior. Tannenbaum and Schmidt argue that the leader should choose an appropriate style of leadership depending on the organisational circumstances, thereby positioning their leadership model as a contingency one. However, the authors do not develop the contextual side of their model and the focus is very much on leadership behaviours, rather than the interaction of individual and environmental factors.

Perhaps the best known theory of leadership style is 'The Managerial Grid' developed by Blake and Mouton (1964). This was later re-titled 'The Leadership Grid' (Blake and McCanse, 1991). These researchers proposed a two-dimensional theory. The two dimensions are a concern for people and a concern for production. The two axes have a minimum (low) score of one and a maximum (high) score of nine. Leaders are observed (or given a question-naire) and then plotted on the grid. Depending on where they are positioned on the grid, particular descriptions of leadership follow. Someone positioned as a (1,1) leader is involved in 'impoverished management'. Such a person has lit-tle concern for people or results. 'Country club management' (1,9) is the term used to describe a leader who has a high concern for people, but little concern for results. The opposite form of leadership (9,1) in which the leader's concern is for results with little time for people is called 'authority–compliance man-agement'. In the centre of the grid is 'middle-of-the-road management' (5,5), which denotes moderate concern for people and results. The (9,9) leadership style is termed 'team management', which denotes an equally high concern for both people and production. This style relies on interdependence between lead-ers and followers through a common stake in the organisation's purpose. This interdependence creates relationships based on mutual trust and respect leading to commitment. Blake and Mouton regard 'team management' as the leader-ship style that is most effective and they recommend it for every situation. Blake and Mouton's Leadership Grid is a simple panacea and as such is easy to refute as a universal theory of leadership. For example, the sort of leadership suited to a co-operative organization is unlikely to be the sort of leadership required in moments of extreme danger. That said, the nature of much work at the start of the twenty-first century with skilled workforces, increased people management legislation, greater measurement of results, and greater closeness to customers makes it an approach with considerable appeal.

Although trait theories have been around for a long time and have a natural appeal (as they are based around what leaders are and do), they are easy to criti-cise. Bryman (1992) offers a critique of trait and style approaches to leadership. His first criticism relates to the problem of causality. This criticism is the diffi-culty that researchers have connecting leadership behaviours to outcomes. For example, consider Margaret Thatcher. Most people accept, regardless of their political views or feelings about her policies, that she exhibited some leadership qualities and that she did much to change the country. These changes include a social change towards greater individualism, less altruism, and more greed. But was she the cause? This was a time of considerable technological change. Computers were finding a place in almost every type of gadget. Sony Walkmans were a 'must have' accessory. Cars came with radios and cassette players. In addition, the number of television channels and radio stations dramatically increased. All of these things might be thought of as factors in the greater individualisation of society and would have happened regardless of who was Prime Minister. How then, can we ascribe causality on to Margaret Thatcher?

Bryman also considers the problem leadership style theories have explaining informal leadership. Informal leadership refers to the everyday influencing that goes on in organisations. Leadership is not just about 'Great Men'[1] in positions of power, it is much subtler and occurs everywhere. Theories of leadership traits and styles focus on the designated leader of a group (Shackleton, 1995), that is, formal leadership. Crucially, the formal leader may not be the most influential in the minds of the followers and the styles of formal and informal leaders may be very different. If this is so, then it would be a mistake to use leadership style theories to explain the impact of informal leaders.

Finally, of course, there are the criticisms of Grint (1997). This group of leadership theories largely ignore contextual issues (a behaviour suited to one environment may not be suitable in another environment) and they assume that it is possible to be knowledgeable about the leader, which is not necessarily the case.

## Situational

Hersey and Blanchard's situational leadership theory (Hersey and Blanchard, 1988) is an extension of Blake and Mouton's Managerial Grid but with the focus reversed so that the situation, or context, is dominant. It contains two dimensions (relationship behaviours and task behaviours). Relationship behaviours are those behaviours associated with support, recognition, and encouragement given by leaders to followers. Task behaviour is concerned with the amount of direction provided by the leader. These dimensions produce a two by two grid containing four styles: structuring (telling), coaching (selling), encouraging (participating), and delegating. Different versions of the theory use different labels for three of the styles. One way in which this theory differs to style approaches is that it does not assume that there is one best style of leadership. Instead, it suggests that leaders should change their styles to suit the demands of the situation. The appropriateness of the style depends on the readiness of followers. When followers are ready (i.e. they are motivated to do the work and have the necessary knowledge, skills, and abilities), encouraging and delegating styles are appropriate. When followers are less ready, structuring and coaching are more suitable. Hersey and Blanchard argue that as subordinates (followers) become more mature (this refers to the peoples' ability and motivation to carry out a task), less guidance (i.e. structuring and coaching) is required and instead the leader can focus on encouragement and delegation. Thus, the readiness of followers dictates the sorts of behaviours leaders should adopt. And the emphasis of leaders is a diagnosis of followers' maturity. Sadly, Hersey and Blanchard's situational leadership theory has not attracted much research attention. One study by Vecchio (1987) does offer some guarded support. This researcher studied high school teachers and head teachers in the USA. The results showed that the model fitted best with practice in situations of low maturity (when structuring and coaching was called for), but did not fit at all in high maturity situations.

Hersey and Blanchard's theory of situational leadership remains a popular approach to leadership in the classroom and it is widely used on management development courses (Shackleton, 1995). Shackleton (1995) suggests that its prescriptive and intuitive appeal strikes a chord with the audience as it appears to echo what managers have learnt from experience. Another reason why a situational approach might be well received by practitioners is that it accords with the human tendency to assign causality to situational factors. A consistent finding in the psychology literature is that people attribute causality for their own actions to situational factors, and causality for other people's actions to the person (Heider, 1958; Kelley, 1967). Hence, when people are encouraged to think about their own leadership development, an approach that concentrates on situational factors is likely to have considerable appeal. Nevertheless, the situational approach to leadership is a largely ignored domain, with much focus going instead to contingency approaches.

## Contingent

One of the earliest, and certainly one of the most cited, contingency theories of leadership was developed by Fiedler (1967). Broadly, his theory suggests that leadership style depends on the needs of the situation. Fiedler's theory draws upon earlier leadership theories and uses them within a contingency framework. For example, when describing a suitable leadership style, Fiedler says that this has two components, relationship-oriented and task-oriented, which are strongly reminiscent of Blake and Mouton's approach. The cornerstone of Fiedler's theory is a questionnaire (containing sixteen bipolar adjectives) that describes the leader's 'least preferred coworker' (LPC). The LPC is the person the leader least liked of all the people he or she has worked with. Someone's LPC can be scored either high or low, that is, a positive or negative description of the person. A high (positive feeling towards the) LPC indicates that the leader is people-oriented, whereas a low (negative feelings towards the) LPC indicates that the leader is task-oriented. Left like this, the questionnaire would enable the leader to plot his or her leadership style on a two by two grid similar to Blake and Mouton. But Fiedler develops his theory to include three elements of the situation that can be either favourable or unfavourable to the leader. These three elements are 'group atmosphere', 'task structure', and 'position power'. Fiedler (1972) combines these three situational factors to produce eight leadership situations. To these octants, Fiedler advocates a suitable fit between the leader's style and the situation. In summary, task-oriented leaders are predicted to perform better in situations with a good group atmosphere and structured tasks or when there is a poor group atmosphere and unstructured tasks. People-oriented perform better in the reverse of these situations. In other words, a people-oriented style of leadership is more effective in moderately favourable situations, whereas a task-oriented style of leadership is more effective in extreme situations. The position power situational dimension seems to act as a mediator. An interesting aspect of Fiedler's theory is that assumes that the LPC preference of the leader is a trait-like quality. As such, it is difficult, if not impossible, to alter or adapt consciously it to suit the needs of the situation.

Fiedler's contingency theory of leadership has attracted many studies. Meta-analyses of these studies (Peters, Hartke and Pohlmann, 1985; Strube and Garcia, 1981) conclude that the studies have provided data to support the theory, although studies in laboratory conditions yield much better data than studies in the field. Despite these findings, many criticisms can be levelled at the theory. Primarily, the model is relatively simplistic. It contains just one dimension of leadership behaviour (LPC) and just three dimensions of the situation. These dimensions can be deconstructed and shown to be flawed as a universal theory. For example, the measurement of the leader's perceptions of his or her LPC depends, crucially, on the characteristics of particular LPCs. Some might be technically and socially inept, whereas others might not. The theory also suffers have the prescriptive problem that it describes situations, but does not inform the leader of how to change things to improve his or her own leadership. Rather like trait theory, the LPC dimension is not malleable and therefore someone either is or is not the right leader for the situation.

A contingency theory of leadership that argues that leaders can change their style of leadership to suit the situation is known as 'Path–Goal' theory. This approach is an offshoot of the expectancy theory of motivation. As a theory of leadership, expectancy theory is most closely associated with the work of House (House, 1971; House and Mitchell, 1974). Expectancy theory is based on the idea that peoples' actions are determined by their calculation of the expectancy (i.e. the perception that effort will result in performance), instrumentality (i.e. the perception that performance will be rewarded), and valence (the value of the outcome) in the situation. Central to the path–goal theory of leadership is the idea that leaders can (and should) manipulate workers' perceptions of these dimensions. Echoing earlier theories, leaders can adopt four types of behaviour to achieve this manipulation: instrumental (or directive), supportive, participative, and achievement-oriented. House (1971) argues that the effective leader is the one who can determine which style is the most appropriate in the situation and then adapt his or her own style to suit.

There have been many studies of path–goal theory. By and large, these studies support the theory, especially in situations of low task structure when an instrumental style of leadership is associated with greater worker satisfaction, motivation, and satisfaction with the leader. However, an association between worker performance and instrumental leadership style was not found in similar situations as would have been predicted by the theory (Indvik, 1986, cited in Shackleton, 1995). Although there have been many studies of this theory, most of these have tended to examine particular pieces of the theory and much of it remains untested. Another criticism of the theory is that of causality (Bryman, 1992). Whilst studies have shown associations between leadership style and follower satisfaction or performance, it is uncertain whether the leadership style causes the outcome, or whether the situation shapes the leadership behaviour. For example, a study by Greene (1979) showed that follower performance caused the leader to act in different ways, rather than vice versa. Finally, as demonstrated earlier, leadership style is a trait-like quality and as such resistant to change. This raises the question of how much leaders might be able to manipulate and alter their style of leadership and the various costs of doing so. There are dangers that the leader who continually changes his or her style might be seen as shifty or dishonest.

## Constitutive

Grint's final division of leadership envisages an approach to leadership in which it is not possible to capture either the person or the place objectively. As we have seen, most of the extant leadership theories simplify these dimensions so severely that the theories become panaceas with limited usefulness. More recent approaches have changed tack and sought to understand why 'leadership' eludes objective capture and the implications of this. One approach has been advocated by Wheatley (1992, 1999). Her approach to leadership has its roots in quantum mechanics, complex adaptive systems, living systems theory, and chaos theory. It inquires into the metaphorical links between these scientific perspectives and leadership. She notes that in the quantum world, 'relationship' is the key determiner of everything: 'subatomic particles come into form and are observed only as they are in relationship to something else' (Wheatley, 1999, p. 11). She then draws on uncertainty, self-regulation, strange attractors, and the wholeness of beings to describe leadership as a dynamic, 'amorphous phenomenon' (p.13) in which participation, awareness, relationships, and self-regulation are dilemmas to be resolved.

Grint's constitutive approach uses social constructivism and linguistic interpretation to provide insight about leadership. He rejects the idea that it is possible to form an objective account of either people or situations. Instead, he argues, as there are as many 'truths' about a person or a situation as there are observers; truth emerges from a competition between various accounts and interpretations. He says that these interpretations do not have equal weight. Some are more dominant than others and become the accepted view, regardless of the 'reality' of the person or the situation. Hence, 'we may never know what the true essence of a leader or the situation actually is and must often base our actions and beliefs on the accounts of others from whom we can (re)constitute our version of events' (Grint, 1997, p. 6). The practical implications of this approach are not a million miles away from the theories considered earlier in this paper: 'In terms of leadership development, the approach suggests that the ancient study of rhetoric provides one significant element of leadership training since it may be persuasive powers that hold the key to leadership success. Political networking, interpersonal skills, material wealth, and negotiating skills are the hallmark of this approach' (p. 6) ... 'this does not mean that leadership is whatever anyone wants it to be; it is what certain powerful 'voices' make it. All voices may be equal but some are more equal than others' (p. 9).

These approaches offer radical insight into the nature of leadership but, despite the long history of some of the underpinning ideas such as Plato's rhetorical skill, these are ideas in formation rather than the more fully developed theories examined earlier. Nevertheless, they capture some characteristics of leadership, such as the complexity, multi-dimensional, and individual interpretation of leadership, which previous theories have long struggled to accommodate.

## Note

1. Apologies about the inherent sexism in the term 'Great Men', but this is a phrase commonly used in the literature to denote the trait approach. As this paper is an introduction to leadership theories and you may want to read more on the subject, one of my goals was to introduce you to the language of the field.

## References

Blake, R. and McCanse, A.A. (1991) *Leadership Dilemmas: Grid Solutions*, Houston, TX, Gulf Publishing.

Blake, R. and Mouton, J.S. (1964) *The Managerial Grid*, Houston, TX, Gulf Publishing.

Bryman, A. (1992) *Charisma and Leadership in Organizations*, London, Sage.

Daft, R.L. (1999) *Leadership: Theory and Practice*, Fort Worth, TX, The Dryden Press.

Daft, R.L. (2001) *The Leadership Experience* (2nd edn), Fort Worth, TX, Harcourt College Publishers.

Fiedler, F.E. (1967) *A Theory of Leadership*, New York, McGraw-Hill.

Fiedler, F.E. (1972) 'The effects of leadership training and experience: A contingency model interpretation', *Administrative Science Quarterly*, vol. 17, pp. 453–470.

Greene, C.N. (1979) 'Questions of causation in the path–goal theory of leadership', *Academy of Management Journal*, vol. 22, pp. 22–41.

Grint, K. (1997) *Leadership: Classical, Contemporary, and Critical Approaches*, Oxford, Oxford University Press.

Heider, F. (1958) *The Psychology of Interpersonal Relations*, New York, John Wiley.

Hersey, P. and Blanchard, K.H. (1988) *Management of Organizational Behavior* (5th edn), Englewood Cliffs, NJ, Prentice-Hall.

House, R.J. (1971) 'A path–goal theory of leadership effectiveness', *Administrative Science Quarterly*, vol. 16, pp. 321–38.

House, R.J. and Mitchell, T.R. (1974) 'Path goal theory of leadership', *Journal of Contemporary Business*, pp. 81–97.

Indvik, J. (1986, August) 'Path–goal theory of leadership: A meta-analysis', paper presented at the Academy of Management Conference.

Kelley, H.H. (1967) 'Attribution theory in social psychology' in D. Levine (ed.) *Nebraska Symposium on Motivation, Vol 15*, Lincoln, NE, University of Nebraska Press.

Kirkpatrick, S.A. and Locke, E.A. (1991) 'Leadership: Do traits matter?' *The Executive*, vol. 5, pp. 48–60.

Lewin, K. (1939) 'Field theory and experiment in social psychology: Concepts and methods', *American Journal of Sociology*, vol. 44, pp. 868–96.

Lewin, K. and Lippett, R. (1938) 'An experimental approach to the study of autocracy and democracy: A preliminary note', *Sociometry*, vol. 1, pp. 292–300.

Lewin, K., Lippett, R. and White, R.K. (1939) 'Patterns of aggressive behaviour in experimentally created social climates', *Journal of Social Psychology*, vol. 10, pp. 271–301.

Lord, R.G., De Vader, C.L. and Alliger, G.M. (1986) 'A meta-analysis of the relation between personality traits and leadership perceptions: An application of validity generalization procedures', *Journal of Applied Psychology*, vol. 71, pp. 402–10.

Mann, R.D. (1959) 'A review of the relationships between personality and performance in small groups', *Psychological Bulletin*, vol. 56, pp. 241–70.

Peters, L.H., Hartke, D.D. and Pohlmann, J.T. (1985) 'Fiedler's contingency theory of leadership: An application of the meta-analysis procedures of Schmidt and Hunter', *Psychological Bulletin*, vol. 97, pp. 224–85.

Shackleton, V. (1995) *Business Leadership*, London, Routledge.

Stogdill, R.M. (1948) 'Personal factors associated with leadership: A survey of the literature', *Journal of Psychology*, vol. 25, pp. 35–71.

Stogdill, R.M. (1974) *Handbook of Leadership*, New York, The Free Press.

Strube, M.J. and Garcia, J.E. (1981) 'A meta-analytic investigation of Fiedler's contingency model of leadership effectiveness', *Psychological Bulletin*, vol. 90, pp. 307–21.

Tannenbaum, R. and Schmidt, W.H. (1958) 'How to choose a leadership pattern', *Harvard Business Review*, vol. 36, pp. 95–101.

Vecchio, R.P. (1987) 'Situational leadership theory: An examination of a prescriptive theory', *Journal of Applied Psychology*, vol. 72, pp. 444–451.

Wheatley, M.J. (1992) *Leadership and the New Science* (1st edn), San Francisco, Berrett-Koehler.

Wheatley, M.J. (1999) *Leadership and the New Science* (2nd edn), San Francisco, Berrett-Koehler.

# What Leaders Really Do

*John P. Kotter*

Leadership is different from management, but not for the reasons most people think. Leadership isn't mystical and mysterious. It has nothing to do with having 'charisma' or other exotic personality traits. It is not the province of a chosen few. Nor is leadership necessarily better than management or a replacement for it.

Rather, leadership and management are two distinctive and complementary systems of action. Each has its own function and characteristic activities. Both are necessary for success in an increasingly complex and volatile business environment.

Most U.S. corporations today are overmanaged and underled. They need to develop their capacity to exercise leadership. Successful corporations don't wait for leaders to come along. They actively seek out people with leadership potential and expose them to career experiences designed to develop that potential. Indeed, with careful selection, nurturing, and encouragement, dozens of people can play important leadership roles in a business organization.

But while improving their ability to lead, companies should remember that strong leadership with weak management is no better, and is sometimes actually worse, than the reverse. The real challenge is to combine strong leadership and strong management and use each to balance the other.

Of course, not everyone can be good at both leading and managing. Some people have the capacity to become excellent managers but not strong leaders. Others have great leadership potential but, for a variety of reasons, have great difficulty becoming strong managers. Smart companies value both kinds of people and work hard to make them a part of the team.

But when it comes to preparing people for executive jobs, such companies rightly ignore the recent literature that says people cannot manage *and* lead. They try to develop leader-managers. Once companies understand the fundamental difference between leadership and management, they can begin to groom their top people to provide both.

Kotter, J.P. (1990) 'What leaders really do', Harvard Business Review, May–June, pp. 103–11.

# The Difference between Management and Leadership

Management is about coping with complexity. Its practices and procedures are largely a response to one of the most significant developments of the twentieth century: the emergence of large organizations. Without good management, complex enterprises tend to become chaotic in ways that threaten their very existence. Good management brings a degree of order and consistency to key dimensions like the quality and profitability of products.

Leadership, by contrast, is about coping with change. Part of the reason it has become so important in recent years is that the business world has become more competitive and more volatile. Faster technological change, greater international competition, the deregulation of markets, overcapacity in capital-intensive industries, an unstable oil cartel, raiders with junk bonds, and the changing demographics of the work force are among the many factors that have contributed to this shift. The net result is that doing what was done yesterday, or doing it 5 per cent better, is no longer a formula for success. Major changes are more and more necessary to survive and compete effectively in this new environment. More change always demands more leadership.

Consider a simple military analogy: a peacetime army can usually survive with good administration and management up and down the hierarchy, coupled with good leadership concentrated at the very top. A wartime army, however, needs competent leadership at all levels. No one yet has figured out how to manage people effectively into battle; they must be *led*.

These different functions – coping with complexity and coping with change – shape the characteristic activities of management and leadership. Each system of action involves deciding what needs to be done, creating networks of people and relationships that can accomplish an agenda, and then trying to ensure that those people actually do the job. But each accomplishes these three tasks in different ways.

Companies manage complexity first by *planning and budgeting* – setting targets or goals for the future (typically for the next month or year), establishing detailed steps for achieving those targets, and then allocating resources to accomplish those plans. By contrast, leading an organization to constructive change begins by *setting a direction* – developing a vision of the future (often the distant future) along with strategies for producing the changes needed to achieve that vision.

Management develops the capacity to achieve its plan by *organizing and staffing* – creating an organizational structure and set of jobs for accomplishing plan requirements, staffing the jobs with qualified individuals, communicating the plan to those people, delegating responsibility for carrying out the plan, and devising systems to monitor implementation. The equivalent leadership activity, however, is *aligning people*. This means communicating the new direction to those who can create coalitions that understand the vision and are committed to its achievement.

Finally, management ensures plan accomplishment by *controlling and prob-lem solving* – monitoring results versus the plan in some detail, both formally and informally, by means of reports, meetings, and other tools; identifying deviations; and then planning and organizing to solve the problems. But for leadership, achieving a vision requires *motivating and inspiring* – keeping people moving in the right direction, despite major obstacles to change, by appealing to basic but often untapped human needs, values, and emotions.

A closer examination of each of these activities will help clarify the skills leaders need.

## Setting a Direction vs. Planning and Budgeting

Since the function of leadership is to produce change, setting the direction of that change is fundamental to leadership.

Setting direction is never the same as planning or even long-term planning, although people often confuse the two. Planning is a management process, deductive in nature and designed to produce orderly results, not change. Setting a direction is more inductive. Leaders gather a broad range of data and look for patterns, relationships, and linkages that help explain things. What's more, the direction-setting aspect of leadership does not produce plans; it creates vision and strategies. These describe a business, technology, or corporate culture in terms of what it should become over the long term and articulate a feasible way of achieving this goal.

Most discussions of vision have a tendency to degenerate into the mystical. The implication is that a vision is something mysterious that mere mortals, even talented ones, could never hope to have. But developing good business direc-tion isn't magic. It is a tough, sometimes exhausting process of gathering and analyzing information. People who articulate such visions aren't magicians but broad-based strategic thinkers who are willing to take risks.

Nor do visions and strategies have to be brilliantly innovative, in fact, some of the best are not. Effective business visions regularly have an almost mundane quality, usually consisting of ideas that are already well known. The particular combination or patterning of the ideas may be new, but sometimes even that is not the case.

For example, when CEO Jan Carlzon articulated his vision to make Scandinavian Airline Systems (SAS) the best airline in the world for the fre-quent business traveler, he was not saying anything that everyone in the airline industry didn't already know. Business travelers fly more consistently than other market segments and are generally willing to pay higher fares. Thus focusing on business customers offers an airline the possibility of high margins, steady business, and considerable growth. But in an industry known more for bureaucracy than vision, no company had ever put these simple ideas together and dedicated itself to implementing them. SAS did, and it worked.

What's crucial about a vision is not its originality but how well it serves the interests of important constituencies – customers, stockholders, employees – and how easily it can be translated into a realistic competitive strategy. Bad visions tend to ignore the legitimate needs and rights of important constituencies – favoring, say, employees over customers or stockholders. Or they are strategically unsound. When a company that has never been better than a weak competitor in an industry suddenly starts talking about becoming number one, that is a pipe dream, not a vision.

One of the most frequent mistakes that over-managed and underled corporations make is to embrace 'long-term planning' as a panacea for their lack of direction and inability to adapt to an increasingly competitive and dynamic business environment. But such an approach misinterprets the nature of direction setting and can never work.

Long-term planning is always time consuming. Whenever something unexpected happens, plans have to be redone. In a dynamic business environment, the unexpected often becomes the norm, and long-term planning can become an extraordinarily burdensome activity. This is why most successful corporations limit the time frame of their planning activities. Indeed, some even consider 'long-term planning' a contradiction in terms.

In a company without direction, even short-term planning can become a black hole capable of absorbing an infinite amount of time and energy. With no vision and strategy to provide constraints around the planning process or to guide it, every eventuality deserves a plan. Under these circumstances, contingency planning can go on forever, draining time and attention from far more essential activities, yet without ever providing the clear sense of direction that a company desperately needs. After awhile, managers inevitably become cynical about all this, and the planning process can degenerate into a highly politicized game.

Planning works best not as a substitute for direction setting but as a complement to it. A competent planning process serves as a useful reality check on direction-setting activities. Likewise, a competent direction-setting process provides a focus in which planning can then be realistically carried out. It helps clarify what kind of planning is essential and what kind is irrelevant.

## Aligning People vs. Organizing and Staffing

A central feature of modern organizations is interdependence, where no one has complete autonomy, where most employees are tied to many others by their

work, technol                    hierarchy. These linkages present
a special chal                    t to change. Unless many individuals line u          e direction, people will tend to
fall all over c                    re overeducated in management
and undered                    tting people moving in the same
direction ap                    lem. What executives need to do,
however, is r                    n.

Manager                    ems that can implement plans as
precisely and efficiently as possib            this requires a number of potentially complex decisions. A company must choose a structure of jobs and reporting relationships, staff it with individuals suited to the jobs, provide training
for those who need it, communicate plans to the work force, and decide how
much authority to delegate and to whom. Economic incentives also need to be
constructed to accomplish the plan, as well as systems to monitor its implementation. These organizational judgments are much like architectural decisions.
It's a question of fit within a particular context.

Aligning is different. It is more of a communications challenge than a design
problem. First, aligning invariably involves talking to many more individuals than
organizing does. The target population can involve not only a manager's subordinates but also bosses, peers, staff in other parts of the organization, as well as
suppliers, governmental officials, or even customers. Anyone who can help implement the vision and strategies or who can block implementation is relevant.

Trying to get people to comprehend a vision of an alternative future is also
a communications challenge of a completely different magnitude from organizing them to fulfill a short-term plan. It's much like the difference between a
football quarterback attempting to describe to his team the next two or three
plays versus his trying to explain to them a totally new approach to the game to
be used in the second half of the season.

Whether delivered with many words or a few carefully chosen symbols,
such messages are not necessarily accepted just because they are understood.
Another big challenge in leadership efforts is credibility – getting people to
believe the message. Many things contribute to credibility: the track record of
the person delivering the message, the content of the message itself, the communicator's reputation for integrity and trustworthiness, and the consistency
between words and deeds.

Finally, aligning leads to empowerment in a way that organizing rarely does.
One of the reasons some organizations have difficulty adjusting to rapid changes
in markets or technology is that so many people in those companies feel relatively powerless. They have learned from experience that even if they correctly
perceive important external changes and then initiate appropriate actions, they
are vulnerable to someone higher up who does not like what they have done.
Reprimands can take many different forms: 'That's against policy' or 'We can't
afford it' or 'Shut up and do as you're told'.

Alignment helps overcome this problem by empowering people in at least two ways. First, when a clear sense of direction has been communicated throughout an organization, lower level employees can initiate actions without the same degree of vulnerability. As long as their behavior is consistent with the vision, superiors will have more difficulty reprimanding them. Second, because everyone is aiming at the same target, the probability is less that one person's initiative will be stalled when it comes into conflict with someone else's.

# Motivating People vs. Controlling and Problem Solving

Since change is the function of leadership, being able to generate highly energized behavior is important for coping with the inevitable barriers to change. Just as direction setting identifies an appropriate path for movement and just as effective alignment gets people moving down that path, successful motivation ensures that they will have the energy to overcome obstacles.

According to the logic of management, control mechanisms compare system behavior with the plan and take action when a deviation is detected. In a well-managed factory, for example, this means the planning process establishes sensible quality targets, the organizing process builds an organization that can achieve those targets, and a control process makes sure that quality lapses are spotted immediately, not in 30 or 60 days, and corrected.

For some of the same reasons that control is so central to management, highly motivated or inspired behavior is almost irrelevant. Managerial processes must be as close as possible to fail-safe and risk-free. That means they cannot be dependent on the unusual or hard to obtain. The whole purpose of systems and structures is to help normal people who behave in normal ways to complete routine jobs successfully, day after day. It's not exciting or glamorous. But that's management.

Leadership is different. Achieving grand visions always requires an occasional burst of energy. Motivation and inspiration energize people, not by pushing them in the right direction as control mechanisms do but by satisfying basic human needs for achievement, a sense of belonging, recognition, self-esteem, a feeling of control over one's life, and the ability to live up to one's ideals. Such feelings touch us deeply and elicit a powerful response.

Good leaders motivate people in a variety of ways. First, they always articulate the organization's vision in a manner that stresses the values of the audience they are addressing. This makes the work important to those individuals. Leaders also regularly involve people in deciding how to achieve the organization's vision (or the part most relevant to a particular individual). This gives people a sense of control. Another important motivational technique is to support employee efforts to realize the vision by providing coaching, feedback, and role modeling, thereby helping people grow professionally and enhancing their self-esteem. Finally, good leaders recognize and reward success, which not only gives people a sense of accomplishment but also makes them feel like they belong to an organization that cares about them. When all this is done, the work itself becomes intrinsically motivating.

The more that change characterizes the business environment, the more that leaders must motivate people to provide leadership as well. When this works, it tends to reproduce leadership across the entire organization, with people occupying multiple leadership roles throughout the hierarchy. This is highly valuable, because coping with change in any complex business demands initiatives from a multitude of people. Nothing less will work.

Of course, leadership from many sources does not necessarily converge. To the contrary, it can easily conflict. For multiple leadership roles to work together, people's actions must be carefully coordinated by mechanisms that differ from those coordinating traditional management roles.

Strong networks of informal relationships – the kind found in companies with healthy cultures – help coordinate leadership activities in much the same way that formal structure coordinates managerial activities. The key difference is that informal networks can deal with the greater demands for coordination associated with nonroutine activities and change. The multitude of communication channels and the trust among the individuals connected by those channels allow for an ongoing process of accommodation and adaptation. When conflicts arise among roles, those same relationships help resolve the conflicts. Perhaps most important, this process of dialogue and accommodation can produce visions that are linked and compatible instead of remote and competitive. All this requires a great deal more communication than is needed to coordinate managerial roles, but unlike formal structure, strong informal networks can handle it.

Of course, informal relations of some sort exist in all corporations. But too often these networks are either very weak – some people are well connected but most are not – or they are highly fragmented – a strong network exists inside the marketing group and inside R&D but not across the two departments. Such networks do not support multiple leadership initiatives well. In fact, extensive informal networks are so important that if they do not exist, creating them has to be the focus of activity early in a major leadership initiative.

# Creating a Culture of Leadership

Despite the increasing importance of leadership to business success, the on-the-job experiences of most people actually seem to undermine the development of attributes needed for leadership. Nevertheless, some companies have consistently demonstrated an ability to develop people into outstanding leader-managers. Recruiting people with leadership potential is only the first step. Equally important is managing their career patterns. Individuals who are effective in large leadership roles often share a number of career experiences.

Perhaps the most typical and most important is significant challenge early in a career. Leaders almost always have had opportunities during their twenties and thirties to actually try to lead, to take a risk, and to learn from both triumphs and failures. Such learning seems essential in developing a wide range of leadership skills and perspectives. It also teaches people something about both the difficulty of leadership and its potential for producing change.

Later in their careers, something equally important happens that has to do with broadening. People who provide effective leadership in important jobs always have a chance, before they get into those jobs, to grow beyond the narrow base that characterizes most managerial careers. This is usually the result of lateral career moves or of early promotions to unusually broad job assignments. Sometimes other vehicles help, like special task-force assignments or a lengthy general management course. Whatever the case, the breadth of knowledge developed in this way seems to be helpful in all aspects of leadership. So does the network of relationships that is often acquired both inside and outside the company. When enough people get opportunities like this, the relationships that are built also help create the strong informal networks needed to support multiple leadership initiatives.

Corporations that do a better-than-average job of developing leaders put an emphasis on creating challenging opportunities for relatively young employees. In many businesses, decentralization is the key. By definition, it pushes responsibility lower in an organization and in the process creates more challenging jobs at lower levels. Johnson & Johnson, 3M, Hewlett-Packard, General Electric, and many other well-known companies have used that approach quite successfully. Some of those same companies also create as many small units as possible so there are a lot of challenging lower level general management jobs available.

Sometimes these businesses develop additional challenging opportunities by stressing growth through new products or services. Over the years, 3M has had a policy that at least 25 per cent of its revenue should come from products introduced within the last five years. That encourages small new ventures, which in turn offer hundreds of opportunities to test and stretch young people with leadership potential.

Such practices can, almost by themselves, prepare people for small- and medium-sized leadership jobs. But developing people for important leadership positions requires more work on the part of senior executives, often over a long period of time. That work begins with efforts to spot people with great leadership potential early in their careers and to identify what will be needed to stretch and develop them.

Again, there is nothing magic about this process. The methods successful companies use are surprisingly straightforward. They go out of their way to make young employees and people at lower levels in their organizations visible to senior management. Senior managers then judge for themselves who has potential and what the development needs of those people are. Executives also discuss their tentative conclusions among themselves to draw more accurate judgments.

Armed with a clear sense of who has considerable leadership potential and what skills they need to develop, executives in these companies then spend time planning for that development. Sometimes that is done as part of a formal succession planning or high-potential development process; often it is more informal. In either case, the key ingredient appears to be an intelligent assessment of what feasible development opportunities fit each candidate's needs.

To encourage managers to participate in these activities, well-led businesses tend to recognize and reward people who successfully develop leaders. This is rarely done as part of a formal compensation or bonus formula, simply because it is so difficult to measure such achievements with precision. But it does become a factor in decisions about promotion, especially to the most senior levels, and that seems to make a big difference. When told that future promotions will depend to some degree on their ability to nurture leaders, even people who say that leadership cannot be developed somehow find ways to do it.

Such strategies help create a corporate culture where people value strong leadership and strive to create it. Just as we need more people to provide leadership in the complex organizations that dominate our world today, we also need more people to develop the cultures that will create that leadership. Institutionalizing a leadership-centered culture is the ultimate act of leadership.

# Part II
## Effective Leadership

# The Five Practices of Exemplary Leadership

## James M. Kouzes and Barry Z. Posner

Leadership is ultimately about creating a way for people to contribute to making something extraordinary happen.

*(Alan Keith, Genentech)*

'When I walked in the door on my first day', Dick Nettell told us, 'we had four hundred people working really, really hard, but they weren't winning. We had people who were walking around looking like they ran over their dogs on the way to work. It was very, very sad.' As the new site executive for Bank of America's Consumer Call Center in Concord, California, Dick found 'rep scores' (the key performance measure) 21 percentage points behind the top performing call center and 18 points behind the next lowest performer. Fifty-five percent of employees felt that they were in an environment in which they could not speak their minds, and 50 percent believed that nothing was going to happen even if they did.

It's Dick's firm belief that 'everybody wants to win. Everybody wants to be successful. Everybody comes to work trying to make a difference.' But the call center employees suffered from 'management whiplash'. The constant turnover in leadership and changes in priorities had been sending them down the path of poor performance. Dick said that when he started asking about the comparisons with other centers, 'All I heard were the reasons why we couldn't do this or that. If there were an Olympic excuse-making team, we would be gold medallists. People were very disempowered.' So Dick set out to change all that.

Dick set aside three entire days just for talking and listening to people. He gathered as much data as he could from these interviews and elsewhere. 'If you keep your eyes open and periodically actually shut your mouth, and you have the courage to turn the mirror around on yourself', said Dick, 'it's amazing what you can learn and how you can change things.'

He met with the call center's senior managers and support staff in a large basement conference room and presented his findings. Then he handed out

Kouzes, J.M. and Posner, B.Z. (2007) 'The five practices of exemplary leadership'. From Kouzes, J.M. and Posner, B.Z. The Leadership Challenge (4th edn), San Francisco, Wiley, pp. 3–25.

stacks of Post-it notepads and asked the group to write down five adjectives that described the center at that time. He repeated this process two more times, asking them to write down five adjectives that described how they thought their peers would describe the center and what they thought the associates, or customer service representatives, would say. Each time, their responses were written on an easel. It was a bleak picture. Words such as *demotivated, volatile, imprecise, failing, disorganized, frustrating, not fun, constantly changing priorities, lack of appreciation, too many changes,* and *not enough coaching* appeared on the lists. Even so, there were some positive comments about the people, such as *dedicated, energetic,* and *supportive.*

Then Dick asked them to go through the process once more, this time describing how they would *like* the call center to look in the future. 'If you could wave a magic wand', he asked the group, 'in three to five years how would you like the center to be described?' The language they used to express their hopes, dreams, and aspirations painted a dramatically different picture from the one Dick found when he came aboard: *amazing results, world class, a model for others to follow, a unique place to work, partnership, opportunities to learn and grow, true passion for our customers.* Armed with this list of aspirations Dick and the management team began to craft a vision, mission, and set of values (which they called commitments). The resulting vision and mission read as follows:

### OUR VISION OF THE FUTURE...
■ We will be seen as a *World Class Call Center* and the standard against which others are measured – one with true passion for our customers.
■ We will be acknowledged across the franchise as a model to follow, where every associate truly feels like a partner, has an equal opportunity to learn and grow, and understands their personal impact on our overall success.
■ We will be viewed as a unique place to work, an organization that drives amazing results while having fun along the way.

### OUR MISSION IS...
■ To provide an experience that consistently 'delights' our customers every single minute of every single day.

Over the next six weeks Dick held twenty-two forty-five minute state-of-the-center meetings with every team in the call center. 'Here's our vision, here's what we're committed to', Dick would say to begin raising awareness of the issues, and then he'd ask, 'Does this make sense to you? Is there something we need to change?' Then Dick told them about his own beginnings in Bank of America. He told them about how he started as a garage helper, worked his way up to be an automobile fleet manager, and eventually found his way into senior management. He told them, 'I'm here at the call center because I want to be here', and then related the story of how he had retired as the bank's corporate services executive and decided to come back.

He said he woke up early one morning and realized that something was missing in his life. 'At four in the morning you can't lie to yourself', he told them. 'I realized that I'm really passionate about working with folks to get them to think differently about themselves. What was missing in my life was the ability to make a difference in people's lives. It may sound corny, but I love to be able to work with people so that they can be the best they can be.' So Dick reached out to an executive he admired at the bank and asked about the chance of coming back. He got his wish when the opportunity to take on the Concord Call Center came along. Everyone in those state-of-the-center meetings, when they heard Dick's story, realized that they had a champion on their side, a genuine leader who would enable them to turn their aspirations into actuality. They understood that Dick was there because he wanted to be there, not because the call center was on some career path to a higher position.

At those meetings Dick challenged everyone to take the initiative to make the new vision a reality. 'You've lost the right to suffer in silence', he said. 'If you have an issue, open your mouth. I want you to talk to your managers, talk to my communications person, talk to me, or visit AskDick.com. Think about sitting in my chair. Give me ideas and proposals that I have the authority to approve.' Dick made it clear that from then on changing the call center was everybody's business. 'You have to be a part of this', he said. 'You want to be like a partner, then you've signed up for some responsibility in the process.' Dick's challenge made it clear that things were going to change, and that the associates were empowered to act. 'Everybody should have that equal opportunity to succeed and learn and know what it feels like to win', Dick said, and 'once you've done that – you've got people well positioned – get the hell out of their way and watch them rock and roll.'

To maintain the momentum, Dick began holding monthly 'town hall' meetings. To make that happen he had to challenge the way things are normally done – it's tough to pull call center people off the phone, even once a month. So they do two half-hour town halls each month, with half the center attending one, and the other half coming to the other. At each one, Dick constantly reiterates the mission, commitments, and vision – that's a ritual with him. He gives a 'you said, we did' report. Then there's a discussion of current initiatives. For example, the month that we visited Dick, the new-hire onboarding process, the upcoming associate survey, and clothing guidelines were the topics of discussion. Following the initiative discussion is a report on the month's performance. Each town hall concludes with 'Celebrating Heroes', a time for individuals who have made significant contributions to the center to be publicly recognized. And it's not just Dick and his managers doing the recognizing. Associates also get time on the agenda to celebrate peers for living the values of the bank and keeping the commitments they've made to each other.

Recognition and celebration are a big deal to Dick. When he arrived at the Concord Call Center, very little of either was going on, so Dick put it on the agenda. Every Wednesday, for example, is 'Pride Day', when people wear company logo merchandise and you see a lot of red, blue, and white bank shirts. Although Pride Day was started before Dick arrived, he added new dimensions to the ritual. For starters, there's the fifteen-minute spirit huddle; once a month every one of the team managers has to bring at least one associate with them, and in the huddles the managers recognize their local heroes. You'll also see people wearing spirit beads. Dick came up with the idea because he wanted something really visible yet inexpensive enough that they could do a lot of it. The beads come in different colors, but on every string hangs a medallion with the same word: PRIDE.

PRIDE is Dick's motto; it stands for Personal Responsibility In Delivering Excellence. That medallion suspended from the gold, blue, and green beads symbolizes what all the values, vision, and mission are about to Dick. They're about taking pride in what you do. And when Dick conducts quarterly coaching sessions with each of his direct reports, they talk about PRIDE, and mission, and vision, and values. Another thing they talk about is how other people see them as leaders. 'When we turn that mirror around', he asks, 'is there a match to what we're saying? How do we spend our time every day? Do our goals match our commitments?' It's in these discussions that Dick gets down to aligning actions with the values of the center.

Despite the tremendous progress they've made in becoming a model call center, and toward keeping the commitments that they've made to each other, Dick still believes that 'every day is opening day.' He said, 'It doesn't matter what you did yesterday. Each and every decision and action is a moment of truth. You say something and what do people see? The two have to be aligned. It's all about the video matching the audio.'

And for Dick the challenge continues, for he knows that every day will present him and the organization with some wonderful chance to try something new: 'In today's environment, if you want to be successful, doing things the same way just won't get it done, period. Expectations continue to be raised, by our shareholders, by our managers, and by our customers. And if we're not willing to be innovative and do things differently, we're going to have the competition pass us like we're sitting still on the freeway.'

Dick demonstrates exemplary leadership skills, and he shows us how leaders can seize the opportunities to bring out the best in others and guide them on the journey to accomplishing exceptionally challenging goals. He serves as a role model for leaders who want to get extraordinary things done in organizations.

## Leadership Opportunities are Everywhere

Leadership can happen anywhere, at any time. It can happen in a huge business or a small one. It can happen in the public, private, or social sector. It can happen in any function. It can happen at home, at school, or in the community.

The call to lead can come at four o'clock in the morning, or it can come late at night. The energy and motivation to lead can come in ways you'd least expect. While Dick Nettell's most recent personal-best leadership grew out of a need to again challenge himself, Claire Owen's leadership best grew out of necessity.

Claire Owen is founder and Leader of Vision & Values of the SG Group in London, England, a 110-person firm that's a collection of four businesses designed to meet the marketing and human resource recruitment needs of agencies and corporations. Stopgap, the United Kingdom's first specialist freelance marketing agency and the SG Group's original business, began because the marketing agency Claire was working in at the time went into receivership. She had a four-week-old baby and a huge mortgage, and was wondering what was going to happen next. But Claire was also worried about what would happen to her client, with whom they were midway through an important promotion. Her concern for her client overrode her personal concerns, so she called her contacts there, told them what was happening, and agreed on what they were going to do.

'I said to the client, "Look, you are up you-know-where without a paddle, but don't panic. I will provide you with a stopgap."' So the account manager and I provided them with a temporary solution, and finished off running the promotion. I thought at the end of that, gosh, there is something here, providing people with a temporary marketing solution. But I knew *I* didn't want to be that temporary solution. I had had enough of printers, and creatives, and copywriters, so I thought maybe I could find other people to do the doing and I would just put them together with the client.

When Stopgap opened its doors there wasn't another business out there that was doing what Claire proposed. 'We created the marketplace that we operate in', she said. 'When we started up, nobody was providing freelance marketers. You could get locum (temporary) doctors, teachers, lawyers, dentists, and vets. In most professions you could get a temp, interim, whatever you like, but you couldn't in marketing.' The fact that there was no other business like hers was fine with Claire. 'I hate the predictable', she told us. 'I hate doing things the way everyone else does. Whatever I do I like to do something different. I never wanted to be a me-too company from day one.'

Claire is very outspoken about her lack of respect for the traditional ways the recruitment industries have been run. 'I had been a candidate myself, and I had been so mistreated by the recruitment consultancy that I wanted to challenge the rules the recruitment industry was playing by', she told us. 'If I could change those practices then I'd be proud to work in this field, and that is what I did.'

For Claire the most fundamental rules had to do with how they operated. 'I wanted an open and transparent business that people could trust', she said. 'Whether it was about our fee structure, or the fact that we never send a candidate to a job before telling them everything about the organization, we operate by the principle of total transparency. We might say to a candidate, "This looks like a great job for your career, but the location is terrible." '

The early days were tough. There were a lot of naysayers. Because Claire was so outspoken about her views of the industry, competitors were particularly harsh. Claire remembers one time when a competitor looked at her, wagged his finger, and told her that she would never be a success in the business. She just laughed and said, 'You don't know how wrong you are.'

Success for Claire is not defined by a specific revenue amount or a specific head count. Quite simply, Claire said, 'I wanted to run a business that had a phenomenal reputation.' Her vision was that there would be Stopgaps all over the country, as there are Reeds (the U.K. leader in specialist recruitment, training, and HR consultancy) – an outlet on every corner so to speak. She knew they were never going to be a High Street recruitment consultancy, but she wanted Stopgap to be everywhere and to be a company that people wanted to do business with. Claire said that she's not a dreamer, but closer to the truth is that she is living her dream every day. For her the future is now.

Rather than waiting to run the business the way she thinks it should be run, she's bringing it to life every day of the week.

A clear set of values guides the daily decisions and actions that Claire and her staff make. These values came from walking in the shoes of her staff and their candidates. These wouldn't work, however, if they weren't shared values. As Claire told us, 'People have said to me time and time again, "I wouldn't work for any other recruitment consultancy. The only reason I'm sitting here is because I like these values. They're the same as mine." '

'That's music to my ears', Claire said. 'We're not everybody's cup of tea. People come and work for us because they want to make a difference to people. They want to help people. It's what they do.'

'We are a very, very candidate-driven business', Claire told us. But even more important to her than the candidate is her staff. She fervently believes that if you take care of your staff, they will take care of the candidate; if the staff takes care of the candidate, the candidate will take care of the client; and if the candidate takes care of the client, the client will return to the SG Group for more business. Claire puts her staff first, knowing that they are the ones that ultimately determine the reputation of the company.

As you'd expect, staff turnover at the SG Group is extremely low. People rarely leave the business, and if they do they are always welcomed back should they choose to return. 'Friendship is the glue that keeps people here. Why would I want to leave when my best mates work with me? Someone once said to me, "Don't take this the wrong way, Claire, but coming to work is a bit like going to a coffee morning." I asked her what she meant, and she said, "I am with people I like, and we can socialize. And yes, we do the job." I thought that was wonderful. They love coming to work because of the people that are here.'

The values of helping and caring for clients and staff are by no means permission to coddle people and allow them to do whatever they want. Claire is very clear that she expects the values to be lived, not just talked about. They are as much a discipline as any other operational values. 'If you want customers to have a certain experience', says Claire, 'you have got to have people who can deliver on that experience. It's a darn sight easier if you employ people who have the values that you want to give your customers.'

Clearly the SG Group values aren't just posters on the wall – they are the guidelines the group uses in everything they do. For example, there is the 'First Tuesday in the Month' meeting. It's actually never held on the first Tuesday, but that's what it was called when they were first held and the name has stuck. It happens once a month from 9:00 a.m. to 10:00 a.m., and everybody comes. In that meeting they share the company's financials. Everybody learns what the business turned over, and the profit made or loss taken. They talk about where the business has come from, so people don't forget about their important clients. They share any marketing that's going on. They share a lot of people things – who's joining, who's leaving, who's got an anniversary this month, and anything else that affects staff. And they always have the 'grapevine' – a time when people can ask about things they might have heard about and want to know if it's really happening. They film the meeting, so if someone has to miss it they can watch it on DVD.

Then there's the Friday meeting. It's a look back at the week, a sharing of good things and bad things that went on during the week. There's also the Thursday Breakfast Club, which happens every other Thursday. That's a forum for consultants to talk about candidates and clients, and to just share in depth the issues they're having. Notes from these meetings are often posted in the lavatory so that they are visible at all times – you never know when you might come up with a solution to someone's problem. Finally, there is a staff newsletter that goes out every other week for more personal needs, like someone wanting details of a great Mexican restaurant, a good plumber, or a flatmate.

Being physically present is important for Claire. She asked her staff what they wanted from her, and they told her 'that they just wanted to see more of me, to have time to talk to me, to see me wandering around'. Claire radiates energy. When you're around her you have no doubt that she cares deeply about the business, and, in particular, about the people in the business. Claire fully understands the potency of her physical presence. 'You see that I get excited about things', she pointed out to us – not that there was any doubt – 'and people go, "Well, Claire is excited by it, so I'm going to get excited by it. She believes it and she thinks it is going to be great – well I think it's going to be great." That's really all I do.'

Claire also realizes that if her enthusiasm isn't genuine, it's going to have a negative effect. 'If it's an act', she said, 'they'll see right through it. People really respect you for who you are, and they don't want you to be someone you are not. They prefer to see who you are, the real you.'

The SG Group has a positively charged atmosphere that is fueled by numerous recognitions and celebrations. These are the informal kinds at which people toast personal successes, anniversaries, and births of babies. Every month staff members nominate people who have gone the extra mile. Anybody can nominate anybody. Every month all the nominations are considered, 99 percent are approved, and every winner gets a silver envelope placed on their desk thanking them for going the extra mile and presenting usually between 25 and 50 Stopgap Points. Each point is worth about £1, and they can convert the points into whatever they want to spend it on. The SG Group also has a very flexible benefits scheme called 'Mind, Body, Soul'. Nothing is formal, and staff create things for themselves. The whole idea is that each person is different and they can customize the plan to fit their needs. For some it's a gym membership, for others it's health insurance, and for others it's personal coaching. The entire scheme celebrates the individuality of each person.

The marketplace for freelance marketers has grown more and more competitive. 'You can never get complacent', Claire said. 'As a business we are always, always thinking, "What else can we do to stay ahead?"' But something that won't change is Claire Owen's leadership philosophy. 'We are human beings', she said. 'We don't have employees. We don't have staff. We have people, and people have emotions, and people have needs. If you are happy you do a better job. If you are excited about the business, and if you are excited about where it is going and what is happening in it, then there is a buzz, a physical buzz. It's my job to create that kind of place.'

# The Five Practices of Exemplary Leadership

Since 1983 we've been conducting research on personal-best leadership experiences, and we've discovered that there are countless examples of how leaders, like Dick and Claire, mobilize others to get extraordinary things done in virtually every arena of organized activity. We've found them in profit-based firms and nonprofits, manufacturing and services, government and business, health care, education and entertainment, and work and community service. Leaders reside in every city and every country, in every position and every place. They're employees and volunteers, young and old, women and men. Leadership knows no racial or religious bounds, no ethnic or cultural borders. We find exemplary leadership everywhere we look.

From our analysis of thousands of personal-best leadership experiences, we've discovered that ordinary people who guide others along pioneering journeys follow rather similar paths. Though each experience we examined was unique in expression, every case followed remarkably similar patterns of action. We've forged these common practices into a model of leadership, and we offer it here as guidance for leaders as they attempt to keep their own bearings and steer others toward peak achievements.

As we looked deeper into the dynamic process of leadership, through case analyses and survey questionnaires, we uncovered five practices common to personal-best leadership experiences. When getting extraordinary things done in organizations, leaders engage in these Five Practices of Exemplary Leadership:

- Model the Way
- Inspire a Shared Vision
- Challenge the Process
- Enable Others to Act
- Encourage the Heart

The Five Practices [ ... ] aren't the private property of the people we studied or of a few select shining stars. Leadership is not about personality; it's about behavior. The Five Practices are available to anyone who accepts the leadership challenge. And they're also not the accident of a unique moment in history. The Five Practices have stood the test of time, and our most recent research confirms that they're just as relevant today as they were when we first began our investigation more than twenty-five years ago.

## Model the Way

Titles are granted, but it's your behavior that wins you respect. As Tom Brack, with Europe's SmartTeam AG, told us, 'Leading means you have to be a good example, and live what you say.' This sentiment was shared across all the cases that we collected. Exemplary leaders know that if they want to gain commitment and achieve the highest standards, they must be models of the behavior they expect of others. *Leaders model the way.*

To effectively model the behavior they expect of others, leaders must first be clear about guiding principles. They must *clarify values.* As Lindsay Levin, chairman for Whites Group in England, explained, 'You have to open up your heart and let people know what you really think and believe. This means talking about your values.' Leaders must find their own voice, and then they must clearly and distinctively give voice to their values. As the personal-best stories illustrate, leaders are supposed to stand up for their beliefs, so they'd better have some beliefs to stand up for. But it's not just the leader's values that are important. Leaders aren't just representing themselves. They speak and act on behalf of a larger organization. Leaders must forge agreement around common principles and common ideals.

Eloquent speeches about common values, however, aren't nearly enough. Leaders' deeds are far more important than their words when one wants to determine how serious leaders really are about what they say. Words and deeds must be consistent. Exemplary leaders go first. They go first by *setting the example* through daily actions that demonstrate they are deeply committed to their beliefs. As Prabha Seshan, principal engineer for SSA Global, told us, 'One of the best ways to prove something is important is by doing it yourself and setting an example.' She discovered that her actions spoke volumes about how the team needed to 'take ownership of things they believed in and valued'. There wasn't anything Prabha asked others to do that she wasn't willing to do herself, and as a result, 'while I always trusted my team, my team in turn trusted me.' For instance, she wasn't required to design or code features but by doing some of this work she demonstrated to others not only what she stood for but also how much she valued the work they were doing and what their end user expected from the product.

The personal-best projects we heard about in our research were all distinguished by relentless effort, steadfastness, competence, and attention to detail. We were also struck by how the actions leaders took to set an example were often simple things. Sure, leaders had operational and strategic plans. But the examples they gave were not about elaborate designs. They were about the power of spending time with someone, of working side by side with colleagues, of telling stories that made values come alive, of being highly visible during times of uncertainty, and of asking questions to get people to think about values and priorities.

Modeling the way is about earning the right and the respect to lead through direct involvement and action. People follow first the person, then the plan.

## Inspire a Shared Vision

When people described to us their personal-best leadership experiences, they told of times when they imagined an exciting, highly attractive future for their organization. They had visions and dreams of what *could* be. They had absolute and total personal belief in those dreams, and they were confident in their abilities to make extraordinary things happen. Every organization, every social movement, begins with a dream. The dream or vision is the force that invents the future. *Leaders inspire a shared vision.* As Mark D'Arcangelo, system memory product marketing manager at Hitachi Semiconductor, told us about his personal-best leadership experience, 'What made the difference was the vision of how things could be and clearly painting this picture for all to see and comprehend.'

Leaders gaze across the horizon of time, imagining the attractive opportunities that are in store when they and their constituents arrive at a distant destination. They *envision exciting and ennobling possibilities*. Leaders have a desire to make something happen, to change the way things are, to create something that no one else has ever created before. In some ways, leaders live their lives backward. They see pictures in their mind's eye of what the results will look like even before they've started their project, much as an architect draws a blue-print or an engineer builds a model. Their clear image of the future pulls them forward. Yet visions seen only by leaders are insufficient to create an organized movement or a significant change in a company. A person with no constituents is not a leader, and people will not follow until they accept a vision as their own. Leaders cannot command commitment, only inspire it.

Leaders have to *enlist others in a common vision*. To enlist people in a vision, leaders must know their constituents and speak their language. People must believe that leaders understand their needs and have their interests at heart. Leadership is a dialogue, not a monologue. To enlist support, leaders must have intimate knowledge of people's dreams, hopes, aspirations, visions, and values. Evelia Davis, merchandise manager for Mervyns, told us that while she was good at telling people where they were going together, she also needed to do a good job of explaining why they should follow her, how they could help reach the destination, and what this meant for them. As Evelia put it, 'If you don't believe enough to share it, talk about it, and get others excited about it then it's not much of a vision!'

Leaders breathe life into the hopes and dreams of others and enable them to see the exciting possibilities that the future holds. Leaders forge a unity of purpose by showing constituents how the dream is for the common good. Leaders stir the fire of passion in others by expressing enthusiasm for the compelling vision of their group. Leaders communicate their passion through vivid language and an expressive style.

Whatever the venue, and without exception, the people in our study reported that they were incredibly enthusiastic about their personal-best projects. Their own enthusiasm was catching; it spread from leader to constituents. Their belief in and enthusiasm for the vision were the sparks that ignited the flame of inspiration.

## Challenge the Process

Every single personal-best leadership case we collected involved some kind of challenge. The challenge might have been an innovative new product, a cutting-edge service, a groundbreaking piece of legislation, an invigorating campaign to get adolescents to join an environmental program, a revolutionary turnaround of a bureaucratic military program, or the start-up of a new plant or business. Whatever the challenge, all the cases involved a change from the status quo. Not one person claimed to have achieved a personal best by keeping things the same. All leaders *challenge the process*.

Leaders venture out. None of the individuals in our study sat idly by waiting for fate to smile upon them. 'Luck' or 'being in the right place at the right time' may play a role in the specific opportunities leaders embrace, but those who lead others to greatness seek and accept challenge. Jennifer Cun, in her role as a budget analyst with Intel, noted how critical it is for leaders 'to always be looking for ways to improve their team, taking interests outside of their job or organization, finding ways to stay current of what the competition is doing, networking, and taking initiative to try new things'.

Leaders are pioneers. They are willing to step out into the unknown. They *search for opportunities to innovate, grow, and improve.* But leaders aren't the only creators or originators of new products, services, or processes. In fact, it's more likely that they're not: innovation comes more from listening than from telling. Product and service innovations tend to come from customers, clients, vendors, people in the labs, and people on the front lines; process innovations, from the people doing the work. Sometimes a dramatic external event thrusts an organization into a radically new condition. Leaders have to constantly be looking outside of themselves and their organizations for new and innovative products, processes, and services. 'Mediocrity and status quo will never lead a company to success in the marketplace', is what Mike Pepe, product marketing manager at O3 Entertainment, told us. 'Taking risks and believing that taking them is worthwhile', he went on to say, 'are the only way companies can "jump" rather than simply climb the improvement ladder.'

When it comes to innovation, the leader's major contributions are in the creation of a climate for experimentation, the recognition of good ideas, the support of those ideas, and the willingness to challenge the system to get new products, processes, services, and systems adopted. It might be more accurate, then, to say that leaders aren't the inventors as much as they are the early patrons and adopters of innovation.

Leaders know well that innovation and change involve *experimenting and taking risks.* Despite the inevitability of mistakes and failures leaders proceed anyway. One way of dealing with the potential risks and failures of experimentation is to approach change through incremental steps and small wins. Little victories, when piled on top of each other, build confidence that even the biggest challenges can be met. In so doing, they strengthen commitment to the long-term future. Not everyone is equally comfortable with risk and uncertainty. Leaders must pay attention to the capacity of their constituents to take control of challenging situations and become fully committed to change. You can't exhort people to take risks if they don't also feel safe.

It would be ridiculous to assert that those who fail over and over again eventually succeed as leaders. Success in any endeavor isn't a process of simply buying enough lottery tickets. The key that unlocks the door to opportunity is learning. Claude Meyer, with the Red Cross in Kenya, put it to us this way: 'Leadership is learning by doing, adapting to actual conditions. Leaders are constantly learning from their errors and failures.' Life is the leader's laboratory, and exemplary leaders use it to conduct as many experiments as possible. Try, fail, learn. Try, fail, learn. Try, fail, learn. That's the leader's mantra. Leaders are learners. They learn from their failures as well as their successes, and they make it possible for others to do the same.

## Enable Others to Act

Grand dreams don't become significant realities through the actions of a single person. It requires a team effort. It requires solid trust and strong relationships. It requires deep competence and cool confidence. It requires group collaboration and individual accountability. To get extraordinary things done in organizations, leaders have to *enable others to act*.

After reviewing thousands of personal-best cases, we developed a simple test to detect whether someone is on the road to becoming a leader. That test is the frequency of the use of the word *we*. In our interviews, we found that people used *we* nearly three times more often than *I* in explaining their personal-best leadership experience. Hewlett-Packard's Angie Yim was the technical IT team leader on a project involving core team members from the United States, Singapore, Australia, and Hong Kong. In the past, Angie told us, she 'had a bad habit of using the pronoun *I* instead of *we*', but she learned that people responded more eagerly and her team became more cohesive when people felt part of the *we*. 'This is a magic word', Angie realized. 'I would recommend that others use it more often.'

Leaders *foster collaboration and build trust*. This sense of teamwork goes far beyond a few direct reports or close confidants. They engage all those who must make the project work – and in some way, all who must live with the results. In today's virtual organizations, cooperation can't be restricted to a small group of loyalists; it must include peers, managers, customers and clients, suppliers, citizens – all those who have a stake in the vision.

Leaders make it possible for others to do good work. They know that those who are expected to produce the results must feel a sense of personal power and ownership. Leaders understand that the command-and-control techniques of traditional management no longer apply. Instead, leaders work to make people feel strong, capable, and committed. Leaders enable others to act not by hoarding the power they have but by giving it away. Exemplary leaders *strengthen everyone's capacity* to deliver on the promises they make. As Kathryn Winters learned working with the communications department at NVIDIA Corporation, 'You have to make sure that no one is outside the loop or uninvolved in all the changes that occur.' She continually ensures that each person has a sense of ownership for his or her projects. She seeks out the opinions of others and uses the ensuing discussion not only to build up their capabilities but also to educate and update her own information and perspective. 'Inclusion (not exclusion)', she finds, 'ensures that everyone feels and thinks that they are owners and leaders-this makes work much easier'. Kathryn realized that when people are trusted and have more discretion, more authority, and more information, they're much more likely to use their energies to produce extraordinary results.

In the cases we analyzed, leaders proudly discussed teamwork, trust, and empowerment as essential elements of their efforts. A leader's ability to enable others to act is essential. Constituents neither perform at their best nor stick around for very long if their leader makes them feel weak, dependent, or alienated. But when a leader makes people feel strong and capable – as if they can do more than they ever thought possible – they'll give it their all and exceed their own expectations. Authentic leadership is founded on trust, and the more people trust their leader, and each other, the more they take risks, make changes, and keep organizations and movements alive. Through that relationship, leaders turn their constituents into leaders themselves.

## Encourage the Heart

The climb to the top is arduous and long. People become exhausted, frustrated, and disenchanted. They're often tempted to give up. Leaders *encourage the heart* of their constituents to carry on. Genuine acts of caring uplift the spirits and draw people forward. In her personal-best leadership experience Ankush Joshi, the service line manager with Informix USA, learned that 'writing a personal thank-you note, rather than sending an e-mail, can do wonders'. Janel Ahrens, marcom manager with National Semiconductor, echoed Ankush's observation. Janel would make notes about important events in other people's lives and then follow up with them directly after or simply wish them luck prior to an important event. Every person was 'genuinely touched that I cared enough to ask them about how things are going'. She told us that in her organization 'work relationships have been stronger since this undertaking'. Janel's and Ankush's experiences are testimony to the power of a 'thank you'.

*Recognizing contributions* can be one-to-one or with many people. It can come from dramatic gestures or simple actions. One of the first actions that Abraham Kuruvilla took upon becoming CEO of the Dredging Corporation of India (a government-owned private-sector company providing services to all ten major Indian ports) was to send out to every employee a monthly newsletter (*DCI News*) that was full of success stories. In addition, he introduced, for the first time, a public-recognition program through which awards and simple appreciation notices were given out to individuals and teams for doing great work. Abraham made sure that people were recognized for their contributions, because he wanted to provide a climate in which 'people felt cared about and genuinely appreciated by their leaders'.

It's part of the leader's job to show appreciation for people's contributions and to create a culture of *celebrating values and victories*. In the cases we collected, we saw thousands of examples of individual recognition and group celebration. We've heard and seen everything from handwritten thank-yous to marching bands and 'This Is Your Life'–type ceremonies.

Recognition and celebration aren't about fun and games, though there is a lot of fun and there are a lot of games when people encourage the hearts of their constituents. Neither are they about pretentious ceremonies designed to create some phony sense of camaraderie. When people see a charlatan making noisy affectations, they turn away in disgust. Encouragement is, curiously, serious business. It's how leaders visibly and behaviorally link rewards with performance. When striving to raise quality, recover from disaster, start up a new service, or make dramatic change of any kind, leaders make sure people see the benefit of behavior that's aligned with cherished values. Leaders also know that celebrations and rituals, when done with authenticity and from the heart, build a strong sense of collective identity and community spirit that can carry a group through extraordinarily tough times.

## Leadership is a Relationship

Our findings from the analysis of personal-best leadership experiences challenge the myth that leadership is something that you find only at the highest levels of organizations and society. We found it everywhere. These findings also challenge the belief that leadership is reserved for a few charismatic men and women. Leadership is not a gene and it's not an inheritance. Leadership is an identifiable set of skills and abilities that are available to all of us. The 'great person' – woman or man – theory of leadership is just plain wrong. Or, we should say, the theory that there are only a few great men and women who can lead others to greatness is just plain wrong. Likewise, it is plain wrong that leaders only come from large, or great, or small, or new organizations, or from established economies, or from start-up companies. We consider the women and men in our research to be great, and so do those with whom they worked. They are the everyday heroes of our world. It's because there are so many – not so few – leaders that extraordinary things get done on a regular basis, especially in extraordinary times.

To us this is inspiring and should give everyone hope. Hope, because it means that no one needs to wait around to be saved by someone riding into town on a white horse. Hope, because there's a generation of leaders searching for the opportunities to make a difference. Hope, because right down the block or right down the hall there are people who will seize the opportunity to lead you to greatness. They're your neighbors, friends, and colleagues. And you are one of them, too.

There's still another crucial truth about leadership. It's something that we've known for a long time, but we've come to prize even more today. In talking to leaders and reading their cases, there was a very clear message that wove itself throughout every situation and every action. The message was: *leadership is a relationship*. Leadership is a relationship between those who aspire to lead and those who choose to follow. It's the quality of this relationship that matters most when we're engaged in getting extraordinary things done. A leader-constituent relationship that's characterized by fear and distrust will never, ever produce anything of lasting value. A relationship characterized by mutual respect and confidence will overcome the greatest adversities and leave a legacy of significance. [ ... ]

# Primal Leadership: The Hidden Driver of Great Performance

5

*Daniel Goleman, Richard Boyatzis and Annie McKee*

When the theory of emotional intelligence at work began to receive widespread attention, we frequently heard executives say – in the same breath, mind you – 'That's incredible', and, 'Well, I've known that all along.' They were responding to our research that showed an incontrovertible link between an executive's emotional maturity, exemplified by such capabilities as self-awareness and empathy, and his or her financial performance. Simply put, the research showed that 'good guys' – that is, emotionally intelligent men and women – finish first.

We've recently compiled two years of new research that, we suspect, will elicit the same kind of reaction. People will first exclaim, 'No way', then quickly add, 'But of course'. We found that of all the elements affecting bottom-line performance, the importance of the leader's mood and its attendant behaviors are most surprising. That powerful pair set off a chain reaction: The leader's mood and behaviors drive the moods and behaviors of everyone else. A cranky and ruthless boss creates a toxic organization filled with negative underachievers who ignore opportunities; an inspirational, inclusive leader spawns acolytes for whom any challenge is surmountable. The final link in the chain is performance: profit or loss.

Our observation about the overwhelming impact of the leader's 'emotional style', as we call it, is not a wholesale departure from our research into emotional intelligence. It does, however, represent a deeper analysis of our earlier assertion that a leader's emotional intelligence creates a certain culture or work environment. High levels of emotional intelligence, our research showed, create climates in which information sharing, trust, healthy risk-taking, and learning flourish. Low levels of emotional intelligence create climates rife with fear and anxiety. Because tense or terrified employees can be very productive in the short term, their organizations may post good results, but they never last.

Goleman, D., Boyatzis, R. and McKee, A. (2001) 'Primal leadership: The hidden driver of great performance', Harvard Business Review, December, pp. 42–51.

Our investigation was designed in part to look at how emotional intelligence drives performance – in particular, at how it travels from the leader through the organization to bottom-line results. 'What mechanism', we asked, 'binds the chain together?' To answer that question, we turned to the latest neurological and psychological research. We also drew on our work with business leaders, observations by our colleagues of hundreds of leaders, and Hay Group data on the leadership styles of thousands of executives. From this body of research, we discovered that emotional intelligence is carried through an organization like electricity through wires. To be more specific, the leader's mood is quite literally contagious, spreading quickly and inexorably throughout the business.

We'll discuss the science of mood contagion in more depth later, but first let's turn to the key implications of our finding. If a leader's mood and accompanying behaviors are indeed such potent drivers of business success, then a leader's premier task – we would even say his primal task – is emotional leadership. A leader needs to make sure that not only is he regularly in an optimistic, authentic, high-energy mood, but also that, through his chosen actions, his followers feel and act that way, too. Managing for financial results, then, begins with the leader managing his inner life so that the right emotional and behavioral chain reaction occurs.

Managing one's inner life is not easy, of course. For many of us, it's our most difficult challenge. And accurately gauging how one's emotions affect others can be just as difficult. We know of one CEO, for example, who was certain that everyone saw him as upbeat and reliable; his direct reports told us they found his cheerfulness strained, even fake, and his decisions erratic. (We call this common disconnect 'CEO disease'.) The implication is that primal leadership demands more than putting on a game face every day. It requires an executive to determine, through reflective analysis, how his emotional leadership drives the moods and actions of the organization, and then, with equal discipline, to adjust his behavior accordingly.

That's not to say that leaders can't have a bad day or week: Life happens. And our research doesn't suggest that good moods have to be high-pitched or nonstop – optimistic, sincere, and realistic will do. But there is no escaping the conclusion that a leader must first attend to the impact of his mood and behaviors before moving on to his wide panoply of other critical responsibilities. In this article, we introduce a process that executives can follow to assess how others experience their leadership, and we discuss ways to calibrate that impact. But first, we'll look at why moods aren't often discussed in the workplace, how the brain works to make moods contagious, and what you need to know about CEO disease.

# No Way! Yes Way

When we said earlier that people will likely respond to our new finding by saying 'No way', we weren't joking. The fact is, the emotional impact of a leader is almost never discussed in the workplace, let alone in the literature on leadership and performance. For most people, 'mood' feels too personal. Even though Americans can be shockingly candid about personal matters – witness the *Jerry Springer Show* and its ilk – we are also the most legally bound. We can't even ask the age of a job applicant. Thus, a conversation about an executive's mood or the moods he creates in his employees might be construed as an invasion of privacy.

We also might avoid talking about a leader's emotional style and its impact because, frankly, the topic feels soft. When was the last time you evaluated a subordinate's mood as part of her performance appraisal? You may have alluded to it – 'Your work is hindered by an often negative perspective', or 'Your enthusiasm is terrific' – but it is unlikely you mentioned mood outright, let alone discussed its impact on the organization's results.

And yet our research undoubtedly will elicit a 'But of course' reaction, too. Everyone knows how much a leader's emotional state drives performance because everyone has had, at one time or another, the inspirational experience of working for an upbeat manager or the crushing experience of toiling for a sour-spirited boss. The former made everything feel possible, and as a result, stretch goals were achieved, competitors beaten, and new customers won. The latter made work grueling. In the shadow of the boss's dark mood, other parts of the organization became 'the enemy', colleagues became suspicious of one another, and customers slipped away.

Our research, and research by other social scientists, confirms the verity of these experiences. (There are, of course, rare cases when a brutal boss produces terrific results.) [ ... ] The studies are too numerous to mention here but, in aggregate, they show that when the leader is in a happy mood, the people around him view everything in a more positive light. That, in turn, makes them optimistic about achieving their goals, enhances their creativity and the efficiency of their decision making, and predisposes them to be helpful. Research conducted by Alice Isen at Cornell in 1999, for example, found that an upbeat environment fosters mental efficiency, making people better at taking in and understanding information, at using decision rules in complex judgments, and at being flexible in their thinking. Other research directly links mood and financial performance. In 1986, for instance, Martin Seligman and Peter Schulman of the University of Pennsylvania demonstrated that insurance agents who had a 'glass half-full' outlook were far more able than their more pessimistic peers to persist despite rejections, and thus, they closed more sales. (For more information on these studies and a list of our research base, visit www.eiconsortium.org.)

Many leaders whose emotional styles create a dysfunctional environment are eventually fired. (Of course, that's rarely the stated reason; poor results are.) But it doesn't have to end that way. Just as a bad mood can be turned around, so can the spread of toxic feelings from an emotionally inept leader. A look inside the brain explains both why and how.

# The Science of Moods

A growing body of research on the human brain proves that, for better or worse, leaders' moods affect the emotions of the people around them. The reason for that lies in what scientists call the open-loop nature of the brain's limbic system, our emotional center. A closed-loop system is self-regulating, whereas an open-loop system depends on external sources to manage itself. In other words, we rely on connections with other people to determine our moods. The open-loop limbic system was a winning design in evolution because it let people come to one another's emotional rescue – enabling a mother, for example, to soothe her crying infant.

The open-loop design serves the same purpose today as it did thousands of years ago. Research in intensive care units has shown, for example, that the comforting presence of another person not only lowers the patient's blood pressure but also slows the secretion of fatty acids that block arteries. Another study found that three or more incidents of intense stress within a year (for example, serious financial trouble, being fired, or a divorce) triples the death rate in socially isolated middle-aged men, but it has no impact on the death rate of men with many close relationships.

Scientists describe the open loop as 'interpersonal limbic regulation'; one person transmits signals that can alter hormone levels, cardiovascular functions, sleep rhythms, even immune functions, inside the body of another. That's how couples are able to trigger surges of oxytocin in each other's brains, creating a pleasant, affectionate feeling. But in all aspects of social life, our physiologies intermingle. Our limbic system's open-loop design lets other people change our very physiology and hence, our emotions.

Even though the open loop is so much a part of our lives, we usually don't notice the process. Scientists have captured the attunement of emotions in the laboratory by measuring the physiology – such as heart rate – of two people sharing a good conversation. As the interaction begins, their bodies operate at different rhythms. But after 15 minutes, the physiological profiles of their bodies look remarkably similar.

Researchers have seen again and again how emotions spread irresistibly in this way whenever people are near one another. As far back as 1981, psychologists Howard Friedman and Ronald Riggio found that even completely nonverbal expressiveness can affect other people. For example, when three strangers sit facing one another in silence for a minute or two, the most emotionally expressive of the three transmits his or her mood to the other two – without a single word being spoken.

The same holds true in the office, boardroom, or shop floor; group members inevitably 'catch' feelings from one another. In 2000, Caroline Bartel at New York University and Richard Saavedra at the University of Michigan found that in 70 work teams across diverse industries, people in meetings together ended up sharing moods – both good and bad – within two hours. One study asked teams of nurses and accountants to monitor their moods over weeks; researchers discovered that their emotions tracked together, and they were largely independent of each team's shared hassles. Groups, therefore, like individuals, ride emotional roller coasters, sharing everything from jealousy to angst to euphoria. (A good mood, incidentally, spreads most swiftly by the judicious use of humor. [ ... ])

Moods that start at the top tend to move the fastest because everyone watches the boss. They take their emotional cues from him. Even when the boss isn't highly visible – for example, the CEO who works behind closed doors on an upper floor – his attitude affects the moods of his direct reports, and a domino effect ripples throughout the company.

## Call that CEO a Doctor

If the leader's mood is so important, then he or she had better get into a good one, right? Yes, but the full answer is more complicated than that. A leader's mood has the greatest impact on performance when it is upbeat. But it must also be in tune with those around him. We call this dynamic *resonance*. [ ... ]

We found that an alarming number of leaders do not really know if they have resonance with their organizations. Rather, they suffer from CEO disease; its one un-pleasant symptom is the sufferer's near-total ignorance about how his mood and actions appear to the organization. It's not that leaders don't care how they are perceived; most do. But they incorrectly assume that they can decipher this information themselves. Worse, they think that if they are having a negative effect, someone will tell them. They're wrong.

As one CEO in our research explains, 'I so often feel I'm not getting the truth. I can never put my finger on it, because no one is actually lying to me. But I can sense that people are hiding information or camouflaging key facts. They aren't lying, but neither are they telling me everything I need to know. I'm always second-guessing.'

People don't tell leaders the whole truth about their emotional impact for many reasons. Sometimes they are scared of being the bearer of bad news – and getting shot. Others feel it isn't their place to comment on such a personal topic. Still others don't realize that what they really want to talk about is the effects of the leader's emotional style – that feels too vague. Whatever the reason, the CEO can't rely on his followers to spontaneously give him the full picture.

## Taking Stock

The process we recommend for self-discovery and personal reinvention is neither newfangled nor born of pop psychology, like so many self-help programs offered to executives today. Rather, it is based on three streams of research into how executives can improve the emotional intelligence capabilities most closely linked to effective leadership. [ ... ] In 1989, one of us (Richard Boyatzis) began drawing on this body of research to design the five-step process itself, and since then, thousands of executives have used it successfully.

Unlike more traditional forms of coaching, our process is based on brain science. A person's emotional skills – the attitude and abilities with which someone approaches life and work – are not genetically hardwired, like eye color and skin tone. But in some ways they might as well be, because they are so deeply embedded in our neurology.

A person's emotional skills do, in fact, have a genetic component. Scientists have discovered, for instance, the gene for shyness – which is not a mood, per se, but it can certainly drive a person toward a persistently quiet demeanor, which may be read as a 'down' mood. Other people are preternaturally jolly – that is, their relentless cheerfulness seems preternatural until you meet their peppy parents. As one executive explains, 'All I know is that ever since I was a baby, I have always been happy. It drives some people crazy, but I couldn't get blue if I tried. And my brother is the exact same way; he saw the bright side of life, even during his divorce.'

Even though emotional skills are partly inborn, experience plays a major role in how the genes are expressed. A happy baby whose parents die or who endures physical abuse may grow into a melancholy adult. A cranky toddler may turn into a cheerful adult after discovering a fulfilling avocation. Still, research suggests that our range of emotional skills is relatively set by our mid-twenties and that our accompanying behaviors are, by that time, deep-seated habits. And therein lies the rub: The more we act a certain way – be it happy, depressed, or cranky – the more the behavior becomes ingrained in our brain circuitry, and the more we will continue to feel and act that way.

That's why emotional intelligence matters so much for a leader. An emotionally intelligent leader can monitor his or her moods through self-awareness, change them for the better through self-management, understand their impact through empathy, and act in ways that boost others' moods through relationship management.

The following five-part process is designed to rewire the brain toward more emotionally intelligent behaviors. The process begins with imagining your ideal self and then coming to terms with your real self, as others experience you. The next step is creating a tactical plan to bridge the gap between ideal and real, and after that, to practice those activities. It concludes with creating a community of colleagues and family – call them change enforcers – to keep the process alive. Let's look at the steps in more detail.

'Who do I want to be?' Sofia, a senior manager at a northern European telecommunications company, knew she needed to understand how her emotional leadership affected others. Whenever she felt stressed, she tended to communicate poorly and take over subordinates' work so that the job would be done 'right'. Attending leadership seminars hadn't changed her habits, and neither had reading management books or working with mentors.

When Sofia came to us, we asked her to imagine herself eight years from now as an effective leader and to write a description of a typical day. 'What would she be doing?' we asked. 'Where would she live? Who would be there? How would it feel?' We urged her to consider her deepest values and loftiest dreams and to explain how those ideals had become a part of her everyday life.

Sofia pictured herself leading her own tight-knit company staffed by ten colleagues. She was enjoying an open relationship with her daughter and had trusting relationships with her friends and coworkers. She saw herself as a relaxed and happy leader and parent and as loving and empowering to all those around her.

In general, Sofia had a low level of self-awareness: She was rarely able to pinpoint why she was struggling at work and at home. All she could say was, 'Nothing is working right.' This exercise, which prompted her to picture what life would look life if everything were going right, opened her eyes to the missing elements in her emotional style. She was able to see the impact she had on people in her life.

'Who am I now?' In the next step of the discovery process, you come to see your leadership style as others do. This is both difficult and dangerous. Difficult, because few people have the guts to tell the boss or a colleague what he's really like. And dangerous, because such information can sting or even paralyze. A small bit of ignorance about yourself isn't always a bad thing: Ego-defense mechanisms have their advantages. Research by Martin Seligman shows that high-functioning people generally feel more optimistic about their prospects and possibilities than average performers. Their rose-colored lenses, in fact, fuel the enthusiasm and energy that make the unexpected and the extraordinary achievable. Playwright Henrik Ibsen called such self-delusions 'vital lies', soothing mistruths we let ourselves believe in order to face a daunting world.

But self-delusion should come in very small doses. Executives should relentlessly seek the truth about themselves, especially since it is sure to be somewhat diluted when they hear it anyway. One way to get the truth is to keep an extremely open attitude toward critiques. Another is to seek out negative feedback, even cultivating a colleague or two to play devil's advocate.

We also highly recommend gathering feedback from as many people as possible – including bosses, peers, and subordinates. Feedback from subordinates and peers is especially helpful because it most accurately predicts a leader's effectiveness, two, four, and even seven years out, according to research by Glenn McEvoy at Utah State and Richard Beatty at Rutgers University.

Of course, 360-degree feedback doesn't specifically ask people to evaluate your moods, actions, and their impact. But it does reveal how people experience you. For instance, when people rate how well you listen, they are really reporting how well they think you hear them. Similarly, when 360-degree feedback elicits ratings about coaching effectiveness, the answers show whether or not people feel you understand and care about them. When the feedback uncovers low scores on, say, openness to new ideas, it means that people experience you as inaccessible or unapproachable or both. In sum, all you need to know about your emotional impact is in 360-degree feedback, if you look for it.

One last note on this second step. It is, of course, crucial to identify your areas of weakness. But focusing only on your weaknesses can be dispiriting. That's why it is just as important, maybe even more so, to understand your strengths. Knowing where your real self overlaps with your ideal self will give you the positive energy you need to move forward to the next step in the process – bridging the gaps.

'How do I get from here to there?' Once you know who you want to be and have compared it with how people see you, you need to devise an action plan. For Sofia, this meant planning for a real improvement in her level of self-awareness. So she asked each member of her team at work to give her feedback – weekly, anonymously, and in written form – about her mood and performance and their affect on people. She also committed herself to three tough but achievable tasks: spending an hour each day reflecting on her behavior in a journal, taking a class on group dynamics at a local college, and enlisting the help of a trusted colleague as an informal coach.

Consider, too, how Juan, a marketing executive for the Latin American division of a major integrated energy company, completed this step. Juan was charged with growing the company in his home country of Venezuela as well as in the entire region – a job that would require him to be a coach and a visionary and to have an encouraging, optimistic outlook. Yet 360-degree feedback revealed that Juan was seen as intimidating and internally focused. Many of his direct reports saw him as a grouch – impossible to please at his worst, and emotionally draining at his best.

Identifying this gap allowed Juan to craft a plan with manageable steps toward improvement. He knew he needed to hone his powers of empathy if he wanted to develop a coaching style, so he committed to various activities that would let him practice that skill. For instance, Juan decided to get to know each of his subordinates better; if he understood more about who they were, he thought, he'd be more able to help them reach their goals. He made plans with each employee to meet outside of work, where they might be more comfortable revealing their feelings.

Juan also looked for areas outside of his job to forge his missing links – for example, coaching his daughter's soccer team and volunteering at a local crisis center. Both activities helped him to experiment with how well he understood others and to try out new behaviors.

Again, let's look at the brain science at work. Juan was trying to overcome ingrained behaviors – his approach to work had taken hold over time, without his realizing it. Bringing them into awareness was a crucial step toward changing them. As he paid more attention, the situations that arose – while listening to a colleague, coaching soccer, or talking on the phone to someone who was distraught – all became cues that stimulated him to break old habits and try new responses.

This cueing for habit change is neural as well as perceptual. Researchers at the University of Pittsburgh and Carnegie Mellon University have shown that as we mentally prepare for a task, we activate the prefrontal cortex – the part of the brain that moves us into action. The greater the prior activation, the better we do at the task.

Such mental preparation becomes particularly important when we're trying to replace an old habit with a better one. As neuroscientist Cameron Carter at the University of Pittsburgh found, the prefrontal cortex becomes particularly active when a person prepares to overcome a habitual response. The aroused prefrontal cortex marks the brain's focus on what's about to happen. Without that arousal, a person will reenact tried-and-true but undesirable routines: The executive who just doesn't listen will once again cut off his subordinate, a ruthless leader will launch into yet another critical attack, and so on. That's why a learning agenda is so important. Without one, we literally do not have the brainpower to change.

'How do I make change stick?' In short, making change last requires practice. The reason, again, lies in the brain. It takes doing and redoing, over and over, to break old neural habits. A leader must rehearse a new behavior until it becomes automatic – that is, until he's mastered it at the level of implicit learning. Only then will the new wiring replace the old.

While it is best to practice new behaviors, as Juan did, sometimes just envisioning them will do. Take the case of Tom, an executive who wanted to close the gap between his real self (perceived by colleagues and subordinates to be cold and hard driving) and his ideal self (a visionary and a coach).

Tom's learning plan involved finding opportunities to step back and coach his employees rather than jumping down their throats when he sensed they were wrong. Tom also began to spend idle moments during his commute thinking through how to handle encounters he would have that day. One morning, while en route to a breakfast meeting with an employee who seemed to be bungling a project, Tom ran through a positive scenario in his mind. He asked questions and listened to be sure he fully understood the situation before trying to solve the problem. He anticipated feeling impatient, and he rehearsed how he would handle these feelings.

Studies on the brain affirm the benefits of Tom's visualization technique: Imagining something in vivid detail can fire the same brain cells actually involved in doing that activity. The new brain circuitry appears to go through its paces, strengthening connections, even when we merely repeat the sequence in our minds. So to alleviate the fears associated with trying out riskier ways of leading, we should first visualize some likely scenarios. Doing so will make us feel less awkward when we actually put the new skills into practice.

Experimenting with new behaviors and seizing opportunities inside and outside of work to practice them – as well as using such methods as mental rehearsal – eventually triggers in our brains the neural connections necessary for genuine change to occur. Even so, lasting change doesn't happen through experimentation and brainpower alone. We need, as the song goes, a little help from our friends.

'Who can help me?' The fifth step in the self-discovery and reinvention process is creating a community of supporters. Take, for example, managers at Unilever who formed learning groups as part of their executive development process. At first, they gathered to discuss their careers and how to provide leadership. But because they were also charged with discussing their dreams and their learning goals, they soon realized that they were discussing both their work and their personal lives. They developed a strong mutual trust and began relying on one another for frank feedback as they worked on strengthening their leadership abilities. When this happens, the business benefits through stronger performance. Many professionals today have created similar groups, and for good reason. People we trust let us try out unfamiliar parts of our leadership repertoire without risk.

We cannot improve our emotional intelligence or change our leadership style without help from others. We not only practice with other people but also rely on them to create a safe environment in which to experiment. We need to get feedback about how our actions affect others and to assess our progress on our learning agenda.

In fact, perhaps paradoxically, in the self-directed learning process we draw on others every step of the way – from articulating and refining our ideal self and comparing it with the reality to the final assessment that affirms our progress. Our relationships offer us the very context in which we understand our progress and comprehend the usefulness of what we're learning.

## Mood over Matter

When we say that managing your mood and the moods of your followers is the task of primal leadership, we certainly don't mean to suggest that mood is all that matters. As we've noted, your actions are critical, and mood and actions together must resonate with the organization and with reality. Similarly, we acknowledge all the other challenges leaders must conquer – from strategy to hiring to new product development. It's all in a long day's work.

But taken as a whole, the message sent by neurological, psychological, and organizational research is startling in its clarity. Emotional leadership is the spark that ignites a company's performance, creating a bonfire of success or a landscape of ashes. Moods matter that much.

# Leadership Competency Models

6

*George P. Hollenbeck, Morgan W. McCall Jr. and Robert F. Silzer*

[ ... ]

Dear Rob,

Our debate on the value of leadership competency models at the 2003 SIOP conference raised a number of issues, but the sound and the fury of the debate did not provide for the kind of reasoned discussion that the issues deserve. An exchange of letters should allow us to share our views on the pluses and minuses of the widespread use of leadership competency models. In this first letter, we lay out our belief that the competency movement is based on a set of questionable assumptions, and that using competency models as the foundation for human resource (HR) systems means that those systems are built on sand. We argue that the wholesale adoption of competency-based HR practices has hindered more than it has helped the advancement of leadership development. And, perhaps worse than shaky systems and processes, the most dangerous impact of competencies is that their very popularity has prevented the search for more useful alternatives.

With the commitment to competencies of so many in our profession today, we risk being seen as the enemy of *competence*. Nothing could be further from the truth. The heresy we propose is that the enchanting song of the competency sirens has lured us into dangerous rocks. It is time to put wax in our ears and seek a better route.

Our field seems to become enchanted with techniques and methods from time to time, from sensitivity training to management by objectives (MBO). Marv Dunnette in his 1966 classic 'Fads, Fashions, and Folderol' called these fads – 'those practices and concepts characterized by capriciousness and intense, but short-lived interest – such things as brainstorming, Q technique, level of aspiration, role playing, need theory, grids of various types, adjective checklists, two factor theory, Theory X and Theory Y, social desirability, response sets and response styles, need hierarchies, and so on and so on'. If Marv were writing his article today, his list most certainly would include competency models. But while the folly of enchantments has been portrayed in literature for centuries,

Hollenbeck, G.P., McCall Jr, M.W. and Silzer, R.F. (2006) 'Leadership competency models', Leadership Quarterly, vol. 17, pp. 398–413.

our ability to recognize them and subsequently break their spell apparently has not improved.

## Underlying Assumptions of Leadership Competency Models

What is wrong with leadership competency models? For starters, they are a 'best practice' that defies logic, experience, and data. Looking first at the logic, the assumptions on which competency models are used do not hold up under analytic scrutiny, nor are they consistent with simple observation of leaders. It seems to us that there are at least four basic and problematic underlying assumptions of leadership competency models:

1. A single set of characteristics adequately describes effective leaders (and consequently, those characteristics predict behavior which in turn predicts effectiveness);
2. Each of these characteristics is independent of the others and of the context, therefore having more of each of these characteristics is independent of the others and of the context, therefore having more of each of these characteristics makes a person a better leader (that is, they are additive, and effective leaders are the simple sum of their parts);
3. Because senior management usually blesses competencies and sometimes even helps generate them, they are the most effective way to think about leader behavior;
4. When HR systems are based on competencies, these systems work effectively.

**Assumption 1. A single set of characteristics adequately describes effective leaders.** As a descendant of the long-discredited 'great man' theory, competency models raise again the specter of one set of traits, abilities, and behaviors (a.k.a. KSAs or knowledge, skills, and abilities) that make up *the* 'great leader'. One need not be a researcher to find fault with this assumption – everyday observation will suffice. Even a casual review of effective leaders demonstrates convincingly how different they are from each other. Effective leaders come in all sizes and shapes (Bennis and Nanus, 1985; Kotter, 1988) with tapestries of strengths and weaknesses that they apply in complex combinations to get the work of the organization done. No one set, whether 15 or 20 or 180, includes all the potentially useful competencies, and even if they did, no one person has them all.

Even the 'contingency' competency models (i.e., ones that specify that competencies 1, 3, and 5 are required in situation A; and competencies 2, 4, and 6 are required in situation B) fail the common sense test. Even if one assumes that unique clusters of competencies are required to enact each specific strategy, the logic is defeated when more than one leadership strategy can be effective in a given contingent situation.

**Assumption 2.** Each of these characteristics is independent of the others and of the context, so therefore having more of each of these characteristics makes a person a better leader.

Effective leaders are not the sum of a set of competencies, however long or broad the list. Leaders, like the rest of us, are particular mixtures of pluses and minuses, the effectiveness of which changes over time and with the circumstances. Our derailment research (McCall, 1998; McCall and Hollenbeck, 2002) demonstrates all too well that strengths can become weaknesses (and therefore that every competence is also an incompetence), that effectiveness depends on how various *combinations* of strengths are used, and that different strengths and weaknesses come in and out of focus at different times in different jobs. What matters is not a person's sum score on a set of competencies, but how well a person uses whatever talents he or she has to get the job done. Leaders do not come in neat, additive packages.

**Assumption 3.** Because senior management usually blesses competencies and sometimes even helps generate them, they are the most effective way to think about leader behavior.

The fact that senior management accepts and even supports competency models brings about a peculiar kind of circular logic: 'They accept the model, so it is correct; the model is correct, thus they accept it.' We are reminded here again of Dunnette's fads and fashions that seem to feed on themselves for some period of time, uncritically accepted because they are uncritically accepted. Even if they are not valid, the temptation is great to go with 'the devil we know'. The elegant applications of competencies have in many cases earned for HR the apparent respect and support of top management. This appreciation is so valued that, when we expressed some reservations about competency models, one HR development specialist exclaimed, 'We finally have a tool that is getting lots of visibility and acceptance of senior management and you people start criticizing it.'

**Assumption 4. When HR systems are based on competencies, these systems actually work effectively.**

Competency models are very attractive to the HR practitioner. Selection, training, compensation, and other systems can be designed around a finite set of competencies, each of which can be dealt with as a separate 'whole' as well. We have become quite good at measuring competency 2, 13, and 167; and we have a number of techniques for developing each of them. The resulting HR processes can be designated, communicated, and integrated. On the surface they make sense. They look scientific and can be marketed as such.

In fact, competency models have been useful as the basis for selection and training for lower-level jobs where there is a tight coupling between worker characteristics and behaviors, and between those behaviors and subsequent results. Most would agree that mechanical jobs do require mechanical competencies, and that a single set of behaviors on a production line can produce a quality set of results. But the linkage of traits – behaviors – results breaks down as we go up the ranks, until we get to the senior leadership positions where success can come in seemingly infinite guises.

The sophistication and elegance of the competency-based HR processes is beguiling, and practitioners assume that they work. In the leadership ranks, however, that assumption flies in the face of the evidence around us. As we look across the business scene, we see little evidence that these systems, in place for years now, are producing more and better leaders in organizations. Walter Wriston's 1970 comment that it was easier to find $100 million than a competent executive was echoed more recently in a survey of U.S. Fortune 500 companies rated 'competent global leader' ahead of all other business needs for the future with nearly all (85%) indicating that they did not have enough of them (Gregorson, Morrison, and Black, 1998). And not only are leaders in short supply the ones who have emerged have not met the test. Finkelstein (2003) declares 'we are suffering an epidemic of leadership failure.' Charan and Useem (2002) in an analysis of failures of 14 major US companies find executive shortcomings behind the 'ten big mistakes' that companies make and that 'CEOs offer every excuse but the right one: their own errors.'

We do not argue that competencies cannot be useful in a minimum standards approach to leadership development. Schein (1996) argues for just such an approach – that there are minimum competencies that any leader should have. But minimum standards are not what we seek in our leaders, nor can they explain what differentiates minimally effective leaders from the excellent ones. Most organizations at least aspire to leadership excellence.

Models that defy logic and common sense are not necessarily all bad if the results they produce in practice outweigh the costs. We argue that yes, competency models have been useful, but their uncritical acceptance has had consequences that outweigh the benefits. And even the visibility and acceptance of senior management so earnestly valued by HR professionals is an illusion. But before presenting our view of the unanticipated consequences of the competency model fad, we thought it might be useful to give you a chance to address the issues we have raised thus far.

Sincerely,
George P. Hollenbeck
Morgan W. McCall, Jr.

# Letter 2

[...]
Dear George and Morgan,

Thank you for your recent letter. You certainly have stimulated my thinking, not only from our SIOP debate on whether competency models have helped or hindered leadership development but also from your past contributions to the field of leadership. I am looking forward to this exchange of letters exploring the usefulness of competency models and searching for some common ground or integration of our views.

## Understanding Historical Foundations

Let me try to outline how I think we got to our present state regarding competency models. The field of Industrial and Organizational Psychology has historically placed a great deal of emphasis on understanding work behavior by focusing on job duties and tasks (Harvey, 1991). Organizations tended to develop leaders by moving people through predictable job positions and career paths. It was essentially development by job experience. This seemed to make some sense at the time because jobs, career ladders, and organizational structures were very stable and predictable over time. So being able to do the tasks in job A predicted being able to do the tasks in job B. Outside of cognitive abilities, we were not very good then at measuring individual differences that influenced work performance.

In the 1970s, as you know, things began to change when the results of the assessment center work at AT&T (Bray, Campbell, and Grant, 1974) began to influence the field. I clearly remember my consulting experience in the mid-1970s of helping to design and install assessment centers at Merrill Lynch where George was the human resources executive. Initially, assessment centers were a state-of-the-art tool that focused on measuring people against underlying job performance dimensions in order to select people into specific positions, but the emphasis soon switched to more person-centered variables, such as initiative and interpersonal skills, to select and develop leaders. This was the start of a more widespread focus on knowledge, skills, and abilities (KSA) dimensions and a diminishing interest in job dimensions.

Then in the 1980s, organizations and jobs started changing more rapidly and assessment centers evolved to select and develop people for a larger family of jobs such as management positions, and not just for a specific position. The dimensions became less job specific, more general, and more person-centered. For example, we moved first to selecting subordinates for the more general 'making decisions' and then to the person-centered 'seasoned judgment'. About the same time, selection initiatives switched from expensive and complex job analyses to a simpler process that skipped the job analysis and went directly to identifying the KSAs required to do the job. This not only was a more straightforward process but also encouraged the switch to person-centered variables for both selection and development. At the same time, we saw an emerging research focus on how personality and ability variables impact work performance. Given the rapidly changing business environment and the globalization of business, at the time it made sense to try to develop people independently of specific jobs since those jobs were often likely to be eliminated or drastically redesigned. There was little point in selecting and developing leaders for specific positions if those positions were unlikely to exist in a few years.

So in the 1990s there was a rush to design person-centered models initially referred to as 'management models' of performance. Later this evolved to the more useful 'leadership competency models'. The intent was to look for fundamental KSAs that would identify fungible individuals who could be effective in a range of leadership positions.

However, there has been a long history of identifying person characteristics that are related to leadership success (Silzer, 2002). Many well-known I/O psychologists over the years have identified the characteristics that they think are important to effectiveness although they have used different labels, such as attributes (Office of Strategic Services, 1948), executive dimensions (Dunnette, 1971; Hemphill, 1959), management dimensions (Bray et al., 1974), assessment dimensions (Thornton and Byham, 1982), competencies (McClelland, 1975), and global executive competencies (Kets de Vries, 1999; McCall and Hollenbeck, 2002). Many of these KSAs were carefully identified based on available research.

Initially, dimensions or competencies were developed for a specific organization and were carefully researched and designed. Typically, they were developed and cross-validated on different populations. However, as the competency approach gained acceptance and became 'fashionable', the rigor of the design and development process was compromised or lost in many initiatives. Unfortunately, many consultants in and out of our field became self-declared experts (but with little expertise). This has led to deterioration in the quality of some competency models. But let us not throw out a useful tool because of some inept practitioners.

## The Action is in the Interaction

As an extension of the historical trend outlined above, there has been considerable discussion about the importance and impact of person characteristics versus situational variables on leadership. You have wisely cited the drawbacks of a 'great man' theory of leadership; there are equally serious shortcomings to the 'great times' theory of leadership. I think we can agree that leadership effectiveness is influenced by both person and situational variables.

However, I would go further and underscore the importance of the interaction between these two sets of variables. As we have learned in the long-standing nature versus nurture debate in psychology, behavior is the product of not only person attributes and situational variables, but also the interaction between them, in that specific situations can provide the opportunity to express particular personal predispositions. For example, a socially extroverted person is more likely to demonstrate and leverage her interpersonal skills in a situation that involves extensive interaction with other people than by working alone.

I suspect that quite a bit of variance in leadership effectiveness is probably in the interaction of these variables. Learning ability probably interacts with new or challenging work situations to allow an individual to stretch himself and quickly grasp essential situational information in order to take effective action or as Fulkerson (2003) describes 'delivering first time results in first time situations'. I think the same reasoning holds for the interaction of competencies and leadership situations. To be effective, many leaders not only need to have some learning abilities but they also need to be put in situations where they can learn new things. Remember the Bray et al. (1974) finding that talented people who get stretch assignments early in their career are more likely to be successful higher in the organization. Neither the skills nor the stretch assignments alone produce this outcome.

## Why Competency Models are Helpful

Competency models have been helpful to both individuals and organizations in developing leadership skills. Competencies help individuals by

- Summarizing the experience and insight of seasoned leaders,
- Specifying a range of useful leader behaviors,
- Providing a tool that individuals can use for their self-development, and
- Outlining a leadership framework that can be used to help select, develop, and understand leadership effectiveness.

Competencies, when properly designed, leverage the experience and seasoned insight of leadership incumbents in an organization. The personal experience of a large group of managers and executives gets summarized in a limited number of competencies. The list is intentionally kept to a manageable size of about 10–20 competencies, so people will find it useful and not burdensome or too complex. As a result, the competencies can provide clear guidance on the behaviors that seasoned incumbents think are related to effectiveness. They provide a tremendous educational tool to people trying to learn how to become more effective. I am sure you remember the days when you had to get lucky and work under the right boss who not only had some leadership skills but who was also willing to take time to teach them to you. Competency models in fact serve as a partial backup for that hit or miss approach.

In addition, competencies help individuals understand how effective they and others are as leaders. People can take some personal responsibility and independent action on their own development. Competencies are equally valuable in teaching people how to observe and evaluate the leadership effectiveness of others. They have significantly raised the performance evaluation skills of managers in many organizations.

Organizations have also benefited from the use of competency models. Competencies help organizations by

- Openly communicating which leader behaviors are important,
- Helping to discriminate the performance of individuals,
- Linking leader behaviors to the strategic directions and goals of the business, and
- Providing an integrative model of leadership that is relevant across many positions and leadership situations.

Competency models are a fairly egalitarian way to communicate broadly the leader behaviors that are important in a particular organization. It puts critical information into everyone's hands and reduces some of the secrecy that has plagued organizations and careers. Consequently as a result of this wide distribution of a competency model, individuals are expected to take an interest and some action in developing themselves. The degree to which individuals take some initiative helps organizations to differentiate people on career motivation.

In addition, leadership competencies can provide an integrative model of leadership that can be applied across a range of positions and leadership situations. It is a general map to leadership effectiveness, providing alternate ways of reaching a destination, but it is not a trip ticket that dictates very specific and rigid directions. It is a guiding framework and not an end in itself or an answer key. In one organization with which I have worked, the expected leader behaviors under a particular competency are modified for different leadership levels and contexts. In this case, job level and functional area represent a matrix of leadership situations in the organization, and different expected behaviors are identified for each situation. So different leader behaviors are associated with a level-four operations manager than for a level-two human resources director. Not only does this approach try to identify the interaction of KSAs with leadership situations, but it also outlines how the expected leadership behaviors change for different career paths. An individual can clearly see what new behaviors will be expected if he wants to move up a level or sideways to a different functional area.

However, the competencies should also reflect the leadership skills that are needed to accomplish the organization's strategic objectives. For example, an operations-driven company might emphasize a different set of leadership competencies than a marketing-driven company. An organization going through a transition can focus on those competencies that will be needed not just to get the organization through the transition but also those that will contribute to success in the new end state. For example, the telecommunications industry in the early 1990s began focusing on marketing and customer relations' skills and away from technical engineering and command and control leadership behaviors because of strategic changes in the industry.

## Questionable Assumptions

Now that I have rambled on a bit, I do want to respond more directly to your recent letter. I do question the assumptions that you cite for competency models. Instead of categorizing competency models as fads, I would suggest that they are better placed in the fashions category – 'manners or modes of action taking on the character of habits and enforced by social or scientific norms defining what constitutes the thing to do' (Dunnette, 1966). Many sound, useful tools and approaches can be considered fashions (Marv includes null hypothesis testing and model building for example). Like assessment centers and behavioral interviewing, useful tools can be seen as 'the right thing to do' and widely used. Competency models, even poorly designed ones, are not typically capricious as Marv characterizes fads. Many, if not most, competency efforts are thoughtfully considered, designed, and implemented.

Competency models do not make the assumption that a single set of characteristics adequately describes effective leaders. Supporters of leadership competency models would not argue that competency models are 'the prescription' for effective leadership. They are simply an attempt to leverage the experience, lessons learned, and knowledge of seasoned leaders for the benefit of others and the organization. Everyone is aware that leaders face complex situations and challenges that require the use of a wide range of KSAs and that leaders often use a different set and mix of KSAs moment to moment in their work in order to be effective. In addition, the KSAs that might have been important in the past may become less important in the present while other new KSAs emerge as important. In your letter you do not disagree with any of the KSAs that typically show up on these lists. Most of them do have a rational connection to leadership behavior – that is one reason why they have become fashionable: they make logical sense to the corporate managers and executives that develop and use them. It may also be why you have provided your own list of global executive competencies in your recent book (McCall and Hollenbeck, 2002). Surely your list was never intended to be a single comprehensive list of the KSAs that are needed.

You also say that competency models assume that the competencies are independent of each other and with the leadership context. In fact, most users of competency models understand that the KSAs are interactive. Who has not thought about the interactions and tradeoffs of thinking skills with interpersonal skills? We all are aware of the downsides of having only one of these skills without enough of the other. I agree that some strengths can be used in isolation, be over used or misused, and in fact can limit a leader's effectiveness in some situations where a different set or mix of skills may be more effective. However, it seems a little absurd to say 'every competence is also an incompetence'. I think you have taken a helpful idea and overplayed it. Leadership effectiveness is related to what competencies a person uses in different situations and how those competencies get balanced and integrated depending on the situational context. The action is in the interaction and balance of competencies, how the leader uses those competencies, and how appropriate they are in a specific situation. Every situation is different in some ways so a leader needs to quickly read the situation and then utilize the appropriate competencies.

Many competency models for leaders in management and executive positions were created by the incumbents in those positions and even cross-validated on another similar group. They are used by managers and executives because they make some logical sense. No one has ever said that it is 'the answer' to thinking about leadership behavior. It is a tool that huge numbers of people have found useful. It would be great to have a model of leadership behavior that includes not only relevant KSAs, but also critical situational variables and the interactions between KSAs and situations. However, no one has produced such a comprehensive model beyond the attempts of Fiedler (1967), Vroom (2000), and a few others – which are too simplistic to accommodate the complexity of variables that a leader must consider. And of course if someone did produce such a model, no one would use it because it would be too complex. Keep in mind that while we can hypothesize about these complex interactions, leaders keep requiring tools and models to be simple and easy to use. And many of them have found competency models as a good start on a way to think about some fundamental leadership variables.

Finally, I think it is unlikely that HR practitioners assume that all HR systems built around competency models are automatically effective. Clearly, the way an HR system is implemented often has more impact on the system's effectiveness than the underlying model. Many leaders would certainly emphasize the importance of execution (Bossidy and Charan, 2002). A competency model can be a useful organizing framework for some HR systems just as MBO models have been for performance appraisal.

You also argue that there has been widespread leadership failure. I am not sure I agree. Do not forget that a leader can be effective in some situations and not others. So citing a few situations where failure of leadership was identified only means that a particular person in a particular situation was not effective. On the whole there has been an amazing number of effective leaders, particularly in the business world. But at any time an effective leader can face a situation that he cannot effectively handle. That does not make him an ineffective leader in general but only ineffective in that particular situation. So an executive or manager who has been effective in a leadership position for three years or more years probably is an effective leader even if in the fourth year he cannot rise to new leadership challenges. I hope you are not saying that in order to be an effective leader a person needs to be highly effective in every leadership situation. Only a few people have been seen as an effective leader for a broad range of situations. We already can identify people who are best suited for leadership positions that require the turnaround of a business while other people may be best suited for a staff leadership role. These are simple examples of matching a person's KSAs to a particular leadership context. We need to further pursue this direction more in order to get better at selecting and developing leaders.

Many companies that have well-developed competency models would strongly argue that the competency approach has significantly increased the leadership skills in the organization (Silzer and Douma, 1998). In many organizations competency approaches have raised the basic leadership skills of many managers and executives.

I do take issue with your statement that we should pursue 'competence and not competencies'. I think you are making a distinction without a difference. On a basic level, competency is defined as competence (*Merriam-Webster's Collegiate Dictionary*, 2002). What you may intend is to encourage people to focus on outcomes, such as demonstrating leadership behavior, and not on inputs. You may be thinking of KSAs in an academic sense like classic individual difference variables in psychology. However, I would suggest that well-designed competency models do focus on behavioral outcomes. For example a leadership competency might be 'to address and resolve all conflicts that occur in a group of direct reports'. Surely someone who demonstrates this competency would be seen as competent in this area.

I was glad to see that you agree that competencies can be useful in identifying some leadership skills and that they can be useful in selection and training systems. Of course there are leadership positions and situations that require a more complex set and mix of KSAs, particularly at the top of an organization. Many executives might find a competency model too simplistic for them, and that is reasonable given that many executive positions are extraordinarily complex. In fact many of them are highly unique not only because they deal with a unique set of relationships, business challenges, and leadership situations but also because executives often change the position to better suit their own KSAs. Although, as you know, it is not uncommon to find that a key reason why many executives fail in senior positions is because they are ineffective at building relationships and influencing others – a basic competency found in many leadership competency models. So what you may dismiss as too basic for an executive can often be an important behavior that can help him be successful.

Leadership effectiveness is in some ways similar to the effectiveness of a home builder. A builder has to have a wide range of KSAs such as knowledge of building materials, skills in physically putting down foundations and putting up walls, and influencing skills. However, the builder must also be very aware of the specific situation surrounding each home such as the desires and personality of the client, the composition and layout of a particular piece of land, and the weather conditions. An understanding of the interactions between his own KSAs and the situational variables are often critical to building a home that succeeds. Competencies are a basic tool kit of a builder or a leader. Surely the world-renown builders, such as the architect Phillip Johnson, operate in a highly complex environment that requires much more sophisticated skills, but a more typical home builder probably gets by with not much more than the basic builder KSAs and a basic understanding of situational issues. Both may be seen as effective for the situations that they have to handle. Similarly leadership competencies are basic building blocks that help people become more effective leaders. I would caution us not to see leadership effectiveness solely through the lens of a senior executive.

Thanks again for helping me to see some of these issues more clearly. I look forward to hearing from you.

Sincerely,
Rob Silzer

[Editor's note: A further exchange of letters on this subject has been omitted.]

### References

Bennis, W. and Nanus, B. (1985) *Leaders: The strategies of Taking Charge*, New York, Harper and Row.

Bossidy, L. and Charan, R. (2002) *Execution: The Discipline of Getting Things Done*, New York, Crown.

Bray, D., Campbell, R. and Grant, D. (1974) *Formative Years in Business: A Long Term AT&T Study of Managerial Lives*, New York, Wiley.

Charan, R. and Useem, J. (May 27 2002) 'Why companies fail', *Fortune*, pp. 50–62.

Dunnette, M. (1966) 'Fads, fashions, and folderol in psychology', *American Psychologist*, vol. 21, pp. 343–52.

Dunnette, M. (1971) 'The assessment of managerial talent' in McReynolds, P. (ed.) *Advances in Psychological Assessment, Vol. 2*, Palo Alto, Science and Behavior Books.

Fiedler, F. (1967) *A Theory of Leadership Effectiveness*, New York, McGraw Hill.

Finkelstein, S. (2003) *Why Smart Executive Fail*, New York, Penguin.

Fulkerson, J. (December 2003) 'Developing global high potential executives', A presentation at the meeting of the New York Metropolitan Applied Psychology Association, New York City.

Gregorson, A.J., Morrison, A.J. and Black, J.S. (1998) 'Developing leaders for the global frontier', *Sloan Management Review*, vol. 40, no. 1, pp. 21–32.

Harvey, R. (1991) 'Job analysis' in Dunnette, M. and Hough, L. (eds) *Handbook of Industrial and Organizational Psychology, Vol. 2*, Palo Alto, Consulting Psychologists Press.

Hemphill, J. (1959) 'Job descriptions for executives', *Harvard Business Review*, vol. 37, no. 5, pp. 55–67.

Kets de Vries, M. (1999) *The New Global Leaders*, San Francisco, CA, Jossey-Bass.

Kotter, J.P. (1988) *The Leadership Challenge*, New York, Free Press.

McCall, M.W. (1998) *High Flyers: Developing the Next Generation of Leaders*, Boston, MA, Harvard Business School Press.

McCall, M.W. and Hollenbeck, G.P. (2002) *Developing Global Executives: The Lessons of International Experience*, Boston, MA, Harvard Business School Press.

McClelland, D. (1975) *Power: The Inner Experience*, New York, Irvington.

*Merriam-Webster's Collegiate Dictionary* (2002) Springfield, MA, Merriam-Webster.

Office of Strategic Services (1948) *The Assessment of Men*, New York, Rinehart.

Schein, E. (1996) 'Three cultures of management: The key to organizational learning', *Sloan Management Review*, vol. 38, no. 1, pp. 9–20.

Silzer, R. (2002) *The 21st Century Executive: Innovative Practices for Building Leadership at the Top*, San Francisco, CA, Jossey-Bass.

Silzer, R. and Douma, R. (April 1998) 'Partnership on strategic selection and development: Building a high growth, high technology Generation X company', A presentation at the Annual Conference of the Society of Industrial and Organizational Psychology, Dallas.

Thomton, G. and Byham, W. (1982) *Assessment Centers and Managerial Performance*, Orlando, Academic Press.

Vroom, V. (2000) 'Leadership and the decision making process', *Organizational Dynamics*, vol. 28, no. 4, pp. 82–94.

# Part III
## Leadership: Image or Substance?

# Bringing Humility to Leade[rship]

7

*J. Andrew [Morris, Céleste M. Broth]eridge*
*and John C. [Urbanski]*

[ ... ]

Organizational discourse over the past century has become preoccupied with the notion of leaders and leadership. Indeed, a basic search of the word *leader* in the ABI/Inform search engine yielded 388,122 documents, 50,947 of which were in scholarly journals with the remaining appearing in magazines, trade publications, newspapers, and assorted reports. Recent perspectives from both scholarly and popular sources indicate that leaders have begun to take a certain widespread notoriety, having gained a charismatic-like appeal and a significant increase in social status much in the same way that Hollywood stars or professional athletes have become icons in the cult of celebrity that surrounds them. Leaders have been referred to as idols (*The Economist*, 2002), heroes (Bennis, 1988; Bowles, 1997; Collins, 2000; Raelin, 2003; Shelton, 1996), saviors (Khurana, 2002), warriors and magicians (Tallman, 2003), and omnipotent and omniscient demi-gods (Gabriel, 1997; Noer, 1994). Leaders have become imbued with 'a saviorlike essence in a world that constantly needs saving' (Rost, 1991, p. 94). This glorification of leaders has increased despite continuing evidence that the actions of many leaders are far from heroic.

This apparent obsession with the charismatic appeal of individual leaders stands in contrast with a small but growing call for humility in leadership. Although humility may be perceived as a form of personal weakness (Exline and Geyer, 2004), it may well serve as *the* marker of a leader's intrinsic desire to serve (Collins, 2001a, 2001b; Smith et al., 2004). Recent research by Collins (2001a, 2001b) provided strong evidence for the utility of humility in leadership. He found that consistently high performing organizations shared several important characteristics, the most counterintuitive of which was that great companies were led by Level 5 leaders; that is, individuals who possessed a blend of humility and strong personal will. In coining the term Level 5 leadership, Collins suggested

Morris, A.J., Brotheridge, C.M. and Urbanski, J.C. (2005) 'Bringing humility to leadership', *Human Relations*, vol. 58, no. 10, pp. 1323–50.

that Level 5 leaders were still ambitious but that their primary focus was the success of the organization rather than their personal success.

Collins proposed that leadership by those who possess true humility may bring significantly greater benefits to the organization relative to benefits realized from CEOs of the 'celebrity' variety. Collins (2001a) provided particulars of these benefits when they identified those organizations belonging to the 'Great' rather than merely the 'Good' cohort. Specifically, the superior performance of the organization led by the 'humble' CEO is continually sustained over long periods, often spanning decades. Second, the organization is quite often the benchmark performer in its particular industry. Third, if the humble leader retires, resigns, or otherwise leaves the helm of the organization, the sustained superior performance of the organization continues long past the tenure of the humble leader. Finally, 'embarrassments' such as mistresses, theft for personal gain, 'cooking the books', excessive perquisites, etc., do not seem to arise in connection with the leadership of the 'humble' CEO.

Humility in leadership serves several potential functions. First, humility may influence leaders to behave in a manner that is primarily other-enhancing, rather than self-enhancing. Second, possession of humility may shield the CEO from needing to receive public adulation, and may cause him or her to shun such attention. Similarly, as argued by Vera and Rodriguez-Lopez (2004), humility as a leadership trait may contribute to organizational performance through its impact on organizational learning and organizational resilience.

Given its potential importance in generating organizational and leader effectiveness, humility may offer a new lens through which to view and understand the leadership process. Although considered by some organizational scholars to be a quaint notion from the past (e.g. Northhouse, 1997), the idea that certain personal traits influence a leader's effectiveness, particularly when framed as competencies, remains compelling (Kirkpatrick and Locke, 1991; Kochanski, 1997). This article attempts to extend the list of the critical competencies or traits required for successful organizational leadership by arguing for the inclusion of humility in this list.

It appears that the relationship between humility and leadership has been considered primarily in the popular press rather than in empirical research. As a result, the concept of humility has not been precisely defined in the academic literature. Several authors in the behavioral and organizational sciences have considered how certain variables may influence levels of humility. Others have discussed some potential benefits of humility for organizations, such as providing a source of competitive advantage. Most of these proposals, however, stem from anecdotal sources and have not yet been anchored in the scientific literature. In this article, we attempt to address this gap in the academic literature by providing a precise conceptualization of the concept of humility, which we then apply to the process of leadership. To introduce humility to the organizational discourse, we draw as broadly as possible from diverse sources to develop a three-dimensional conceptualization of humility that differentiates it from related but distinct constructs. Indeed, this article draws heavily upon the new and emerging bodies of research known as positive psychology (Peterson and Seligman, 2004; Seligman, 2002) and its organizational application labeled positive organizational psychology (Cameron et al., 2003) to better understand how personal strengths and virtues lead to positive deviance in leadership. Unlike previous leadership approaches such as servant and transformational leadership, our focus is not only on leadership behaviors but also the underlying psychological mechanisms associated with such human virtues as humility. We then examine research in psychology and leadership as a means of identifying individual differences that are likely to predict humility and the specific leadership behaviors that may result from high levels of humility.

## The Celebrity CEO: Rise and Fall

In his examination of leadership effectiveness over a 20-year period, Khurana (2002) found that CEOs were increasingly being viewed in the popular press as superheroes that single-handedly spawned organizational success. This celebrity status of CEOs rose (Donovan et al., 2002; Maccoby, 2000) as socially elite CEOs became the focus of news stories and society pages, heroes in comic books (Francq and Van Hamme, 1994), best-selling biographers, and highly sought-after public speakers (Collins, 2000; Huczynski, 1993). As argued by Chen and Meindl (1991), 'these images feed and expand our appetites for leadership products, appealing not only to our collective commitments to the concept but fixating us in particular on the personas and characteristics of leaders themselves' (p. 522). Leaders began to be treated as heroes not necessarily because of anything that they did, but simply because they were leaders. The visibility of leaders, in essence, their charismatic appeal, and their subsequent willingness to search for and bask in the glow of public adulation was what mattered, not necessarily the outcomes of their behavior which may be significantly overstated in value, or even detrimental to the organization or its members. Both Haigh (2003) and Khurana (2002) argued that the notion of celebrity CEO was promoted by a conflation of the relationship between a company's celebrity CEO and its associated increases in stock value. The popular belief that leadership meant motivating employees to do what they otherwise would not do, possibly through inspiring, emotionally charged visions, may have perpetuated this cult of the great leader. This romance with leadership may also be the result of a widespread interest in leaders whose charismatic appeal creates followers who cling to them like groupies to a pop star (Howell and Shamir, 2005; Meindl, 1993; Sankowsky, 1995; Tourish and Pinnington, 2002). More broadly, however, it may also be the product of competitive capitalist markets in which 'the construction of highly individualized selves is promoted' (Willmott, 1997, p. 1345) and instrumental interaction becomes the norm as people worship at the feet of the corporation (Bowles, 1997).

Recently, however, society's fascination with leaders (see *The Economist,* 2002) has given way to anger, frustration, and feelings of betrayal as scandals ranging from Enron, WorldCom, Tyco, Bre X, and Credit Suisse First Boston to Credit Lyonnais (*The Economist,* 2003b) began to dominate the business news. These circumstances resulted in a dearth of leadership (Nagle, 1995), leading some to ask, 'Where are all the leaders?' (Seib, 1998, p. A20). In the same vein, Raelin (2003) argued that, although 'charismatics can charm the masses with their rhetoric and can draw the big picture; they tend to be grandiose and distrustful' (p. 46). As explained by Khurana (2002), the almost singular focus on charismatic leadership and its associated deference to a single individual has provided an unstable and precarious foundation for organizational performance and leaves little room for rationality as a basis for organizational decision-making. Furthermore, as argued by Raelin (2003), the romantic notion of charisma may actually 'deprive a community of its own power and utility. Leadership is needed that subsists without charismatics, or heroes' (p. 46).

This notion of the celebrity CEO as heroic stands in sharp contrast to the traditional notion of a hero, a person who is willing to make the personal sacrifices necessary so that others may benefit. Paragons of this latter notion of hero are many and include Nelson Mandela, Pope John Paul II, and Mother Teresa, individuals who have sacrificed much so that many others might benefit. Paradoxically, unlike celebrity CEOs, the more effort made to raise the truly heroic in status, the more these *traditional heroes* seem to avoid having the spotlight shine on their efforts, often becoming self-effacing, as well as attempting to divert credit to others. Thus, as used in this article, the words *hero* and *celebrity* become disparaging, while the word *anti-hero* refers to the non-celebrity status of an alternative type of leader (Badaracco, 2002; Macht, 2002; Polleys, 2002). As noted in *The Economist* (2003a), 'Humility is in, arrogance is out…There is more emphasis on under-promising and overdelivering' (p. 4). These are ordinary individuals who quietly lead by maintaining a low profile and acting with modesty, restraint, patience, mutuality, and care. Support for this perspective can be found in the personal characteristics of CEOs from the top 25 market value added companies for the year 2002 according to *Chief Executive.* The success of these companies was attributed to their CEO's personal humility, dependability, and consistency (Griffith, 2002). In like manner, at the annual conference of the Society for Human Resource Management, the former mayor of New York, Rudolph Giuliani, argued that leadership required humility (Schramm, 2002). Also, in a recent *USA Today* article, Stephen Covey asserted that 'humility is one of the characteristics of the people at the very top…They're more teachable, they're more open, they often show more reverence and respect for other people' (Flick, 2002, p. 1). In sum, the popular press has served as a type of barometer of societal attitudes in which emphasis has shifted from the worship and adulation of celebrity CEOs to their distrust and denigration.

# Understanding Humility

Humility has long been a subject of contemplation across numerous cultures. Indeed, our review suggests the existence of at least four eras of development in thinking regarding the concept of humility: historical, monotheistic, enlightenment, and modern. These are considered below.

## Historical View of Humility

Some of the earliest writings on humility come from the Greek Stoic tradition and the teachings of Buddhism and Taoism (Peterson and Seligman, 2004). Although early Greek philosophers considered humility to be a virtue (i.e. an excellence in behavior, a capacity or power, and a way of being), in general, it was not greatly emphasized (Sandage and Wiess, 2001). Comte-Sponville (2001) suggested that humility's place in Greek thought was due less to arrogance than to a deep and profound understanding of human limitation. That is, humility was not paramount in the Greek tradition since rightly educated individuals were all too aware of their personal limitations. In essence, humility's place in human affairs was so obvious that it was considered to be a starting point for the virtuous life not an end in itself. Stoic philosophy made this point very clearly in, for example, the opening chapter of *The art of living:* 'Happiness and freedom begin with a clear understanding of one principle: Some things are within our control, and some things are not' (Lebell, 1995, p. 3).

Buddhist and Taoism teachings also recognized humility as important to human excellence. However, eastern thought approached humility not so much as an understanding of personal limits but, rather, as a need to let go of the self and connect with a greater reality (Peterson and Seligman, 2004). For example, Buddhism considered the cause of human suffering to be *Samudaya* (craving) which, in turn, was caused by individual misperception or ignorance of the self (Mishra, 2004). To end suffering, one followed *Margo* (the path of enlightenment). Two key elements of the eight-fold path to enlightenment were right view and right intention. Right view involved awareness of things as they really were, whereas right intention involved freeing oneself from selfishness, which was partly achieved through humble thought.

Like Buddhism, Taoism approached humility as a losing of the self. In particular, humility was valued in the Taoist tradition because it was believed that leader effectiveness was largely determined by the leader's ability to *let go* in order to achieve harmony with Tao. For example, Chapter 66 (Mitchell translation, 1988, p. 66) of the *Tao Te Ching* reads:

All streams flow to the sea
Because it is lower than they are.

Humility gives it its power.
If you want to govern the people,
You must place yourself below them.
If you want to lead the people,
You must learn how to follow them ...

## Monotheistic View of Humility

The monotheistic traditions of Judaism, Islam, and Christianity offered an alternative perspective of humility. These traditions generally conceptualized humility as submission before and to God (Murray, 2001). An essential paradox in Christianity is that humility is considered to be the avenue to glory (Spiegel, 2003). Humility's central role in Christian texts greatly influenced how humility was traditionally conceived in western culture (Comte-Sponville, 2001; Sandage and Wiess, 2001; Spiegel, 2003); that is, that humility is a state of humbleness that involves 'having or showing a low estimate of one's own importance' (Pearsall and Trumble, 1996, p. 689). For example, Paul (Romans 12:3) advised, 'one should not think of themselves more highly than you ought.' Further, in Philippians 2:1–4, Paul counseled his readers to, 'in humility consider others better than yourselves'. This positioned humility in opposition to selfish ambition and vain conceit and provided the foundation for the conceptualization of humility as reflecting 'an unselfishness that counters the temptation to vanity' (Grundmann, 1972, p. 14). Later church fathers concurred with this view of humility. For example, Augustine wrote, 'wherever there is humility there is also charity', since humility leads to love and all true love presupposes humility. Thus, within the Christian tradition, it is through humility that one comes to see others as people worthy of love and compassion (Comte-Sponville, 2001). Correspondingly, the word *Muslim* means one who surrenders.

## Enlightenment Views of Humility

Many philosophers of the enlightenment period either took exception to Christianity's understanding of humility or were disdainful of it. Nietzsche (1974), for example, believed that man had no need of humility. He reasoned that humility was the virtue of slaves since it necessitated self-abasement. He wrote: 'the masters, noble and brave, have no use for it: to them, all humility is worthy of contempt' (p. 229). Spinoza (1994) argued, however, that humility was a virtue in which the mind has adequate knowledge of itself and realizes that something greater than itself exists. Kant (1964) supported this understanding of humility and considered true humility (as opposed to false humility) to be the awareness of the insignificance of one's moral worth in comparison with the law. In essence, humility was not, 'I'm bad, worthless, and lowly' but, simply, an understanding that 'God is greater' (Furey, 1986; Templeton, 1997). Kant further argued that it was necessary to 'distinguish between having a low opinion of oneself and considering oneself to be as valuable as another. The former is not a virtue: "it is a sign of little spirit and of a servile character"' (Ben-Ze'ev, 2000, p. 521).

## Modern Views of Humility

In the modern era, both philosophers and social scientists suggested that humility is a more complex construct than sometimes believed. For example, the French philosopher Comte-Sponville (2001) suggested that humility should be thought of as the science of the self since humility arises from a trustful understanding of one's strengths and weaknesses. In this manner, humility is an awareness of all that one is and all that one is not. Moreover, Comte-Sponville argued that, if people wished to practice the virtue of humility, they must love the truth more than themselves since all knowledge is a wound to the ego. Enlarging the humility as truth approach, Richards (1992) suggested that humility is best understood as both an accurate assessment of one's abilities and achievements and the ability to keep those assessments in perspective. Similarly, Tangney (2000) viewed humility as involving not only honest self-appraisal but also an ability to forget the self and to appreciate the value of all things. Key to this line of reasoning is the understanding that humility is more than knowledge of self for, as Ben-Ze'ev (2000) argued, it is possible to make an accurate assessment of one's capabilities while at the same time lack humility by considering others to be inferior to oneself. Thus, humility requires both an accurate self-appraisal and a belief that 'all human beings have a positive worth which should be respected' (Ben-Ze'ev, 2000, p. 520).

Writing from the perspective of positive psychology, with its foundations in personality psychology and trait theory, Peterson and Seligman (2004) and others (Tangney, 2000, 2002), argued that humility was best understood as a positive human trait that is both stable and enduring. However, they recognized that humility is also influenced by situational factors. Two points are paramount in this understanding of humility: first, humility does not involve self-disparagement or negativity, only a desire to take an objective look at the self; second, humility implies a willingness to see the self accurately not the actual attainment of accuracy (Peterson and Seligman, 2004). The second point is especially relevant since it recognizes that human beings are subject to a number of perceptual and decision-making biases (Krueger and Mueller, 2002; Simon, 1976; Tversky and Kahneman, 1974).

# A Definition of Humility

Our review of the theological, philosophical, and social psychology literatures suggests that humility is a human virtue that reflects a relatively stable character trait (Vera and Rodriguez-Lopez, 2004). Since all virtues represent an acquired disposition to do that which is right or good (Peterson and Seligman, 2004), humility can be thought of as that crest of human excellence between arrogance and lowliness. Drawing upon this understanding and the rich history of humility thought, we define humility as a personal orientation founded on a willingness to see the self accurately and a propensity to put oneself in perspective. We believe that authentic humility involves neither self-abasement nor overly positive self-regard. This definition involves three connected but distinct dimensions including: (1) self-awareness, (2) openness, and (3) transcendence.

*Self-awareness*: A consistent theme in the literature on the topic of humility has been the recognition that a key element of humility is the ability to understand one's strengths and weaknesses. Although humility may not be a true science of the self as suggested by Comte-Sponville (2001), it is an enduring orientation to objectively appraise one's abilities and limitations.

*Openness*: An implied aspect of knowing one's weaknesses is an awareness of personal limitation or imperfection (Furey, 1986; Kurtz and Ketcham, 1992). As suggested by the Stoic tradition, humility involves knowing that there are things that are beyond one's control (Richards, 1992). This suggests that to be humble is to be open to new ideas and ways of knowing. Thus humility also involves the willingness to learn from others.

*Transcendence*: Transcendence is sometimes thought to require belief in an omnipotent God. However, as argued by Peterson and Seligman (2004), it may mean exceeding one's usual limits so that one can forge a connection to a larger perspective. An example of this is provided by Dennett (1995) who wrote of his sense of the transcendent as he pondered the awe inspiring complexity displayed in nature. In essence, complexity inspires the possibility of a larger reality. We argue that transcendence can best be thought of as an acceptance of something greater than the self. Out of this acceptance comes an understanding of the small role that one plays in a vast universe, an appreciation of others, and a recognition that others have a positive worth. Transcendence brings about having a proper perspective on life.

The application of this three-dimensional conceptualization of humility to leadership does not require that a humble leader be uniformly strong on all three dimensions. However, humility is likely to involve at least some minimum level of self-awareness, openness, and transcendence. For example, leaders with a high level of self-awareness but little or no openness are not likely to be authentically humble. Authentically humble leaders understand their strengths, weaknesses, and limitations, and recognize how dependent they are on forces outside of themselves. Such individuals appreciate that they do not have all the answers and, as a result, actively seek out the contributions of others as a means of overcoming their individual limitations. Simply put, they demonstrate acceptance as well as resolve: acceptance of personal strengths and limitations coupled with a willingness to ask and utilize help from others. Like meekness, humility is 'a self-respect and self-regard that is secure, wise and large enough to take risks by sharing and blending discipline with compassion. Thereby it can embrace its own and others' needs – needs that include, but extend well beyond, simple economic needs and considerations' (Molyneaux, 2003, p. 359). However, in contrast with humility, which is internally focused, modesty is more likely to be externally focused (Peterson and Seligman, 2004). Modest behaviors are designed to diminish the extent to which people draw attention to themselves. For example, award-wining actors who thank their film directors for their success are displaying modesty. In contrast, humility 'refers to the person's own sense that he or she is not the center of the universe' (Peterman and Seligman, 2004, p. 138). Actors who thank their directors but truly believe that they were solely responsible for the film's success are being modest but not humble. This suggests that authentic humility leads to modesty but that modesty may not reflect true humility. As one reviewer of this article noted, the difference between humility and modesty is much like the difference between felt and displayed emotion (Hochschild, 1979). Like displayed emotion, modesty is strongly subject to social rules and norms but may or may not reflect one's true internal state. For example, the most valuable player (MVP) of a winning team who thanks her teammates but truly believes that the winning outcome of the game was due solely to her contributions would be displaying modesty but lacking humility. In turn, the MVP who announced the true extent of her contributions might appear immodest but as long as she correctly noted the contributions of others could not be said to lack humility.

[ ... ]

# Humility and the Leadership Process

Humility is expected to result in leadership behaviors that parallel those of servant leaders. Indeed, Greenleaf (1997) introduced the concept of servant leadership partly as a response to the cult of leadership. According to Greenleaf, servant leaders approach the leadership role from a non-focal position and seek to fulfill the interests of the organization and its members rather than maximize personal ambition. Simply put, service leaders operate out of a motivational basis of 'I serve' as opposed to 'I lead' (Sendjaya and Sarros, 2002). For servant leaders, organizational others take on more importance than oneself. Rather than engaging in behaviors aimed at self-gratification or glorification as would a celebrity CEO, servant leaders work in a facilitative manner to ensure the betterment of the entire organization. They actively engage in the development and preparation of lower level management to assume control of the organization, thus ensuring the perpetuation of the organization's success beyond the individual's own tenure. In doing so, rather than bringing attention to themselves and having glory reflected on them, servant leaders choose to remain in the background and strive to have credit given to followers. These behaviors are consistent with what we would expect from individuals who possess high levels of self-awareness, openness, and transcendence. Indeed, it would appear that humility might be the operating mechanism through which servant leaders function. Thus, humility may serve as a potential motivational basis for servant leadership. In the rich anecdotal information provided by Collins (2001a), there are marked similarities between the behavior of those termed Level 5 leaders and the servant or humble leader. This suggests that leaders with high levels of humility are more likely to be servant leaders.

In addition to its parallels with servant leadership, humility is consistent with an emerging emphasis on authentic leadership (Luthans and Avolio, 2003; May et al., 2003). In proposing the concept of authentic leadership, Avolio and his associates (Avolio et al., 2004) defined the essence of authenticity as 'know thyself' (p. 802). According to these authors, authentic leaders exhibit self-awareness, which includes being able to: accurately assess their strengths and weaknesses, know, accept and remain true to themselves, and acknowledge their limitations. For its part, humility is likely to significantly assist leaders in both engaging in objective self-examination, and also accepting whatever personal shortcomings that they may discover. May et al. (2003) acknowledged the influence of humility on authentic leadership by noting that authentic leaders are humble by nature, and that humility decreases leaders' desire to be the focus of recognition and the center of attention. Finally, George (2003) posited that authentic leaders had a strong desire to serve their followers, a notion that corresponds with servant leadership. In this section, we examine how these concepts of authentic and servant leadership may be expressed in the specific behaviors of humble leaders.

A possible relationship between transformational leadership (Burns, 1978) and humility may also bear investigation. Bass (1985, 1996) suggested that transformational leadership may be split into socialized and personalized components, the primary difference being the orientation of the leader either toward one's self-interests, termed pseudotransformational leadership, based solely on the leader's charisma, or toward organizational and employee interests, identified as true transformational leadership. A significant level of humility may be required for a leader to engage in true transformational leadership. The behaviors and orientation of true transformational leaders stand in contrast to those of pseudotransformational leaders. [ ... T]ransformational leaders engage in egalitarian behavior to serve the interests of the organization rather than oneself, and they attempt to develop and empower others.

Bass and others (Bass, 1985, 1996; Bass and Avolio, 1994a, 1994b) suggested that true transformational leadership consists of four discrete segments (Bass, 1985, 1996), three of which the current authors believe may be influenced by the leader's level of humility. All three require that leaders act in a manner that primarily benefits the organization's and employees' well-being. Briefly, Bass et al. argued that transformational leaders act as role models for employees by engaging in ethical and moral conduct, sharing risks and considering the needs of others before self. In turn, followers admire, respect and trust these leaders, and wish to emulate them. Second, transformational leaders provide intellectual stimulation for followers, encouraging creativity and 'thinking out of the box', refraining from public criticism of followers for mistakes or for ideas that diverge from those of the leader, and including followers in identifying problems and, subsequently, creating solutions for them. Finally, transformational leaders provide individualized attention to followers, acting as coach and mentor in order to continually develop employees to successively higher levels of competency. This includes delegating responsibility to employees as a developmental tool, and fostering a work climate that supports and facilitates these development activities.

Pseudotransformational leaders operate through the use of charismatic power, which is exploitative in nature and aimed primarily at serving leaders' self-interests. Although these leaders may exhibit expected transformational behaviors, their focus is self-benefit (Bass, 1996). As noted by Bass (1996), these individuals are often impulsive, aggressive, narcissistic and impetuous. Again, [ ... ] these individuals disregard the rights and feelings of others, are exploitative, and are self-promoting (Bass, 1996). As stated earlier, we suggest that humility provides leaders with an 'other' rather than 'self' orientation. This 'other' orientation would assist leaders in manifesting behaviors from these three segments, and would preclude the use and exhibition of self-aggrandizing, exploitative, self-benefiting behavior.

# Supportive Relationships with Others

A substantial body of research points to the importance of supportive relationships in the workplace, particularly those that exist between managers and their employees (e.g. Hofstede et al., 1993; Seers et al., 1983). Since leaders with high levels of humility are likely to avoid being competitive with others in a zero-sum game and to avoid disrespectful behaviors such as ridiculing, interrupting, or coercing others, they are more likely to form supportive relationships with their employees (Richards, 1992). This is especially probable since humble people value both themselves and others, and, as expressed by the eighteenth-century theologian, Samuel Johnson, 'He that overvalues himself will undervalue others, and he that undervalues others will oppress them' (quoted in Myers, 1987, p. 131). Thus, humble leaders are more likely to adopt a stance of egalitarianism rather than superiority or servility in their communications with others. This perspective is consistent with Lee et al.'s (2003) research in which individuals who scored high on their honesty–humility scale were much less likely to exploit or harm others. Furthermore, authentic leaders are likely to be supportive of their followers by being fair in dealings with followers, continually emphasizing the growth of followers, acting in the best interests of others, and considering their needs before coming to any decisions (Luthans and Avolio, 2003; May et al., 2003). Thus, it is likely that leaders with high levels of humility are supportive of those around them. [ ... ]

# Power

Humility may also impact the leadership process through a leader's accumulation, use, and sharing of power. Leaders with a preference for personalized power (i.e. those at the lower levels of power motivation) are more likely to use power for the betterment of self (McClelland, 1975). Use of personalized power tends to be manifested through dominance–submission as well as win–lose relationships between the leader and others. Personal satisfaction for these leaders stems from winning, specifically, by conquering others. Research indicates that a preference for personalized power is often related to excesses in personal behavior (McClelland, 1975). These excesses in behavior manifest themselves in the acquisition of prestige possessions such as automobiles and *objets d'art,* indulgence in substance abuse, ruthless behavior when combined with low affiliation needs, a propensity to engage in non-romantic sexual activity, and impulsive acts of aggression, among others (McClelland, 1975; McClelland et al., 1972).

At higher levels of power motivation (i.e. socialized power), power is used to influence others to achieve organizational success for the betterment of all rather than for self-promotion or glorification. Socialized power is characterized by a concern for group goals and the achievement of group goals through the efforts of group members. Associated behaviors include: identifying goals that motivate others, facilitating the development of competent organizational members, assisting the group in formulation of goals, and providing any resource the group may require in order to achieve group goals. Leaders with a socialized power motivation appear to be much more likely to engage in a style of leadership involving leading people to lead themselves (Manz and Sims, 1991). Unlike heroic leaders who may single-handedly make decisions, leaders with socialized power are more likely to develop employees to the point where they need very little direction from their leader. Thus, they engage in many of the behaviors that Collins (2001a) associated with Level 5 leaders such as power-sharing and the development of power in employees so that their organizations may continue to thrive even after the leader's departure. The foregoing discussion suggests that humility and the use of socialized power are positively related, and that leaders with high levels of humility are more likely to encourage employee participation and involvement than their counterparts. [ ... ]

# Future Directions and Conclusion

In sum, this article has explored the theological, philosophical, and social psychology literatures in order to develop a clear conceptualization of humility. We have offered several potential predictors of humility and indicated the specific ways in which humility may impact the leadership process. [ ... ] Humility [ ... ] is expected to generate servant leader-type behaviors such as engaging in supportive relationships, presenting a socialized power motivation, and leading through participation. [ ... ]

------ *References* ------

Avolio, B.J., Gardner, W.L., Walumba, F.O., Luthans, F. and May, D.R. (2004) 'Unlocking the mask: A look at the process by which authentic leaders impact follower attitudes and behaviors', *The Leadership Quarterly,* vol. 15, pp. 801–23.

Badaracco, J.L., Jr (2002) *Leading Quietly: An Unorthodox Guide to Doing the Right Thing,* Boston, MA, Harvard Business School Press.

Bass, B.M. (1985) *Leadership and Performance Beyond Expectations,* New York, Free Press.

Bass, B.M. (1996) *A New Paradigm of Leadership: An Inquiry into Transformational Leadership,* Alexandria, VA, US Army Institute for the Behavioral and Social Sciences.

Bass, B.M. and Avolio, B.J. (eds) (1994a) *Improving Organizational Effectiveness through Transformational Leadership,* Thousand Oaks, CA, Sage.

Bass, B.M. and Avolio, B.J. (1994b) 'Transformational leadership and organizational culture', *International Journal of Public Administration,* vol. 17, nos 3–4, pp. 541–52.

Bennis, W. (1988) 'The leader as hero', *Executive Excellence,* vol. 5, no. 3, pp. 3–4.

Ben-Ze'ev, A. (2000) *The Subtlety of Emotions,* Cambridge, MA, MIT Press.

Bowles, M. (1997) 'The myth of management: Direction and failure in contemporary organizations', *Human Relations,* vol. 50, pp. 779–803.

Burns, J.M. (1978) *Leadership,* New York: Harper and Row.

Cameron, K., Dutton, J. and Quinn, R. (2003) *Positive Organizational Scholarship: Foundations of a New Discipline,* San Francisco, CA, Berrett-Koehler.

Chen, C.C. and Meindl, J.R. (1991) 'The construction of leadership images in the popular press: The case of Donald Burr and People Express', *Administrative Science Quarterly,* vol. 36, pp. 521–51.

Collins, D. (2000) *Management Fads and Buzzwords: Critical-Practical Perspectives.* London, Routledge.

Collins, J. (2001a) *Good to Great: Why Some Companies Make the Leap and Others Don't*, New York, Harper Business.

Collins, J. (2001b) 'Level 5 leadership: The triumph of humility and fierce resolve', *Harvard Business Review*, vol. 79, no. 1, pp. 67–77.

Comte-Sponville, A. (2001) *A Small Treatise on the Great Virtues*, New York, Henry Holt and Company.

Dennett, D. (1995) *Darwin's Dangerous Idea: Evolution and the Meanings of Life*, New York, Simon and Schuster.

Donovan, D., Bird, A., Buchanan, R., Rogers, P. and Blenko, M. (2002) 'Putting your leader where it counts', *European Business Journal*, vol. 24, no. 3, pp. 144–50.

*The Economist* (2002) 'Leaders: Fallen idols', *The Economist*, vol. 363, no. 8271, p. 11.

*The Economist* (2003a) 'Survey: Tough at the top', *The Economist*, vol. 369, no. 8347, p. 4.

*The Economist* (2003b) 'Leaders: Another scandalous year. Business behavior', *The Economist*, vol. 369, no. 8355, p. 14.

Exline, J. and Geyer, A. (2004) 'Perceptions of humility: A preliminary study', *Self & Identity*, vol. 3, no. 2, pp. 95–115.

Flick, H. (2002) 'Recipe for humble pie provided', *MSU Memo,* 14 June. Available at: [http://msuinfo.ur.msstate.edu/msu_memo/1998/06–15–98/humility.htm].

Francq, P. and Van Hamme, J. (1994) *Chronique BD gest [Largo winch 13. Le prix de l'argent]*. H. Brussels, Dupuis-Reperages.

Furey, R.J. (1986) *So I'm Not Perfect: a Psychology of Humility*, New York, Alba House.

Gabriel, Y. (1997) 'Meeting God: When organizational members come face to face with the supreme leader', *Human Relations*, vol. 50, pp. 315–42.

George, B. (2003) *Authentic Leadership: Rediscovering the Secrets to Creating Lasting Value*, San Francisco, CA, Jossey-Bass.

Greenleaf, R.K. (1997) *Servant Leadership: A Journey into the Nature of Legitimate Greatness*, Mahwah, NJ, Paulist Press.

Griffith, V. (2002) 'Steady as they go', *Chief Executive,* 2002, *184.* Available at: [http://www.chiefexecutive.net/depts/performancemeasurement/184.htm].

Grundmann, W. (1972) in G. Friedrich and W. Bromiley (eds) *Theological Dictionary of the New Testament,* Vol. 8, Grand Rapids, MI, Eerdmans, pp. 1–26.

Haigh, G. (2003) *Bad Company: The Cult of the CEO* (Quarterly Essay #10), Melbourne, Black Inc.

Hochschild, A.R. (1979) 'Emotion work, feeling rules, and social structure', *American Journal of Sociology*, vol. 85, pp. 551–75.

Hofstede, G., Bond, M.H. and Luk, C.L. (1993) 'Individual perceptions of organizational cultures: A methodological treatise on levels of analysis', *Organization Studies*, vol. 14, pp. 483–503.

Howell, J. and Shamir, B. (2005) 'The role of followers in the charismatic leadership process', *Academy of Management Review*, vol. 30, pp. 96–112.

Huczynski, A.A. (1993) *Management Gurus: What Makes Them and How to Become One*, London, Routledge.

Kant, I. (1964) *The Metaphysical Principles of Virtue* (trans. J. Ellington), New York, Library of Liberal Arts/Bobbs-Merrill.

Khurana, R. (2002) *Searching for a Corporate Savior: The Irrational Quest for Charismatic CEOs*, Princeton, NJ, Princeton University Press.

Kirkpatrick, S.A. and Locke, E.A. (1991) 'Leadership: Do traits matter?' *Academy of Management Executive*, vol. 5, no. 2, pp. 48–60.

Kochanski, J. (1997) 'Competency-based management', *Training and Development*, vol. 51, pp. 41–4.

Krueger, J. and Mueller, R. (2002) 'Unskilled, unaware, or both? The contribution of social-perceptual skills and statistical regression to self-enhancement biases', *Journal of Personality and Social Psychology*, vol. 82, pp. 180–88.

Kurtz, E. and Ketcham, K. (1992) *The Spirituality of Imperfection: Storytelling and the Journey to Wholeness*, New York, Bantam Books.

Lebell, S. (1995) *The Art of Living: The Classic Manual on Virtue, Happiness, and Effectiveness.* A

*New Interpretation*, New York, HarperCollins.

Lee, K., Gizzarone, M. and Ashton, M. (2003) 'Personality and the likelihood to sexually harass', *Sex Roles*, vol. 49, pp. 59–69.

Luthans, F. and Avolio, B.J. (2003) 'Authentic leadership: A positive development approach' in K.S. Cameron, J.E. Dutton and R.E. Quinn (eds) *Positive Organizational Scholarship*, San Francisco, CA, Berret-Koehler, pp. 241–58.

Maccoby, M. (2000) 'Narcissistic leaders: The incredible pros, the inevitable cons', *Harvard Business Review* , vol. 78, no. 1, pp. 68–78.

McClelland, D. (1975) *Power: The Inner Experience*, New York, Irvington.

McClelland, D.C., Davis, W.N., Kalin, R. and Wanner, E. (1972) *The Drinking Man*, New York, The Free Press.

Macht, J. (2002) 'Letting the air out of celebrity leaders', *Business 2.0*, vol. 3, no. 3, p. 94.

Manz, C. and Sims, H. (1991) 'Superleadership: Beyond the myth of heroic leadership', *Organizational Dynamics*, vol. 19, no. 4, pp. 18–35.

May, D.R., Chan, A., Hodges, T. and Avolio, B.J. (2003) 'Developing the moral component of authentic leadership', *Organizational Dynamics*, vol. 32, pp. 247–60.

Meindl, J.R. (1993) 'Reinventing leadership: A radical, social psychological approach' in J.K. Murnighan (ed.) *Social Psychology in Organizations: Advances in Theory and Research*, Englewood Cliffs, NJ, Prentice Hall, pp. 89–118.

Mishra, P. (2004) *An End to Suffering: The Buddha in the World*, New York, Farrar, Straus and Giroux.

Mitchell, S. (1988) *Tao Te Ching: A New English Version*, New York, Harper and Row.

Molyneaux, D. (2003) ' "Blessed are the meek, for they shall inherit the earth": An aspiration applicable to business?' *Journal of Business Ethics*, vol. 48, pp. 347–63.

Murray, A. (2001) *Humility: The Journey toward Holiness*, Bloomington, MN, Bethany House.

Myers, D.G. (1987) 'Yin and yang in psychological research and Christian belief', *Perspectives on Science and Christian Faith*, vol. 39, pp. 128–39.

Nagle, B.A. (1995) 'Wanted: A leader for the 21st Century', *Industry Week*, vol. 244, no. 21, p. 29.

Nietzsche, F. (1974) *Beyond Good and Evil: Prelude to a Philosophy of the Future (The Complete Works of Friedrich Nietzsche)* (trans. H. Zimmerman), New York, Gordon Press.

Noer, D. (1994) 'Images of cowboys and leaders', *Executive Excellence*, vol. 11, no. 12, p. 11.

Northhouse, P.G. (1997) *Leadership: Theory and Practice,* Thousand Oaks, CA, Sage.

Pearsall, J. and Trumble, B. (eds) (1996) *The Oxford English Reference Dictionary* (2nd edn), Oxford, Oxford University Press.

Peterson, C. and Seligman, M. (2004) *Character Strengths and Virtues: A Handbook and Classification*, New York, Oxford University Press.

Polleys, M.S. (2002) 'One university's response to the anti-leadership vaccine: Developing servant leader', *Journal of Leadership Studies*, vol. 8, no. 3, pp. 117–33.

Raelin, J.A. (2003) 'The myth of charismatic leaders', *Training and Development*, vol. 57, no. 3, pp. 46–51.

Richards, N. (1992) *Humility*, Philadelphia, PA, Temple University Press.

Rost, J.C. (1991) *Leadership for the Twenty-First Century*, New York, Praeger.

Sandage, S. and Wiess, T. (2001) 'Contextualizing models of humility and forgiveness: A reply to Gassin', *Journal of Psychology and Theology*, vol. 29, no. 3, pp. 201–11.

Sankowsky, D. (1995) 'The charismatic leader as narcissist: Understanding the abuse of power', *Organizational Dynamics*, vol. 23, no. 4, pp. 57–72.

Schramm, J. (2002) 'Humility is key to leadership', *People Management*, vol. 8, no. 14, p. 11.

Seers, A., McGee, G.W., Serey, T.T. and Graen, G.B. (1983) 'The interaction of job stress and social support: A strong inference investigation', *Academy of Management Journal*, vol. 26, pp. 273–84.

Seib, G.F. (1998) 'Crises abound, so where are all the leaders?' *Wall Street Journal*, Eastern edition, 2 September, p. A20.

Seligman, M. (2002) *Authentic Happiness: Using the New Positive Psychology to Realize Your Potential for Lasting Fulfillment*, New York, Free Press.

Sendjaya, S. and Sarros, J. (2002) 'Servant leadership: Its origin, development, and application in organizations', *Journal of Leadership and Organizational Studies*, vol. 9, no. 2, pp. 57–65.

Shelton, K. (1996) 'Many leaders, many heroes', *Executive Excellence*, vol. 13, no. 4, p. 2.

Simon, H. (1976) *Administrative Behavior* (3rd edn), New York, Free Press.

Smith, B., Montagon, R. and Kuzmenko, T. (2004) 'Transformational and servant leadership: Content and contextual comparisons', *Journal of Leadership and Organizational Studies*, vol. 10, no. 4, pp. 80–91.

Spiegel, J.S. (2003) 'The moral irony of humility', *Logos: A Journal of Catholic Thought and Culture*, vol. 6, pp. 131–50.

Spinoza, B. (1994) 'The ethics' in *A Spinoza Reader: The Ethics and Other Works* (trans. E. Curley), Princeton, MA, Princeton University Press.

Tangney, J.P. (2000) 'Humility: Theoretical perspectives, empirical findings, and directions for future research', *Journal of Social and Clinical Psychology*, vol. 19, pp. 70–82.

Templeton, J. (1997) *Worldwide Laws of Life*, Philadelphia, PA, Templeton Foundation Press.

Tourish, D. and Pinnington, A. (2002) 'Transformational leadership, corporate cultism and the spirituality paradigm: An unholy trinity in the workplace?' *Human Relations*, vol. 55, pp. 147–72.

Tversky, A. and Kahneman, D. (1974) 'Judgment under uncertainty: Heuristics and biases', *Science*, September, pp. 1124–131.

Vera, D. and Rodriguez-Lopez, A. (2004) 'Humility as a source of competitive advantage', *Organizational Dynamics*, vol. 33, no. 4, pp. 393–408.

Willmott, H. (1997) 'Rethinking management and managerial work: Capitalism, control, and subjectivity', *Human Relations*, vol. 50, pp. 1329–359.

# The Constructions of Social Constructionism

## 8

*Jörgen Sandberg*

This chapter describes the main features of the social constructionist research approach. A weakness in a wide range of social constructionist studies is the articulation of the assumptions underlying social constructionism. These are often treated superficially, which opens the way for various misunderstandings about constructionism (Hacking, 1999). Therefore, the purpose of this chapter is [ ... ] to provide an elaboration [ ... ] of the basic assumptions underlying social constructionism [ ... ].

The first part of the chapter considers some common features, as well as the differences and tensions that exist between different research approaches used in social constructionism. The second part elaborates a social phenomenological approach to social constructionism [ ... ]. In particular, it identifies and describes some of the most basic assumptions underlying a social phenomenological approach, and looks at how social construction is regarded from this standpoint.

## What is Social Constructionism?

For the last two decades, the label 'social construction'[1] has been used [ ... ] widely in the social sciences. The general tenet within social constructionism is that reality is not objective and given, but is socially constructed. More specifically, it is argued that all aspects of social reality such as male, female, family, identity, sexuality, genius, creativity, management, money, organization and leadership can be seen as socially defined through ongoing actions, negotiations and agreements. However, social constructionism is not a single unified approach but is made up of a large variety of disparate research approaches (Gergen, 1994; Schwandt, 1994; Danzinger, 1997). [ ... ]

Sandberg, J. (2001) 'The constructions of social constructionism' in Sjöstrand, S.-E., Sandberg, J. and Tyrstrup, M. (eds) Invisible Management: The Social Construction of Leadership, London, Thomson Learning, pp. 28–48.

# Common Features in Social Constructionism

Despite the great variety of approaches, there are above all four themes that unify the [ ... ] research approaches under the label of social constructionism. In particular, what unifies them is a rejection of the assumptions underlying prevalent research approaches in the social sciences: a dualistic ontology, an objectivistic epistemology, the individual as the foundation of knowledge, and language as a mirror of objective reality. This chapter will first describe the general meaning of these assumptions and then discuss why advocates of a social constructionist stance reject them.

## Dualistic Ontology

Assuming a dualistic ontology means treating subject and object as two separate and independent entities. A dualistic ontology implies a division of research objects into two main separate entities: a subject in itself and an object in itself (cf. Giorgi, 1994). For example, within theories of occupational competence, competence in a particular type of work is identified by looking at the worker and the work as two separate entities. Thereafter, an attempt is made to identify the specific attributes, such as knowledge and skills, that are inherent to the worker and what activities are inherent to the particular work he or she accomplishes (Sandberg, 1994). Similarly, corporate strategy is defined and described by seeing organization and environment as two separate entities. First, the inherent qualities of the organization such as its strengths and weaknesses are described, and then the inherent qualities of the environment such as the threats and opportunities that it offers (Smircich and Stubbart, 1985).

## Objectivistic Epistemology

The assumption of an objectivistic epistemology stipulates that beyond human consciousness there is an objective reality. Its qualities and the meaning we experience are assumed to be inherent to reality itself. Objective reality is thus seen as given and the ultimate foundation for all our knowledge. Through systematic scientific observations and careful monitoring of the extent to which our theories correspond to the particular aspect of objective reality we are investigating, it is assumed that we will come closer to this true picture of reality.

## Individualistic Epistemology

Assuming an individualistic epistemology means regarding the individual as the primary creator and possessor of knowledge about reality. The individual is then also regarded as the basic research object. Researchers with an empirical orientation (empiricism) assume that knowledge is produced through the sense experiences of individuals, while researchers with a rationalistic orientation (rationalism) assume that individuals produce knowledge through their inherent reason and their capacity to process and organize incoming sense experiences.

## Language as a Mirror of Objective Reality

The core idea of this assumption is that language can represent or, as Rorty (1979) argued, 'mirror' reality in an objective fashion. The relationship between language and reality is thus seen as a relationship of correspondence. As it is assumed that language has the capacity to represent reality, it is treated as a representational system available to the researchers in their endeavour to describe reality objectively.

These assumptions guide advocates of prevalent research approaches in fundamental ways, when it comes to designing and conducting their own research. In particular, research approaches governed by these assumptions focus either on the individual and/or the environment, and treat the individual and the environment as two separate entities, each with their own inherent qualities. For example, the most common approaches in leadership (Yukl, 1994) try either to identify and describe leadership (a) by focusing on the specific behaviours of leaders and/or the attributes such as knowledge, skills, attitudes and personal traits that the individual leaders possess, or (b) by focusing on situational factors such as the characteristics of the particular leadership task, the staff, the department and the organization in which the leadership is performed. In the former case, leadership is defined in terms of a specific set of attributes inherent to a person; in the latter it is defined by situational factors, that is, a specific set of situational factors requiring a specific type of leadership. Often these two approaches are combined: a specific set of situational factors postulate a specific set of attributes possessed by the leader.

Advocates of social constructionist approaches reject the above assumptions for several reasons. First and most importantly, instead of assuming a dualistic ontology that implies a division of subject and object, advocates of social constructionism regard subject and object as an inseparable relation. As Giorgi (1992) expressed it:

> There are not two independent entities, objects and subjects existing in themselves which later get to relate to each other, but the very meaning of subject implies a relationship to an object and to be an object intrinsically implies being related to subjectivity. (p. 7)

The problem of separating subject and object was originally pointed out by phenomenologists such as Husserl (1970[1900–01]) and Heidegger (1981[1927]), and later by a series of other researchers such as Schutz (1945,

1953), Berger and Luckmann (1966), Bourdieu (1990), Giddens (1984, 1993) and Searle (1995). Husserl argued that as subjects we are always related to reality through our lived experience of that reality. Heidegger developed Husserl's argument by suggesting that not only is reality mediated through our lived experience, but that it is also mediated through the specific culture, historical time and language in which we are situated.

A number of other researchers in areas such as critical theory, literature theory and social theory have reached similar conclusions to Heidegger. Critical theorists have suggested that our descriptions of reality are often coloured by taken-for-granted ideologies (Alvesson and Willmott, 1996). Advocates of literature theory have argued that such descriptions are furnished by established cultural conventions concerning specific narrative genres and speech codes (Bruner, 1996). Feminist studies have suggested that the dominating theoretical framework for producing knowledge is moulded by and saturated with male imagery (Richardson, 1995). Social scientists have shown that our descriptions of reality are not objective but are socially produced (Danzinger, 1997).

Advocates of these research approaches in social constructionism thus claim that it is not possible to produce objective descriptions of reality. Instead, their basic argument is that our descriptions are always coloured by our specific historical, cultural and linguistic understanding of reality. Thus instead of assuming an objectivistic epistemology in terms of the existence of a given and objective reality, advocates of a social constructionist approach claim that reality is socially constructed by continuous negotiation between people about what their reality is.

The assumption that reality is socially constructed also means a shift from an individualistic to a social epistemology. It is in our relationship to each other that we produce and reproduce reality. More specifically, from the above argument that reality is socially constructed it follows that the social interactions between individuals, rather than the individual mind, is the primary vehicle for developing knowledge. Finally, the assumption that reality is socially constructed means that language is not seen as a representational system that can be used to classify and name objective reality. Instead, language is seen as socially constructed. Thus, language does not achieve its meaning primarily through a correspondence with objective reality, but through the way we socially define and use it in different practices.

Finally, the basic claim of social constructionism, that reality is socially constructed through our activities, does not mean that we continuously produce new realities. Rather, the opposite applies. The fact that our activities are mediated through a specific culture, historical time and language implies that we, to a large extent, reproduce rather than produce reality.

In much the same way that the earlier assumptions guide the advocates of prevalent research approaches, the common assumptions that underlie social constructionist approaches guide its advocates to design and conduct research in specific ways. One of the most fundamental ways in which the assumptions underlying social constructionism govern its specific approaches, is by treating subject and world as an inseparable relation.

For example, within social constructionist approaches, leadership is regarded as a relational or intersubjective phenomenon. First, leadership is seen as inter-subjective in terms of an interactive wholeness between the leader and the led (Hosking and Morley, 1991; Hosking, Dachler and Gergen, 1995; Sandberg and Targama, 1998). More specifically, the leader and the led are seen as part of a social process in which particular forms of leadership are constructed and reproduced over time. Second, leadership is regarded as intersubjective in terms of different forms of conversation or discourse about leadership, such as those that occur within specific organizations, industries, research literature, media and cultures (Calás and Smircich, 1991; Chen and Meindl, 1991; Gemmill and Oakley, 1992; Jönsson, 1995; Alvesson and Willmott, 1996). For instance, Chen and Meindl (1991) explored the construction of leadership over time by investigating how different forms of media produced and reproduced the leadership of Donald Burr and *People Express* between 1981 and 1986.

By regarding leadership as socially constructed, the primary research focus for identifying and describing leadership concerns how certain aspects of leadership are produced and reproduced through the interaction between the leader and the led – that is, both in terms of particular constructions of leadership, and the processes of producing and reproducing these constructions. Moreover, language often becomes a focal point in social constructionist approaches, due to the assumption that we are compelled to report our experiences of reality through a commonly shared language. The way in which we define and use language therefore becomes central to the investigation and understanding of how we construct reality. The focus on language as a central vehicle in constructing leadership is particularly salient in those studies that explore leadership as produced and reproduced through conversation and discourse.

# Differences and Tensions in Social Constructionism

Given the great variety of research approaches housed under the roof of social constructionism, there are naturally not only unifying themes but also significant differences and tensions between the different approaches. Three central differences and areas of tension in descriptions of the social construction of reality are micro versus macro levels of social construction; the role of language; and the nature of the relationship between subjectivity and objectivity.

## Micro versus Macro Level of Social Construction

It is possible to distinguish two major foci within social constructionism (Knorr-Certina, 1981; Engeström and Middleton, 1996). One set of research approaches, which includes ethnomethodology, symbolic interaction and cultural psychology, puts its primary focus on the locally constructed reality that is to be found mainly in face-to-face interaction. Another set of approaches, which includes various forms of institutional theory and theories of culture, focuses primarily on a more generally constructed type of reality such as 'the labour market' and 'kinship'. However, a growing number of researchers, such as Knorr-Certina (1981), Callon and Latour (1981), Giddens (1984), Bourdieu (1990), Sjöstrand (1993) and Engestrom and Middleton (1996), advocate integrating the micro and macro levels in order to understand how reality is socially constructed.

Approaches that focus on face-to-face interaction only, fail to recognize how that interaction is framed by the larger culture and institutionalized context of which it is a part, while an exclusive focus on the broader social context and culture, fails to recognize how that social context and that culture are produced and maintained in our daily face-to-face interactions.

## The Role of Language in Social Construction

As was argued before, a general view among social constructionist approaches is that language is not a representational system for classifying and labelling external reality, but that it is instead part of social reality. The debate within social constructionism deals with the extent to which language is part of socially constructed reality, and in what sense it is so. Those who place the strongest emphasis on language are the post-structuralists. Following Derrida (1981[1972], 1998), it is claimed that meaning expressed through language does not refer to an external reality. Derrida (1981[1972]) argues further that a specific sign or word within language does not achieve its meaning in relation to an external reality, but only in relation to other words, that is, the meaning of a word is constructed through the play of differences between words. And since meaning is constructed within language, reality appears as language.

A somewhat weaker, albeit still strong emphasis on language is proposed by advocates of discursive approaches. For example, Gergen (1994) argued that social constructionism does not deny:

> the world out there more generally [ ... ]. Once we attempt to articulate 'what there is', however, we enter the world of discourse. At that moment the process of construction commences, and this effort is inextricably woven into processes of social interchange and into history and culture. (p. 72)

The argument that we construct reality through language and discursive practices implies that they are in focus when exploring the social construction of reality.

Although a number of researchers regard language and discursive practices as the primary vehicle in the social construction of reality, there are also many others such as Wittgenstein (1953), Berger and Luckmann (1966), Habermas (1972), Giddens (1984), Bourdieu (1990), Chaiklin and Lave (1993) and Searle (1995) who place less emphasis on language. Giddens (1984), for example, claimed that reality is only partly constructed through discursive practices, or what he called 'discursive consciousness'. He claims instead that the greater part of the social construction of reality takes place in 'practical consciousness'.

> Practical consciousness consists of all the things which actors know tacitly about how to 'go on' in the context of social life without being able to give them direct discursive expression.

In his theory of practice Bourdieu (1990) argued along lines similar to Giddens. More specifically, in elaborating the concept of habitus as a theory for bridging the distinction between individual and social, Bourdieu argued that habitus is primarily bodily rather than discursive. Moreover, as Bourdieu (1990), Engeström (1993) and even Derrida in his later writings (see Debrix, 1999) have pointed out, various forms of material conditions, such as economic capital and material tools, are also central components in social construction, since they constrain and enable the social construction of reality in specific ways.

## The Nature of the Relationship between Subject and Object

As was described earlier, most social constructionists embrace a relational ontology, in the sense that subject and object are regarded as inextricably related. However, there is tension between those researchers who put the focus on the subject pole and those who focus on the object pole of the relation, and there is an ongoing debate between the two sides. The theoretical path within constructionism originating from Piaget (1954) and Kelly (1955) in cognitive psychology (Schwandt, 1994; Gergen, 1995) falls close to the subjective pole. Post-structuralists who tend to equate reality with language, as well as researchers who mainly adopt a discursive approach, also come close to the subjective side. A number of institutional theorists, on the other hand, are closely related to the objective pole.

Researchers such as Berger and Luckmann (1966), Bourdieu (1990) and Giddens (1984) are critical of these approaches, whose primary focus falls on either the subject or the object pole of the relation. The greatest risk in taking a strong subjectivistic or objectivistic stance here is that the indissoluble relation between subject and object may be neglected. For example, a strong focus on individuals may fail to take into account the way in which institutions such as money, property, marriage and leadership influence the subjective construction of reality. Taking a strong subjective stance also implies the risk of falling into idealism. On the other hand, a strong objective focus may fail to take into account how these institutions are subjectively produced and reproduced, and thus lead to realism.

# A Social Phenomenological Approach to Social Constructionism

[ ... ] The aim of the rest of this chapter is to further elaborate and describe the most central features of a social phenomenological approach to social constructionism. This elaboration will be based primarily on Berger and Luckmann's (1966) theory of social construction. [ ... ]

# Life-World as the Basis for the Social Phenomenological Approach to Social Constructionism

The basis for a social phenomenological approach to social constructionism is the notion of life-world, stipulating that subject and world are inextricably related through the subject's lived experience of the world. [ ... ]

Bengtsson (1989, p. 72) captured the basic idea of life-world, that subject and world are inseparable through the subjects' experience of the world as follows:

> [ ... ] even if life-world is objective both in the sense that it is a shared world and in the sense that it transcends (exceeds) the subject, that is, its qualities are not qualities within the subject, it is likewise inseparable from a subject, namely, the subject who experiences it, lives and acts in it. The world is always there in the first person from the perspective of my space and time here and now.

As Bengtsson (ibid.) points out, life-world is the subject's experience of reality, at the same time that it is objective. It is not objective, however, in the sense of being an objective reality independent of the subject. Instead, it is objective in the sense that it is an intersubjective world. We share it with other subjects through our experience of it, and we are constantly involved in negotiation with other subjects about reality in terms of our intersubjective sense-making of it. The agreed meaning constitutes the objective reality. Furthermore, life-world is objective in the sense that it transcends its subjects. This is because its qualities are not solely tied to the subjects' lived experience of it. At the same time, however, it is inseparable from the subjects through their experience of it. For example, most European countries have agreed to have daylight saving and move the clock one hour ahead for the period of March to October. Daylight saving thus becomes an objective fact through this agreement. Even if some of us try to ignore the agreed daylight saving time, we encounter difficulty in doing so because its qualities extend beyond our experience of clock time.

As became apparent in the above example, subjective and objective realities reflect each other. On the one hand, a basic condition for individuals to survive in society is that their subjective reality corresponds with objective reality. If my subjective construction of clock time deviates considerably from the general construction of clock time, I encounter difficulties in getting by. On the other hand, the construction of objective reality must correspond to the subjectively constructed reality. If not, a particular constructed reality will not achieve the status of objective reality. It is first when there is a correspondence between a number of subjectively constructed realities, such as agreement among most countries in Europe concerning the introduction of daylight saving, that an objective reality can appear.

However, subjective and objective reality can never correspond completely, because objective reality always exceeds subjective reality in a number of ways. One reason for this is the division of labour, which gives rise to a particular distribution of knowledge of reality among members of a society. For instance, even if a trade unionist and a board member of a company are in agreement that the failure of their company to produce a desirable profit stems from a leadership problem, their construction of leadership and the solution to that problem may differ. Another central factor is our social position, such as class and gender in the social structure in which we live and act. If the trade unionist is a woman and comes from the working class, and the board member is a man who comes from the upper class, this may mean an even larger difference in their construction of the problem of leadership. Moreover, other factors such as differences in culture and the geographical area (urban or rural) in which a person has grown up and lives, or differences in age, may also lead to a lower level of correspondence between the subjective and objective construction of reality. For example, Hofstede's (1980) study of cultural differences in 40 countries illustrates that the construction of leadership varies from culture to culture.

## Subjective and Objective Reality as a Dialectic Wholeness

But how can reality exist as subjective and objective at the same time? As well as Berger and Luckmann, both Bourdieu and Giddens have each offered a comprehensive account of the problem of the simultaneity of subjective and objective experience. Through his concept of *habitus,* Bourdieu (1981, 1990) tried to describe the inextricable relation between subject and object. According to his view, every action brings together two states of history: objectified history and embodied history in the form of habitus. Objective reality exists in terms of an objectified history accumulated in material objects such as machines and buildings and in immaterial objects such as theories and customs. Subjective reality exists as embodied history, which consists of an internalized objectified history or objective reality. In our activities and actions, objectified and embodied history appears simultaneously in habitus. As Bourdieu (1981) exemplified it:

> A man who raises his hat in greeting is unwittingly reactivating a conventional sign inherited from the Middle Ages, when as Panoflosky reminds us, armed men used to take off their helmets to make clear their peaceful intentions. (p. 305)

What Bourdieu's example shows is that the habitus of 'greeting' is part of objectified history or objective reality, while at the same time it is part of embodied history or subjective reality, in the sense that 'greeting' carries the agent's action and is carried by the agent simultaneously.

In his theory of structuration, Giddens (1984, 1993) gives a similar account of how subjective and objective reality can exist simultaneously. In his view, the dialectic relation between subjective and objective reality can be described as a duality of structure. By duality of structure he means 'that social structure is both constituted by human agency and yet is at the same time the very *medium* of this constitution' (Giddens, 1993, p. 128). The theory of duality of structures can also be illustrated by Bourdieu's example of greeting, where we see how the social structure of greeting is produced by the man who raises his hat to the person he meets, while at the same time the social structure of greeting produces the way in which the two people interact when they meet each other.

The simultaneous dialectic between subjective and objective reality is also the most central feature of Berger and Luckmann's (1966) theory of social construction. In the social construction of reality, they see an ongoing dialectical process between subjective and objective reality, which can be described in terms of externalization, objectivation and internalization.

Externalization means that we produce our reality through activities such as talking, thinking, building, managing, curing, eating, writing and driving. The agreement on daylight saving time is an externalization of human activities. Objectivation means that we experience our activities as having an objective existence independent of ourselves as individual subjects. For instance, the agreed change in time is experienced as objective because it influences our daily life in various ways. Internalization refers to the socialization process whereby we become part of the reality we have produced. For example, we internalize daylight saving time by living and acting according to that time. These three dialectical elements appear not sequentially, but simultaneously. At the same time that we act in accordance with the stipulated daylight saving time, we externalize, objectify and internalize it. More precisely, by following this time, we reproduce it; and because of our doing so, daylight saving time achieves the status of objective reality, which we internalize by being socialized into daylight saving time.

## Socialization: From Subjective to Objective Construction of Reality

Although we participate simultaneously in the societal dialectics between subjective and objective reality, there is a sequential time span in which each one of us becomes part of these societal dialectics. The starting-point for this is the internalization process, the immediate experience of an activity that expresses meaning, that is, as a manifestation of someone else's subjective processes that become subjectively meaningful to me. Through the externalization, this person's subjectivity becomes objectively available to me, and thus also meaningful to me irrespective of whether my interpretation is in line with the other's intention.

There are two central processes by which an individual internalizes society: primary and secondary socialization. Primary socialization is the first and most fundamental step in the internalization of the construction of objective reality. In primary socialization we internalize the most basic constructions of reality such as language, greetings, mother, father and gender that regulate the most common activities and interactions among people. Secondary socialization includes any of the subsequent socialization processes by which individuals internalize central aspects of reality, such as professions, and institutions such as money, banks and tax authorities.

A central feature in both primary and secondary socialization is that the internalization of roles and attitudes from significant others such as parents, relatives, friends and teachers becomes progressively abstracted to roles and attitudes in general. When the generalized other has been incorporated into consciousness, a symmetrical relation between objective and subjective reality is established. As Berger and Luckmann (1966) expressed it: 'What is real "outside" corresponds with what is real "within"' (p. 153).

An important conclusion to be drawn from the above discussion is that our experience of reality as meaningful is not primarily a result of our own sense-making of it. Rather, meaningfulness originates in the process by which we as individuals internalize the reality in which others already act and live. In other words, the socially constructed reality that we internalize becomes our framework for making sense of reality. This means that those activities and actions in which individuals are involved, achieve their meaning through the specific social constructions of reality that they have internalized via primary and secondary socialization.

From the above description, it may appear as though the interaction between subjects in the process of constructing reality is primarily harmonious and symmetrical. This, however, is not always the case. As was pointed out earlier, the symmetry between subjective and objective reality can never be complete, because there is always more objective than subjective reality available. In addition, the interaction is largely asymmetrical, in terms of both knowledge and power (Foucault, 1972). This asymmetry is obvious between parents–children and teacher–pupil, but is also particular salient in leadership. In Berger and Luckmann's words (1966):

> He (sic) who has the largest stick has the better chance of imposing his definitions of reality. This is a rather safe assumption to make with regard to any larger collectivity, although there is always the possibility of politically disinterested theoreticians convincing each other without recourse to the cruder means of persuasion. (p. 127)

## The Role of Language in the Social Construction of Reality

In the social phenomenological approach, language plays a crucial role in the social construction of reality. However, while language is fundamental to the social construction of reality, it is at the same time socially constructed itself. As Searle (1995) argued, language can be seen as the most basic socially constructed institution, since all other socially constructed institutions presuppose language. Therefore, before the role of language in the social construction of reality is discussed in more detail, there follows a brief description of how language is socially constructed.

Language can be characterized as a system of vocal signs. It is produced when we externalize ourselves through specific forms of vocal expression. Through vocal expressions, language becomes objectively available to others, and objectified as having an objective and independent existence. We are also concerned about constructing the same language. For example, we often correct each other when we deviate from objective language. Some countries have also gone so far as to establish language authorities whose aim it is to monitor, and in some cases even dictate, how a particular language develops. This concern for constructing a single language is based on the idea that the social construction of reality presupposes an objective language. A high correspondence between subjective and objective language construction is a prerequisite for achieving a high correspondence between subjective and objective constructions of other aspects of reality.

The need to have a strong correspondence between the subjective and objective construction of reality becomes particularly obvious when we learn an additional language in order to communicate adequately. To achieve a high level of correspondence, a successful internalization of language is fundamental in both primary and secondary socialization. In the first phases of primary socialization, there is a big distance between subjective and objective language. Gradually, subjective and objective languages begin to come closer and closer together. The same applies to secondary socialization. For example, to become a corporate leader in a Swedish company the person concerned has to internalize the specific language and vocabulary developed and used by Swedish leaders when exercising leadership.

If language, then, is socially constructed, what role does it play in the social construction of other aspects of reality? From a social phenomenological perspective (e.g. Berger and Luckmann, 1966; Giddens, 1984; Bourdieu, 1990; Searle, 1995), language plays the following roles in the social construction of reality:

- it objectifies our experiences by categorizing and organizing them into meaningful wholes;
- it functions to a large extent as interpretative schemes of reality in the sense that our experiences of reality are objectified through language;
- through the objectivation of our experiences, it functions as a storage room for our accumulated experiences; and
- it works as the primary medium through which our accumulated experiences are transmitted between people and between generations, that is, between subjective and objective reality.

It is primarily in conversations between people that language plays an important role in the social construction of reality. The construction of reality through conversation is often described as discourses (Potter and Whetherell, 1987). However, the term 'discourse' does not have one single meaning, but is defined and used in a whole range of ways (Mills, 1997). In its most general sense, discourse can be described as a particular set of linguistic expressions, statements and concepts that form a kind of wholeness of particular topics.

In an overview of discourse studies in organization and management, Alvesson and Karreman (1998) identified two key dimensions. One dimension refers to the extent to which discourse determines the construction of reality and enjoys a wide range of advocates, from those who assume that discourse determines the construction of reality completely to those who regard discourse as relatively independent of the construction of social reality. As was argued in the first part of the chapter, social phenomenology falls between the end positions on this dimension. The second key dimension refers to the level of discourse, from local discourse in which most face-to-face conversations take place, to mega discourse such as general conversation about medicine or leadership in the Western world. The second dimension corresponds to a large degree with Berger and Luckmann's (1966) description of the legitimation of socially constructed reality as being objective. This correspondence can be used as a further exemplification of the role of language and discourse in the social construction of reality.

Following Berger and Luckmann (ibid.), legitimation can be seen as a second-order objectivation of our construction of reality. These authors distinguish four levels of legitimation. The first is described as a pre-theoretical and taken-for-granted stipulating that 'this is the way we do things here'. This level in particular provides a basic vocabulary which legitimates the social construction in question, and parallels a range of discourse studies in Alvesson and Kärreman's (1998) overview that emphasise the importance of detailed studies of local discourse in the understanding of particular social constructions of reality, such as leadership.

At the second level of legitimation, rudimentary theoretical statements are introduced. Proverbs and different forms of words of wisdom are commonly used. This second level of legitimation parallels the studies cited by Alvesson and Kärreman (ibid.), in which researchers acknowledge not only the need to be sensitive to specific expressions and statements used in local discourse, but also the need to go beyond local discourse and to make comparisons with other similar discourses in order to find broader discourse patterns. For example, instead of focusing only on the leadership discourse of a specific company, we could also investigate discourses of recruitment, incentives, training and career planning in an effort to explore in greater depth how leadership is socially constructed in that company.

The third level of legitimation provides more explicit theories on a range of institutions, which in turn often provide a more comprehensive framework to legitimate a specific social construction of reality. This level corresponds with the discourse researchers in Alvesson and Kärreman's (ibid.) overview present, which focuses on the higher-level discourses that order more local discourses into an integrated frame constituting a particular institution. For example, a higher-level discourse of leadership is often provided by business schools, leadership institutes and research literature.

Finally, a particular construction of reality is legitimated at a fourth level, comprised of overarching theories. These theories integrate a range of related activities into a meaningful whole, or what Berger and Luckmann (1966) labelled a 'symbolic universe'. The aim of this symbolic universe is to produce an exhaustive framework that gives meaning to, and justifies the existence of a range of related institutionalized activities. The symbolic universe corresponds to what Alvesson and Kärreman (1998) called 'mega discourse'. Mega discourse refers to the most general and standardized ways of conversing about certain practices, such as leadership. The market economy can be regarded as one mega discourse in which different forms of leadership discourse take place.

# Concluding Remarks

The aim of this chapter has been to describe the main features of social constructionism and to provide some background for the analysis [ ... ] of how leadership is socially constructed in different arenas. I first looked at the different research approaches covered by the label of social constructionism, to explore what they have in common and what differences and tensions exist among them. I then examined the basic features of a social phenomenological approach in greater detail, with a view to highlighting the theoretical framework behind the analysis of leadership in the chapters that follow.

A central claim arising from this more detailed examination of the social phenomenological approach is that the social construction of reality consists first and foremost of an ongoing reproduction, rather than an ongoing production, of reality. Using Bourdieu's (1981, 1990) terminology, the social construction of reality is largely a reproduction of objectified history embodied in our subjective activities in the form of habitus. No sooner are we born than we begin to internalize and embody reality as an objectified history. The more we become part of reality, through primary and secondary socialization, the more we begin to reproduce it ourselves. It is when we as subjects are first able to reproduce objective reality through our activities that we are regarded as fully fledged members of socially constructed reality.

That individuals to a large extent reproduce reality does not mean that they are some kind of mechanical robots that have been programmed in a certain way through socialization into society. We also have an ability to stand back and reflect on our performance, and to become aware of the ways in which our activities and actions are a result of what we have internalized through our participation in society. In other words, through reflection we are able to discover that society is a social construction rather than something given by nature. If we have created society, it also means that we can change it. However, changing requires an awareness and knowledge about how we socially construct reality, and its specific aspects such as leadership. Without such knowledge, we are more or less doomed to reproduce society in its present form. [ ... ]

---

## *Note*

1. In social science, the terms 'constructivism' and 'constructionism' are sometimes used interchangeably. But as Gergen (1985) and others have pointed out, these terms have quite different origins. The term 'constructivism' is used primarily with reference to the Piagetian theory of perception, while 'constructionism' refers mainly to Berger and Luckmann's (1966) work on how reality is socially constructed. As the main focus in this book is on theories more closely linked to Berger and Luckmann than to Piaget, the term 'constructionism' is used.

_____ *References* _____

Alvesson, M. and Kärreman, D. (1998) 'Discourses and Grand Discourse. Discourse and the Study of Organizations', paper Presented at the Conference Organizational Discourse: Pretext, Subtext and Context, London, UK.

Alvesson, M. and Willmott, H. (1996) *Making Sense of Management. A Critical Introduction*, London, Sage.

Bengtsson, J. (1989) 'Fenomenologi: Vardagsforskning, existensfilosofi, hermeneutik' in P. Månson (ed.) *Moderna Samhällsteorier: Traditioner Riktningar Teoretiker*, Stockholm, Prisma, pp. 67–108.

Berger, P.L. and Luckmann, T. (1981[1966]). *The Social Construction of Reality*, Harmondsworth, Penguin.

Bourdieu, P. (1981) 'Men and machines' in Knorr-Certina, K. and Cicourel, A.V. (eds) *Advances in Social Theory and Methodology. Toward an Integration of Micro- and Macro-Sociologies*, Boston, MA, Routledge.

Bourdieu, P. (1990) *The Logic of Practice*, Cambridge, Polity Press.

Bruner, J. (1996) *The Culture of Education*, Cambridge, Harvard University Press.

Calás, M.B. and Smircich, L. (1991) 'Voicing seduction to silence leadership', *Organization Studies*, vol. 4, pp. 567–602.

Callon, M. and Latour, B. (1981) 'Unscrewing the big Leviathan: How actors macro-structure reality and how sociologists help them to do so' in Knorr-Certina, K. and Cicourel, A.V. (eds) *Advances in Social Theory and Methodology. Toward an Integration of Micro- and Macro-Sociologies*, Boston, MA, Routledge.

Chaiklin, S. and Lave, J. (1993) *Understanding Practice. Perspectives on Activity and Context*, Cambridge, Cambridge University Press.

Chen, C.C. and Meindl, J.R. (1991) 'The construction of leadership images in the popular press: The case of Donald Burr and People Express', *Administrative Science Quarterly*, vol. 36, pp. 521–51.

Danzinger, K. (1997) 'The varieties of social construction', *Theory & Psychology*, vol. 3, pp. 399–416.

Debrix, F. (1999) 'Specters of postmodernism: Derrida's Marx, the new International and the return of situationism', *Philosophy & Social Criticism*, vol. 1, pp. 1–21.

Derrida, J. (1981[1972]) *Positions* (trans. Alan Bass), London, The Athlone Press.

Derrida, J. (1998) *Rösten och fenomenet*, Stockholm, Thales.

Engeström, Y. (1993) 'Developmental studies of work as a testbench of activity theory: The case of primary care medical practice' in Chaiklin, S. and Lave, J. (eds) *Understanding Practice. Perspectives on Activity and Context*, Cambridge, Cambridge University Press.

Engeström, Y. and Middleton, D. (1996) *Cognition and Communication at Work*, Cambridge, Cambridge University Press.

Foucault, M. (1972) *The Archeology of Knowledge*, London, Routledge.

Gemmill, G. and Oakley, J. (1992) 'Leadership: An alienating social myth?' *Human Relations*, vol. 2, pp. 113–29.

Gergen, K. (1994) *Realities And Relationships. Soundings in Social Construction*, Cambridge, Harvard University Press.

Giddens, A. (1984) *The Constitution of Society. Outline of the Theory of Structuration*, Cambridge, Polity Press.

Giddens, A. (1993) *New Rules of Sociological Methods. A Positive Critique of Interpretative Sociologies*, Cambridge, Polity Press.

Giorgi, A. (1992) *The Theory, Practice and Evaluation of the Phenomenological Method as a Qualitative Research Procedure for the Human Sciences*, Quebec, Université Du Québec A Montréal.

Giorgi, A. (1994) 'A phenomenological perspective on certain qualitative research methods', *Journal of Phenomenological Psychology*, vol. 25, pp. 191–220.

Habermas, J. (1972) *Knowledge and Human Interest*, London, Heinemann.

Heidegger, M. (1981[1927]) *Varat och tiden*, vols 1–2 (trans. Richard Matz), Lund, Doxa.

Hofstede, G. (1980) *Culture's Consequences: International Differences in Work-Related Values*, Beverly Hills, Sage.

Hosking, D-M. and Morley, I.E. (1991) *A Social Psychology of Organizing*, New York, Harvester Wheatsheaf.

Hosking, D-M., Dachler, P.H., and Gergen, K.J. (1995) *Management and Organization: Relational Alternatives to Individualism*, Aldershot, Avebury.

Husserl, E. (1970[1900–01]). *Logical Investigations,* vol. 2 (trans. J.N. Findlay), London, Routledge and Kegan Paul.

Jönsson, S. (1995) *Goda utsikter. Svenskt Management in perspektiv*, Stockholm, Nerenius & Santérus.

Kelly, G.A. (1955) *The Psychology of Personal Construct*, New York, Norton.

Knorr-Certina, K. (1981) 'The micro-sociological challenge of macro-sociology: toward a reconstruction of social theory and methodology' in Knorr-Certina, K. and Cicourel, A.V. (eds) *Advances in Social Theory and Methodology. Toward an Integration of Micro- and Macro-Sociologies*, Boston, MA, Routledge.

Mills, S. (1997) *Discourse*, London, Routledge.

Piaget, J. (1954) *The Construction of the Reality in the Child*, New York, Basic Books.

Potter, J. and Wetherell, M. (1987) *Discourse and Social Psychology: Beyond Attitudes and Behaviour*, London, Sage.

Richardson, L. (1995) 'Poetics, dramatics, and transgressive validity: The case of the skipped line', *The Sociological Quarterly,* vol. 4, pp. 695–710.

Rorty, R. (1979) *Philosophy and the Mirror of Nature*, Princeton, NJ, Princeton University Press.

Sandberg, J. (1994) *Human Competence at Work: An Interpretative Approach*, Göteborg, Bas.

Sandberg, J. and Targama, A. (1998) *Ledning och förståelse. Ett kompetensper-spektiv på organisationer*, Lund, Studentlitteratur.

Schutz, A. (1945) 'On multiple realities', *Philosophy and Phenomenological Research, A Quarterly Journal,* vol. 5, pp. 533–75.

Schutz, A. (1953) 'Common-sense and scientific interpretation of human action', *Philosophy and Phenomenological Research,* vol. 14, pp. 1–37.

Schwandt, T.A. (1994) 'Constructivist, interpretivist approaches to human inquiry' in Denzin, N.K. and Lincoln, Y.S. (eds) *Handbook of Qualitative Research,* Thousand Oaks, CA, Sage, pp. 118–37.

Searle, J.R. (1995) *The Construction of Social Reality*, New York, Free Press.

Sjöstrand, S-E. (1993) 'The socioeconomic institutions of organizing: Origin, emergence, and reproduction', *The Journal of Socio-Economics,* vol. 4, pp. 323–52.

Smircich, L. and Stubbart, C. (1985) 'Strategic management in an enacted world', *Academy of Management Review,* vol. 4, pp. 724–36.

Wittgenstein, L. (1953). *Philosophical Investigations*, Blackwell, Oxford.

Yukl, G. (1994). *Leadership in Organizations*, Englewood Cliffs, NJ, Prentice Hall.

# The Virtual Leader Construct: The Mass Mediatization and Simulation of Transformational Leadership

# 9

## David M. Boje and Carl Rhodes

## Introduction

Ronald McDonald, clown icon of the McDonald's Corporation, holds two 'official' executive positions. On 23 August 2003 he was appointed as McDonald's *Chief Happiness Officer* and his name was listed next to the other corporate officers in the 2003 Annual Report (McDonald's, 2004, p. 22). Less than a year later, on 16 April 2004, he was given the additional responsibility of *Ambassador for an Active Lifestyle*. At first glance it might seem odd that a clown be granted such positions – after all, he is not an 'actual' leader in the sense that leaders are considered exclusively to be flesh-and-blood humans. Contra such established wisdom, in this article we explore what happens when leaders and leadership becomes virtualized through the mass media.

The article develops the concept of the 'virtual leader construct'. This is a leader who is virtual, first in terms of being virtuous in relation to culturally accepted archetypes of leadership excellence, and second in terms of not being an actual embodied human being.[1] In this sense, virtuality is understood in contrast to actuality – while that which is actual can be located in the material world, that which is virtual has no materiality. In terms of virtual leadership, this distinction is between the leader who corresponds to an actual person, and the leader who is fictional or fictionalized. Note here that we regard the virtual leader as one who can fulfill an important leadership function – in part this is because they are 'real

Boje, D.M. and Rhodes, C. (2005) 'The virtual leader construct: The mass mediatization and simulation of transformational leadership', Leadership, vol. 1, no. 4, pp. 407–28.

without being actual' (Deleuze and Guattari, 1994, p. 156). This virtual leader is a 'construct' because she or he is an image or idea that is created by systematically fitting gestures, voice, and other virtues together to generate an impression or model. This Virtual Leadership Construct (VLC) provides a vehicle for handlers and organizers to speak intent through a simulation.

One of the most prevalent sites for the virtualization of leaders is the fast food industry. In this article we seek to theorize the VLC by examining its emergence in three major organizations from that industry. The first is the massive US-based hamburger restaurant chain Wendy's where former chief executive Dave Thomas was recreated in an extended series of advertisements following his retirement. The second is KFC where former owner 'Colonel' Harland Sanders was resuscitated, in a cartoon version, as the iconic figure for the organization's advertising. The third is McDonald's, where Ronald McDonald holds 'official' corporate roles and is used explicitly to promote and communicate the organization's vision. [ ... ]

We analyze virtual leaders as forms of *simulacra* – copies or imitations that become realer than real (see Deleuze, 1983, 52–53). Drawing on Baudrillard's (1983) discussion of the *orders of simulacra,* we argue that virtual leaders can exist at different levels of the virtualization, which enact different forms of substitution for traditional leadership. At these different levels, Dave Thomas's virtual leadership is an attempt to become an imitation of himself; Colonel Sanders's is an attempt to become a re-representation of the colonel that is increasingly distanced from the actual person; and Ronald McDonald is a leadership construct who bears no direct relation to any actual or specific leader. In each case we analyze the way that the virtualized and resemiotized leader has, or has not, helped the organization achieve the transformation leadership requirements emerging from the crisis that the fast food industry has faced in recent years – that is, the public backlash against the nutritional content of fast food and its effects of people's health.
[ ... ]

# The Orders of the VLC

In his book *Simulations,* Jean Baudrillard (1983) discusses what he calls the three orders of simulacra. Baudrillard's concern is with the different 'symbolic orders' that have emerged in different stages of history. Here the 'symbolic order' refers to the dominant way that the relationships between representations or signs and reality are understood. This leads Baudrillard to conclude that 'the domination of the sign within contemporary society has led ... to a situation whereby the idea that reality can in some way be grounded in terms of the authenticity of the material object can no longer hold' (Hancock, 1999, p. 166). As Baudrillard discusses, there are three different orders that have successively developed since the end of feudalism in Europe.

Baudrillard (1983) argues that with the Renaissance and the growth of the bourgeoisie as a new class in Europe, the relationship between signs and reality began to radically alter. This period saw the emergence of the first order of simulacra. This is an order of the *counterfeit* where representations of objects are understood as imitations. In this case there is a clear demarcation between a representation and an original. Using examples of art works and architecture, Baudrillard shows that the counterfeit is separate from the original – it is an *imitation*. These simulacra are still grounded in an assumption that there is something actual which is being copied.

With the industrial era, Baudrillard claims that the dominant symbolic order changed. This second order of simulacra is that of *production*. Here, new mass-production technologies enabled representations to go beyond being just imitations or counterfeits. Instead, the emergence of mass production, for the first time, meant that objects could be endlessly reproduced as copies of each other without needing to be related to any notion of an original. In this second order, the difference between the original and that which is represented is significantly widened because the mass-produced item is only ever a reproduction of an image of itself. It has no original.

Baudrillard associates the contemporary era with the third order of simulacra. Here, the rapid expansion of digital technology has meant that there is no longer any discernable difference between representations and originals. The movement Baudrillard proposes is one that takes us from authenticity and presence to the domination of simulacra – copies without originals that replace an actual reality with a simulated *hyperreality*.

Baudrillard's epochalization of simulation from the Renaissance to the industrial revolution to today has been described as his most imaginative and provocative claim, as well as his least defensible one (Karreman, 2001). In what Kellner (1989) refers to as 'semiological determinism', Baudrillard suggests that the development of the social order is determined by relations of signification and symbolic exchange. Despite such criticisms, in this article we take up Baudrillard's framework in the way that it 'presupposes the potential co-existence of different orders of simulacra' rather than seeing them as 'belonging to successive phases of history' (Karreman, 2001, p. 104; see also Deetz, 1994). In attempting to understand and theorize virtuality, it is therefore viable to retain the framework provided in Baudrillard's orders of simulacra, while letting go of his insistence on their epochal associations. Doing so leaves a theorization of three increasing levels of virtuality. These being first-order simulacra where simulation is recognizable as a representation, second-order simulacra where the boundary between originality and representation is blurred, and third-order simulacra where the model has no relation with a discernable original (Lane, 2000).

We use these three orders to explore the different extent to which leaders can be virtualized in the mass media and the effects of this in terms of the resemiotization of leadership. We use the examples of Wendy's, KFC and McDonald's to exemplify three orders of VLC. The first order is where the VLC is an imitation of an actual human leader – this is the order that Wendy's has experimented with. The second order is where the VLC is a mass-produced image that aberates the representation of an actual human leader – this is the order seen in KFC's Colonel Sanders. The third order is where the VLC operates as a leader, but bears no relation whatsoever to a human leader – this is the order of Ronald McDonald. As well as using the fast food industry to explore how the three orders of VLC work in relation to transformational leadership, we also suggest that each successive order has the potential to develop an increasingly potent (and problematic) form of VLC. This arises because the more virtualized the leader, the more malleable his or her character, the greater capacity she or he has for double narration.

## First-Order VLC – Wendy's Dave Thomas

In 1989 Dave Thomas, the founder of the Wendy's hamburger restaurant chain, began appearing in Wendy's television commercials. Between 1989 and his death in 2002, he appeared in all of the company's commercials. He was even listed in the *Guinness Book of World Records* for the longest-running advertising campaign featuring the founder of a company. This was an unprecedented mass mediatization of a corporate leader.

Before becoming the star of Wendy's TV commercials, Dave Thomas was better known as the founder of Wendy's Old Fashioned Hamburgers – a company that he founded on 15 November 1969. As the head of Wendy's, Thomas led its franchising in the early 1970s, took it public in 1976 (with 500 locations), and later transformed it into Wendy's International Inc. As of September 2004, Wendy's had 5,854 outlets in the Unites States and 718 elsewhere in the world. It also owns Tim Hortons with 2,632 outlets and Baja Fresh Mexican Grill with 305 outlets (Finan, 2005).

After ceasing his day-to-day management role in 1982, Thomas took up the position of chairman. In was in 1989, however, that he started an even more dramatic role as Wendy's spokesperson in their comical, sometimes whacky ('aw-shucks') TV commercials.[2] These commercials presented Thomas not as a suited corporate leader, but as a 'regular guy'. Dressed in a short-sleeved white shirt and a red tie, the commercials would find Thomas in very unlikely situations such as driving a racing car while the actual driver ate a burger. Thomas's transition from business man to the star of television commercials marked a significant shift in his leadership function. Indeed, while corporate leaders are seldom very well known to the public, 'wearing a Wendy's apron, Thomas was one of the nation's most recognized television spokesmen' (CNN Money, 2002).

Thomas's transition from CEO to celebrity status television spokesperson is indicative of a transition toward the first order of the VLC. Through the commercials,

Thomas became an image of his former self and, importantly, this was an image of leadership divorced from his corporate role as a manager and executive. The TV Thomas was an imitation or counterfeit of his alter ego as a corporate leader. As Baudrillard (1983) remarks, the counterfeit marks a place where theatre takes over social life. It is in this way that Thomas's commercials became theatrical – he was playing the role of himself as a regular guy, rather than as an extremely successful and wealthy entrepreneur. As a symbol for Wendy's he was still very much 'tied somehow to the world' (Baudrillard, 1983, p. 85) but he was not tied completely to his alter ego corporate self. There is an alteration between the mass media Thomas and the boardroom Thomas, but the difference between them does not disturb the fact that they are one and the same actual person.

In his new role and with his new media fame, Thomas's leadership capacity changed. As he was beginning to be virtualized he took on more of a mythical role in establishing Wendy's as an organization guided by old-fashioned values and common sense business practice. Indeed Wendy's is attempting to lionize Thomas's VLC in the image of a folk hero claiming that

> The long running Dave Thomas® campaign made Dave one of the nation's most recognizable spokesmen. North Americans loved him for his down-to-earth, homey style. As interest in Dave grew, he was often asked to talk to students, business or the media about free enterprise, success and community services.[3]

Even after Thomas's death Wendy's continues to draw on his character in its public image. His picture appears on the main page of Wendy's website[4] with the caption: 'father, founder, friend'. In Wendy's stores too, there are posters featuring Thomas's face. The current advertisement campaign has the by-line: 'prepared Dave's way'.

In relation to transformational leadership, Wendy's used Thomas's VLC to establish a particular image for the corporation and to promulgate its corporate values. In terms of our opening question of what happens when a corporate leader becomes virtualized, for Wendy's the answer was that the VLC was able to create a corporate image that supported its ongoing success. Even to this day the organization uses Thomas as a bedrock of its way of doing business. As Wendy's current chairman and CEO Jack Schuessler recently said: 'quality is a way of doing business that must extend ... throughout the entire enterprise. Dave Thomas declared that years ago when he declared the words "Quality is our Recipe"' (cited in Finan, 2005, p. 4). In terms of transformational leadership, Thomas's VLC focused on setting an example to others through his down to earth style (Bass, 1999) as well as propagating a set of organizational values (House and Shamir, 1993). These are functions that still live on after his death, and are enabled in part because of how his saturated media persona became so well known. Indeed, Thomas's own values are still used by the organization: 'quality is our recipe', 'do the right thing', 'treat people with respect', 'profit is a not a dirty word', and 'give something back'. The first of these values is registered by Wendy's as a trademark and is used as a marketing slogan.

While the virtualized Thomas retained a leadership function, his VLC capacity was never fully realized in terms of contributing to the leadership of organizational level transformation. This is because the 'nice guy' VLC Thomas, while providing the corporation with a vehicle to narrate its values and image, did not fully realize a capacity for double narration. The VLC Thomas was still very much rooted in the epic story of the corporation and did not provide any substantial new narratives. For example, Wendy's have not used the Thomas VLC in direct relation to the health crisis facing the fast food industry. In part this may be because while Thomas had become his own theatric VLC, this image was not further transitioned or developed after Thomas died in 2002. Wendy's response to the fast food industry's health-consciousness crisis happened after that. This challenge has, however, been given specific attention by Wendy's. Seven press releases were listed on Wendy's website in 2004 – every single one of them was about an initiative the organization had taken in relation to the nutritional value of its food – from salads, to baked potatoes, to low-carbohydrate burgers.

Wendy's has become involved in a range of activities to help generate a more health-conscious image. In August 2004 Wendy's partnered with the American Dietetic Association in a nutrition education program. The plan was to develop tools and materials to help customers understand the nutritional contents of the various items on Wendy's menu. In December of the same year the 'Combo Choices' menu was introduced allowing customers to substitute part of the standard meal for healthier options such as replacing french fries with a baked potato or a salad. In the kid's meal, low-fat milk can be substituted for the normal soft drink. In January 2005 fresh fruit was put on the menu.

In terms of VLC, what we find with Wendy's is an attempt to approach the first order of VLC through the mass mediatization of Thomas. By making him a house-hold name as a regular guy, Wendy's were able create an image of corporate leadership distanced from the goings on in the board room and the stock market, and instead to have a leader who could promote the traditional values that it aspired to. The result is that Thomas is still a VLC, but in a fairly minimal way, and without being used directly in relation to the changes going on in the industry.

## Second-Order VLC – KFC's Colonel Sanders

While Dave Thomas approached being a first order for VLC at Wendy's, it is Colonel Sanders, the iconic image of KFC, who takes this leadership in the direction of the second order. The development of the Colonel's virtualization, however, does pass through the first order, as we shall see. The story of

KFC starts in 1952 when the original Harland Sanders (born on 9 September 1890), who was at the time living on his social security cheque, decided to devote his life to opening a chicken franchising business that he called Kentucky Fried Chicken. Sanders had for a long time been a cook – indeed, his title of Colonel was not earned through military service but was given to him in 1935 by the then Governor of Kentucky Ruby Laffoon for his contribution to Kentucky cuisine. By 1964, when Sanders sold the business to investors for US$2 million, Kentucky Fried Chicken had 600 outlets. In 1969 the company went public with Sanders being the first shareholder. Today KFC has more than 11,000 restaurants in more than 80 countries and territories. It is also part of Yum! Brands Inc., the world's largest restaurant system with more than 32,500 KFC, A&W All-American Food(tm), Taco Bell, Long John Silver's and Pizza Hut restaurants.[5]

Although officially ending his ownership of Kentucky Fried Chicken more than 30 years ago, Colonel Sanders has still been very much a part of the corporation. He quickly came out of retirement to be paid an annual salary as a corporate spokesperson. This was a move which saw him being increasingly mediatized through his new role as a pitchman in television commercials. For example, in one commercial the Colonel was kidnapped by a 'housewife' and interrogated in an abandoned ware-house; but he still refused to give up his famous eleven herbs and spices secret recipe. Sanders also had a candid, individualistic style, and a theatrical presence. Together this made him a frequent TV talk show guest. He continued to travel 250,000 miles a year and do TV ads until his death in 1980. Up until this point, Sanders, like Thomas at Wendy's, had only started to become a first order VLC. He represented the corporation's espoused values through his being mass mediatized as a heroic leader with a unique and virtuous character. While Thomas was the regular guy, Sanders was the eccentric southern gentleman replete with white suit, red shoe lace tie and exaggerated white beard. He gave the organization an aura of authenticity with his 'secret' herbs and spices and his living out of the American dream through his epic rags-to-riches story. Even today, his photograph appears on the main page of KFC's website with the banner: 'the Colonel Welcomes You to KFC'.[6] His stylized image also graces the containers in which the food is served.

For the ten years after his death the image of Colonel Sanders only played a minor role at Kentucky Fried Chicken. His picture still appeared in the stores, and there was still the secret recipe, but there was no more mass media coverage through advertisements and television appearances. In 1990, however, things changed as the older campaign was revived with Sanders look-alikes. Still operating as a first-order VLC, the new theatric VLC was an imitation of Sanders's imitation of himself. It did not prove successful. Things changed, however, when on 9 September 1993 an animated version of Sanders was released. It was also in this period that the company changed its branding from Kentucky Fried Chicken to KFC, thus removing the word 'fried'. The new Sanders was even more virtualized to meet the requirements of the new brand strategy. He was a cartoon colonel replete with his familiar string tie, goatee, white suit and cane. Actor Randy Quaid provided the voice.

What KFC did was to restylize a deceased corporate founder's first-order VLC, by contemporalizing his virtual essence for a new generation of consumers, systematically orchestrated in an animated Colonel. The resemiotized leader, however, became increasingly distanced from the actual person that it was representing. In Baudrillard's (1983) terms his second-order simulacrum liquidated the reality of the first order and absorbed its appearance. In this order, rather than an imitative theatre there is a repetitive production whereby the simulacra became increasingly distanced from the actual originals so as to become copies of themselves – as in the case of mass production. In terms of VLC, however, the animated Colonel failed to take on leadership qualities, rendering him instead more of foolish cartoon.[7] He was narrated as both the founder of the organization and as a cartoon character, but the second narration lacked any form of leadership. While the first-order VLC colonel performed a leadership function in terms of embodying the corporation's values, the animated Colonel moved toward the second order of simulacrum, but lost his leadership edge. Gone were the individualized style and the personal embodiment of virtues – the new colonel continued to fulfill a marketing function, but not a leadership one. This colonel was mass mediatized and virtualized but, in the process, his leadership capacity was significantly diminished.

Like most fast food restaurants, in recent years KFC has faced an increasing number of problems associated with its high-fat products – when Kentucky Fried Chicken changed its name to KFC, the frying did not stop. KFC still offers its 'original recipe' chicken, more than 60 per cent of the energy value of which can come from fat. There are now also salads and lower-fat sandwiches on the menu. There are also the familiar partnerships with sports celebrities – in KFC's case golfer Annika Sorenstam, baseballer Barry Bonds and American football players Jim McMahon and William 'The Refrigerator' Perry. Despite this, KFC continues to face problems in relation to the dietary value and production processes of its food. In November 2003 KFC retracted advertisements which claimed that eating KFC was healthy. The advertisement in question stated that a skinless chicken breast has only 3 grams of fat. Complaints to the Fair Trading Commission in the United States claimed that most KFC consumers do not eat skinless and un-battered chicken, and the advertisements were therefore deceptive. To make matters worse, in 2003 Pamela Anderson (former Baywatch star), dressed in lettuce leaf-bikini in billboard ads,[8] joined the boycott of KFC by the 'People for the Ethical Treatment of Animals' (PETA).[9]

Despite the corporation's continued use of the Colonels' image to establish a sense of authenticity, his 'leadership' has been able to do little to respond to the current health crisis. His re-narration into the animated Colonel no longer represents the founder's leadership virtues, so while he is virtualized in the second order, the term VLC ceases to apply. In relation to our opening question of what happens when a leader is virtualized, in the case of Colonel Sanders the increasing levels of virtualization meant that his simulacrum was less and less able to provide a leadership function.

## Third-Order VLC – McDonald's Ronald McDonald

With Dave Thomas we saw a movement toward a first-order VLC. In Colonel Sanders we saw the unrealized potential for a second-order VLC. It is in Ronald McDonald, however, that we see the most successful VLC and the one who is the most virtualized.[10] Ronald has appeared in many incarnations since his humble beginnings as an entertainer at a Washington D.C. franchise of McDonald's in the early 1960s. Today American children rank him as second only to Santa Claus as the most recognizable person (Royle, 2000) thanks to the massive media coverage of his character in television advertisements, live shows, merchandising and videos.

Ronald's leadership capacity is clearly demonstrated in the series of events following the death of CEO Jim Cantalupo on 19 April 2004. Ironically, Cantalupo (a cheeseburger and fries lover), died of heart failure just when he was to celebrate McDonald's most highly successful corporate reorientation: to become a nutritious and fitness-conscious chain. As CEO, Cantalupo was tasked with turning around a corporation that had just had 14 consecutive months of same store sales decline, a stock price that was at the lowest point in nearly a decade, and a downgrading of its credit rating by Standard and Poor. In less than 16 months as CEO, Cantalupo's campaign introduced salads and other nutritional food sources, slowed franchise proliferation, and refocused McDonald's toward a 'back to basics' approach of customer service. The result was increased same store sales, and reversal of the sagging stock price (stock rose 70.8 per cent during Cantalupo's tenure as CEO, from US\$16.08 in December 2002 to US\$27.46 in April 2004).

By 6 a.m. on the day of Cantalupo's death, the Board convened (in teleconference, but with several members attending in person) to implement its formal succession plan. By 7 a.m. Charlie Bell was the new CEO.[11] Bell's story, as it was publicized by McDonald's, told of a rags-to-riches American dream (even though he was Australian) that saw him start his career as a 15-year-old fry clerk who made the climb to CEO. This was a reversal of the *McJob* image of dead end, no skill work in fast food outlets.[12]

Immediately following Bell's appointment, Ronald took on yet another leadership task. The Board commissioned full-page advertisements of Ronald commemorating Cantalupo. The advertisements presented a photo of Ronald in human clown form, with a tear running down his right cheek. As the tear made his clown makeup run, there was a caption that read: 'we miss you Jim'.[13]

The advertisement, distributed just two days after Cantalupo's death, appeared in eight major news outlets, including the *Wall Street Journal,* the *New York Times* and *USA Today.* Translated versions were placed in major dailies around the world. What is most interesting about the tear advertisement is that it was Ronald, not Charlie Bell (the new CEO) or a Board member, who gave emotional expression to corporate grief. As we will explore, this is an indicative demonstration that Ronald has achieved the status of a third-order VLC. In the 'Ronald's tear' example, Ronald had the charismatic influence to appeal to people around the world, and to meet the strategic goal of sustaining corporate image cohesion in a time of crisis.

Ronald, more than the other VLCs in the fast food industry, plays a special role in corporate transformation. In terms of the challenges of changing consumer preferences and public opinion about fast food, McDonald's has been particularly singled out. The extensive publicity surrounding the 2004 movie *Supersize Me* is a salient example of this. The movie is a documentary that follows director and star Morgan Spurlock as he ate nothing but McDonald's food for 30 days. As a result he gained 28.5 pounds in weight, became impotent and was warned by doctors that his endeavor was a serious health risk. McDonald's has also faced a variety of lawsuits about its alleged contribution to obesity (Bradford, 2003). With McDonald's being the largest fast food franchise with over 30,000 outlets in 121 nations, the industry leader was taking the most heat.

The use of Ronald in the tear advertisements is an important illustration of his leadership, but his real transformation role is his leadership of McDonald's attempt to transform into a champion for nutrition and fitness. Ronald, as he is incarnated by more than 250 actors who play him around the world in his new live show (*Get Moving with Ronald*), and animation-Ronald appearing in commercials and on tray liners, is doing what actual transformational leaders do: he is influencing people to ensure the organization achieves its strategic corporate objectives (Kapica, 2004). His leadership involves espousing the company's vision (Shamir et al., 1993), influencing outsiders to have a favorable impression of the corporation (Yukl, 1999), showing determination and confidence, setting an example (Bass, 1999), and communicating enthusiasm and inspiration (Rafferty and Griffin, 2004). In so doing, however, he has realized a double narration whereby he continues to present the older image of McDonald's as a fast food restaurant, but has also created a new image that is highly questioning of the company's fast food legacy.

Ronald's malleable character has been exploited to enable him to better meet McDonald's leadership challenges. Indeed, by him being such a character, McDonald's has achieved a resemiotization that has significantly altered the meanings and effects of its leadership. In a series of six films featuring Ronald released between 1998 and 2002, Ronald's character was significantly modified from the persona of a clown entertainer to that of super-hero clown who transmuted one material into another, changed the weather with a breath, and commanded animals with a thought. This new Ronald was adventurous and heroic, displaying the transformational leadership characteristics of creativity, risk taking and experimentation (Bass, 1999). Further, unlike Dave Thomas and Colonels Sanders, the executives were keen to ensure that Ronald did not appear too much of a salesman, but rather wanted him to be edgy, timely, and more in step with popular culture (Kramer, 1999). In the final three films Ronald's character also symbolically represents the corporation's desired image of fitness and health. The actor who plays the new Ronald is thinner, more athletic, and more active – he even uses a treadmill. Resemiotized in the mass media, the VLC Ronald communicates the organization's vision in his very being.

While KFC and Wendy's virtualized former owners in comedic, even clown-like ways, with Ronald, McDonald's has gone the full way toward a third-order VLC. Ronald approaches being a hyper-real leader in that he is generated by a model of a 'real without origin' (Baudrillard, 1983, p. 2). What this means is that while the first two orders of VLC retain the epic narrative associated with a single leader, with Ronald 'the system puts an end to the myth of its origin and to all the referential values it has itself secreted along the way' (p. 113) such that 'the contradiction between the real and the imaginary is effaced' (p. 142). He even cries human tears. In Baudrillard's terms, Ronald's leadership approaches an aesthetic hallucination of reality (p. 148). What this means for the corporation is that Ronald can perform a much greater variety of leadership functions because he is no longer constrained by the limitations of an actual person – while he in part imitates and extends the function of transformational leadership, he does not need to imitate any actual person, and as a result his capacity for double narration is advanced. Corporate power never had it so good.

Like Wendy's and KFC, however, McDonald's did have a heroic leader who founded and grew the organization – this was Ray Kroc who retired from McDonald's in 1969 and passed away in 1984. Like the other two organizations, McDonald's did experiment with using Kroc in first- and third-order simulacra. As a corporate leader Kroc became a lionized, larger-than-life, epic character who was promoted through his autobiography and other books written about him (see Kroc and Anderson, 1976; Love, 1986/1995). As reported in an authorized biography (Westman and Molina, 1980) he was even used as the inspiration for the animated character 'Mayor of McDonaldland'. These uses of Kroc do indicate a level of virtualization. Further, if work by Boas and Chain (1976), Schlosser (2001), and Kincheloe (2002) is any indication, there is a discernable gap between Kroc's epic heroic construct and the actual person called Kroc. The original Kroc was not the grandfatherly, nice guy he was double narrated to be. Instead he was an aggressive, hard-hitting strategist, who plotted expansion in what he called the 'war room'.

McDonald's had at least two potential VLCs, Ronald and Kroc, but, different to Wendy's and KFC, it was the fictional Ronald who was fully developed by the corporation. The reason for this, we suggest, is that when Kroc's epic narrative had ceased to be useful to the corporation, a fictional and more virtualized, yet still heroic, leader was better suited to its needs. What made McDonald's famous was its Taylorized, standardized, routinized and efficiency-focused work practices – practices that were replicated irrespective of cultural or geographic location (see Ritzer, 1993/2002). It was only after Kroc's death in 1984 that the restaurant was able to bring in regional menu variations to address localized tastes. The predictability that made McDonald's successful in the first instance had to be modified. In fact, going global, and keeping up with consumer changes in diet, made staying the same (what made McDonald's great) a liability. People began to see standardized uniformity as boring, insipid and too controlling.[14] The aggressive expansion policies and hardball, 'war room' tactics of Kroc (Boas and Chain, 1976) continued, long after his death, until the corporation took a spiraling downturn in the late 1990s. It was precisely then that the new Ronald, replete with his fitness programs and updated image, began to appear. The third-order VLC worked hand in hand with the corporation to lead it out of financial problems and to be renarrated as a more health-conscious, fitness-friendly corporation.

[ ... ]

# Conclusion

What we have proposed in this article is that the VLC is a new way that corporations are beginning to lead and influence people in the global era, where mediatized images are almost more real than their 'real' counterparts. The VLC begins with the theatrical production of leaders, either as animated or imitative live characters, and extends to VLCs who do not originate from actual leaders at all. As the global socioeconomic context of the corporation changes, such as in the example of pressures on the fast food industry to provide more nutritious and healthy food, VLCs can be modified to convey the right signals for employees and consumers, as with Ronald McDonald.[15] Furthermore, they can begin to 'speak for themselves' as a means of counteracting dominant organizational discourse.

For corporations VLCs help to resolve the issue of how leaders in a global economy can become omnipresent: one leader cannot be everywhere, but a mediatized VLC can. On a minimal level as a recognized leader retires or passes away, the VLC can become a simulated embodiment of established leadership virtues. More maximally, the VLC can resemiotize leadership so as to invent virtues and images of leadership that did not inhere in retired or deceased leaders. When handlers orchestrate and organize a VLC, what gets generated can become copied, recopied, and restylized until it emerges as a story that becomes autonomous from its foundations – a VLC fit for a hyper-real world. The science fiction dream is that with advances in media technology, the virtual becomes an increasingly important part of the real. It is still too early to conclude what such an extension of reality might mean for leadership. However, as the fast food examples demonstrated, when leadership heads in this direction it begins to function through different means. No longer the sole domain of the actual human being, leadership can and is taking on new virtualized forms.

As we have been arguing, the arrival of the VLCs marks a shift in the potential power of corporate leadership. This shift entails a movement away from power as it might be channeled through individual persons and moves toward a radical recentering of leadership power to the VLC. In the case of McDonald's this might be seen, at one extreme, as a form of positive power in that it has enabled broader social and cultural concerns about the health value of fast food to directly influence the conduct of the organization. In this sense virtual leadership can be seen to pressure corporations to imitate what is socially expected from them. Conversely, another extreme would suggest that VLCs are a means for corporations to indirectly and surreptitiously enhance their power while reducing transparency. Although McDonald's has done the most, each of the organizations discussed in this article have changed their images and their menus to add healthier food items. Despite this, they still offer the same unhealthy items and justify the effects of this through a liberal philosophy of providing 'free' choice.

It is our argument that the VLC is located between these two extremes of being culturally influenced and being conspiratorially produced. Further, this in-betweenness is a result of the double narration of the VLC. Clearly organizations such as the ones discussed here will create brand icons as a means of enhancing their control over their organizations and their market positions. At the same time, the double narration suggests that VLC behavior is not fully determined by corporate desire. The important point is that given the social saturation of organizations and the ongoing corporate focus on marketing, VLCs may well become increasingly important facets of leadership. It is the operation of this leadership and how it is located between narrowly defined corporate agendas and the broader needs of society that will influence the organizational and social landscape to come.

## Notes

1. Etymologically, *virtue* and *virtual* both originate in the Latin word *virtus* which refers to strength, courageousness, and excellence. This clearly relates to the modern sense of *virtue* as meaning admirable moral qualities. It also relates to the modern *virtual*, i.e. that which, although not actual, still contains the essential characteristics and virtues of the actual.
2. Industry analysts and company officials said the advertisements helped the company rebound from a difficult period in the mid-1980s when earnings sank.

3. Quoted from the special section of the Wendy's website devoted to Dave Thomas's legacy (http://www.wendys.com/dave/flash.html).
4. See http://www.wendys.com/w-1-0.shtml
5. These data come from the KFC website: http://www.kfc.com/about
6. See http://www.kfc.com
7. For more on this point see http://www.filmtracks.com/home/mascots_thesis/kfc.html
8. CNN Money Line (21 October 2003) on-line photo and article available at: http://money.cnn.com/2003/10/17/news/companies/pamela_kfc/?cnn=yes; also see the BBC article and photo at http://news.bbc.co.uk/l/hi/england/merseyside/2932505.stm
9. PETA claims that KFC suppliers drug and scald chickens, and sear off their beaks with hot blades before slaughtering them in an inhumane manner.
10. It is worth noting that McDonald's is not the only fast food chain to use a clown as an advertising icon. For example, in 1979 Burger King created a cartoon character eponymously named Burger King. This character appeared to be a parody or imitation of Ronald McDonald. He was a costumed clownish character who had a magical kingdom (patterned after 'McDonaldland' using the theme of 'King Arthur'). The 'Burger King Kingdom' characters are 'Sir Shakes-A-Lot' a milkshake character similar to McDonald's 'Grimace'; 'Duke of Doubts', a rogue stealing burgers like McDonald's 'Hamburglar'; the 'Wizard of Fries' is a robot with a French fry's head, whereas McDonaldland's 'CosMc' is a robot with an alien's head, and so forth. The project was abandoned by 1981, leaving the animated 'Burger King' all alone. The key difference, however, is that while the Burger King clowns did symbolically represent the firm, they were not imbued with leadership characteristics and did not perform any leadership function.
11. Sadly, Charlie Bell died in January of 2005 from colorectal cancer at the age of 44. Although he is credited with introducing McDonald's new healthy menu options, Guy Russo CEO of McDonald's Australia is quoted as saying: 'When people would ask [Charlie] how he was he would say, "fat and happy" and the only exercise he did was jumping to conclusions' (cited from *The Sydney Morning Herald,* 20 January 2005, available at: http://www.smh.com.au/news/Business/Charlie-Bell-a-fat-and-happy-boy-from-Oz/2005/01/20/1106110860641.html?oneclick=true).
12. The 11th edition of Merriam–Webster's *Collegiate Dictionary,* published in June 2003, defines a *McJob* as 'a low-paying job that requires little skill and provides little opportunity for advancement'. Similar definitions appear in the *Oxford, Random House,* and *American Heritage* dictionaries. The term *McJob* was coined by the Canadian novelist Douglas Coupland (1991) in his novel *Generation X.* Coupland defines a *McJob* as 'A low-pay, low-prestige, low-dignity, low-benefit, no-future job in the service sector. Frequently considered a satisfying career choice by people who have never held one' (p. 5).
13. The tear ad (without caption) as it ran in color version in *USA Today* on 21 April 2004 can be seen at http://www.adage.com/images/random/ronald0421_big.jpg
14. See for example, an analysis by Jacques Pepin at http://www.time.com/time/time100/profile/kroc3.html
15. Although the VLC is clearly a public figure, she or he can still be expected to have a direct influence in employees. Employees of fast food restaurants are also likely to be their customers, so they do experience the organization's marketing. Further, given that the front-line staff at fast food restaurants are generally teenagers and young adults, they either are, or have recently been, the main target of much of the marketing (see Boje and Rhodes, forthcoming).

## References

Bass, B.M. (1999) 'Two decades of research and development in transformational leadership', *European Journal of Organizational Psychology,* vol. 8, pp. 9–32.
Baudrillard, J. (1983) *Simulation,* New York, Semiotext(e).

Boas, A.M. and Chain, S. (1976) *Big Mac: The Unauthorized Story of McDonald's*, New York, E.P. Dutton.

Bradford, L. (2003) 'Fat foods: back in court: novel legal theories revive the case against McDonald's', *Time On Line Edition*, 11 August. Available at: http://www.time.com/time/insidebiz/article/0,9171,1101030811–472858,00.html

CNN Money (2002) 'Wendy's founder dead at 69', 8 January. Available at: http://money.cnn.com/2002/01/08/companies/wendys_obit/

Deetz, S. (1994) 'Representative practices and the political analysis of corporations' in Kovacic, B. (ed.) *Organizational Communication: New Perspectives*, Albany, NY, SUNY Press, pp. 209–42.

Deleuze, G. (1983) 'Plato and the Simulacrum', *October* 27, pp. 52–3.

Deleuze, G. and Guattari, F. (1994) *What is Philosophy?* London, Verso.

Finan, K. (2005) 'Wendy's: The state of the enterprise', *Wendy's Magazine.* Available at: http://www.wendys-invest.com/main/enterprise1204.pdf

Hancock, P. (1999) 'Baudrillard and the metaphysics of motivation: A reappraisal of corporate culturalism in the light of the work and ideas of Jean Baudrillard', *Journal of Management Studies*, vol. 36, no. 2, pp. 155–75.

House, R.J. and Shamir, B. (1993) 'Toward the integration of transformational, charismatic, and visionary theories' in Chemers, M. and Ayman, R. (eds) *Leadership Theory and Research: Perspectives and Directions*, New York, Academic Press, pp. 81–107.

Kapica, C. (2004) 'The role of quick serve restaurants in wellness. Kapica is director of McDonald's corporation's global nutrition', slide presentation to 26th American Overseas Dietetic Association Conference, 27 March, Nicosia, Cyprus. Slides available on-line at: http://www.cydadiet.org/april2004/cathyKapica.pdf

Karreman, D. (2001) 'The scripted organization: Dramaturgy from Burke to Baudrillard' in Westwood, R. and Linstead, S. (eds) *The Language of Organization,* London, SAGE, pp. 89–111.

Kellner, D. (1989) *Jean Baudrillard: From Marxism to Postmodernism and Beyond*, Stanford, CA, Stanford University Press.

Kincheloe, J.L. (2002) *The Sign of the Burger: McDonald's and the Culture of Power*, Philadelphia, PA, Temple University Press.

Kramer, L. (1999) 'McDonald's execs explore makeover for Ronald icon', *Advertising Age*, vol. 70, no. 34, pp. 14–18.

Kroc, R. and Anderson, R. (1976) *Grinding It Out: The Making of McDonald's*, Chicago,IL, Henry Regnery Company.

Lane, R.J. (2000) *Jean Baudrillard*, London, Routledge.

Love, J.F. (1986/1995) *McDonald's: Behind The Arches*, New York, Bantam Books.

McDonald's Corporation (2004) *McDonald's 2003 Summary Annual Report.* Available at: http://www.mcdonalds.com/corp/invest/pub/annual_report.html

Rafferty, A.E. and Griffin, M.A. (2004) 'Dimensions of transformational leadership: Conceptual and empirical extensions', *The Leadership Quarterly*, vol. 15, pp. 329–54.

Ritzer, G. (1993/2002) *The McDonaldization of Society*, Newbury Park, CA, Pine Forge Press.

Royle, T. (2000) *Working for McDonald's in Europe: The Unequal Struggle*, London, Routledge.

Schlosser, E. (2001) *Fast Food Nation: The Dark Side of the All-American Meal*, Boston, MA, Houghton Mifflin.

Shamir, B., House, R.J., and Arthur, M.B. (1993) 'The motivational effects of charismatic leadership: A self-concept based theory', *Organizational Science*, vol. 4, pp. 577–94.

Westman, P. and Molina, M. (1980) *Ray Kroc, Mayor of McDonaldland*, Minneapolis, MN, Dillon Press.

Yukl, G. (1999) 'An evaluative essay on current conceptions of effective leadership', *European Journal of Work and Organizational Psychology*, vol. 8, pp. 33–48.

# Part IV
## Exploring Followership

# Followership: The Theoretical Foundation of a Contemporary Construct

# 10

*Susan D. Baker*

This article presents the theoretical foundation of followership. The words *follower* and *followership* are increasingly used in discussions of leadership and organizations, and many think that the field of followership began in 1988 with Kelley's 'In Praise of Followers'. Followership research began in 1955, and literature in the social sciences discussed followers and followership for decades prior. By examining why leadership rather than followership is emphasized; discussing antecedents, early theory, and research about followership; and identifying common themes found in the literature, this article provides the foundation that has been missing in contemporary discussion of the followership construct.

Almost 20 years ago, Kelley's article, 'In Praise of Followers', was published in *Harvard Business Review* (1988). It received wide attention in both academic and popular presses for its seemingly novel proposal that followers had an active role to play in organizational success: Success was not solely dependent on dynamic leaders. The idea that followers could be more than passive subordinates was echoed in the next decade by Chaleff's (1995) work about courageous followers.

These two publications by Kelley (1988) and Chaleff (1995) became the primary works on which subsequent discussions of followership were based. A small but growing body of work about followership developed into a field of its own, asserting that leadership could no longer be studied in isolation or with only a small nod to followers. Citing Kelley and Chaleff, theorists proposed behaviors, styles, and characteristics of effective followers and posited interdependency in the leader–follower relationship.

Baker, S.D. (2007) 'Followership: The theoretical foundation of a contemporary construct', Journal of Leadership and Organizational Studies, vol. 14, no. 1, pp. 50–60.

As theorists and selected researchers moved forward in their discussion of followership, few looked back across the decades preceding Kelley's (1988) work. The purpose of this article is to provide a theoretical foundation for the field of followership and to examine the roots from which it developed in the United States in the twentieth century management literature. By discussing why management theorists focused on leaders rather than followers, identifying the early voices of followership theory, describing followership's antecedents, and identifying the common themes found in the literature, this article acknowledges the origins of followership theory and begins to set the foundation missing in contemporary discussions of the followership construct. It also acknowledges the limited followership-centric literature in the twenty-first century and identifies contemporary exploration of a common followership theme by leadership theorists. It concludes by proposing further areas for research in followership.

It is important to note that the body of followership literature, distinct from what is traditionally viewed as leadership literature, is small. A search of 26 electronic databases produced approximately 480 unique citations for the period 1928 through September 2004 (Baker, 2006); approximately 50 more have been added through December 2006. About half of the citations were relevant to the field of management, and the great majority of the citations were written by American authors and about American organizations. The citations included opinion pieces as well as articles published in popular and trade magazines and academic and scholarly journals. In general, followership theory developed in the latter half of the twentieth century. With limited exception, the few dissertations and articles written about followership in the first few years of the twenty-first century have explored facets of followership theory posited in earlier decades.

The number of leadership citations in comparable publications dwarfs the body of followership literature. Why has there been so much emphasis on leadership and so little on followership? The next part of the article examines this question.

# Why is the Focus on Leaders Rather Than Followers?

From leadership theories as early as Great Man down to the 1970s, the common view of leadership was that leaders actively led and subordinates, later called followers, passively and obediently followed. As Follett (1996) observed in 1933, her contemporaries thought that one was 'either a leader or nothing of much importance' (p. 170). Why were followers ignored as the spotlight shone so brightly on leaders?

In the early days of civilization, there were no leadership theories – only leaders and their followers. Early leaders were Great Men who functioned in a preindustrial and prebureaucratic period (Daft, 1999). The leadership talents and skills that set the Great Men apart from other humans were assumed to be inborn; natural abilities were thought to be inherited, not acquired (Galton, 1900). Those who did not inherit these abilities had no chance to acquire them. The Great Men had their followers, troops, or devotees who followed in their footsteps, obeyed their directives, and faithfully mimicked their actions.

## Heroic Leaders

In a similar fashion, Burns (1978) saw leadership literature as dealing with historically heroic or demonic figures, where fame was equated with importance. The followers of the heroic leaders were the 'drab powerless masses' (p. 3). This was the predominant idea about leaders and followers as the United States of America transformed from a rural, agricultural economy into an urban, industrial one in the latter part of the nineteenth century. The business enterprises that arose then followed the model of Great Man leadership. Follett (1960) described the business leader of that era as a 'masterful man carrying all before him by the sheer force of his personality' (p. 310). She painted a stark picture of the leader–follower dynamic:

> Can you not remember the picture ... of the man in the swivel chair? A trembling subordinate enters, states his problem; snap goes the decision from the chair. This man disappears only for another to enter. And so it goes. The massive brain in the swivel chair all day communicates to his followers his special knowledge. (p. 311)

That view continued into the 1970s when Hollander (1974) described the then-current view of followers as 'nonleaders ... an essentially passive residual category' (p. 23).

## Idealized Leader Overshadows Followers

Hollander (1974) argued that the primary role filled by an organizational leader was that of executive or manager who directed the activities of others. Other leader roles such as change agent, adjudicator, and problem solver were overshadowed by the director's role. He further observed that leaders were thought to 'hold' a position of authority, which led to thinking of the position as a fixed, static role. The fixed leader role was idealized, and its idealization led to making a sharp and distinct difference between leader and followers. With this distinction in mind, the fixed position of leader was honored, and the role that it contained received less attention. Hollander suggested that were people to view the leader position as less fixed and more fluid, they would have a better understanding of the leader's roles and would think more about leader–follower relations rather than only about leaders.

Vanderslice (1988) similarly saw a problem in operationalizing leadership 'in individualistic, static, and exclusive positional roles' (p. 683). She observed that people thought of planning, decision making, and task responsibility as the province of those who filled the leader roles and wondered if these functions could be achieved without 'invoking role-defined static power differentials' (p. 683). Meindl, Ehrlich, and Dukerich (1985) believed that their culture held a view of a heroic, romanticized leader to whom was attributed all glory or all failure. Their concept of idealized leader overshadowed the follower.

## Social Change Affects Followers

Social change in the United States and elsewhere also shaped people's views of followers. Although in the early 1930s Follett discussed the interdependence of leaders and followers, the active role of followers, the situational authority of those closest to the task or problem at hand, and the win-win nature of constructive conflict, her views were lost in the milieu surrounding World War II. The world at that time embraced hierarchical, authoritarian structures that were built on a win-lose proposition that had but one purpose: to conquer an enemy. Lived in epic proportions, leadership was embodied in Great Men such as Roosevelt, Churchill, Stalin, and Hitler.

The organizations that prospered in America during and after World War II were mostly vertical organizational hierarchies (Useem, 1996). These postwar American corporations helped foster the 'golden age' of prosperity within the United States (Smith and Dyer, 1996, p. 51), and the economy they led was admired and envied by 'most of the rest of the world' (Kaysen, 1996, p. 3). As America achieved economic dominance in this era, corporations promised life-long job security to employees in exchange for their loyalty, obedience, and hard work. Nothing more was asked of followers, and there was no need to examine the leader–follower relationship while economic conditions were stable. The leader's actions, not those of the followers, were instrumental to the company's success (Berg, 1998).

By the early 1980s, American industry had experienced a crisis that transformed its stable nature. The advent of a global economy; advancing technology; changes in the American labor force; and the ongoing dynamic between business, labor, and government that introduced many contractual obligations into the employment relationship were several of the forces putting pressure on the status quo of the modern corporate system. Applied in an era of reduced resources, these pressures gave birth to the takeover and downsizing trends of the 1980s and 1990s.

As corporate organizational structures flattened, power and responsibility were delegated to a wider range of people, including the traditionally dependent followers. Leaders expected more initiative and risk taking from their followers (Lippitt, 1982). But as these business organizations struggled to reform themselves, leaders found that their followers were ill equipped to take initiative or to collaborate with their superiors (Berg, 1998). Followers saw the challenge but avoided the risk of new responsibilities for which they had no training or support (Lippitt, 1982). When the need arose for a more active follower, the model of the omniscient leader and obedient, passive follower or subordinate was too entrenched to allow those subordinates to embrace a new role of active followership. Instead, the focus was recentered on leadership: developing new leadership skills and even developing those leadership skills in followers. There was no focus on the leader–follower relationship or on the demands placed on each role (Berg, 1998).

The demise of the psychological contract and the organizational pressures resulting from the downsizing trends of the 1980s and 1990s were viewed by some as an opportunity for employees to craft a new psychological contract by taking a partnership role with their leaders (Potter, Rosenbach, and Pittman, 1996). Nonetheless, the image of the 'drab powerless masses' that Burns (1978, p. 3) described as followers in the historic leadership literature was slow to change. Berg (1998) reported that participants in his Leadership and Followership workshops conducted in the early 1990s used words like 'sheep', 'passive', 'obedient', 'lemming', and 'serf' (p. 29) to describe followers, and he attributed these negative associations to the organizational and psychological demeaning of the follower role.

## Moving to a View of Active Followers

Although management scholars in the first decades of the twentieth century were slow to recognize and discuss followers, theorists in other behavioral science fields were not. In psychoanalysis and psychology, Freud in 1921 and Fromm in 1941 identified a psychological link between leader and followers; Erikson discussed a link between leader and followers in 1975 (Hollander, 1992b). In anthropology, Mead (1949) discussed the importance of examining the psychological relationships between leader, lieutenant, and follower; the effect those psychological relationships had in the lives of the individuals; and cultural and anthropological factors that affected the individuals and their roles.

In sociology, Sanford (1950) observed that 'leadership is an intricate relation between leader and followers' (p. 183) and that leaders had to meet their followers' needs to maintain a desirable relationship with them. Homans (1950) discussed the 'human group' and posited a connection between a leader and a group by whose norms the leader must live (pp. 425–29). In 1961 Homans was among the early writers to describe a process of exchange between leader and group members in which both parties give and take resources (Bargal and Schmid, 1989). It gave recognition to the group member, or follower, as well as to the leader. Homans's work laid the foundation for social exchange theory, which was antecedent to transactional leadership theory (Hollander and Offermann, 1990) and one of the forebears of active followership theory.

## The Early Voices of Active Followership Theory

The theorists who began bridging the concepts of passive subordinates and active followers included those of social psychologist Hollander and his associates. In 1955, Hollander and Webb (1955) argued that *leader and follower* was not an either/or proposition in which leaders and followers were found at opposite ends of a continuum. They proposed that the qualities associated with leadership and followership were interdependent. They conducted one of the earliest empirical studies about leaders and followers and concluded that nonleaders were not desirable as followers and that qualities of followership needed to be considered as a component of good leadership. Building on Homans's work about social exchange processes, Hollander and Julian (1969) reviewed then-recent studies and concluded that leadership encompassed a 'two-way influence relationship' (p. 390) that contained an 'implicit exchange relationship' (p. 395) between leaders and followers over time.

In 1974 Hollander advanced this line of thought when he authored 'Processes of Leadership Emergence'. In it he framed the central arguments about leaders and followers that arose from the traditional view of follower as subordinate:

> It is commonly assumed that a cleavage exists between those who lead and those who follow, and that being a follower is not being a leader. ... Only some members of a group have 'leadership qualities' ... and stand out as 'leaders.' ... Followers are treated essentially as 'nonleaders,' which is a relatively passive residual category. (pp. 20–21)

In his work, Hollander (1974) raised questions and identified topics that became central themes and issues in active followership literature. These included the ideas that leader and follower were roles and processes that should not be confused with the people filling them; that at least some of the time and to some extent, leaders were also followers; and that the behaviors needed to fill a leader's role at a particular time were not limited to leaders alone and that followers could also have those behaviors. Other concepts identified by Hollander that reappeared later in active followership literature included drawing a distinction about the source of a leader's authority and its affect on followers, the two-way influence process between leader and follower, and the role of the situation in the leader–follower relationship.

Other early voices spoke and wrote about leaders and followers but did not affect active followership theory. In these works, the authors urged leaders to focus on followers as a way of improving managers' leadership skills; they did not study followers in and of themselves. Wortman (1982) called these works 'leadership studies that incorporate data about followers' (p. 373).

A few researchers did follow in Hollander's footsteps by examining the leader–follower relational component of active followership. Herold (1977) used a laboratory study to demonstrate how each party could influence the other party's behavior in a leader–follower relationship or dyad. He contributed to the growing body of literature that supported the idea that leader effectiveness must look beyond analyzing the effects of leader behavior on subordinates; subordinate effects on leader behavior must also be considered.

Frew (1977) contributed to followership theory by focusing on the importance of followers to a leader's success and by developing the first instrument that measured followership. His contributions were only beginning steps, though, because he examined followers to determine what kinds of leadership styles they preferred in their supervisors. His conclusions focused on making leaders more effective and improving organizational effectiveness by reducing managerial error; followers were not the focus of his conclusions. Additionally, although he studied followers and followership, he did not define the terms.

Steger, Manners, and Zimmerer (1982) advanced followership theory by proposing the first followership model built on two dimensions: followers' desire for self-enhancement and followers' desire for self-protection. Nine followership styles resulted from the followers' high, medium, or low attraction to each of the dimensions. Although they noted that 'we are all followers in some way' (p. 22), Steger et al. did not provide definitions of *follower* or *followership,* although they did state that a followership theory would offer a taxonomy of subordinates' behavioral reactions to leaders.

Steger et al. (1982) raised two important issues that resurfaced in later decades as key issues in active followership theory: organizational structure and the use of power. In their view, a hierarchical structure was a given, and the only question was how much freedom the organization gave a manager to reward or punish subordinates. Power was not shared with followers; it was a managerial tool. Depending on a follower's style, a manager used direct power, supportive and developmental power, or devious and manipulative power to motivate followers to support organizational change.

Although Steger et al. (1982) took beginning steps in discussing follower behaviors and attributes, they also focused on followers as a means of improving managerial performance. They asserted that as managers moved up through the organizational hierarchy they encountered different types of 'followerships'

(p. 51) and that management training was needed to help a manager understand different follower styles and how to motivate the followers.

To reduce the complexity of leadership contingency theory, Zierdan (1980) proposed that the contingency model should focus on subordinates rather than a manager. In his model, a manager established performance and emotional objectives for his subordinates as well as ways to measure the objectives. The manager in this model needed to be aware of subordinates' attitudes and feelings and use that information to make informed decisions in the contingency framework. Tjosvold, Andrews, and Jones (1983) conducted an empirical study about causal links between leaders and subordinates, focusing on leaders' cooperative and competitive behaviors. The study suggested that to improve their own success, to improve subordinates' reactions to their leadership, to increase subordinates' satisfaction, and to build morale leaders should emphasize common goals held by leader and subordinates, help subordinates achieve their goals, encourage subordinate learning and development, exchange information and resources, and share the rewards of their combined efforts.

## Theoretical Antecedents to Active Followership

The theorists and researchers described above were influenced by theorists in other disciplines. Recognition of followers and development of active followership literature had its roots in social exchange, attribution, and small group theories that grew out of the disciplines of sociology and psychology. The theories and observations found therein were eventually woven into the fabric of organizational behavior and followership literature.

*Social exchange theories.* Exchange theories posited that social interaction was a form of exchange in which a group member contributed to the group at a cost to himself or herself and received benefits from the group at a cost to the group. The exchange continued as long as members found it mutually beneficial (Bass, 1990). Homans's (1950, 1974) work was among the foundation blocks of the theory. His work was followed by that of Hollander (1974) and Hollander and Julian (1969), who noted that 'an entire interpersonal system' (Hollander and Julian, 1969, p. 393) must be included in the evaluation of a leader's effectiveness. They developed theories about the implicit nature of the social exchange processes and applied them to leaders and followers. In their view of the leader–follower transaction, leaders provided benefits such as direction, and followers responded with increased esteem for and responsiveness to the leader. Recognition of this transaction led to transactional theories of leadership, which generally focused on a follower's perceptions and expectations of a leader.

Transactional leadership was named and popularized by historian Burns (1978). In this leadership theory, he recognized a 'leadership act' (p. 20) in which one initiated an exchange with another. Their interaction was short-term and nonbinding. Burns contrasted this to another point on his leadership continuum, a point that he called 'transforming leadership' (p. 20). In that leadership act, leader and follower interacted to transform each other and raise each other to higher moral levels. In Burns's theory, followers were recognized as important players in the leadership act.

The Leader-Member Exchange Model (LMX) was a social exchange theory that arose in the 1970s and provided another way to view followers. Developed by Graen, Scandura, Uhl-Bien, and others, it focused on the leader–follower dyad and examined how exchange processes affected the dyadic relationship over time (Schriesheim, Castro, Zhou, and Yammarino, 2001). As the dyadic relationship developed over time, informal exchanges between leader and follower replaced the formal exchanges required by the organization. The leader relied less on power and influence to negotiate with a follower for whom he or she had increasing trust. The leader began to share power and influence with the follower, empowering the follower to exercise more influence over the leader. LMX theory and its focus on the leader–follower dyad paralleled the discussion of the relational nature of the leader–follower role in the psychology literature: Both drew attention to the follower. Citing Graen and Uhl-Bien's (1995) classification of leadership theories into the three domains of leader, follower, and relationship, Howell and Shamir (2005) asserted that 'while LMX theory emphasizes the importance of all three domains, its main contribution has been to shift the focus from the leadership domain to the relationship domain' (p. 98).

*Attribution and small group theories.* Arising in the 1970s, attribution theories presented a different framework through which to view the leader–follower relationship. These theories posited the importance of recognizing leaders' and followers' perceptions about leadership rather than focusing solely on a leader's traits or how he or she acted. Each leader and follower was thought to have his or her own implicit leadership theory about what a leader does and how he or she behaves. Either personal internal traits or external constraints were thought to cause the behaviors (Bass, 1990). Over time the focus of implicit leadership theories shifted from leaders' perceptions to followers' perceptions.

Meindl et al.'s (1985) research advanced attribution theory by proposing that leadership was a romantic and heroic concept thoroughly 'entrenched' (p. 78) in the social fabric. Society's emphasis on leadership grew as business systems became large, complex, and difficult to understand. Observers, unable to understand the intricacies of a complex system of multilevel networks, attributed organizational success or failure to something more easily understandable – a person, in particular a leader, to whom was attributed control and responsibility. Further, Meindl et al. found that not only organizational outcomes but also the performance of entire industries were attributed to leaders' actions. The authors suggested that people's 'infatuation' (p. 100) with the romantic, heroic, mystical view of leadership might be necessary to sustain followership and to motivate individuals to respond to the organization's needs and goals. Attribution theory did move in that direction, as Hollander and Offermann (1990) observed in 1990 that the focus was on 'follower attributions of leaders that make followers respond' (p. 84) positively or negatively to the leader. Although attribution theory started with psychological research about the area of cognition, it began to integrate organizational research about leader–follower relations (p. 85).

Social scientists studied the behavior of members of small groups in the hopes of discerning patterns and principles that could be applied to larger groups. The small group was seen as a microcosm of society at large; its small size made detailed study possible (Homans, 1974). The study of relationships between group leader and small group members provided insight into leaders and subordinates in business settings on a larger scale.

While other fields were exploring social interactions in groups and cognitive approaches to leaders and followers, the field of management looked at interaction between supervisors – also called *bosses* – and their subordinates. With few exceptions, not until the 1980s did management literature adopt the term *follower*. Graham (1988) observed that in the emerging discussion of transformational leadership a distinction was drawn between *leader* or *manager* and *supervisor*. She drew a similar distinction between *follower* and *subordinate,* basing her argument on Hunt's (1984) application of French and Raven's (1959) classification of the bases of social power. Hunt proposed that leadership derived from the personal-power bases of expert and referent power but supervision derived from the position-power bases of reward, coercion, and legitimacy. Similarly Graham separated followers from subordinates by the degree of free choice that they exercised. She called subordinates those who followed orders because they feared punishment, had been promised rewards, or wanted to fulfill a contractual obligation.

## Active Followership Gains Acceptance

Writing at the same time as Graham, Kelley published 'In Praise of Followers' in 1988 and proposed that followers deserved praise and deserved to be studied. He reframed the arguments introduced in earlier generations and, by promoting a positive concept of followers and active followership, he recast management literature's traditionally negative image of the passive subordinate. He also linked follower effectiveness with organizational success. Kelley's article moved the heretofore theoretical and academic discussion of effective followers into the popular press. Similarly, Chaleff's (1995) book, *The Courageous Follower,* gained widespread popular acceptance. Chaleff recognized the danger that could derive from hierarchically bestowed leader power. He proposed a new model of leader–follower relations that was built on a leader's courage to be less than dominant and a follower's courage to be more dominant. In his model, the courageous follower had to be willing to assume responsibility, to serve, to challenge the leader, to participate in change processes when needed, and even to oppose leaders whose acts harmed the organization.

# Themes in Followership Literature

Scholars writing about followership over the years sounded a similar note: There was a dearth of work about followership when compared to leadership. As early as 1978, Burns observed that one of the 'most serious failures' (p. 3) in the study of leadership was the separation of leadership and followership literatures. In 1982 Heller and Van Til called it a 'novelty' to link the concepts, noting that not only were leadership and followership rarely discussed as 'co-equal concepts' but that discussion of followership by itself was rare (pp. 405–06). Gilbert (1985) saw little management literature on how to be a good follower but volumes on leadership and motivation. Gilbert and Hyde (1988) observed that obsession with the 'romance of leadership' and 'dependence on the "ability to motivate"' (p. 962) were two major reasons for lack of research about followership. Lundin and Lancaster (1990) wrote that thousands of pages had been written about leadership but very few written about followership. Brown and Thornborrow (1996) observed that literature about followers and followership was 'not extensive' (p. 5) and was written mostly by American authors who wrote from an American perspective. Berg (1998) saw an 'overwhelming emphasis' (p. 28) in corporations and schools on leadership and development of leadership skills while followership received little attention. Bjugstad, Thach, Thompson, and Morris (2006) saw followership as an 'understudied discipline' (p. 304), and Goffee and Jones (2006) observed that 'the analysis of followership has barely begun' (p. 23).

In the work of those who did study followership, several themes were apparent. They included the idea that followers and leaders were roles, that followers were active rather than passive, and that leaders and followers shared a common purpose. A fourth theme, the relational nature of follower and leader, received great attention in the followership literature. This theme is receiving renewed attention in the leadership literature.

## Followers and Leaders are Roles, Not People with Inherent Characteristics

In proposing guidelines for studies about mental health and leadership that were to be conducted in the early 1950s, Mead (1949) identified the relationship between leaders, lieutenants, and followers as an important area of the studies. She questioned the psychological relationships and the roles that each individual played.

Hollander (1974) defined a *role* as 'a set of behaviors which are appropriate for a position which an individual fills' (p. 19). He believed that a leader's characteristics should fill the demands of the role and that followers were not permanently confined to their follower roles. Heller and Van Til (1982) asserted that 'leadership and followership are best seen as roles in relation' (p. 406). Kelley (1991) stated that followership and leadership were roles, not people, and that most managers played the roles of both follower and leader (Kelley, 1988). Berg (1998) described participants in his workshops as managers who also filled the role of followers in their organizations.

## Followers are Active, Not Passive

In the early twentieth century, followers in America were viewed as passive, obedient, and having nothing to contribute but manual labor. In the post–World War II era, followers were seen as obedient, dependent, and loyal to a leader or company – but still with only labor to contribute. In neither case were followers held in high regard. The values of obedience and loyalty were further tarnished by the aberrant behavior and actions of the Nazi followers of Adolph Hitler during World War II.

Contrary to that traditional view of followers as passively obedient people, other theorists in the twentieth century held a different view: They widely agreed that followers were an active party in the leader–follower relationship. Going against the grain of her time, Follett (1996) proposed that followers had an active role in keeping the leader 'in control of a situation' (p. 170). They did this by offering suggestions, by sharing their difficulties with work as well as their successes at work, by not being a 'yes, yes' subordinate, and by not being passively obedient (pp. 170–72). Heifetz (1999) echoed Follett by observing that the 'best leadership … generates people who are willing to take responsibility' (p. 20).

Barnard (1987) theorized that the subordinate held the power to a leader's authority: Without a subordinate's cooperation and assent, the leader had no authority. Extending Barnard's idea, Litzinger and Schaefer (1982) theorized that because followers could withhold or grant their obedience to a leader, the leader was constrained to act in ways that the follower found consistent with organizational goals. They argued that the leader must therefore be a follower – of the organizational goals as understood by his or her own followers – and further that being a good follower helped to prepare one to be a good leader. Although they believed that a 'personal history of good followership' (p. 81) was critical to good leadership, it alone was not sufficient to determine a leader's success.

Also citing Barnard (1987), Hansen (1987) was one of the first to write about the active follower in his study of first-line supervisor effectiveness. Hansen linked supervisor effectiveness to subordinates' willingness to follow the wishes of the supervisor. He described 'active followership' (p. 44) as subordinates' granting legitimacy to their supervisor's orders and directions. More broadly, Hollander and Offermann (1990) described both leadership and followership as active roles. Hollander (1992a, 1992b) reiterated that point and added that followers could initiate activity and had the potential to make major contributions to successful leadership.

Burns (1978) drew distinctions among passive followers, who offered 'undiscriminating support' in exchange for favors; participatory followers, who wanted to belong to the leadership group and selectively bargained to exchange their support for favors; and close followers of leaders who were in reality subleaders but still dependent on the leader (p. 68). Kelley (1988) separated the effective from the ineffective follower. Distinctive characteristics of Kelley's effective follower included enthusiasm, intelligence, and self-reliant participation. Additionally, effective followers saw their role as one that was 'legitimate, inherently valuable, even virtuous' (p. 143).

## Followers and Leaders Share a Common Purpose

In an interdependent relationship, follower and leader should hold some things in common. Follett (1996) argued that followers and leaders must follow a common purpose on which their work is focused. Burns (1978) wrote that leaders and followers had 'inseparable functions' (p. 20) but different roles. Gilbert (1985) coined the term *psychological commitment* (p. 452), akin to the organizational psychological contract, that described an implicit contract between boss and subordinate on very effective work teams. In such a commitment, both boss and subordinate exhibit a commitment to the organization's goals as well as to the success of each other. Hollander (1992a) theorized that a leader must engage followers in 'mutually satisfying and productive enterprises' (p. 74). Vecchio (1997) observed that followers and leaders are interconnected and share responsibility for meeting goals.

## The Relational Nature of Followers and Leaders

From the early writings of Follett (1960) and the early studies of Mead (1949) to contemporary authors, followership theorists recognized the interconnection between follower and leader and advocated the importance of examining the relationship between them. The relationship was described as interdependent rather than either/or (Hollander and Webb, 1955), a two-way influence process (Hollander and Julian, 1969), and reciprocal and complex (Burns, 1978). Herold (1977) saw the relationship as one in which dyadic partners influenced each other's behaviors and attitudes, and Frew (1977) observed that much of a supervisor's success was dependent on his or her acceptance by the staff. Heller and Van Til (1982) discussed a participative leadership–followership model and said that leaders and followers should be studied in relation to one another, not separately. Gilbert (1990) saw the relationship as one of partners. Hollander restated his contention that the leader–follower relationship was interdependent (1992a) and reciprocal (1992b), involving two-way support and influence (1997). He further believed that the 'usual expectation' (1997, p. 13) that the follower role was passive with little power did not fit with the concept of active followers.

Berg (1998) promoted the idea of a collaborative follower–leader relationship. Potter et al. (1996) promoted the idea of a partnership relationship between leaders and followers in which follower initiatives were as important as leader initiatives, and Pittman, Rosenbach, and Potter (1998) described the best leader–follower relationship as a partnership. Kelley (1991) also promoted the idea of follower–leader partnership. In his version of partnership, both follower and leader were individually and collectively responsible for the actions of the organization, and both roles had equal weight.

As followership theorists discussed the relational nature of leader and follower, positing the interdependency of leader and follower and the idea of leader–follower partnerships, leadership theorists also discussed leader–follower relations but from a leader-centric perspective. Contingency theories posited a link between a follower's actions and a leader's behavior, and situational theories of leadership focused on a leader's ability to motivate workers or followers through situational control and design (Baker 2006). Substitutes for leadership theory questioned the importance of leaders in all situations (Gronn, 2003). LMX theory was one of the few leadership theories to recognize the follower's role in 'the leadership processes' (Howell and Shamir, 2005, p. 98) and to posit that both leader and follower shared responsibility for the success of their relationship (Howell and Shamir, 2005).

Recently, leadership scholars Howell and Shamir (2005) echoed the decades-long call of followership theorists to examine the relational nature of leaders and followers. In their analysis of the role of followers in the charismatic leadership process, Howell and Shamir noted that 'beyond paying lip service to the importance of followers, few scholars have attempted to theoretically specify and empirically assess the role of followers in the leadership process' (p. 96). They called for study of effective followers and concluded that 'understanding followers is as important as understanding leaders' (p. 110).

Authentic leadership is a new construct that is being promoted by scholars to create positive leadership that can combat the post-9/11 'increase in societal challenges' as well as the concurrent 'decrease in ethical leadership' (Cooper, Scandura, and Schriesheim, 2005, p. 476). Citing Howell and Shamir's (2005) call for inclusion of followers in leadership models, Gardner, Avolio, Luthans, May, and Walumbwa (2005) developed a model of 'authentic leadership and followership'. Part of their model emphasized the importance of self-identity in authentic followers. Lord and Brown (2001) and Collinson (2006) also discussed follower self-concept as a factor in the leader–follower relationship. Gardner et al. and Lord and Brown used a more leader-centric lens for their views and Collinson used a more follower-centric lens.

Other issues traditionally found in leadership literature and applied to leaders have recently been applied to followers. Vecchio (2002) noted that although gender advantage had been explored in leadership theory it had not been explored in followership theory. Eagly (2005) emphasized followers in her discussion of gender impact on leaders' building of relational authenticity with their followers.

The dark side of leaders is another issue addressed in leadership literature. Demonstrating another aspect of the relational nature of leaders and followers, authors have recently raised the question of the mutual account-ability of both followers and leaders for bad leadership (Kellerman, 2004) and toxic leadership (Lipman-Blumen, 2005). Howell and Shamir (2005) discussed followers' responsibility for negative aspects displayed by leaders in personalized charismatic relationships.

## Summary

This article has identified and presented the theoretical foundation of the construct of followership. Leadership scholars can look back across a century of theory and research works to identify origins, name founding fathers, trace movements and eras, discuss practical applications of older studies, and propose new avenues for future research in the field of leadership. Until now, those studying followership could not accomplish the same tasks because there have been no uniform acknowledgement and treatment of the body of literature that formed followership's roots. This article establishes that foundation for followership by examining why emphasis was placed on leaders almost to the exclusion of followers, identifying the antecedents from which followership theory developed, naming early followership theorists and researchers and discussing their work, and identifying the common themes in their work.

This presentation discusses the transition from the traditional view of a passive, unthinkingly obedient subordinate who was led by a Great Man to a contemporary image of an active, participative, effective follower who must be studied in relation to his or her leader. The theorists constructing the image of active follower shared four basic tenets of active followership theory: (a) that followers and leaders are roles, not people with inherent characteristics; (b) that followers are active, not passive; (c) that followers and leaders share a common purpose; and (d) that followers and leaders must be studied in the context of their relationship. [ ... ]

## References

Baker, S.D. (2006) ;The effect of leader-follower agreement on team effectiveness', *Dissertation Abstracts International*, vol. 6, no. 03, A. (UMI No. 3209933).

Bargal, D. and Schmid, H. (1989) 'Recent themes in theory and research on leadership and their implications for management of human services', *Administration in Social Work*, vol. 13, pp. 37–54.

Barnard, C. (1987) 'The theory of authority' in Boone, L.E. and Bowen, D.D. (eds) *The Great Writings in Management and Organizational Behavior* (2nd edn), New York, McGraw-Hill, pp. 92–104.

Bass, B.M. (1990) *Bass & Stogdill's Handbook of Leadership* (3rd edn), New York, Free Press.

Berg, D.N. (1998) 'Resurrecting the muse: Followership in organizations' in Klein, E.B., Gabelnick, F. and Herr, P. (eds) *The Psychodynamics of Leadership*, Madison, CT, Psychosocial Press, pp. 27–52.

Bjugstad, K., Thach, E.C., Thompson, K.J. and Morris, A. (2006) 'A fresh look at followership: A model for matching follower-ship and leadership styles', *Journal of Behavioral and Applied Management*, vol. 7, pp. 304–19.

Brown, A.D. and Thornborrow, W.T. (1996) 'Do organizations get the followers they deserve? *Leadership & Organization Development Journal*, vol. 17, pp. 5–11.

Burns, J.M. (1978) *Leadership*, New York, Harper and Row.

Chaleff, I. (1995) *The Courageous Follower: Standing up to and for Our Leaders*, San Francisco, CA, Berrett-Koehler.

Collinson, D. (2006) 'Rethinking followership: A post-structuralist analysis of follower identities', *The Leadership Quarterly*, vol. 17, pp. 179–89.

Cooper, D.C., Scandura, T. and Schriesheim, C.A. (2005) 'Looking forward but learning from our past: Potential challenges to developing authentic leadership theory and authentic leaders', *The Leadership Quarterly*, vol. 16, pp. 475–93.

Daft, R.L. (1999) *Leadership Theory and Practice*, Fort Worth, TX, Dryden.

Eagly, A.H. (2005) 'Achieving relational authenticity in leadership: Does gender matter? *The Leadership Quarterly*, vol. 16, pp. 459–74.

Follett, M.P. (1960) 'Management as a profession' in Merrill, H.F. (ed.) *Classics in Management*, New York, American Management Association, pp. 309–22.

Follett, M.P. (1996) 'The essentials of leadership' in Graham, P. (ed.) *Mary Parker Follett: Prophet of Management*, Boston, MA, Harvard Business School Publishing, pp: 163–77.

French, J.R.P. and Raven, B. (1959) 'The bases of social power' in Cartwright, D. (ed.) *Studies in Social Power*, Ann Arbor, University of Michigan, Institute of Social Research.

Frew, D.R. (1977) 'Leadership and followership', *Personnel Journal*, vol. 56, pp. 90–97.

Galton, F. (1900) *Hereditary Genius: An Inquiry into Its Laws and Consequences* (2nd American edn), New York, D. Appleton.

Gardner, W.L., Avolio, B., Luthans, F., May, D.R. and Walumbwa, F. (2005) 'Can you see the real me? A self-based model of authentic leader and follower development', *The Leadership Quarterly*, vol. 16, pp. 342–72.

Gilbert, G.R. (1985) 'Building highly productive work teams through positive leadership', *Public Personnel Management*, vol. 14, pp. 449–54.

Gilbert, G.R. (June 1990) 'Effective leaders must be good followers, too', *Government Executive*, vol. 22, p. 58.

Gilbert, G.R. and Hyde, A.C. (1988) 'Followership and the federal worker', *Public Administration Review*, vol. 48, pp. 962–68.

Goffee, R. and Jones, G. (2006) 'The art of followership', *European Business Forum*, vol. 25, pp. 22–26.

Graen, G.B. and Uhl-Bien, M. (1995) 'Relationship-based approach to leadership: Development of leader-member exchange (LMX theory) over 25 years: Applying a multi-level multi-domain perspective', *The Leadership Quarterly*, vol. 6, pp. 219–47.

Graham, J.W. (1988) 'Chapter 3 commentary: Transformational leadership: Fostering follower autonomy, not automatic followership' in Hunt, J.G., Baliga, B.R., Dachler, H.P. and Schriesheim, C.A. (eds) *Emerging Leadership Vistas*, Lexington, MA, Lexington Books, pp. 73–79.

Gronn, P. (2003) 'Leadership: Who needs it? *School Leadership and Management*, vol. 23, pp. 267–90.

Hansen, T.L., Jr (1987) 'Management's impact on first-line supervisor effectiveness', *SAM Advanced Management Journal*, vol. 52, pp. 41–45.

Heifetz, R.A. (1999) 'Leadership vs. authority', *Across the Board*, vol. 36, pp. 19–20.

Heller, T. and Van Til, J. (1982) 'Leadership and followership: Some summary propositions', *Journal of Applied Behavioral Sciences*, vol. 18, pp. 405–14.

Herold, D.M. (1977) 'Two-way influence processes in leader-follower dyads', *Academy of Management Journal*, vol. 20, pp. 224–37.

Hollander, E.P. (1974) 'Processes of leadership emergence', *Journal of Contemporary Business*, vol. 3, pp. 19–33.

Hollander, E.P. (1992a) 'The essential interdependence of leadership and followership', *Current Directions in Psychological Science*, vol. 1, pp. 71–74.

Hollander, E.P. (1992b) 'Leadership, followership, self, and others', *The Leadership Quarterly*, vol. 3, pp. 43–54.

Hollander, E.P. and Julian, J.W. (1969) 'Contemporary trends in the analysis of leadership processes', *Psychological Bulletin*, vol. 71, pp. 387–97.

Hollander, E.P. and Offermann, L.R. (1990) 'Relational features of organizational leadership and followership' in Clark, K.E. and Clark, M.B. (eds) *Measures of Leadership*, West Orange, NJ, Leadership Library of America, pp. 83–97.

Hollander, E.P. and Webb, W.B. (1955) 'Leadership, follower-ship, and friendship: An analysis of peer nominations', *Journal of Abnormal and Social Psychology*, vol. 50, pp. 163–67.

Homans, G.C. (1950) *The Human Group*, New York, Harcourt Brace and World.

Homans, G.C. (1974) *Social Behavior* (Revised edn), New York, Harcourt Brace Jovanovich.

Howell, J.M. and Shamir, B. (2005) 'The role of followers in the charismatic leadership process: Relationships and their consequences', *Academy of Management Review*, vol. 30, pp. 96–112.

Hunt, J.G. (1984) *Leadership and Managerial Behavior* (Modules in Management), Chicago, IL, Research Science Associates.

Kaysen, C. (ed.) (1996) *The American Corporation Today*, New York, Oxford University Press.

Kellerman, B. (2004) *Bad Leadership: What It Is, How It Happens, Why It matters*, Boston, MA, Harvard Business School Publishing.

Kelley, R.E. (1988) 'In praise of followers', *Harvard Business Review*, vol. 66, pp. 142–48.

Kelley, R.E. (1991) 'Combining followership and leadership into partnership' in Kilmann, R.H., Kilmann, I. and Associates (eds) *Making Organizations Competitive: Enhancing Networks and Relationships across Traditional Boundaries*, San Francisco, CA, Jossey-Bass, pp. 195–220.

Lipman-Blumen, J. (2005) *The Allure of Toxic Leaders: Why We Follow Destructive Bosses and Corrupt Politicians – and How We Can Survive Them*, Oxford, UK, Oxford University Press.

Lippitt, R. (1982) 'The changing leader-follower relationships of the 1980s', *Journal of Applied Behavioral Sciences*, vol. 18, pp. 395–403.

Litzinger, W. and Schaefer, T. (1982) 'Leadership through followership', *Business Horizons*, vol. 25, pp. 78–81.

Lord, R.G. and Brown, D.J. (2001) 'Leadership, values, and subordinate self-concepts', *The Leadership Quarterly*, vol. 12, pp. 133–52.

Lundin, S.C. and Lancaster, L.C. (1990) 'Beyond leadership... The importance of followership', *The Futurist*, vol. 24. no. 3, pp. 18–22.

Mead, M. (1949) 'Problems of leadership and mental health', *World Federation for Mental Health Bulletin (1949–1952)*, vol. 1, no. 6, pp. 7–12.

Meindl, J.R., Ehrlich, S.B. and Dukerich, J.M. (1985) 'The romance of leadership', *Administrative Science Quarterly*, vol. 30, pp. 78–102.

Pittman, T.S., Rosenbach, W.E. and Potter, E.H., III. (1998) 'Followers as partners: Taking the initiative for action' in Rosenbach, W.E. and Taylor, R.L. (eds) *Contemporary Issues in Leadership*, Boulder, CO, Westview, pp. 107–20.

Potter, E.H., III, Rosenbach, W.E. and Pittman, T.S. (1996) 'Leading the new professional' in Taylor, R.L. and Rosenbach, W.E. (eds) *Military Leadership: In Pursuit of Excellence* (3rd edn), Boulder, CO, Westview, pp. 145–52.

Sanford, F.H. (1950). *Authoritarianism and Leadership*, Philadelphia, Institute for Research in Human Relations.

Schriesheim, C.A., Castro, S.L., Zhou, X.T. and Yammarino, F.J. (2001) 'The folly of theorizing "a" but testing "b": A selective level-of-analysis review of the field and a detailed leader-member exchange illustration', *The Leadership Quarterly*, vol. 12, pp. 515–51.

Smith, G.D. and Dyer, D. (1996) 'The rise and transformation of the American corporation' in Kaysen, C. (ed.) *The American Corporation Today*, New York, Oxford University Press, pp. 28–73.

Steger, J.A., Manners, G.E., Jr and Zimmerer, T.W. (1982) 'Following the leader: How to link management style to subordinate personalities', *Management Review*, vol. 71, pp. 22–28, 49–51.

Tjosvold, D., Andrews, R. and Jones, H. (1983) 'Cooperative and competitive relationships between leaders and subordinates', *Human Relations*, vol. 36, pp. 1111–24.

Useem, M. (1996) 'Corporate education and training' in Kaysen, C. (ed.) *The American Corporation Today*, New York, Oxford University Press, pp. 292–326.

Vanderslice, V.J. (1988) 'Separating leadership from leaders: An assessment of the effect of leader and follower roles in organizations', *Human Relations*, vol. 41, pp. 677–696.

Vecchio, R.P. (1997) 'Effective followership: Leadership turned upside down' in Vecchio, R.P. (ed.) *Leadership: Understanding the Dynamics of Power and Influence in Organizations*, Notre Dame, IN, University of Notre Dame Press, pp. 114–23.

Vecchio, R.P. (2002) 'Leadership and gender advantage', *The Leadership Quarterly*, vol. 13, pp. 643–71.

Wortman, M.S., Jr (1982) 'Strategic management and changing leader-follower roles', *Journal of Applied Behavioral Sciences*, vol. 18, pp. 371–83.

Zierdan, W.E. (1980) 'Leading through the follower's point of view', *Organizational Dynamics*, vol. 8, pp. 27–46.

# What Every Leader Needs to Know About Followers

# 11

## Barbara Kellerman

There is no leader without at least one follower – that's obvious. Yet the modern leadership industry, now a quarter-century old, is built on the proposition that leaders matter a great deal and followers hardly at all.

Good leadership is the stuff of countless courses, workshops, books, and articles. Everyone wants to understand just what makes leaders tick – the charismatic ones, the retiring ones, and even the crooked ones. Good followership, by contrast, is the stuff of nearly nothing. Most of the limited research and writing on subordinates has tended to either explain their behavior in the context of leaders' development rather than followers' or mistakenly assume that followers are amorphous, all one and the same. As a result, we hardly notice, for example, that followers who tag along mindlessly are altogether different from those who are deeply devoted.

In reality, the distinctions among followers in groups and organizations are every bit as consequential as those among leaders. This is particularly true in business: In an era of flatter, networked organizations and cross-cutting teams of knowledge workers, it's not always obvious who exactly is following (or, for that matter, who exactly is leading) and how they are going about it. Reporting relationships are shifting, and new talent-management tools and approaches are constantly emerging. A confluence of changes – cultural and technological ones in particular – have influenced what subordinates want and how they behave, especially in relation to their ostensible bosses.

It's long overdue for leaders to acknowledge the importance of understanding their followers better. In these next pages, I explore the evolving dynamic between leaders and followers and offer a new typology for determining and appreciating the differences among subordinates. These distinctions have critical implications for how leaders should lead and managers should manage.

Kellerman, B. (2007) 'What every leader needs to know about followership', Harvard Business Review, December, pp. 84–91.

# A Level Playing Field

Followers can be defined by their behavior – doing what others want them to do. But for the purposes of this article, and to avoid confusing what followers do with who they are, I define followers according to their rank: They are low in the hierarchy and have less power, authority, and influence than their superiors. They generally go along to get along, particularly with those in higher positions. In the workplace, they may comply so as not to put money or stature at risk. In the community, they may comply to preserve collective stability and security – or simply because it's the easiest thing to do.

History tells us, however, that subordinates do not follow all the time. As the ideas of the Enlightenment took hold in the eighteenth century, for instance, ordinary people (in industrialized societies especially) became less dependent on kings, landowners, and the like, and their expectations changed accordingly – as did their sense of empowerment. The trend continues. Increasingly, followers think of themselves as free agents, not as dependent underlings. And they act accordingly, often withholding support from bad leaders, throwing their weight behind good ones, and sometimes claiming commanding voices for those lower down in the social or organizational hierarchy.

Witness the gradual demise of communism (and totalitarianism) in the former Soviet Union, Eastern Europe, and now China. And consider the social and political upheavals, all of them antiauthority, in the United States and elsewhere during the 1960s and 1970s. Similarly, there has been a dispersion of power at the highest levels of American business, partly because of changes in the cultures and structures of corporations as well as the advance of new technologies.

CEOs share power and influence with a range of players, including boards, regulators, and shareholder activists. Executives at global companies must monitor the activities of subordinates situated thousands of miles away. And knowledge workers can choose independently to use collaborative technologies to connect with colleagues and partners in other companies and countries in order to get things done. The result is reminiscent of what management sage Peter Drucker suggested in his 1967 book *The Effective Executive:* In an era dominated by knowledge workers rather than manual workers, expertise can – and often does – trump position as an indicator of who is really leading and who is really following.

# Types of Followers

Over the years, only a handful of researchers have attempted to study, segment, and speak to followers in some depth. To various degrees, Harvard Business

School professor Abraham Zaleznik, Carnegie Mellon adjunct professor Robert Kelley, and executive coach Ira Chaleff have all argued that leaders with even some understanding of what drives their subordinates can be a great help to themselves, their followers, and their organizations. Each researcher further recognized the need to classify subordinates into different types. (See the sidebar 'Distinguishing Marks: Three Other Follower Typologies'.)

Zaleznik classified subordinates into one of four types according to two sets of variables – dominance versus submission and activity versus passivity. His research findings intended to inform corporate leaders in particular. By contrast, Kelley and Chaleff were more interested in the welfare of those lower down the corporate ladder. Their work was designed to challenge and counteract what Kelley called the 'leadership myth' – the idea that leaders are all-powerful and all-important.

Kelley classified subordinates into five types according to their levels of independence and activity, but his special interest was in fostering 'exemplary' followers – those who acted with 'intelligence, independence, courage, and a strong sense of ethics'. These individuals are critical to the success of all groups and organizations, he argued. Meanwhile, Chaleff placed subordinates into one of four categories based on the degree to which the follower supports the leader and the degree to which the follower challenges the leader.

All three did pioneering work – and yet, as indicated, it seems to have had little impact on how current leader-follower relationships are perceived. In part, this is because of cultural, organizational, and technological changes that have taken place in just the past few years. Manual laborers, for instance, have been replaced by younger, tech-savvy knowledge workers, who are generally less disposed to be, in Zaleznik's parlance, 'masochistic' or 'withdrawn'.

The most important point of all these typologies, however, is that leader-follower relationships, no matter the situation, culture, or era in which they are embedded, are more similar than they are different. Underlying them is some sort of dominance and some sort of deference. Segmenting followers, then, serves at least two broad purposes: In theory, it enables us all to impose an order on groups and organizations that up to now has been largely lacking. In practice, it allows superiors and subordinates alike to discern who in the group or organization is doing what – and why.

# A New Typology

The typology I've developed after years of study and observation aligns followers on one, all-important metric – level of engagement. I categorize all followers according to where they fall along a continuum that ranges from 'feeling and doing absolutely nothing' to 'being passionately committed and deeply involved'. I chose level of engagement because, regardless of context, it's the follower's degree of involvement that largely determines the nature of the superior-subordinate relationship. This is especially true today: Because of the aforementioned changes in the cultures and structures of organizations, for instance, knowledge workers often care as much if not more about intrinsic factors – the quality of their interpersonal relationships with their superiors, for instance, or their passion for the organization's mission – than about extrinsic rewards such as salary, titles, and other benefits.

A typology based on a single, simple metric – as opposed to the multiple rating factors used by the creators of previous segmenting tools – offers leaders immediate information on whether and to what degree their followers are buying what they're selling: Do your followers participate actively in meetings and proceedings? Do they demonstrate engagement by pursuing dialogues, asking good questions, and generating new ideas? Or have they checked out – pecking away at their BlackBerries or keeping a close eye on the clock? I categorize followers as *isolates, bystanders, participants, activists,* and *diehards.* Let's look at each type.

**Isolates are completely detached.** These followers are scarcely aware of what's going on around them. Moreover, they do not care about their leaders, know anything about them, or respond to them in any obvious way. Their alienation is, nevertheless, of consequence. By knowing and doing nothing, these types of followers passively support the status quo and further strengthen leaders who already have the upper hand. As a result, isolates can drag down their groups or organizations.

Isolates are most likely to be found in large companies, where they can easily disappear in the maze of cubicles, offices, departments, and divisions. Their attitudes and behaviors attract little or no notice from those at the top levels of the organization as long as they do their jobs, even if only marginally well and with zero enthusiasm. Consider the member of the design team at a large consumer goods company who dutifully completes his individual assignments but couldn't care less about the rest of the company's products and processes – he just needs to pay the bills. Or witness the typical American voter – or, more accurately, nonvoter.

In 2004, no fewer than 15 million Americans said they had not gone to the polls because they were 'not interested in the election' or were 'not involved in politics'. Groups or organizations rarely profit from isolates, especially if their numbers are high. Unwittingly, they impede improvement and slow change.

To mitigate the isolates' negative effect on companies, leaders and managers first need to ask themselves the following questions: Do we have any isolates among us, and, if so, how many? Where are they? Why are they so detached? Answering these questions won't be easy given that isolates by their very nature are invisible to the top team. Senior management will need to acquire information from those at other levels of the organization by having informal and formal conversations about managers and employees who seem lethargic or indifferent about their work, the group, or both.

The next step, of course, is to take action. Depending on the reasons for alienation, there may be ways to engage isolates in the workplace. If it's a matter of job satisfaction, a training and development plan might be drawn up. If it's a matter of job stress, a new schedule that allows for several days of work from home might be considered. In any case, leaders and managers will need to consider the return from making such investments in isolates: If it will be low or nonexistent, managers may ultimately decide to part ways with these followers. Employers that are satisfied with those who do an adequate job and no more might choose to keep these types of followers.

**Bystanders observe but do not participate.** These free riders deliberately stand aside and disengage, both from their leaders and from their groups or organizations. They may go along passively when it is in their self-interest to do so, but they are not internally motivated to engage in an active way. Their withdrawal also amounts to tacit support for whoever and whatever constitutes the status quo.

Like isolates, bystanders can drag down the rest of the group or organization. But unlike isolates, they are perfectly aware of what is going on around them; they just choose not to take the time, the trouble, or, to be fair, sometimes the risk to get involved. A notorious example from the public sector is people who refuse to intervene when a crime is being committed – commonly referred to as the Genovese syndrome or the bystander effect. A corporate counterpart might be the account representative at a financial services company who goes along with the new CEO's recently mandated process changes, even as some of her colleagues are being demoted or fired for pointing out inefficiencies in the new system. To speak up or get involved would be to put her own career and reputation on the line at a time when the CEO is still weeding out 'loyal' employees from 'problem' ones.

There are bystanders everywhere – and, like isolates, they tend to go unnoticed, especially in large organizations, because they consciously choose to fly under the radar. In the workplace, silent but productive bystander followers can be useful to managers who just want people to do as they are told – but they will inevitably disappoint those bosses who want people to actually care about the organization's mission. There are ways to bring bystanders along, however. As with isolates, the key is to determine the root causes of their alienation and offer appropriate intrinsic or extrinsic rewards that may increase their levels of engagement, and, ultimately, their productivity. Bystanders, perhaps much more than isolates, may be swayed by such incentives.

**Participants are engaged in some way.** Regardless of whether these followers clearly support their leaders and organizations or clearly oppose them, they care enough to invest some of what they have (time or money, for example) to try to make an impact. Consider the physicians and scientists who developed the painkiller Vioxx: They felt personally invested in producing a best-selling drug for Merck, bringing it to market – and defending it even in the face of later revelations that the drug could create very serious side effects in some users. They were driven by their own passions (ambition, innovation, creation, helping people) – not necessarily by senior managers.

When participants support their leaders and managers, they are highly coveted. They are the fuel that drives the engine. In the workplace, for instance, they can make effective junior partners. When they disapprove of their leaders and managers, however, or when they act as independent agents, the situation gets more complicated. Former Merck CEO Raymond Gilmartin, for instance, was not trained as either a physician or a scientist. So it was easy enough for the people who on paper were his subordinates – the physicians and researchers championing Vioxx – to get ahead of him with a drug that brought the company a whole lot of trouble. (Vioxx was pulled from the market in 2004.)

Gilmartin could have done a much better job of communicating with and learning from these participant followers, perhaps bringing in experts from the outside to consult with him and his knowledge workers as Vioxx was being produced and marketed – and especially as it was being questioned. Indeed, if Gilmartin had understood the leader-follower dynamic even a bit better, he might have been able to help his company avert public relations and legal disasters.

Although Gilmartin's subordinates acted as free agents, they supported him nonetheless – which highlights an important point about followers' attitudes and opinions. When it comes to participant followers, and to the other engaged follower types described later in this article, leaders need to watch them overall and pay particularly close attention to whether their subordinates are for or against them. (The for-or-against question does not even come up for disengaged isolates and bystanders.)

**Activists feel strongly one way or another about their leaders and organizations, and they act accordingly.** These followers are eager, energetic, and engaged. They are heavily invested in people and processes, so they work hard either on behalf of their leaders or to undermine and even unseat them.

When Paul Wolfowitz ran into trouble as president of the World Bank, for instance, it was the activists among his staffers who led the charge against him. As soon as the news broke that Wolfowitz had intervened in a professional situation on behalf of a woman with whom he was having a personal relationship, members of the World Bank Group Staff Association promptly issued a statement: 'The President must acknowledge that his conduct has compromised the integrity and effectiveness of the World Bank Group and has destroyed the staff's trust in his leadership. He must act honorably and resign.'

Activists who strongly support their leaders and managers can be important allies, whether they are direct or indirect reports. Activists are not necessarily high in number, though, if only because their level of commitment demands an expense of time and energy that most people find difficult to sustain. Of course, this same passion also means they can and often do have a considerable impact on a group or organization. Those activists who are as loyal as they are competent and committed are frequently in the leader or manager's inner circle – simply because they can be counted on to dedicate their (usually long) working hours to the mission as their superiors see it.

Some activist followers are effectively encouraged by their superiors to take matters into their own hands. This was the case at Best Buy. CEO Brad Anderson had consistently encouraged 'bottom-up, stealth innovation' at the retail organization, and human resource managers Jody Thompson and Cali Ressler were bold – and smart – enough to take him up on it. They wanted to create policies that would enable a workplace without any fixed schedules – a 'results-oriented work environment', or ROWE. Best Buy employees at all levels of the organization – in the stores and at headquarters – would be free to set their own hours and come and go as they pleased, as long as their work got done. On their own, Thompson and Ressler considered how to make such a policy work, how exactly to measure results in the absence of set hours, how to implement the new processes that might be required, and so forth. In 2003, they presented their ideas to several unit managers who were struggling with complaints from top performers about undesirable and unsustainable levels of stress in the workplace. The managers were open to hearing about ROWE – more important, they were willing to test it in their units. Word gradually spread about the grassroots experiment, building strong support and acceptance in various departments, until it finally reached management's ears – after some parts of the company had already implemented the new policy. The HR managers' program eventually was rolled out companywide.

**Diehards are prepared to go down for their cause – whether it's an individual, an idea, or both.** These followers may be deeply devoted to their leaders, or they may be strongly motivated to oust their leaders by any means necessary. They exhibit an all-consuming dedication to someone or something they deem worthy.

Diehard followers are rare; their all-encompassing commitment means they emerge only in those situations that are dire or close to it. They can be either a strong asset to their leaders or managers or a dangerous liability. Hitler's most ardent disciple from the start was, arguably, Nazi propagandist Josef Goebbels. As conditions in Germany began deteriorating, with the Allies closing in, Goebbels remained close to the leader – straight through to the end: Shortly after the führer committed suicide, Goebbels took the most radical diehard-type step when he and his wife took their lives along with those of their six children. Without Hitler, they considered life not worth living.

Of course, not all diehard followers are so extreme in their devotion. But they are willing, by definition, to endanger their own health and welfare in the service of their cause. Soldiers the world over, for instance, risk life and limb in their commitment to protect and defend. They are trained and willing to follow nearly blindly the orders of their superiors, who depend on them absolutely to get the job done.

Sometimes diehards can be found in more ordinary circumstances, even in traditional organizations in which they are motivated to act in ways judged by others to be extreme. Whistleblowers are a case in point. Usually we think them heroes and heroines. In fact, these diehards can and often do pay a high price for their unconventional behavior. Bunnatine H. Greenhouse, a U.S. Army contracting official who criticized a large, noncompetitive government contract with Halliburton for work being done in Iraq, was punished for being so outspoken. She had initially registered her complaint only to those inside the Army. When this had no effect, she testified in 2005 before the Senate Democratic Policy Committee and described the contract as 'the most blatant and improper contract abuse I have witnessed'. Incensed by her remark, and citing poor performance, the Army removed Greenhouse from her elite Senior Executive Service position and reassigned her to a lesser job.

As I mentioned earlier, attitudes and opinions do not matter much when we are talking about isolates and bystanders, if only because they do little or even nothing. They matter a great deal, however, when we are talking about participants, activists, and diehards. Do these followers support their leader? Or, rank notwithstanding, are they using their available resources to resist people in positions of power, authority, and influence? My typology suggests that good leaders should pay special attention to those who demonstrate their strong support or their vehement opposition. It's not difficult to see the signs – participants and especially activists and diehards wear their hearts on their sleeves.

## Good and Bad Followers

Certain character and personality traits are nearly always associated with being a good leader (integrity, intelligence, and wise judgment, for instance), as are particular skills and capacities (effective communication and decision making, for example). But given the different roles played by leaders and followers, what can reasonably be said about what constitutes a good follower? More to the point, what distinguishes a good follower from a bad one? Here my typology can again be of help.

First and foremost, there is this: Followers who do something are nearly always preferred to followers who do nothing. In other words, isolates and bystanders (little or no engagement, little or no action) don't have much to recommend them. Then again, doing something is not, in and of itself, sufficient, especially in cases of bad leadership. On the one hand, the story of 'Chainsaw Al'

Dunlap, former CEO of Scott Paper and Sunbeam, is one of a powerful leader with a mean streak, an intimidating executive who cultivated a culture of tyranny and misery while realizing success at Scott Paper and failure at Sunbeam. On the other hand, it's the story of isolates and bystanders who were unwilling or unable to stop him from leading so poorly. It's also a tale of participants and activists who did something; trouble was they supported rather than opposed a leader who did not deserve it.

Or consider the extreme case of Darfur, which *New York Times* columnist Nicholas Kristof has long described as a situation in which there is enough blame to go around, including to those among us who have known about the genocide for years but have done nothing to stop it. Kristof praises certain kinds of followers, however – participants and activists who, despite being without power, authority, and influence, did what they reasonably could to stop the murder and mayhem. One such follower was the 12-year-old from a small town in Oregon who, after seeing the film *Hotel Rwanda,* formed a Sudan Club and raised money by selling eggs and washing cars. Another was the doctoral student who in his spare time became the foremost expert on how investments by foreign companies 'underwrite the Sudanese genocide'.

Good followers will actively support a leader who is good (effective and ethical) and will actively oppose a leader who is bad (ineffective and unethical). Good followers invest time and energy in making informed judgments about who their leaders are and what they espouse. Then they take the appropriate action. The senior editors and other newsroom staffers at the *New York Times,* for instance, certainly may have had problems with the way Howell Raines, then the executive editor, was trying to remake the venerable publication and may have chafed at his arrogant leadership style. The tipping point for them, however, was Raines's mismanagement of the scandal involving wayward reporter Jayson Blair – an incident they believed could create lasting damage to an institution to which they were deeply committed and where credibility is everything.

Conversely, bad followers will do nothing whatsoever to contribute to the group or organization. Or they will actively oppose a leader who is good. Or they will actively support a leader who is bad. Clearly Chainsaw Al's lapdogs fall into this last category. Most of the subordinates in his inner circle – those who were closest to him and who arguably could have afforded, professionally and financially, to oppose his ultimately destructive behavior – did nothing to try to shorten his miserable reign.

\*   \*   \*

Contrary to what the leadership industry would have you believe, the relationship between superiors and their subordinates is not one-sided. Nor are followers all one and the same – and they should not be treated as such. Insofar as they can, followers act in their own self-interests, just as leaders do. And while they may lack authority, at least in comparison with their superiors, followers do not lack power and influence.

Spurred by cultural and technological advances, more and more followers are either challenging their leaders or, in many cases, simply circumventing them altogether. Participant, activist, and diehard followers invested in animal rights can, for instance, on their own now mass-send messages via e-mail, collect data using concealed cameras, and post their galvanizing images on various websites. Their work has motivated chains like McDonald's and Burger King to ask their meat and egg suppliers to follow guidelines that include providing extra water, more wing room, and fresh air for egg-laying hens. In 2007, Burger King went a step further and announced that it would buy eggs and pork only from suppliers that did not confine their animals in crates or cages.

As this example and countless others confirm, it's long overdue for academics and practitioners to adopt a more expansive view of leadership – one that sees leaders and followers as inseparable, indivisible, and impossible to conceive the one without the other.

# I Second that Emotion: Effects of Emotional Contagion and Affect at Work on Leader and Follower Outcomes

12

*Stefanie K. Johnson*

[ ... ] One means by which charismatic leaders achieve outstanding outcomes is through the formulation and articulation of a vision (Conger and Kanungo, 1987), and in particular an inspirational vision (Sosik and Dinger, 2007). Another explanation is that charismatic leaders impact followers' motivation through their self-concepts (Shamir, House and Arthur, 1993). An additional mechanism by which charismatic leaders impact followers is through the emotional attachment that they build with followers (Bass, 1985; Bass and Avolio, 1995; Conger and Kanungo, 1994; Gardner and Avolio, 1998; House, 1977; Shamir et al., 1993; Weber, 1920). While transactional leaders emphasize the rational or exchange basis of a leader–follower relationship, charismatic and transformational leaders emphasize the emotional basis of this relationship (Bass, 1985). The current research examines the impact of affect in charismatic leadership.
[ ... ]

## Theoretical Background and Hypothesis Development

Charismatic and transformational leadership theories, primarily based on the work of Bass (1985), House (1977), and Weber (1920) explain the emotional

Johnson, S.K. (2008) 'I Second that emotion: Effects of emotional contagion and affect at work on leader and follower outcomes', Leadership Quarterly.

connection between leaders and followers that results in extraordinary increases in follower performance. House and Shamir (1993) include both of these types of leadership in what they call the neo-charisma paradigm because charisma is a central concept of both charismatic and transformational leadership theories. There are at least three central components of charismatic leadership: attributed charisma, idealized influence, and inspiration motivation (Bass and Avolio, 1994). Attributed charisma is the personal power that charismatic leaders possess. Idealized influence includes leader behavior related to serving as a role model for followers in which a leader stresses values and beliefs, moral behavior, and a strong sense of the collective mission. Inspiration motivation is comprised of those behaviors aimed at adding meaning to followers' work, typically resulting in an increase in follower enthusiasm.

As House, Woycke, and Fodor (1988, p. 101) suggest, 'Transactional [exchange] leaders have their primary effects on follower cognitions and abilities. Charismatic leaders have their major effects on the emotions and self-esteem of followers – the affective motivational variables rather than the cognitive variables.' Shamir et al.'s (1993) theory of charismatic leadership suggests that charismatic leaders achieve their motivating effects by linking follower self-concepts to organizational goals, so followers internalize the organization's mission and vision. The leader's specific behaviors include increasing the intrinsic value of effort, increasing the value of goal accomplishment, creating follower commitment to goals, expressing high expectations for followers to raise followers' self-esteem, and providing an optimistic vision of the future. As Connelly, Gaddis, and Helton-Fauth (2002) note, one of the major underlying assumptions of Shamir et al.'s (1993) theory is that when leaders are engaging in the described behaviors they are expressing positive emotions to motivate the followers.

For example, when charismatic leaders are crafting and delivering speeches to align followers' goals with the organization's goals, providing high expectations for followers, and conveying an optimistic vision for the future their speeches are infused with positive affect. Positive affect is communicated both through the content of what the leader says, and his or her nonverbal behavior during communication (Ashkanasy and Tse, 2000; Bass, 1985; Gardner and Avolio, 1998), which can result in the spread of that positive affect to followers through emotional contagion. Insofar as an emotional response occurs in followers, the leader's behavior can be conceptualized as an affective event for followers [ ... ], which can impact followers' subsequent attitudes and behaviors (Dasborough, 2006).

## Emotional Contagion and Leadership

Emotional contagion is the automatic and unconscious transfer of emotions between individuals (Hatfield, Cacioppo, and Rapson, 1992) that is thought to occur as a result of individuals' tendency to mimic and synchronize the facial expressions, vocalizations, postures, and movements of others which cues the target to experience the emotion that he or she is mimicking (Chartrand and Bargh, 1999). A long line of research in social psychology has demonstrated that exposure to emotional stimuli can affect one's facial expressions (e.g. Lee and Wagner, 2002) and that exhibiting a particular facial expression can elicit the corresponding emotion (Adelmann and Zajonc, 1989). In one study, Friedman and Riggio (1981) found that emotional contagion occurred between two individuals who simply sat and faced each other in silence for two-minutes. More recently, emotional contagion has been examined in a leadership context (Cherulnik et al., 2001; Halverson, 2004; Lewis, 2000; Sy et al., 2005).

For example, Sy et al. (2005) manipulated leaders' moods in self-managing work teams and found that the leaders' moods affected their team members' moods and influenced group affective tone. Emotional contagion from leaders to followers should be particularly strong because leaders are highly salient group members (Connelly et al., 2002). In addition, research suggests that persons of lower status have a heightened awareness of their superiors' feelings (Snodgrass, 1985) and attending to one's feelings makes emotional contagion more likely to occur (Hatfield et al., 1992; Hatfield, Cacioppo, and Rapson, 1994). However, laboratory evidence for emotional contagion from leaders to followers (Cherulnik et al., 2001; Halverson, 2004; Lewis, 2000; Sy et al., 2005) may be enhanced by the strength of the laboratory situation and the absence of external influences. Mischel (1973, 1977) argued that strong situations are likely to elicit similar responses from all individuals. However, in weaker situations other factors, such as individual differences, may also impact the extent to which emotional contagion occurs.

## Susceptibility to Emotional Contagion

While all individuals have the potential to send and receive emotions through emotional contagion, some individuals are more susceptible than others to emotional contagion (Hatfield et al., 1992). Susceptible persons tend to pay close attention to others' emotional expressions, are able to read others' emotional expressions, feel that they are similar to or interrelated with other persons, and tend to mimic facial, vocal, and postural expressions. Because of these behaviors, susceptible individuals are more likely to catch others' emotions. Doherty (1997, p. 149) suggests that 'Susceptibility is best considered the tendency to automatically mimic and synchronize with the expressions of others and, through afferent feedback from the facial and/or skeletal muscular activity, to experience or 'catch' the others' emotions.'

He also stated that genetics, gender, early experience, and personality characteristics all contribute to individual differences in susceptibility to emotional contagion. Susceptibility encompasses one's likelihood to catch five basic emotions: happiness, love, fear, anger, and sadness. People who are more susceptible would more strongly endorse statements such as, 'If someone I'm talking with begins to cry, I get teary-eyed', 'Being with a happy person picks me up when I'm feeling down', 'When someone smiles warmly at me, I smile back and feel warm inside', and 'I get filled with sorrow when people talk about the death of their loved ones.' We suggest that emotional contagion from leaders to followers will occur among followers who are more susceptible to emotional contagion.

> *Hypothesis 1a. The positive relationship between leader positive affect at work and follower positive affect at work will increase as follower susceptibility to emotional contagion increases.*

> *Hypothesis 1b. The positive relationship between leader negative affect at work and follower negative at work affect will increase as follower susceptibility to emotional contagion increases.*

## Follower Affect and Perceptions of Charismatic Leadership

Further, if followers 'catch' their leader's affect, then their subsequent evaluations of their leader and subsequent performance should be influenced by that affect. Research on person perception demonstrates that one's affect at the time a judgment is made can impact his or her perceptions of others. Specifically, individuals perceive others in an affect-congruent manner such that people in good moods perceive others positively, and people in bad moods perceive others negatively (Isen and Baron, 1991). This is thought to occur as a result of the affect-priming principle, which suggests that when an affective state is primed it results in the retrieval of affect-congruent thoughts and memories (Bower, 1981) and through the affect-as-information principle, which suggests that individuals rely on their current affective state when judging a stimulus (Schwarz, 1990). Regardless of the mechanism, a great deal of research has demonstrated that affect influences individuals' impressions of others across a broad range of situations (Isen and Baron, 1991).

Dasborough and Ashkanasy (2002) developed a model specifically relating to the relationship between affect and attributions of leadership. In this model they suggest that follower affect can influence follower attributions of their leader's intentionality. Further, in a laboratory study, Halverson (2004) found that persons in a positive mood tend to perceive their leaders as more charismatic than persons in a less positive mood and persons in a negative mood tend to perceive their leaders as less charismatic than persons in a less negative mood (Halverson, 2004). Likewise, Dasborough (2006) suggests that follower affect influences follower attitudes about their leader and organizational behavior.

It should be noted that the opposite direction of the affect – attributions of leadership relationship has received support in the literature. That is, leaders who are charismatic elicit more positive affect from followers (Dasborough, 2006; McColl-Kennedy and Anderson, 2002), just as follower positive affect impacts attributions of charismatic leadership. Further, leaders who express positive affect are perceived as more effective and charismatic than those who do not (Gaddis, Connelly, and Mumford, 2004; Lewis, 2000; Newcombe and Ashkanasy, 2002), as the expression of positive affect is one of the specific behavioral indicators of charismatic leadership (Bass, 1985). Although these relationships are complex and intertwined, in the current study we focus on the effects of follower affect on attributions of leadership (Figure 12.1).

*Hypothesis 2a. Follower positive affect will be positively related to follower perceptions of charismatic leadership.*

*Hypothesis 2b. Follower negative affect will be negatively related to follower perceptions of charismatic leadership.*

## Performance

Job performance can be conceptualized as the extent to which one exhibits behaviors that further the goals of the organization (Rotundo and Sackett, 2002). This includes both formal, prescribed, task related behavior, or core task behaviors, and informal acts of a prosocial nature that benefit coworkers, supervisors, and/or the organization called organizational citizenship behavior (Smith, Organ, and Near, 1983). Although the initial conceptualization of organizational citizenship behavior included behaviors that were not formally recognized or rewarded by the organization, Organ's reconceptualization of OCB does not require that the behaviors be extra-role (Organ, 1997). Similar, but not identical to OCB, is the concept of contextual performance (Borman and Motowidlo, 1993). Contextual performance includes a set of behaviors that are more likely to be part of one's rewarded work behaviors, and does not require that these behaviors be discretionary (Motowidlo, 2000). These behaviors include persisting on tasks, volunteering or helping others, following rules, and supporting the organization. The current research focuses on contextual performance as a type of OCB.

The relationship between affect and OCB has been examined in a leadership context. George and Bettenhausen (1990) found that leader affect was related to work groups' prosocial behavior. However, that study did not examine the mechanism for that relationship. One possibility is that follower affect may have explained the relationship between leader affect and follower OCB given the relationship between affect and helping behavior (Isen and Baron, 1991). George

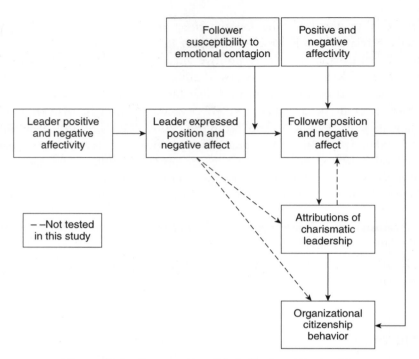

**Figure 12.1**   Proposed model of affect and leadership

and Brief (1992) describe positive affect as a direct antecedent of organizational spontaneity, and research has demonstrated the relationship between positive affect and organizational citizenship behavior (George, 1991; Lee and Allen, 2002). While the relationship between negative affect at work and OCB has not yet been established, research has linked employee negative affect to counterproductive work behaviors (Lee and Allen, 2002). Considering that employees who experience negative affect at work may want to harm their organization, it is unlikely that they will also engage in behaviors that help their organization, such as OCBs. Therefore, it is expected that negative affect at work will be negatively related to OCB.

> *Hypothesis 3a. Follower positive affect will be positively related to follower organizational citizenship behavior.*
>
> *Hypothesis 3b. Follower negative affect will be negatively related to follower organizational citizenship behavior.*

Charismatic leadership has also been conceptually and empirically linked to organizational citizenship behavior (Deluga, 1995; Koh, Steers, and Terborg, 1995). Charismatic leaders are thought to appeal to followers' higher order needs, foster follower dedication to organizational goals, and increase follower self-confidence and self-expectations. These behaviors cause followers to, 'do more than they are expected to do', (Yukl, 1989), 'perform above and beyond the call of duty', (Bass, 1985), take on greater responsibility, perform beyond expectations, and assume leadership roles themselves (Bass and Avolio, 1994). Theory suggests that charismatic leaders will impact organizational citizenship behavior in particular. For example, Bass (1990) argued that when the criteria for the evaluation of performance is ambiguous the leaders' expected influence in defining expectations is more important.

Shamir et al.'s (1993) theory suggests that charismatic leaders are able to motivate followers to exert extra effort by engaging their self-concepts and aligning their goals with the organization's goals. When extrinsic motivation is low, followers of charismatic leaders are more likely to attribute their behavior to internal motivation because their self-concepts have been engaged. In addition, setting high expectations for followers can encourage them to expend extra effort (Shamir et al., 1993). In a large field sample, Sosik (2005) found that leader values and charismatic behavior impacted follower extra effort and organizational citizenship behavior. Koh et al. (1995) found that teachers' perceptions of their principals' charismatic leadership behavior predicted organizational citizenship behavior. Therefore, it is expected that follower attributions of charismatic leadership will relate to their engagement in OCBs.

*Hypothesis 4. Follower perceptions of charismatic leadership will relate positively to follower organizational citizenship behavior.*

# Methods

## Sample

[ ... ]
One hundred twenty-six teachers, from 21 [large public] schools, responded. Only data from 112 teachers from 16 of the schools were usable because the others lacked the corresponding principal data. Among the usable sample, 19 were men (17%), 91 were women (81%), and two people failed to respond (2%). There were four Asian (4%), 11 Black (10%), 14 Hispanic (13%), 80 White (71%), and six teachers who indicated 'other' as their race (5%). Tenure ranged from teachers in their first year to 30 years ($M$=5.58, $SD$=5.66). Groups ranged in size from 1 to 18 ($M$=6.69, $SD$=5.34).

Because education is a very specific industry, it is important to justify the use of principals as organizational leaders, and specifically charismatic leaders. Although principals engage in a great deal of administrative duties, they also work to inspire teachers and the community through the use of inspirational visions. Research has used the principal role, and formulating a new vision for a school, as a setting for creating leadership visions (Strange and Mumford, 2005). As, Bess and Goldman (2001, p. 432) said

> Charismatic leadership is an antidote to discouragement and disengagement, and it seems to have surfaced in many of the least privileged schools, inspiring and energizing teachers and students alike. In the 1980s, Blumberg and Greenfield (1986) and Lightfoot (1983) published widely read volumes of case studies that described how charismatic leaders reestablished educational values in difficult schools. The implied leadership model uses charisma as its frame of reference: strong personalities inspire staff (and sometimes students), resulting in improved school climate, conflict resolution, and better outcomes.

Further, previous research has demonstrated the transformational leader behaviors of school principals (Koh et al., 1995). Based on these previous studies, the examination of charismatic leader behavior from school principals appears to be justified.

## Procedure

This study used a survey methodology. Teachers completed measures of trait positive and negative affect (affectivity), susceptibility to emotional contagion, and positive and negative affect at work. Teachers also rated their principal on charismatic leadership and self-reported organizational citizenship behavior. Principals completed the same measures of trait affect and affect at work as the teachers did. In addition, they completed a Big 5 personality measure for use as a control variable. [ ... ]

# Results

[ ... ]

## Test of Hypotheses

Intercorrelations between the principal and teacher variables are presented in Table 12.1. Hypotheses 1a and 1b examined the interaction between leader affect and work and follower susceptibility to emotional contagion as a predictor of follower positive and negative affect at work. Hypothesis 1a was supported [ ... ] such that as principal positive affect at work increased, so did the relationship between teacher susceptibility to emotional contagion and teacher positive affect at work. Although not hypothesized, the interaction between principal

**Table 12.1** Intercorrelations between teacher variables and principal variables

| | a | M | SD | 1 | 2 | 3 | 4 | 5 | 6 | 7 | 8 | 9 | 10 |
|---|---|---|---|---|---|---|---|---|---|---|---|---|---|
| *Teacher variables* | | | | | | | | | | | | | |
| 1. Positive affect at work | 0.85 | 3.54 | 0.84 | – | | | | | | | | | |
| 2. Negative affect at work | 0.87 | 1.63 | 0.60 | -0.28** | – | | | | | | | | |
| 3. Positive affectivity | 0.92 | 3.78 | 0.77 | 0.80** | -0.24** | – | | | | | | | |
| 4. Negative affectivity | 0.92 | 1.85 | 0.74 | -0.20** | 0.28** | -0.26** | – | | | | | | |
| 5. Susceptibility to EC | 0.79 | 2.58 | 0.44 | 0.03 | -0.02 | 0.01 | 0.10 | – | | | | | |
| 6. Charismatic leadership | 0.96 | 3.71 | 1.08 | 0.34** | -0.35** | 0.37** | -0.19* | 0.06 | – | | | | |
| 7. OCB | 0.90 | 4.21 | 0.56 | 0.47** | -0.23* | 0.44** | -0.16* | 0.18* | 0.31** | – | | | |
| *Principal variables* | | | | | | | | | | | | | |
| 1. Positive affect at work | 0.84 | 4.08 | 0.53 | – | | | | | | | | | |
| 2. Negative affect at work | 0.70 | 1.54 | 0.38 | 0.05 | – | | | | | | | | |
| 3. Positive affectivity | 0.87 | 4.25 | 0.42 | 0.74** | -0.09 | – | | | | | | | |
| 4. Negative affectivity | 0.87 | 1.31 | 0.30 | -0.24 | 0.43 | -0.24 | – | | | | | | |
| 5. Extroversion | 0.84 | 3.49 | 0.65 | 0.49 | -0.29 | 0.58* | -0.22 | – | | | | | |
| 6. Agreeableness | 0.78 | 4.38 | 0.48 | 0.22 | 0.13 | 0.47 | 0.09 | 0.08 | – | | | | |
| 7. Conscientiousness | 0.76 | 3.93 | 0.51 | -0.29 | -0.13 | 0.01 | 0.34 | -0.07 | 0.11 | – | | | |
| 8. Emotional stability | 0.87 | 3.81 | 0.64 | 0.59* | -0.23 | 0.70** | -0.76** | 0.59* | 0.20 | -0.39 | – | | |
| 9. Openness to experience | 0.38 | 4.17 | 0.32 | 0.09 | 0.01 | 0.15 | -0.10 | 0.25 | -0.42 | 0.19 | 0.07 | – | |
| 10. Turnover | – | 3.71 | 2.20 | -0.58** | 0.09 | -0.43 | -0.15 | -0.36 | 0.14 | 0.00 | -0.20 | 0.10 | – |

*Note:* For teachers, $n = 126$. For principals, $n = 16$. $a$ = Cronbach's $a$. *$p$<.05, **$p$<.01.

negative affect at work and teacher susceptibility to emotional contagion was also significant. Figure 12.2 displays this relationship using median splits for principal positive and negative affect at work and teacher susceptibility to emotional contagion. Although there was less support for the aggregation of teacher negative affect at work to the group level, Hypothesis 1b was tested. There was no effect for the interaction between principal negative affect at work, teacher susceptibility to emotional contagion, and teacher negative affect at work ($p>.05$).

Further, because data were gathered on school characteristics, it was possible to examine the relationship between principal positive and negative affect and teacher turnover at the end of the year. Based on the fact that data for the current study were collected 6–9 months before the turnover occurred (since most if not all teachers turnover during the summer months), there is greater support for the notion that principal positive affect led to teacher turnover, rather than turnover leading to principal affect. There was a statistically significant relationship between principal positive affect at work and teacher turnover the following year, although there was no relationship between principal negative affect at work and turnover (Table 12.1). Principals who reported greater positive affect at work had lower levels of turnover the following summer.

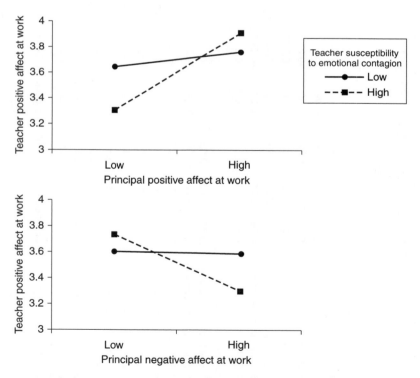

**Figure 12.2**  Relationship between principal affect at work, teacher susceptibility to emotional contagion, and teacher positive affect at work

Hypotheses 2a, 2b and 3a, 3b suggest that teacher positive and negative affect at work would be related to attributions of charismatic leadership and organizational citizenship behavior. Based on the correlational data, both hypotheses were supported. Teacher positive affect at work was positively related to attributions of charismatic leadership and OCB. Teacher negative affect at work was negatively related to attributions of charismatic leadership and OCB. In line with Hypothesis 4, attributions of charismatic leadership were positively related to OCB.
[...]

# Discussion

The current study highlights the importance of emotional contagion and affect at work in a leadership context. Both leader and follower affect related to important outcomes for the principals and teachers in this study. First, leader positive affect at work was related to follower turnover at the end of the year. Second, there was a relationship between leader affect, follower affect, and follower susceptibility to emotional contagion. The positive relationship between leader positive affect at work and follower positive affect at work increased as follower susceptibility to emotional contagion increased. Also, the negative relationship between leader negative affect at work and follower positive affect at work increased as follower susceptibility to emotional contagion increased. Third, follower positive and negative affect at work were linked to attributions of charismatic leadership and OCB. The findings from this research are important to leadership from both a theoretical and practical position.

## Leader Affect

This study provides evidence of the importance of leader affect at work and emotional contagion in terms of organizational outcomes. In addition to the relationship between leader positive affect and follower turnover, leader positive and negative affect at work were related to follower positive affect at work for followers who were more susceptible to emotional contagion. Contrary to expectations, this study did not find any relationship between principal affect at work and follower negative affect at work. It is possible that the lack of within school agreement, the small sample size, restriction of range, or social desirability in responding contributed to the null finding. While previous theory (e.g., Bass, 1985) and laboratory research (Cherulnik et al., 2001; Halverson, 2004; Lewis, 2000; Sy et al., 2005) has linked leader affect to follower affect, this is the first study to extend this relationship to a field setting, adding to the generalizability of this effect.

The findings also suggest that the likelihood that emotional contagion will occur depends on followers' susceptibility to emotional contagion. Although previous laboratory research has found direct relationships of leader affect on follower affect, regardless of susceptibility, it is possible that the strength of the laboratory situation creates an environment where emotional contagion is particularly likely to occur. Indeed, Mischel (1973, 1977) argues that strong situations are likely to elicit similar responses from all individuals. However, in weaker, more complex environments, susceptibility to emotional contagion may be a requirement for emotional contagion to occur.

## Follower Affect

The current research also builds upon the growing body of literature on affect at work. This study found that follower positive and negative affect at work were related to perceptions of charismatic leadership and organizational citizenship behavior. The link between follower affect at work and attributions of charismatic leadership can be explained in terms of research demonstrating that individuals tend to perceive others in an affect-congruent manner (Isen and Baron, 1991). The relationship between positive affect at work and organizational citizenship behavior is also supported by previous research (George, 1991; Lee and Allen, 2002). Finally, followers' perceptions of their leader's charisma were related to their self-reported OCB. Theory asserts that charismatic leaders are able to encourage followers to perform beyond expectations (Bass, 1985), which may involve the performance of organizational citizenship behavior.

However, when these relationships were all examined simultaneously using structural equation modeling, follower positive affect proved to be the most important predictor of attributions of charismatic leadership and OCB. Both positive and negative affect predicted attributions of charismatic leadership, but only positive affect at work related to OCB. Although previous research has demonstrated the relationship between positive affect and OCB, the relationship had not been demonstrated for negative affect. Similarly, the relationship between attributions of charismatic leadership and OCB, which has been demonstrated previously (Koh et al., 1995) did not hold when examining follower positive affect at work, attributions of charismatic leadership, and OCB simultaneously. It is possible that previous findings linking charismatic leadership to OCB can be accounted for by follower positive affect. [ ... ]

It is important to note that the directions of the relationship examined in this study cannot be proven. Indeed, research has demonstrated that follower attitudes about their leader can impact their emotions (McColl-Kennedy and Anderson, 2002). Although the opposite directionality of the relationship between follower affect and attributions of charismatic leadership was tested with structural equation modeling, this study cannot prove that the effects work one way or the other. It is most likely that the relationship between follower affect and attitudes is reciprocal, such that follower affect influences attitudes, and those attitudes impact subsequent affect.

## Implications

[ ... ]

Practically, this research not only examines the importance of leader expressed affect on follower outcomes, but also highlights the importance of follower affect as it relates to attitudes and performance outcomes. Leaders should be advised of the potential effects of their expressed affect and organizations should be made aware of the impact that their employees' affect can have on outcomes. Because followers can pass their affect on to others with whom they work (e.g., Barsade, 2002), leader affect may have a cascading effect on organizations. Therefore, leader affect may have the potential to influence organizational effectiveness, through its impact on follower affect.

Further, the effectiveness of charismatic leaders may depend upon the situations in which they are leading and the types of followers that they are leading. For example, charismatic leaders might be more effective in industries where the expression of positive affect is required, or those industries high in emotional labor. Emotional labor is the, 'management of feeling to create a publicly observable facial and bodily display', (Hochschild, 1983). Such industries include human resource management, healthcare, and sales (see Grandey, 2000 for a review). In industries high in emotional labor leaders would be expected to express positive emotions, making emotional contagion more likely to occur. Indeed, charismatic leaders have proved to be effective in the healthcare industry (e.g., Avolio et al., 2004), sales (Yammarino et al., 1998), and human resource management (Zhu, Chew, and Spangler, 2005).

Conversely, in highly negative situations, having the ability to control negative emotions would also be important for leadership success. Previous research suggests that emotional intelligence and the ability to regulate one's emotions are important for leadership success (Wong and Law, 2002). This may explain, in part, why charismatic leaders are particularly successful in crisis situations (Pillai, 1996). Charismatic leaders might be less successful in non-emotionally charged settings. In addition, a charismatic leaders' success might depend on the type of followers that he or she leads. Followers who are susceptible to emotional contagion might also be more susceptible to the effects of charismatic leaders. Although susceptibility is an individual difference, there are differences by industry. For example, Doherty, Orimoto, Singelis, Hatfield, and Hebb (1995) found that individuals in the medical industry were more susceptible to emotional contagion than those in the military industry.

Doherty et al. (1995) also found differences in gender, such that women were more susceptible to emotional contagion than men. This may suggest that charismatic leaders would be more effective at influencing female followers' emotions than male followers' emotions. Finally, this study has practical implications for the importance of follower affect in organizations. Regardless of leaders' ability to impact followers' emotions through emotional contagion, leaders should be cognizant of other factors influencing followers' emotions. Given the potential effects of follower affect at work on their attitudes and work behaviors, leaders should find ways to increase follower positive affect and decrease follower negative affect at work. In addition to practical implications of these findings, researchers should consider the industry, gender makeup and susceptibility in general of their sample when examining emotional contagion. [ ... ]

## References

Adelmann, P.K. and Zajonc, R.B. (1989) 'Facial efference and the experience of emotion', *Annual Review of Psychology*, vol. 40, pp. 249–80.

Ashkanasy, N.M. and Tse, B. (2000) 'Transformational leadership as management of emotions: A conceptual review' in Ashkanasy, N.M. and Hartel, C.E. (eds) *Emotions in the Workplace: Research, Theory, and Practice*, Westport, CT, Quorum Books/Greenwald Publishing Group, pp. 221–35.

Avolio, B.J., Zhu, W., Koh, W. and Bhatia, P. (2004) 'Transformational leadership and organizational commitment: Mediating role of psychological empowerment and moderating role of structural distance', *Journal of Organizational Behavior*, vol. 25, pp. 951–68.

Barsade, S.G. (2002) 'The ripple effect: Emotional contagion and its influence on group behaviour', *Administrative Science Quarterly*, vol. 47, pp. 644–75.

Bass, B.M. (1985) *Leadership and Performance Beyond Expectations*, New York, Free Press.

Bass, B.M. (1990) *Bass and Stogdill's Handbook of Leadership*, New York, Free Press.

Bass, B.M. and Avolio, B.J. (1994) *Improving Organizational Effectiveness through Charismatic Leadership*, Thousand Oaks, CA, Sage Publications.

Bass, B.M. and Avolio, B.J. (1995) *Manual for the Multifactor Leadership Questionnaire: Rater Form (5X Short)*, Palo Alto, CA, Mind Garden.

Bess, J.L. and Goldman, P. (2001) 'Leadership ambiguity in universities and K-12 schools and the limits of contemporary leadership theory', *The Leadership Quarterly*, vol. 12, pp. 419–50.

Blumberg, A. and Greenfield, W. (1986) *The Effective Principal: Perspectives on School Leadership* (2nd edn), Boston, MA, Allyn and Bacon.

Bower, G.H. (1981) 'Mood and memory', *American Psychologist*, vol. 36, pp. 129–48.

Chartrand, T.L. and Bargh, J.A. (1999) 'The chameleon effect: The perception–behavior link and social interaction', *Journal of Personality and Social Psychology*, vol. 76, pp. 893–910.

Cherulnik, P.D., Donley, K.A., Wiewel, T.S.R. and Miller, S.R. (2001) 'Charisma is contagious: The effect of leaders' charisma on observers' affect', *Journal of Applied Social Psychology*, vol. 31, pp. 2149–59.

Conger, J.A. and Kanungo, R.N. (1987) 'Toward a behavioral theory of charismatic leadership in organizational settings', *Academy of Management Review*, vol. 12, pp. 637–47.

Conger, J.A. and Kanungo, R.N. (1994) 'Charismatic leadership in organizations: Perceived behavioral attributes and their measurement', *Journal of Organizational Behavior*, vol. 15, pp. 439–52.

Connelly, S., Gaddis, B. and Helton-Fauth, W. (2002) 'A closer look at the role of emotions in transformational and charismatic leadership' in Avolio, B.J. and Yammarino, F.J. (eds)

*Transformational and Charismatic Leadership: The Road Ahead, Vol. 2*, Amsterdam, Elsevier, pp. 255–83.

Dasborough, M.T. (2006) 'Cognitive asymmetry in employee emotional reactions to leadership behaviors', *The Leadership Quarterly*, vol. 17, pp. 163–78.

Dasborough, M.T. and Ashkanasy, N.M. (2002) 'Emotion and attribution of intentionality in leader-member relationships', *The Leadership Quarterly*, vol. 13, pp. 615–34.

Deluga, R.J. (1995) 'The relationship between attributional charismatic leadership and organizational citizenship behavior', *Journal of Applied Social Psychology*, vol. 26, pp. 1652–69.

Doherty, R.W. (1997) 'The emotional contagion scale: A measure of individual differences', *Journal of Nonverbal Behavior*, vol. 21, pp. 131–54.

Doherty, R.W., Orimoto, L., Singelis, T.M., Hatfield, E. and Hebb, J. (1995) 'Emotional contagion: Gender and occupational differences', *Psychology of Women Quarterly*, vol. 19, pp. 355–71.

Friedman, H.S. and Riggio, R.E. (1981) 'Effect of individual differences in nonverbal expressiveness on transmission of emotion', *Journal of Nonverbal Behavior*, vol. 6, pp. 96–104.

Gaddis, B., Connelly, S. and Mumford, M.D. (2004) 'Failure feedback as an affective event: Influences of leader affect on subordinate attitudes and performance', *The Leadership Quarterly*, vol. 15, pp. 663–86.

Gardner, W.L. and Avolio, B.J. (1998) 'The charismatic relationship: A dramaturgical perspective', *Academy of Management Review*, vol. 23, pp. 32–58.

George, J.M. (1991) 'State or trait: Effects of positive mood on prosocial behaviors at work', *Journal of Applied Psychology*, vol. 76, pp. 299–307.

George, J.M. and Bettenhausen, K. (1990) 'Understanding prosocial behavior, sales performance, and turnover: A group level analysis in a service context', *Journal of Applied Psychology*, vol. 75, pp. 698–709.

George, J.M. and Brief, A.P. (1992) 'Feeling good–doing good: A conceptual analysis of the mood at work-organizational spontaneity relationship', *Psychological Bulletin*, vol. 112, pp. 310–29.

Grandey, A.A. (2000) 'Emotion regulation in the workplace: A new way to conceptualize emotional labor', *Journal of Occupational Health Psychology*, vol. 5, pp. 95–110.

Halverson, S.K. (2004) 'Emotional contagion in leader – follower interactions', Unpublished doctoral dissertation. Rice University, Houston, TX.

Hatfield, E., Cacioppo, J.T. and Rapson, R.L. (1992) 'Primitive emotional contagion' in Clark, M.S. (ed.) *Review of Personality and Social Psychology, vol. 14*, Newbury Park, CA, Sage, pp. 151–77.

Hatfield, E., Cacioppo, J. and Rapson, R.L. (1994) *Emotional Contagion*, New York, Cambridge University Press.

Hochschild, A.R. (1983) *The Managed Heart*, Berkeley, CA, University of California Press.

House, R.J. (1977) 'A 1976 theory of charismatic leadership' in Hunt, J.G. and Larson, L. L. (eds) *Leadership: The Cutting Edge*, Carbondale, IL, Southern Illinois University Press, pp. 189–207.

House, R.J. and Shamir, B. (1993) 'Toward the integration of transformational, charismatic, and visionary theories' in Chemers, M.M. and Ayman, R. (eds) *Leadership Theory and Research: Perspectives and Directions*, San Diego, Academic Press, Inc., pp. 81–136.

House, R.J., Woycke, J. and Fodor, E.M. (1988) 'Charismatic and noncharismatic leaders: Differences in behavior and effectiveness' in Conger, J.A. and Kanungo, R.N. (eds) *Charismatic Leadership: The Elusive Factor in Organizational Effectiveness*, San Francisco, CA, Jossey-Bass, pp. 98–121.

Isen, A.M. and Baron, R.A. (1991) 'Positive affect as a factor in organizational behavior', *Research in Organizational Behavior*, vol. 13, pp. 1–53.

Koh, W.L., Steers, R.M. and Terborg, J.R. (1995) 'The effects of charismatic leadership on teacher attitudes and student performance in Singapore', *Journal of Organizational Behavior*, vol. 16, pp. 319–33.

Lee, K., and Allen, N.J. (2002) 'Organizational citizenship behavior and workplace deviance: The role of affect and cognitions', *Journal of Applied Psychology*, vol. 87, pp. 131–42.

Lee, V. and Wagner, H. (2002) 'The effect of social presence on the facial and verbal expression of emotion and the interrelationships among emotion components', *Journal of Nonverbal Behavior*, vol. 26, pp. 3–25.

Lewis, K.M. (2000) 'When leaders display emotion: how followers respond to negative emotional expression of male and female leaders', *Journal of Organizational Behavior*, vol. 21, pp. 221–34.

Lightfoot, S.L. (1983) *The Good High School: Portraits of Character and Culture*, New York, Basic Books.

McColl-Kennedy, J.R. and Anderson, R.D. (2002) 'Impact of leadership style and emotions on subordinate performance', *The Leadership Quarterly*, vol. 13, pp. 545–59.

Mischel, W. (1973) 'Toward a cognitive social learning conceptualization of personality', *Psychological Review*, vol. 80, pp. 252–83.

Mischel, W. (1977) 'The interaction of person and situation' in Magnusson, D. and Endler, N.S. (eds) *Personality at the Crossroads: Current Issues in Interactional Psychology*, Hillsdale, NJ, Lawrence Erlbaum Associates, pp. 333–52.

Motowidlo, S.J. (2000) 'Some basic issues related to contextual performance and organizational citizenship behavior in human resource management', *Human Resource Management Review*, vol. 10, pp. 115–26.

Newcombe, M.J. and Ashkanasy, N.M. (2002) 'The role of affect and affective congruence in perceptions of leaders: an experimental study', *The Leadership Quarterly*, vol. 13, pp. 601–14.

Organ, D.W. (1997) 'A reappraisal and reinterpretation of the satisfaction-causes-performance hypothesis', *Academy of Management Review*, vol. 2, pp. 46–53.

Pillai, R. (1996) 'Crisis and the emergence of charismatic leadership in groups: An experimental investigation', *Journal of Applied Social Psychology*, vol. 26, pp. 543–62.

Rotundo, M. and Sackett, P.R. (2002) 'The relative importance of task, citizenship, and counterproductive performance: A policy-capturing approach', *Journal of Applied Psychology*, vol. 87, pp. 66–80.

Schwarz, N. (1990) 'Feelings as information: Informational and motivational functions of affective states' in Higgins, E.T. and Sorrentino, R.M. (eds) *Handbook of Motivation and Cognition: Foundations of Social Behavior, Vol. 2*, New York, NY, Guilford Press, pp. 527–61.

Shamir, B., House, R.J. and Arthur, M.B. (1993) 'The motivational effects of charismatic leadership: A self-concept based theory', *Organizational Science*, vol. 4, pp. 577–94.

Smith, C.A., Organ, D.W. and Near, J.P. (1983) 'Organizational citizenship behavior: Its nature and antecedents', *Journal of Applied Psychology*, vol. 68, pp. 453–63.

Sosik, J.J. (2005) 'The role of personal values in the charismatic leadership of corporate managers: A model and preliminary field study', *The Leadership Quarterly*, vol. 16, pp. 221–44.

Sosik, J.J. and Dinger, S.L. (2007) 'Relationships between leadership style and vision content: The moderating role of need for social approval, self-monitoring, and need for social power', *The Leadership Quarterly*, vol. 18, pp. 134–53.

Strange, J.M. and Mumford, M.M. (2005) 'The origins of vision: Effects of reflection, models, and analysis', *The Leadership Quarterly*, vol. 16, pp. 121–48.

Sy, T., Côté, S. and Saavedra, R. (2005) 'The contagious leader: Impact of the leader's mood on group members, group affective tone, and group processes', *Journal of Applied Psychology*, vol. 90, pp. 295–305.

Weber, M. (1920) *The Theory of Social and Economic Organization* (trans. A.M. Henderson and T. Parsons), New York, Oxford University Press.

Wong, C.S. and Law, K.S. (2002) 'The effects of leader and follower emotional intelligence on performance an attitude: An exploratory study', *The Leadership Quarterly*, vol. 13, pp. 243–74.

Yammarino, F.J., Spangler, W.D. and Dubinsky, A.J. (1998) 'Transformational and contingent reward leadership: Individual, dyad, and group levels of analysis', *The Leadership Quarterly*, vol. 9, pp. 27–54.

Yukl, G.A. (1989) *Leadership in Organizations* (2nd edn), Englewood Cliffs, NJ, Prentice Hall.

Zhu, W., Chew, I.K.H. and Spangler, W.D. (2005) 'CEO transformational leadership and organizational outcomes: The mediating role of human-capital-enhancing human resource management', *The Leadership Quarterly*, vol. 16, pp. 39–52.

# Part V
## Leadership Gestation

# Visionary Leadership and Strategic Management

13

## Frances Westley and Henry Mintzberg

A strange process seems to occur as concepts such as culture and charisma move from practice to research. Loosely used in practice, these concepts, as they enter academia, become subjected to a concerted effort to force them to lie down and behave, to render them properly scientific. In the process they seem to lose their emotional resonance, no longer expressing the reality that practitioners originally tried to capture.

Leadership is another such concept. Somewhere along the line, as Pondy has argued, 'we lost sight of the "deep structure", or meaning of leadership' (1978, p. 90). In attempting to deal with the observable and measurable aspects of leadership behavior, and perhaps to simplify for normative purposes, leadership research has focused on a narrow set of styles – democratic, autocratic, and *laissez-faire,* for example. We agree with Pondy that instead 'we should be trying to document the variety of styles available' (p. 90).

Strategy may also be such a concept. Much effort has been dedicated in strategic management to narrowing it, to pinning it down (as in the attention to 'generic' strategies), likewise to narrowing the process by which it forms (in the attention to 'planning'). Again, in attempting to dissect a living phenomenon, the skeleton may be revealed while the specimen dies.

More recently, the concepts of strategy and leadership have been combined into that of strategic vision. In academia (Bennis, 1982; Mendell and Gerjuoy, 1984) as well as practice (*Business Week,* 1984; Kiechel, 1986). This has been hailed as a key to managing increasingly complex organizations. Consultants have responded with workshops (e.g. Levinson and Rosenthal, 1984) that promise to train managers to be visionary leaders. In general, however, efforts to turn the creation of strategic vision into a manageable process, one that can be researched, taught, and adopted by managers, risk robbing it of its vitality.

Westley, F. and Mintzberg, H. (1989) 'Visionary leadership and strategic management', *Strategic Management Journal*, vol. 10, pp. 17–32.

Of special concern should be the tendency to subsume strategic vision under leadership in general, in other words to perceive it as just another category of leadership style (e.g. 'transformative'; Tichy and Devanna, 1986). Most writings seem to agree that leadership vision, or 'visioning', as the process has sometimes been called, can be broken down into three distinct stages: (1) the envisioning of 'an image of a desired future organizational state' (Bass, 1987, p. 51) which (2) when effectively articulated and communicated to followers (Bennis and Nanus, 1985; Tichy and Devanna, 1986; Gluck, 1984) serves (3) to empower those followers so that they can enact the vision (Sashkin, 1987; Srivastva, 1983; Conger and Kanungo, 1987; Robbins and Duncan, 1987). Such a view posits enormous control in the hands of the individual leader (Bennis and Nanus, 1985; Meindl, Erlich and Dukerich, 1985; Gupta, 1984).

If the field of strategic management is to render the concept of strategic vision suitable for its own purposes it must deal with it in a unique way. That is what we set out to do in this paper, proceeding from three assumptions that differ from those of the traditional leadership literature. First, we assume that visionary leadership is a dynamic, interactive phenomenon, as opposed to a unidirectional process. Second, we assume that the study of strategic vision must take into consideration strategic content as well as the strategic contexts of product, market, issue, process, and organization. Third, we assume that visionary style can take on a variety of different forms. [ ... ]

## Visionary Leadership as Drama

As noted, visionary leadership is increasingly being defined as a process with specific steps, by and large as follows:

vision (idea) → communication (word) → empowerment (action)

The process, in its emphasis on active leadership and unidirectional flow, may be likened to a hypodermic needle, with the active ingredient (vision) loaded into a syringe (words) which is injected into the patient (subordinate) to effect change. Stripped to its essence, this model takes on a mechanical quality which surely robs the process of much of its evocative appeal.

An alternative image of visionary leadership might be that of a drama. Here action and communication occur simultaneously. Idea and emotion, actor and audience, are momentarily united in a rich encounter which occurs on many symbolic levels. Peter Brook (1968), the legendary director of the Royal Shakespeare Company, has suggested that the magic of the theatre lies in that moment when fiction and life somehow blend together. It may be brief, but it is the goal of playwright, director, actor, and audience, the result of 'rehearsal', the 'performance' itself, and the 'attendance' of the audience. Brook, however, finds these words too static, and prefers the French equivalents 'repetition', 'representation' and 'assistance' (p. 154), all of which, coincidentally, have special meanings in English. We wish to suggest that these words may equally be substituted to describe strategic vision, suggesting a dynamic model as follows, each stage of which we then discuss in turn.

repetition    ⇔    representation    ⇔    assistance

(idea)                 (vision)        (emotion and action)

## Repetition

Repetition, according to Brook, beautifully captures the endless practice in which every artist must engage. He notes that Lawrence Olivier would repeat his lines again and again until he had so trained his tongue muscles to say them that he could perform effortlessly (p. 154). Repetition is likewise the musician practising her scales until she can be consistent every time, so that while she performs she can think about the music itself rather than the individual notes.

For the strategic visionary, repetition has a similar role – to develop an intimacy with the subject at hand, to deal with strategy as 'craft', as one of us has noted elsewhere:

> Craft evokes the notions of traditional skill, dedication, perfection through the mastery of detail. It is not so much thinking and reason that spring to mind as involvement, a sense of intimacy and harmony with the materials at hand, developed through long experience and commitment. (Mintzberg, 1987, p. 66)

Like the craftsman, the strategic visionary would appear to develop strategic perception as much through practice and gut-level feel for the business, product, market, and technology, as through conscious cognition. Lee Iacocca 'grew up' in the auto industry. When he left Ford he went to Chrysler because cars were 'in his blood' (Iacocca, 1984, p. 141). Jan Carlzon, hailed as a visionary for his turnaround at SAS airlines, has spent his entire career (beginning in 1968) in the travel business, since 1978 in the airline industry. Consider how Edwin Land describes his invention of the Polaroid camera:

> One day when we were vacationing in Santa Fe in 1943 my daughter, Jennifer, who was then 3, asked me why she could not see the picture I had just taken of her. As I walked around that charming town, I undertook the task of solving the puzzle she had set for me. Within the hour the camera, the film and the physical chemistry became so clear that with a great sense of excitement I hurried to the place where a friend was staying to describe to him in detail a dry camera which would give a picture immediately after exposure.

In my mind it was so real that I spent several hours on this description. (Land, 1972, p. 84)

Reading this description, it is easy to focus on the element of inspiration, of an idea seemingly springing fully blown, from nowhere. What might be forgotten is that Land had spent years in the laboratory perfecting the polarization process, schooling his scientific and inventive abilities, practising and repeating, learning his craft. His inspiration fell on fertile ground, prepared by endless repetition. As Land himself said:

It was as if all that we had done...had been a school and a preparation both for that first day in which I suddenly knew how to make one-step dry photographic process and for the following three years in which we made the very vivid dream into a solid reality. (Wensbergh, 1987, p. 85)

In a sense the strategic visionary practises for the moment of vision, much as the actor practises for the moment of performance. But for strategy to become vision, craft is not enough. Repetition can become deadly, rigidifying innovation into imitation. Strategic visionaries are leaders who use their familiarity with the issues as a springboard to innovation, who are able to add value by building new perceptions on old practices.

## Representation

For the actor, the performance itself is what must transform repetition into success. Brook chooses the word 'representation' to describe this transformation. To represent means to take the past and make it live again, giving it immediacy, vitality. In a sense, representation redeems repetition, turning it from craft into art.

But what corresponds to the work of art for the strategic visionary? It is, of course, the vision itself. But not the vision as a private mental image. Rather, it is the vision articulated, the vision *represented* and communicated, in words and in actions. Just as a leader cannot exist without followers, so too strategic vision cannot exist without being so recognized by followers.

For this reason we equate visionary leadership not just with an idea *per se*, but with the communicated idea. Here we are concerned with the profoundly symbolic nature of visionary leadership. What distinguishes visionary leadership is that through words and actions, the leader gets the followers to 'see' his or her vision – to see a new way to think and act – and so to join their leader in realizing it. *How* the vision is communicated thus becomes as important as *what* is communicated. Edwin Land understood this as well. He argued that inventions have two parts: the product itself, which must be 'startling, unexpected and come to a world which is *not* prepared', and the 'gestalt' in which the product is embedded:

> The second great invention for supporting the first invention is finding how to relate the invention itself to the public. It is the public's role to resist. All of us have a miscellany of ideas, most of which are not consequential. It is the duty of the inventor to build a new gestalt for the old one in the framework of society. And when he does his invention calmly and equitably becomes part of everyday life and no one can understand why it wasn't always there. But until the inventor has done both things [product and gestalt] nothing has any meaning. (Land, 1975, p. 50)

And how is such a gestalt created? Here again, the metaphor of drama is useful. When the actor represents the play, he or she draws upon a variety of verbal and nonverbal resources. The voice, the face, the gesture, the language itself, the timing, the costume, the lighting, the staging, all combine in an intricate weave to arouse and inspire the audience to create a living gestalt. There is much to suggest that the visionary leader shares many of the actor's skills in representing his or her strategic vision.

For example, one is hard-pressed to find an example of a visionary leader who was not also adept at using language. Language has the ability to stimulate and motivate, not only through appeals to logic but also through appeals to emotion (Burke, 1950; Pfeffer, 1981; Edelman, 1964). Rhetoricians since Aristotle have carefully observed the potential of linguistic devices such as alliteration, irony, imagery, and metaphor, among other things, to provoke identification and emotional commitment among listeners. The speeches of famous visionary leaders such as Winston Churchill and Martin Luther King offer good examples of the skillful use of such rhetorical devices, which allow their listeners to 'see' the visions as if they were real. Analysis of Lee Iacocca's leadership in the Chrysler turnaround suggests that much of the power of his strategic initatives resided in his use of metaphors to unite stakeholders behind him (Westley and Mintzberg, 1988). Likewise, Edwin Land inspired his employees not only with his inventions, but also with the evocative imagery with which he surrounded them. In a short statement on photography (Land, 1972), Land suggested that it was a way of retaining the shifting, fleeting world of childhood and thus giving the child 'a new kind of security'. Sharing photographs was to him an act of intimacy; to show someone a photograph you took was to give them a 'deeper insight into you as well as what you discerned'. Land presented his new camera as follows:

> It will help [the photographer] to focus some aspect of his life and in the process enrich his life at that moment. This happens as you focus through the view finder. It's not merely the camera you are focusing: you

are focusing yourself. That's an integration of your personality, right that second. Then when you touch the button, what's inside you comes out. It's the most basic form of creativity. Part of you is now permanent. (Land, 1972, p. 84)

In a similar fashion, Steven Jobs decribed the Macintosh as an 'insanely great' product, which will 'make a difference'. He described his co-workers as 'the people who would have been poets in the sixties and they're looking at computers as their medium of expression rather than language' (Jobs, 1984, p. 18). On the Apple Computer Company itself, Jobs said: 'There's something going on here ... something that is changing the world and this is the epicenter' (Jobs, 1984, p. 18). As Steve Wozniak, the co-founder with Jobs of the Apple Computer Company, tersely noted: 'he can always couch things in the right words' (Patterson, 1985).

In addition to language, the visionary leader can use a range of dramaturgical devices capable of stimulating and arousing responses. Nonverbal elements such as gesture (Hall, 1959), glance (Goffman, 1959), timing (Wrapp, 1967), movement, and props are also able to evoke similar responses. For example, Steve Jobs organized the Apple office as a circle of work areas around a central foyer. There stood a grand piano and a BMW. 'I believe people get ideas from seeing great products', Jobs claimed (Wise, 1984, p. 146).

In sum, the media of communication for the visionary are many and varied. By wedding perception with symbols the visionary leader creates a vision, and the vision, by evoking an emotional response, forms a bridge between leader and follower as well as between idea and action.

## Assistance

Brook argues that for repetition to turn into representation requires more than practice, more than craft, more than the power of word and gesture. An audience is needed. But not a passive audience. It must be active, hence the importance of 'assistance'.

Brook tells of an ingenious experiment to show what audience assistance entails (1968, pp. 27–29). During a lecture to a lay group he asked a volunteer to come to the front and do a reading. The audience, predicting that the volunteer would make a fool of himself, began to titter. But Brook had given the volunteer a passage from Peter Weiss' play on Auschwitz, which recounted with great clarity a description of the dead. The volunteer was too 'appalled' by what he was reading to pay much attention to the titters, and something of his attitude was communicated to the audience. It became quieter. As the volunteer was moved by what he was reading, he delivered the text with exactly the right pacing and intonations, and the audience responded with 'shocked, attentive silence' (p. 28).

Next Brook asked for a second volunteer. This time the text was a speech from Henry V listing the names of English and French dead at the battle of Agincourt. Recognizing Shakespeare, the volunteer launched into a typically amateur rendition: false voice, stilted phrasing, etc. The audience grew restless and inattentive. At the finish Brook asked the audience why the list of the dead at Agincourt did not evoke the same response as the description of the dead at Auschwitz. A lively discussion ensued. Brook then asked the same volunteer to read again, but to stop after each name. During the short silence the audience was to try to put together the images of Auschwitz and Agincourt. The reader began. Brook recounts:

> As he spoke the first name, the half silence became a dense one. Its tension caught the reader, there was an emotion in it, shared between him and them and it turned all his attention away from himself on to the subject matter he was speaking. Now the audience's concentration began to guide him: his inflections were simple, his rhythms true: this in turn increased the audience's interest and so the two-way current began to flow. (p. 29)

Like a performance, a strategy is made into vision by a two-way current. It cannot happen alone, it needs assistance. Elsewhere we have argued that part of what made René Lévesque and Lee Iacocca effective as leaders was the temporal significance of their vision: they appealed powerfully to the specific needs of specific stakeholders at a specific time. Indeed, there are important instances when the 'followers' stimulate the leader, as opposed to the other way around. In most cases, however, it would appear that leader and follower participate together in creating the vision. The specific content – the original idea or perception – may come from the leader (though it need not, as in the case of Levesque), but the form which it takes, the special excitement which marks it, is co-created. As Brook put it: 'there is only a practical difference between actor and audience, not a fundamental one' (1968, p. 150). Recall Land's description of hurrying to tell his friend of his vision of the camera. Why was he not content to keep the idea to himself? For the same reason an actor is not content to perform before the mirror. Vision comes alive only when it is shared.

This is captured dramatically in this century's most infamous example of visionary leadership. Shortly before Adolph Hitler came to power, Albert Speer attended one of his lectures. Arriving skeptical, Speer left a convert.

> I was carried away on the wave of enthusiasm which, one could almost feel this physically, bore the speaker along from sentence to sentence. It swept away any skepticism, any reservations ... Hitler no longer seemed to be speaking to convince; rather, *he seemed to feel that he was expressing what the audience, by now transformed into a single mass, expected of him.* It was as if it were the most natural thing in the world ... .(Speer, 1970, p. 18; italics added)

Thus the visionary leader not only empowers his audience; it also empowers him. On leaving Apple, Steve Jobs was described as 'its heart and soul' (Patterson, 1985) and Lévesque was seen as speaking for the little people of Quebec, the average French Canadians whom he loved.

One final word about our analogy. The early Greek and Roman rhetoricians were particularly sensitive to the need for integrity among those who used the power of word and gesture (Burke, 1950). In this sense visionary leadership is distinct from theatre. The actor can play a different person each month and still be considered a good actor. Ironically, the visionary leader who, through similar inconsistency, is labelled a good actor, risks losing credibility. Even before Steven Jobs left Apple, accusations that he was facile, inconsistent, and lacked integrity surfaced. 'He should be running Walt Disney. That way every day when he has some new idea, he can contribute to something different', one Apple manager complained (Cocks, 1983, p. 26). In contrast, Edwin Land's belief that other people in the organization should have the same rich, varied job as himself, the fact that he used similar symbols to describe his products, his organization, and his own life (as we shall describe in greater detail below) enabled stakeholders to trust him. They knew that the same power he used to move them moved him. It is this integrity – this sense of being truly genuine – which proves crucial to visionary leadership, and makes it impossible to translate into a general formula.

In summary, the use of the metaphor of drama has allowed us to construct an alternative model of visionary leadership, one of dynamic interaction rather than unidirectional flow, a process of craft and repetition rather than simple cognition, brought to bear in the communication of affect as well as effect. Vision as leadership is a drama which takes place in time. As in theatre, a leader can have a 'bad house' – a passive, unresponsive organization. Only at the right time with the right leader and the right audience can strategy become vision and leadership become visionary.

## Varieties of Visionary Leadership

All that we have described so far we believe to be common to visionary leadership in general. But in other regards contexts vary, issues vary, leaders vary. If vision is a drama, then script, direction, actors, staging, and audience may all vary; many combinations can produce vivid, exciting representation.

What drives the strategic visionary? What is the nature of his or her particular attributes, his or her particular ideas?

Firstly, just as recent theories of the mind suggest there is not one but multiple kinds of intelligence (Gardner, 1983), so too the notion of vision seems to involve a variety of mental capacities, what can be called *visionary style*. In particular, vision has been equated with a capacity for 'imagination', 'inspiration', 'insight', 'foresight', and 'sagacity' (*Oxford English Dictionary*). An analysis of some of the visionary leaders we have encountered in our research suggest that individual leaders exhibit characteristic styles in which certain of these capacities are salient, while the others, though present, remain secondary.

Secondly, visionary style is expressed through *strategic process*. We identify two elements of this – its mental origin and its evolution. *Mental origin* refers to that combination of mental and social dynamics, particular to the individual, that gives rise to the vision in the first place. For example, vision may arise primarily through introspection or interaction, or through the combination of the two. *Evolution* refers to the deliberateness and pace of development of the vision. Some visions develop more deliberately, through controlled conscious thought. Others emerge through a less conscious learning process. Also, some appear suddenly (like a visitation), others build up gradually, piece by piece over time in an incremental process. We might also note the aspect of intensity, which refers to the degree to which the vision possesses the visionary and those surrounding him/her, and durability, which refers to the persistance of the vision, ranging even beyond the career of the visionary as it infuses the behaviour of an organization for generations.

Thirdly is the *strategic content* of the vision. Vision may focus on products, services, markets, or organizations, or even ideals. This is its strategic component, the central image which drives the vision. We refer to this as the *core* of the vision. In addition to this, every vision is surrounded by a kind of halo designed to gain its acceptance. It is this component, comprising its symbolic aspects of rhetorical and metaphorical devices, which we refer to as its circumference. Often, however, unless the vision focuses on a very tangible product [ ... ], the line between core and circumference is blurred. We should also note that the value added by the visionary may lie in the circumference alone, the core alone, or in the core and circumference in a gestalt combination. That is, leaders can sometimes charge rather ordinary products or markets, etc. with strategic vision, or create novel products of markets. The most exciting cases, however, inevitably involve novelty of both, integrated together.

Fourthly, and last, there are variations in *external context* that influence the visionary process. The nature of the organization itself can vary, in ownership, in structure, in size, in developmental stage, etc., for example, being public or private, developing entrepreneurial or mature turnaround. So too can the industry and the broader environment, from traditional mass production to contemporary high technology, etc.

In a previous paper (Westley and Mintzberg, 1988), we probed into the relevance especially of the contextual and stylistic factors through a comparison of the visionary leadership of Lee Iacocca and René Lévesque. Here we draw on that material and also extend the analysis to some of the other factors in considering [ ... ] visionary leaders [ ... ]. As shown in Table 13.1, we consider [ ... ] five distinct styles of visionary leadership.

**Table 13.1** Varieties of leadership style

| Characteristic style | Salient capacities | Content | Process | Organization content | Product/market context | Target group |
|---|---|---|---|---|---|---|
| Creator | Inspiration, imagination, foresight | Product focus | Sudden, holistic; introspective, deliberate | Start-up, entrepreneurial | Invention and innovation, tangible products, niche markets | Independent consumer, scientific community |
| Proselytizer | Foresight, imagination | Market focus | Emergent, shifting focus, interactive, holistic | Start-up, entrepreneurial | Tangible product, adaptation, mass market | Collective market, competitor infrastructure |
| Idealist | Imagination, sagacity | Ideals focus | Deliberate, deductive, introspective, incremental | Turnaround, public bureaucracy | Political concepts, zero-sum market | General population, 50% market share |
| Bricoleur | Sagacity, foresight, insight | Product/organization focus | Emergent, inductive, interactive, incremental | Revitalization, turnaround, private and public bureaucracy | Product development; segmented, oligopolistic markets | Government (in Chrysler), union, customers |
| Diviner | Insight, sagacity, inspiration | Service focus | Incremental, sudden crystallization, interactive | Revitalization, bureaucracy | Service development and innovation, mass oligopolistic market | Employees |

## The Creator

The creator visionary is characterized by two qualities: the originality of his or her ideas or inventions and the sudden, holistic quality of their realization. Vision for the creator occurs in moments of inspiration, which seize the leader suddenly and unexpectedly and which become, for that leader, a driving preoccupation, a single-minded focus which evokes, at least metaphorically, the notion of all eyes turned in a single direction. Such vision is often experienced as deriving from a source outside the self, as in the classic case of religious leaders who claim to be the receptacles or channels of divine inspiration. [ ... ]

## The Proselytizer

[ ... ]
The proselytizer is the most dependent of the five visionary styles. While creators rely on others to *enact* their vision, proselytizers depend on others to *stimulate* their vision. [ ... ]

One of the potential pitfalls for proselytizers, however, is that they may come to forget this dependence. With success they may believe that, like creators, their vision is responsible for the existence of their products. [ ... ]

## The Idealist

An idealist is someone who speculates on the ideal, who dreams intensely of perfection and minimizes or ignores the flaws and contradictions of the real. As a visionary capacity idealism must have an appeal, it must crystallize the dreams of a constituency. But, like the creator, the source of the idealist's inspiration is essentially introspective, not interactive. He or she is inspired by ideas, his or her own or those already created. Idealism in its extreme form is no more responsive to social interaction than is the creator's inspired invention. But for the idealist this can present a problem. If the idealistic capacities characteristic of the visionary leader are overdeveloped at the expense of other more interactive capacities, the individual will not long be a leader. Thus the idealistic visionary may have to be a pragmatist, to mix considerable political sagacity with his or her idealism in order to animate the vision, and to avoid alienating stakeholders. Of course, we are more likely to find what we are labelling the idealistic visionary in a missionary-type organization than in a conventional business corporation. [ ... ]

The difficulty for the idealist [ ... ] is that he or she has to sell an abstract concept. [ ... ] All strategists have to manage ideas, often in the form of analysis or debates, simply because every strategy is at its roots no more than an abstract concept that has to be seen in the mind's eye. But some strategies can at least come to life in tangible ways – for example, as products that flow off assembly lines. For others, where this is not true, strategy-making becomes that much more of a vulnerable process. [ ... ]

For idealists to implement their vision they must convince people to accept it in its entirety. They must convince them not only to execute a plan but also to accept the values which undergird that plan. This process may resemble a conversion. But when such an 'ideal' vision is broken into distinct parts it may not be possible to reassemble it later. In the realization of ideals, [ ... ] the whole is greater than the sum of its parts. [ ... ]

## The Bricoleur

The term 'bricoleur' refers to a common figure in France: a man who frequents junkyards and there picks up the stray bits and pieces which he then puts together to make new objects. This image, drawn from Levi-Strauss (1955), was originally intended to be a metaphor for myth-making. Here we use it to suggest both the myth-making capacity of certain visionary leaders and their capacity for building, whether that be organizations, teams, designs or ideologies. In contrast with the creator and to some extent the idealist, the bricoleur's genius resides not in an introspective ability to invent or imagine, but rather in an interactive, social ability to 'read' situations and recognize the essential (insight), to understand and deal with people (sagacity), and to project these essential understandings into the future for promotional purposes (foresight).

[ ... ] The bricoleur is more of a learner than the other strategists so far discussed, and his or her strategies are less deliberate, more emergent. [ ... ]

## The Diviner

The salient capacity of what we are calling the diviner is insight, which comes with great clarity in moments of inspiration. In this respect the diviner is like the creator: his insights have the quality of something new and fresh, of coming into the mind like a visitation. However, unlike the creator, the insights of our diviner visionary tend to focus on process as opposed to product, for example on how to conceive or structure the organization; in fact, in the ability to use his or her capacities to build organizations, the diviner resembles the bricoleur. [ ... ]

Our final type of visionary is again largely inductive, his or her vision – both core and circumference – largely emergent, followed by a more clearly deliberate period of vision enactment. A sharper vision appears here than in the case of [ ... ] the bricoleur, and certainly one that is more original. [ ... ]

# Conclusions

[ ... ] We have suggested that visionary leadership can vary importantly from leader to leader. The style of the leader may vary, as may the content of the leader's vision and the context in which it takes root. The core of the vision may focus on product or service, market, process, organization or ideals; its circumference involves the rhetoric and metaphor of persuasion. The envisioning process may be ignited by introspection or interpersonal interaction. It may be experienced by the leader as deliberate or emergent, and as a sudden visitation or a series of incremental revelations. It may vary in intensity and in duration. The possibilities are enormous; other leaders may reveal other categories. Our intention has not been to present any firm typology so much as to indicate the possibilities for variations in visionary style, and to map out some important dimensions of visionary leadership.

Thus, *strategic vision* is part style, part process, part content, and part context, while *visionary leadership* involves psychological gifts, sociological dynamics and the luck of timing. True strategic visionaries are both born and made, but they are not self-made. They are the product of the historical moment.

Our research suggests that, despite their great skills, it is a mistake to treat leaders [ ... ] as possessing superhuman qualities. They are the product of their times, of their followers, of their opportunities. As times and contexts change the visionaries of yesterday fade into obscurity, or worse, become the villains of today. [ ... ]

We should emphasize that visionary leadership is not always synonymous with good leadership. [ ... ] Leaders in many contexts can be effective without being visionary, and their organizations may be happier places. [ ... ]

Overall, the study of visionary leadership and strategic vision offers the opportunity for a rewarding and revitalizing interchange between the fields of leadership studies and strategic management. Concepts of strategy introduce consideration of market forces, environmental pressures, and organizational imperatives which form the backdrop for visionary initiatives. Against these features it is to their credit that even the gifted individuals we discussed were able to have such an impact on their organizations and on history. Consideration of that impact – more attention to issues of insight and inspiration, communication and commitment – can help to humanize considerations of strategic management while restoring to leadership study itself some of the flavor that Selznick (1957) sought (largely in vain) to instill 30 years ago.

In the closing lines of his book, Brook makes an observation about the relationship between life and the theatre:

In everyday life, 'if' is a fiction, in the
theatre 'if' is an experiment.

In everyday life, 'if' is an evasion, in the
theatre 'if' is the truth.
When we are persuaded to believe in this truth,
then the theatre and life are one.
This is a high aim. It sounds like hard work.
To play needs much more. But when we
experience the work as play, then it is not work
any more.
A play is play. (p. 157)

If we substitute 'organization' for 'life' and 'vision' for 'theatre', we may begin to understand why strategic vision is stimulating so much interest. The
visionary leader is a transformer, cutting through complex problems that leave
other strategists stranded. Visionary leadership encourages innovation – fiction becomes experiment. Visionary leadership inspires the impossible – fiction
becomes truth. In the book *The Soul of a New Machine,* Tracy Kidder quotes a
secretary who worked for the Eagle Team under the visionary Tom West. Asked
why she didn't leave when so overworked and underappreciated, she replied: 'I
can't leave ... I just have to see how it turns out. I just have to see what Tom's
going to do next' (1981, p. 58). Visionary leadership creates drama; it turns
work into play.

## References

Bass, Bernard M. (1987) 'Charismatic and inspirational leadership: what's the difference?'
  *Proceedings of Symposium on Charismatic Leadership in Management,* McGill University,
  Montreal.
Bennis, Warren (1982) 'Leadership transforms vision into action', *Industry Week,* 31 May,
  pp. 54–56.
Bennis, Warren and Burt Nanus (1985) *Leaders: The Strategies for Taking Charge,* New York,
  Harper and Row.
Brook, Peter (1968) *The Empty Space,* Markham, Ontario, Penguin Books.
Burke, K. (1950) *A Rhetoric of Motives,* Englewood Cliffs, NJ, Prentice-Hall.
*Business Week* (1984) 'A new breed of strategic planner', 17 September, pp. 62–68.
Cocks, J. (1983) 'The updated book of Jobs', *Time,* 3 January, pp. 25–27.
Conger, Jay A. and Rabindra N. Kanungo (1987) 'Towards a behavioral theory of charismatic
  leadership in organizational settings', *Academy of Management Review,* vol. 12, no. 4,
  pp. 637–47.
Edelman, M. (1964) *The Symbolic Uses of Politics,* Urbana, IL, University of Illinois Press.
Gardner, H. (1983) *Frames of Mind,* New York, Basic Books.
Gluck, Frederick W. (1984) 'Vision and leadership', *Interfaces,* vol. 14, no. 1, pp. 10–18.
Goffman, Erving (1959) *The Presentation of Self in Everyday Life,* New York, Doubleday, 1959.
Gupta, Anil K. (1984) 'Contingency linkages between strategy and general manager characteristics:
  a conceptual examination', *Academy of Management Review,* vol. 9, pp. 399–412.
Hall, E. (1959) *The Silent Language,* New York, Doubleday.
Iacocca, Lee with William Novak (1984) *Iacocca: An Autobiography,* New York, Bantam Books.
Jobs, Steven (1984) 'What I did for love', *Advertising Age,* 3 September, p. 18.

Kidder, T. (1981) *The Soul of a New Machine,* New York, Aron Books.

Kiechel, W. (1986) 'Visionary leadership and beyond', *Fortune,* 21 July, pp. 127–28.

Land, E. (1972) 'The most basic form of creativity', *Time,* 26 June, p. 84.

Land, E. (1975) 'People should want more from life...', *Forbes,* 1 June, pp. 48–50.

Levinson, H. and S. Rosenthal (1984) *CEO: Corporate Leadership in Action,* New York, Basic Books.

Lévi-Strauss, Claude (1955) 'The structural study of myth', *Journal of American Folklore,* vol. 68, pp. 428–44.

Meindl, James R., Sanford B. Ehrlich and Janet M. Dukerich (1985) 'The romance of leadership', *Administrative Science Quarterly,* vol. 30, pp. 78–102.

Mendell, Jay S. and Herbert G. Gerjuoy (1984) 'Anticipatory management or visionary leadership: a debate', *Managerial Planning,* vol. 33, pp. 28–31, 63.

Mintzberg, Henry (1987) 'Crafting strategy', *Harvard Business Review,* July–August, pp. 66–75.

Patterson, William P. (1985) 'Jobs starts over – this time as a multi millionaire', *Industry Week,* 30 September, pp. 93–98.

Pfeffer, Jeffery (1981) 'Management as symbolic action: the creation and maintenance of organizational paradoxes' in Straw, B.M. (ed.) *Research in Organizational Behavior,* Vol. 3, Greenwich, CT, JAI Press, pp. 1–52.

Pondy, Louis R. (1978) 'Leadership is a language game'. in McCall, M. J. and M. W. Lombardo (eds) *Leadership: Where Else Can We Go?,* Durham, NC, Duke University Press, pp. 87–99.

Robbins, S. R. and Robert B. Duncan (1987) 'The formulation and implementation of strategic vision: a tool for change', paper presented to the seventh Strategic Management Society Conference, Boston, MA, 14–17 October.

Sashkin, Marshall (1987) 'A theory of organizational leadership: vision, culture and charisma', *Proceedings of Symposium on Charismatic Leadership in Management,* McGill University, Montreal.

Selznick, Philip (1957) *Leadership in Administration: A Sociological Interpretation,* New York, Harper and Row.

Speer, A. (1970) *Inside the Third Reich,* New York, Macmillan.

Srivastva, Suresh and Associates (1983) *The Executive Mind,* San Francisco, CA, Jossey-Bass.

Tichy, Noel M. and Mary Anne Devanna (1986) *The Transformational Leader,* New York, John Wiley and Sons.

Wensbergh, Peter C. (1987) *Land's Polaroid,* Boston, MA, Houghton Mifflin.

Westley, F. and H. Mintzberg (1988) 'Profiles of strategic leadership: Lévesque and Iacocca' in Conger, J. and R. Kanungo (eds) *Charismatic Leadership: The Elusive Factor in Organizational Effectiveness,* San Francisco, CA, Jossey-Bass.

Wise, D. (1984) 'Apple's new crusade', *Business Week,* 26 November, pp. 146–56.

Wrapp, H. Edward (1967) 'Good managers don't make policy decisions', *Harvard Business Review,* vol. 45, May–June, pp. 91–99.

# Charisma under Crisis: Presidential Leadership, Rhetoric, and Media Responses before and after the September 11th Terrorist Attacks

14

*Michelle C. Bligh, Jeffrey C. Kohles and James R. Meindl*

## Introduction

The September 11th terrorist attacks on the World Trade Center, the Pentagon, and Flight 93 have been widely perceived as one of the greatest crises in American history. The events of 9/11 surpassed even the attack on Pearl Harbor in the sheer number of lives lost, and represented not an attack on the American military but on the American public. A report released by the Gallup Organization concluded, 'the American psyche was jolted on September 11th, in a way seldom seen before' (Gillespie, 2001, p. 1). This evidence clearly suggests that in the eyes of the public, the terrorist attacks of September 2001 constituted a significant event that shattered American illusions of safety and invulnerability.

Scholars have long studied crisis and crisis management, and the effects of crisis on the leadership relationship (House, Spangler, and Woycke, 1991; Hunt, Boal, and Dodge, 1999; Lord and Maher, 1991; Pillai, 1996; Pillai and Meindl, 1998; Stewart, 1967, 1976). Using previous theory as a guide, we hoped to understand how the events of 9/11 affected the relationship between

Bligh, M.C., Kohles, J.C. and Meindl, J.R. (2004) 'Charisma under crisis: Presidential leadership, rhetoric, and media responses before and after the September 11th terrorist attacks', *Leadership Quarterly*, vol. 15, pp. 211–39.

the President and the American people. Viewing political leadership as a link or connection between the President and the American citizenry, we sought to uncover how the post-9/11 context impacted the nature and strength of this relationship. Previous theoretical and empirical work suggests that the occurrence of a crisis may significantly affect the relationship between a leader and his or her followers (House et al., 1991; Hunt et al., 1999; Pillai, 1996; Pillai and Meindl, 1998). The plethora of emotions felt in the aftermath of a crisis, including shock, confusion, fear, anger, sorrow, and anxiety, can have a potentially devastating effect on individual self-concepts as well as collective national identity. Times of crisis thus enhance the likelihood that followers will want to invest increased faith in leaders, see leaders as more powerful, and identify more with their leaders as a coping mechanism (Madsen and Snow, 1991).

Pearson and Clair (1998) define a crisis as 'a low-probability, high-impact event that threatens the viability of the organization and is characterized by ambiguity of cause, effect, and means of resolution, as well as by a belief that decisions must be made swiftly' (p. 59). Many Americans perceived the events of 9/11 as an attack not only on the Pentagon and the World Trade Center but also as an attack on their fundamental values and beliefs. The President himself reflected this perspective in his 'Enduring Freedom' speech, in which he noted that in the incipient war, 'we defend not only our precious freedoms, but also the freedom of people everywhere to live and raise their children free from fear.' These comments are indicative of the collective response to the attacks as an assault on the American 'way of life', suggesting that the events of 9/11 threatened the very ideology that America represents to many. As President Bush commented on the day of the assaults: 'Today, our fellow citizens, our way of life, our very freedom came under attack.'

We explore how leadership theory might inform our understanding of the President's response to the crisis of 9/11, as well as the collective response of the American people. The tremendous unease and uncertainty brought about by the terrorist attacks presented an opportunity for the President to act in stronger, more decisive, and potentially more meaningful ways (Lord and Maher, 1991; Stewart, 1967, 1976; Yukl, 2002). In addition, these same feelings of uncertainty likely fostered a greater appreciation for the type of 'strong' leadership often associated with charismatic, transformational leaders.

Following Bandura's (2001) notion of proxy control, accepting a leader's interpretation of events and believing in his or her ability to deal with followers' problems relieve followers of the psychological stress and loss of control created in the aftermath of a crisis. Thus, the emergence of more charismatically based forms of leadership can be viewed as a collective coping mechanism, even a palliative (Meindl, 1993), as followers seek to symbolically and emotionally 'restore their own sense of coping ability by linking themselves to a dominant and seemingly effective leader' (Madsen and Snow, 1991, p. 15). Beyer (1999) notes that perceptions of strong needs in followers, such as a shared perception of a crisis, may drive them to 'socially construct and project qualities on a person to satisfy that need' (p. 581).

This collective desire to identify exceptional qualities in a leader suggests that the leader's qualities themselves may be actual or attributed (see also Shamir and Howell, 1999). Prior to the events of 9/11, President George W. Bush was generally not seen as a strong, charismatic leader that people would place their faith in during times of crisis or external threat. Throughout the first nine months of his presidency, a number of questions surrounded Bush's leadership, including the perils of following a president with high charismatic appeal, questions about foreign policy issues, and the lingering cloud of the election vote-counting debacle. In addition, the media often characterized the President as oratorically challenged and frequently disparaged him for his 'troubled relationship with the English language' (Kornblut, 2001).

Prior to the events of 9/11, there were real concerns about Bush's leadership, and many questioned his ability to rise to the challenge in the immediate aftermath of the attacks. Seemingly overnight, however, Americans embraced the President and his leadership. Before the terrorist attacks, 51% of Americans approved of Bush's job performance, whereas after the attacks, his approval ratings jumped to 86%. This 35-point jump in approval rating is the highest ever measured by the Gallup Organization in its over 60 years of polling history (Jones, 2001).

Did the crisis of 9/11 set the stage for a transformation of the leadership process of the presidency and the relationship between the President and the citizenry? Does this apparent transformation following the events of 9/11 entail a shift toward a more charismatically based relationship, as leadership theory might suggest in the wake of a crisis? And can we find evidence of that shift or transformation in the President's leadership via his public rhetoric and in the media's and the public's reactions to that rhetoric?

Recent theorizing regarding political leadership in times of crisis (e.g., Madsen and Snow, 1991), the self-concept and identity processes associated with charismatic leadership (e.g., Shamir, House, and Arthur, 1993), and the relationship between rhetorical style and charisma provided a framework for our investigations. We devised three studies to explore evidence of changes in the President's public discourse in the wake of 9/11, toward a more charismatic rhetorical style on one hand and in tandem with the attention and reception of both the public and the popular mass media to that rhetoric on the other. In Study 1, we sought to determine whether the crisis of 9/11 caused a 'charismatic shift' in the rhetoric of the President. In Study 2, we examine the extent to which the crisis affected the media's portrayal of and response to the President's rhetoric. Finally, in Study 3 we explore the relationship among the President's charismatic rhetoric, the media's portrayal of the President's speeches, and public approval ratings over time. Together, these studies afforded us an opportunity to understand the shifting mutual expectations regarding leadership that were precipitated by the events of 9/11. [ ... ]

# Study 1

## Method

### Sample

The sample comprised 74 of President Bush's major speeches and radio addresses taken directly from the official website of the White House (http://www.whitehouse.gov). The content analysis program we chose automatically divides each speech into 500-word passages for ease of comparison. Smaller snippets of speeches (less than 100 words) were subsequently deleted from the sample, giving us a final sample of 117 passages ranging from 100 to 500 words (58 precrisis and 59 postcrisis). [ ... ] A major speech was defined as a speech that met one of two criteria: (1) It was listed on the official site of the White House as one of the President's major speeches of his administration, or (2) it was delivered to a prime time audience and therefore represented a specific effort by the administration to address the American public. In addition, radio addresses were included to embody the President's weekly communications to the American people. Thus, this sample is representative of the content of speeches that were specifically addressed to the American public, in a variety of different contexts, before and after the crisis.
[ ... ]

### Collective Focus

According to Shamir et al. (1994), the speeches of charismatic leaders will contain more references to collectives, and fewer references to individual self-interest, when compared with the speeches of noncharismatic leaders. Charismatic leaders are thought to 'articulate visions and goals that motivate their followers toward collective action rather than self-interest' (House et al., 1991, p. 368), and engage in selfless actions, such as personal risk taking and self-sacrifice (House et al., 1988; Waldman and Yammarino, 1999). To examine this proposition, we computed a variable that consisted of a speech segment's additive score on collectives and public references, minus the speech's score on self-reference. Thus, this construct reflects a leader's verbal focus on collectives rather than on individuals and self-referential language.

### Temporal Orientation

Shamir et al. (1994) also suggest that charismatic leaders will make more references to the continuity between past and present. To examine this proposition, we constructed an additive index based on the speaker's references to both the present and the past in the same speaking engagement.

## Follower's Worth

Charismatic leaders have been argued to show confidence in their followers and bolster their collective sense of self-efficacy (House et al., 1991; Shamir et al., 1994). We therefore developed a construct including the inspiration dictionary, which includes celebratory terms and words emphasizing desirable moral and personal qualities. In addition, we included the praise dictionary, which includes positive affirmations of a person, group, or abstract entity, and the satisfaction dictionary, which incorporates terms associated with positive affective states and moments of joy and triumph.

## Similarity to Followers

To tap into the idea that charismatic leaders emphasize their identification with and similarity to followers, we constructed a variable that included the following three variables: leveling, familiarity, and human interest. These dictionaries include language used to ignore individual differences and build a sense of completeness, words that specifically focus on human beings and their activities, and everyday words that reflect a speaker's desire to speak on a common level rather than an elevated level.

## Values and Moral Justifications

Shamir et al. (1994) also theorized that charismatic speakers make more references to values and moral justifications. Stated differently, 'by using symbolic language that challenges and appeals to followers' higher level values, a leader can elicit attributions of charisma' (Awamleh and Gardner, 1999, p. 359). Using [re analysis software's] dictionaries for religious terms and inspiration, we were able to identify speech that focuses on the morality of the leader's cause and draws on themes of values and morality to incite followers to identify with the leader's vision of the future.

## Tangibility

A number of scholars have suggested that charismatic leaders will make more references to intangible future goals and fewer references to concrete, tangible outcomes (Conger, 1991; Shamir et al., 1994; Willner, 1984). To test this notion, we created an index consisting of a speaker's concreteness score, or his or her language denoting tangibility and materiality, minus his or her score on variety. Lower variety represents a speaker's preference for precise speech as opposed to flowery or grandiose speech. Thus, in contrast to the other measures, high scores on this construct are theorized to be associated with lower levels of charisma.

## Action

A bold, purposeful vision and a sense of confidence in attaining that vision are considered important elements of charisma (Conger, 1991). Deluga (1998, p. 287) found that presidential proactivity was an 'important ingredient in the charismatic leader's ability to accomplish impressive results'. Maranell (1970) found that charismatic presidents were more active and took significantly stronger actions during their presidencies than noncharismatic presidents. Therefore, charismatic leaders must mobilize followers into action (Fiol et al., 1999; Shamir et al., 1993), conveying a sense of excitement and adventure (Bass, 1990). To reflect this element of charismatic leadership, we added the [software's] aggression and accomplishment dictionaries and then subtracted the passivity and ambivalent dictionaries. These dictionaries reflect a speaker's additive use of words reflecting competition, action, and triumph, minus his or her use of words reflecting hesitation and uncertainty.

## Adversity

Finally, we created an index reflecting a speaker's references to discontent, hardship, and language designed to 'describe or exaggerate the current situation as intolerable' (Conger, 1991, p. 36). A number of theorists have suggested that a core element of charismatic leadership is the leader's ability to define the intolerable nature of the status quo to motivate followers and generate support for a future mission or vision (Fiol et al., 1999). Thus, we developed the construct of adversity to incorporate language reflective of social inappropriateness, downright evil, unfortunate circumstances, and censurable human behavior.

# Results

The overall means, standard deviations, and intercorrelations for each of the constructs are listed in Table 14.1. A one-way multivariate analysis of covariance (MANCOVA) was conducted to examine whether there were significant differences in Bush's speech before and after 9/11 on the variables of interest. The dependent variables included the eight predefined constructs, and the occurrence of the speech segment (pre- or postcrisis) was the independent factor. [ ... ] Overall, we found significant pre- and postcrisis differences on the dependent

**Table 14.1**  Study 1: Means, *SD*s, and intercorrelations for charismatic constructs

| Variables | M | SD | 1 | 2 | 3 | 4 | 5 | 6 | 7 | 8 |
|---|---|---|---|---|---|---|---|---|---|---|
| N=117 | | | | | | | | | | |
| 1. Collective focus | 10.26 | 9.33 | | | | | | | | |
| 2. Temporal orientation | 19.32 | 5.94 | −.01 | | | | | | | |
| 3. Followers' worth | 24.12 | 9.82 | −.13 | .19* | | | | | | |
| 4. Similarity to followers | 160.42 | 16.52 | .06 | −.01 | .11 | | | | | |
| 5. Values/moral justifications | 5.18 | 4.52 | .37** | −.02 | .22* | .21* | | | | |
| 6. Tangibility | 105.73 | 51.78 | −.10 | .08 | −.16 | −.38** | −.38** | | | |
| 7. Action | 12.63 | 10.49 | .21* | −.14 | −.26** | −.20* | .05 | −.07 | | |
| 8. Adversity | 14.53 | 8.63 | .17 | −.24** | −.17 | .16 | .39** | −.51** | .15 | |

*Notes:* *$p < .05$.
      **$p < .01$.

variables after adjusting for differences in speech length. [ ... ] Thus, we can reject the hypothesis that the charismatic content of Bush's speeches was the same before and after the events of 9/11. [ ... ]

Univariate analyses of covariance (ANCOVA) tests were conducted on each of the dependent variables as follow-up tests to the significant MANCOVA. An overview of the mean differences between pre- and postcrisis speeches on each of the constructs [ ... ] is provided in Table 14.2.

[ ... ] The univariate ANCOVA was significant, indicating that Bush's speeches in the wake of the crisis of 9/11 were more likely to refer to collectives and incorporate group-oriented language. [ ... ]

Examination of the nonadjusted pre- and postcrisis means revealed that the President made more references to the past [ ... ], but fewer references to the present [ ... ], in his speeches following the events of 9/11.

[ ... ] Bush's postcrisis speech was significantly more likely to reference leader–follower similarity and engage in speech reflecting familiarity and human interest. [ ... ]

President Bush's speech after the events of 9/11 was indeed significantly more likely to contain references to values, beliefs, and faith-based principles. [ ... ]

President Bush's speeches in the aftermath of the crisis scored lower on [describing tangible, immediate and recognizable matter] suggesting that his speech became markedly less concrete and tangible after the terrorist attacks when compared to speeches from his first nine months in office. [ ... ]

After the crisis, President Bush's speeches became significantly more active and forceful. Bush's postcrisis speeches contained significantly more language

**Table 14.2**   Study 1: Mean comparisons for charismatic constructs pre- and postcrisis

| Charismatic construct | Precrisis mean | SE | Postcrisis mean | SE | Univariate $F(1, 116)$ | $\eta^2$ | Observed power |
|---|---|---|---|---|---|---|---|
| Collective focus | 7.86 | 1.14 | 12.71 | 1.13 | 8.82** | .08 | .84 |
| Temporal orientation | 20.62 | .78 | 18.12 | .78 | 4.96* | .04 | .60 |
| Followers' worth | 25.80 | 1.25 | 22.47 | 1.24 | 3.43 | .03 | .45 |
| Similarity to followers | 156.31 | 1.99 | 164.68 | 1.97 | 8.57** | .07 | .83 |
| Values/moral justifications | 3.51 | .55 | 6.87 | .55 | 18.15*** | .14 | .99 |
| Tangibility | 120.03 | 6.06 | 92.65 | 6.01 | 9.88** | .08 | .88 |
| Action | 8.42 | 1.24 | 16.53 | 1.23 | 20.77*** | .16 | 1.00 |
| Adversity | 9.82 | 1.01 | 19.00 | 1.00 | 39.40*** | .26 | 1.00 |

Notes: Precrisis $n = 58$, Postcrisis $n = 59$. Means reported are adjusted for the covariates.
  *$p < .05$.
  **$p < .01$.
  ***$p < .001$.

reflective of aggression and accomplishment, and fewer words denoting passivity and ambivalence.

Finally, [ ... ] we found support consistent with this idea: The results of the adversity measure indicate that the President's postcrisis speeches contained significantly more frequent references to hardship and adversity.

# Study 2

Having established that the President's speech did become more rhetorically charismatic after the events of 9/11, we sought to determine whether this effect was reflected in the media's response to the President's rhetoric. The media plays a powerful role in disseminating the President's speeches, commenting on their content and delivery, and analyzing how the American public is receiving them. Thus, the media has an important influence on public perceptions of the President, simultaneously shaping and reflecting current opinion (Krosnick and Brannon, 1993; Pan and Kosicki, 1997; Severin and Tankard, 1997). In addition, due to the large social distance between the President and individual Americans, the media acts as the only source of information about the President's actions and leadership style for a large majority of the American public. Therefore, we sought an impartial analysis of the media's portrayal of the President before and after 9/11 to determine whether the differences we uncovered in the charismatic content of the President's speech were reflected in the media.

The purposes underlying Study 2 were threefold. First, we sought to determine if the changes in the President's rhetoric were reflected in the media's commentary on his rhetoric. In essence, similar findings would lend support to the validity of our findings from Study 1, providing evidence that the differences we uncovered in the speech analysis were important or meaningful enough to be picked up on by the media. [ ... ] Second, we sought to understand how the American public was interpreting the increased charismatic rhetoric in the President's speeches. Was the increased charismatic content in the President's speeches subsequently portrayed as more charismatic? In other words, did the media's portrayal of the President mitigate, ignore, or reflect the changes we uncovered in his speeches? And finally, we sought to uncover whether the media, as both a reflection of and an influence on the mood, desires, and needs of the general public, focused increased attention on those aspects of rhetoric that reflect a more charismatically based, transformed relationship with the President.

## Method

### Sample

The sample comprised articles and transcripts from a variety of media outlets, and incorporated newspapers, magazines, and television news programs chosen to represent the information readily available to the American public regarding the President's speech. Articles and transcripts were obtained through *Lexis–Nexus Academic Universe* using a broad keyword search for 'Bush and speech' to access all references to the President's speech from January 20, 2001, to March 11, 2002. To access content readily available to the American public, sources were limited to newspapers serving major U.S. cities included in the *Lexis–Nexus* database, and magazines were limited to *Newsweek, Time,* and *U.S. News & World Report*. In addition, only television news shows on the major networks were included: ABC, CBS, NBC, CNN, Fox News, MSNBC, and PBS. [ ... ]

## Results

Table 14.3 lists the means, standard deviations, and correlations for each of the eight charismatic constructs. To determine whether the media's portrayal of

**Table 14.3**   Study 2: Means, *SDs,* and intercorrelations for charismatic constructs

| Variables | M | SD | 1 | 2 | 3 | 4 | 5 | 6 | 7 | 8 |
|---|---|---|---|---|---|---|---|---|---|---|
| N = 442 | | | | | | | | | | |
| 1. Collective focus | 9.24 | 9.93 | | | | | | | | |
| 2. Temporal orientation | 14.54 | 5.24 | −.08 | | | | | | | |
| 3. Followers worth | 12.37 | 5.75 | −.16** | .09 | | | | | | |
| 4. Similarity to followers | 147.59 | 15.99 | .01 | .22** | .13** | | | | | |
| 5. Values/ moral justifications | 3.17 | 3.99 | .37** | −.03 | .17** | .11* | | | | |
| 6. Tangibility | 116.14 | 55.47 | .12* | −.07 | −.15** | −.29** | −.20** | | | |
| 7. Action | .77 | 10.01 | .54** | −.18** | −.02 | −.08 | .25** | .07 | | |
| 8. Adversity | 12.37 | 6.42 | .06 | −.20** | −.11* | −.09 | .21** | −.28** | .07 | |

*Note:* * p < .05.
      ** p < .01.

President Bush mirrored his increase in charismatic rhetoric, we conducted a one-way MANCOVA with crisis as the predictor and the same eight charismatic constructs as the criteria. [ ... ] The combined charismatic dependent variables were significantly affected by the occurrence of the crisis [ ... ]. Thus, we can reject the hypothesis that the media's portrayal of the President's speeches was the same before and after the events of 9/11. [ ... ]

The media's analysis of the President's rhetoric contained significantly more references to collectives in the wake of the crisis. In addition, the media's comments on the President's speeches contained more references to his similarity to followers and his focus on human interest. Other significant differences in the media's portrayal of the President after 9/11 include more references to his active, action-oriented language and significantly less commentary on tangible, immediate, concrete, and everyday elements when referring to the President's speeches. In addition, the media's commentary on the President's rhetoric reflected an increased focus on values and morals, and contained significantly less temporally oriented language. Finally, as in Study 1, language reflecting the President's emphasis on followers' worth actually decreased slightly after the crisis, although not significantly so.

# Study 3

The public's judgment of presidential performance plays an important role in policy formation and implementation, as perceptions of presidential popularity partly regulate his ability to influence political events (Krosnick and Brannon, 1993). As Groeling and Kernell (1998, p. 1063) put it, we live in an era in which 'presidents' fortunes increasingly depend on their public support'. The important influence of public polling on the presidency has even led Brace and Hinckley (1993, p. 382) to coin the term 'the public relations presidency' as a reflection of the importance of popular support on the presidency.

In the days and weeks following the crisis of 9/11, Bush's approval ratings skyrocketed to a level that is unprecedented in modern polling history. An analysis of past presidential high points shows that these ratings usually show at least some drop-off shortly after the peak and more sustained decay over time, making Bush's pattern of sustained high ratings throughout this time remarkable by comparison (Jones, 2001). Given these results, it is clear that at least in the public's eye, President George W. Bush's leadership in the wake of the crisis represented a marked improvement over his demonstrated leadership prior to the crisis.

An analysis of high presidential approval ratings over the past five decades illustrates how difficult these gains are to sustain for any appreciable amount of time. Historically, drops of five percentage points or more usually happen shortly after the peak of approval. Prior to George W. Bush, only Lyndon Johnson was able to sustain his approval rating within five points of his highest score for more than a month. In addition, seven of the last eight presidents saw their high ratings decline by at least five points in the very next poll (Jones, 2002). Although presidents such as Franklin Delano Roosevelt and the elder George Bush experienced marked rallying effects immediately after the United States entered into war, research has shown that these rally effects tend to be very short-lived and situationally dependent (see [ ... ] Brody, 1991; Meernik and Waterman, 1996). These historical trends suggest that changes in Bush's leadership style, as reflected in more charismatic speech content and its reflection in the media, might be partially responsible for his ability to sustain these high ratings in the wake of the crisis. To test this idea, we conducted a formal analysis of the public's approval ratings of the President over time, relating them to the crisis event of 9/11, his charismatic rhetoric, and the response of the mass media.

## Method

### *Sample and Procedure*

To examine whether or not the changes in speech and media content were associated with an increase in Bush's public opinion ratings, we first obtained

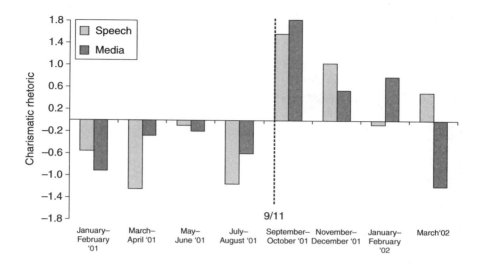

**Figure 14.1**   Charismatic rhetoric of speech and media constructs before and after 9/11

*Note:* This composite plot comprises the six standardized constructs that showed significant change (*p* < .01) before and after 9/11 in Study 1 and Study 2. In addition, Tangibility was reverse coded so that, along with the other constructs, larger numbers reflect higher levels of charismatic rhetoric.

longitudinal presidential approval ratings (encompassing the first 14 months of Bush's presidency) from three of the top polling organizations: (1) *ABC News* and *The Washington Post;* (2) *CNN/USA Today/*Gallup; and (3) *Newsweek* (conducted by Princeton Survey Research Associates). All three of these polling organizations conduct nationwide telephone surveys that ask adult Americans the identical question, 'Do you approve or disapprove of the way George W. Bush is handling his job as President?'

[ ... ]

## Results

[ ... ]

Time-series plots demonstrating trends in overall charismatic rhetoric in the speech and media data sets are shown in Figure 14.1. The results of the [ ... ] analysis show a significant positive coefficient for both the crisis and the combined charisma variables (*p* < .01). The effect of the crisis appears strong and significant in both the speech and the media samples [ ... ]. These results indicate that the occurrence of the crisis was associated with an average polling increase of approximately 16 points after the crisis (see Figure 14.2). The [ ... ] test for the effect of the charismatic index was also significant in both the

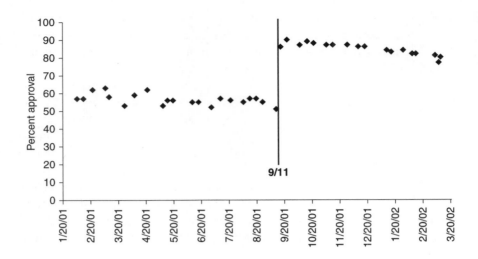

**Figure 14.2**  Public approval ratings before and after 9/11
*Note:* Ratings are averages of responses to the question, 'Do you approve or disapprove of
the way George W. Bush is handling his job as President?' from three separate agencies:
*ABC News* and the *Washington Post; CNN/USA Today/*Gallup; and *Newsweek.*

speech and media samples [ ... ], indicating that the charismatic content of the
previous week was associated with remaining fluctuations in the polls after controlling for the effect of the crisis.

## Discussion

Overall, our results confirm that the occurrence of the 9/11 crisis led to a
change in the rhetoric of the President's communications with the American
public: His rhetoric in the days and weeks following the crisis featured language
that has been theoretically linked to charismatic leadership. Furthermore, and
in parallel, the media's portrayal of the President after 9/11 also incorporated
more charismatic language. Finally, both changes were associated with more
favorable public opinions regarding the President's leadership. Taken together,
these results suggest that the crisis of 9/11 may have transformed the relationship between the President and the U.S. citizenry toward something that is, by
degree, more heavily grounded in charismatic leadership processes than was the
case before the crisis. [ ... ]

Clearly, the President's speeches during the 6-month period after the crisis
did contain detectably more rhetorically charismatic features. But what does
this shift in rhetoric imply about his charismatic stature? Did the President's

underlying personality actually become more charismatic since the early days of his administration, finally blossoming during the days and weeks following the crisis? That seems like a patently remote possibility. As personality-oriented analyses of charismatic leadership indicate (e.g., House et al., 1991), deeply held, enduring motive patterns distinguish between more and less charismatic leadership personalities. Still, it is possible to understand the emergence of charismatic leadership as the result of someone who rises to the special challenges of an extraordinary situation, as in the crisis-responsive model offered by Boal and Bryson (1987) and its partial empirical test by Hunt et al. (1999). It may be that the President had the 'right stuff' all along, with the crisis of 9/11 finally revealing a side of his (charismatic) personality not previously exposed to the American public. This hypothesis is difficult to test at this point, because as far as we know, formal analyses or clinical assessments of President Bush's latent or manifest personality have not been publicly available.

To what extent are the speeches of a president a reflection of his underlying, charismatic personality? Whatever the underlying personality of a president, it is his public persona that is most likely to have an impact on the leadership perceptions of the majority of U.S. citizens. And that public persona is largely created by the public speeches that he delivers (Hart, 1987). One might suggest that professional speechwriters largely control the rhetorical content of what a president delivers in a public speech. Perhaps the President's speechwriters simply crafted the President's speeches in a time of crisis to create the illusion of a more charismatic leader. On the other hand, it may simply be that President Bush is rhetorically more charismatic in his public communications, responding to the needs of the American people who in a time of crisis seek out more 'charismatic' talk.

Leadership represents an intersection of forces and factors associated with the leader, the followers, and the context in which they are embedded. Charismatic leadership also reflects this intersection, as it is not simply or completely defined by the 'charismatic' personality of the leader. What audiences impute as charisma surely depends on the circumstances: In extraordinary situations, a small amount of vision and invocation of collective needs may go a long way in compensating for unpersuasive or awkwardly delivered presentations. The evolution of Bush's rhetoric after the 9/11 crisis represents a compelling case of how leaders can utilize language to galvanize support for overarching causes, almost independently of the original crisis. Within the context of a threatening crisis, when followers feel an acute desire for a charismatically appealing leader, and when a leader adopts a more charismatic style of rhetorical communication – driven to do so either by force of his or her own personality or perhaps by a more strategic goal to create an appealing public persona – surely, the possibilities for the emergence of charismatic leadership are enhanced.

In the present research, we see evidence of this process occurring around the crisis of 9/11. First, the President's decision to act in the wake of the crisis created the need to justify these actions and incite the American people to action, resulting in an increased use of charismatically oriented themes in his rhetoric. Second, the psychological impact of the attacks on the American consciousness created the need for many Americans to identify with and believe in the morality and efficacy of the presidency. Increased media emphasis on the President's charismatic rhetoric may have been in response to the public's need for decisive action, punishment of enemies, and more expressive articulation of collective values and ideals. Taken together, these combined factors represent a potentially fertile ground for charismatic leadership emergence. How great that potential is and how long it lasts are things that perhaps only time will tell.

Several of our findings warrant additional comment. Contrary to our expectations, the President's support for followers' sense of worth actually decreased in the wake of the crisis, and the media similarly focused slightly less on the President's support for followers after 9/11. Several factors may help to explain these findings. First, the events of 9/11 constituted a tremendous crisis in both scope and impact. Therefore, it is perhaps entirely expected that the President's speeches after this tremendous tragedy would incorporate less references to joy, celebration, and positive language. Sigelman, Stoker, and Deering's (2002) content analysis of Bush's post-9/11 radio addresses supports this interpretation. After 9/11, their analyses revealed elevated levels of distress, anxiety, and depression in the President's speeches, reflecting a leader 'thrown off his emotional stride' (p. 20) as he attempted to cope with the aftermath of the tragedy. It is our belief that the President did refer to the worth of the American people after the crisis, but this finding was likely overshadowed by language designed to define the intolerance of the current situation, the evil nature of those responsible for the events of 9/11, and the necessity for war. As the President commented three days after the tragedy:

> It is said that adversity introduces us to ourselves. This is true of a nation as well. In this trial, we have been reminded, and the world has seen, that our fellow Americans are generous and kind, resourceful and brave. We see our national character in rescuers working past exhaustion; in long lines of blood donors; in thousands of citizens who have asked to work and serve in any way possible ... in these acts, and in many others, Americans showed a deep commitment to one another, and an abiding love for our country. Today, we feel what Franklin Roosevelt called 'the warm courage of national unity'.

Our findings suggest that in times of severe crisis and tragedy, positive language such as this is important but may be overshadowed by the need to recognize the horror of the current situation, those responsible for creating it, and the need for change to create a better future.

[ ... ]

--------------------------- *References* ---------------------------

Awamleh, R. and Gardner, W.L. (1999) 'Perceptions of leader charisma and effectiveness: The effects of vision content, delivery, and organizational performance', *The Leadership Quarterly*, vol. 10, no. 3, pp. 345–73.

Bandura, A. (2001) 'Social cognitive theory: An agentic perspective', *Annual Review of Psychology*, vol. 52, pp. 1–26.

Bass, B.M. (1990) *Bass and Stogdill's Handbook of Leadership: Theory, Research, and Managerial Applications* (3rd edn), New York, Free Press.

Beyer, J.M. (1999) 'Two approaches to studying charismatic leadership: Competing or complementary? *The Leadership Quarterly*, vol. 10, pp. 575–88.

Boal, K.B. and Bryson, J.M. (1987) 'Charismatic leadership: A phenomenological and structural approach' in Hunt, J.G., Baliga, B.R., Dachler, H.P. and Schriesheim, C.A. (eds) *Emerging Leadership Vistas*, Lexington, MA, D.C. Heath, pp. 11–28.

Brace, P. and Hinckley, B. (1993. 'Presidential activities from Truman through Reagan: Timing and impact', *The Journal of Politics*, vol. 55, no. 2, pp. 382–98.

Brody, R. (1991) *Assessing the President: The Media, Elite Opinion, and Public Support*, Stamford, CT, Stamford University Press.

Conger, J. (1991) 'Inspiring others: The language of leadership', *Academy of Management Executive*, vol. 5, no. 1, pp. 31–45.

Deluga, R.J. (1998) 'American presidential proactivity, charismatic leadership, and rated performance', *The Leadership Quarterly*, vol. 9, no. 3, pp. 265–91.

Fiol, C.M., Harris, D. and House, R. (1999) 'Charismatic leadership: Strategies for effecting social change', *The Leadership Quarterly*, vol. 10, no. 3, pp. 449–82.

Gillespie, M. (November 19 2001) 'Terrorism reaches status of Korean and Vietnam wars as most important problem', *Poll Analyses*. Retrieved 12 December, 2001, from http://www.gallup.org.

Groeling, T. and Kernell, S. (1998) 'Is network news coverage of the president biased? *Journal of Politics*, vol. 60, no. 4, pp. 1063–87.

Hart, R.P. (1987) *The Sound of Leadership: Presidential Communication in the Modern Age*, Chicago, IL, University of Chicago Press.

House, R.J., Spangler, W.D. and Woycke, J. (1991) 'Personality and charisma in the US presidency: A psychological theory of leader effectiveness', *Administrative Science Quarterly*, vol. 36, pp. 364–95.

House, R.J., Woycke, J. and Fodor, E.M. (1988) 'Charismatic and noncharismatic leaders: Differences in behavior and effectiveness' in Conger, J.A. and Kanungo, R.N. (eds) *Charismatic Leadership*, San Francisco, CA, Jossey-Bass, pp. 98–121.

Hunt, J.G., Boal, K.B. and Dodge, G.E. (1999) 'The effects of visionary and crisis-responsive charisma on followers: An experimental examination of two kinds of charismatic leadership', *The Leadership Quarterly*, vol. 10, no. 3, pp. 423–48.

Jones, J.M. (November 7 2001) 'Bush's high approval ratings among most sustained for presidents', *Poll Analyses*. Retrieved 22 December 2001, from http://www.gallup.org.

Jones, J.M. (March 21 2002) Bush approval showing only slight decline six months after record high. *Poll Analyses*. Retrieved March 23, 2002 from http://www.gallup.org.

Kornblut, A.E. (February 12 2001). 'As a speaker, Bush is gaining command. Confidence, effort improve delivery', *Boston Globe (A1)*.

Krosnick, J.A. and Brannon, L.A. (1993) 'The impact of the Gulf War on the ingredients of presidential evaluations: Multidimensional effects of political involvement', *American Political Science Review*, vol. 87, no. 4, pp. 963–75.

Lord, R.G. and Maher, K.J. (1991) *Leadership and Informational Processing: Linking Perceptions and Performance*, Boston, MA, Unwin Hyman.

Madsen, D. and Snow, P.G. (1991) *The Charismatic Bond: Political Behavior in Time of Crisis*, Cambridge, MA, Harvard University Press.

Maranell, G.M. (1970) 'The evaluation of presidents: An extension of the Schlesinger polls', *Journal of American History*, vol. 57, pp. 104–13.

Meernik, J. and Waterman, P. (1996) 'The myth of the diversionary use of force by American presidents', *Political Research Quarterly*, vol. 49, no. 3, pp. 573–590.

Meindl, J.R. (1993) 'Reinventing leadership: A radical, social psychological approach' in Murnighan, K. (ed.) *Social Psychology in Organizations: Advances in Theory and Research*, Englewood Cliffs, NJ, Prentice-Hall, pp. 89–118.

Pan, Z. and Kosicki, G.M. (1997) 'Priming and media impact on the evaluations of the president's performance', *Communication Research*, vol. 24, pp. 3–30.

Pearson, C.M. and Clair, J.A. (1998) 'Reframing crisis management', *Academy of Management Review*, vol. 23, no. 1, pp. 59–76.

Pillai, R. (1996) 'Crisis and the emergence of charismatic leadership in groups: An experimental investigation', *Journal of Applied Social Psychology*, vol. 26, no. 6, pp. 543–62.

Pillai, R. and Meindl, J.R. (1998) 'Context and charisma: A "meso" level examination of the relationship of organic structure, collectivism, and crisis to charismatic leadership', *Journal of Management*, vol. 24, no. 5, pp. 643–64.

Severin, W.J. and Tankard, J.W. (1997) *Communications Theories: Origins, Methods, and Uses in the Mass Media*, New York, Longman.

Shamir, B., Arthur, M.B. and House, R.J. (1994) 'The rhetoric of charismatic leadership: A theoretical extension, a case study, and implications for research', *The Leadership Quarterly*, vol. 5, no.1, pp. 25–42.

Shamir, B., House, R.J. and Arthur, M.B. (1993) 'The motivational effects of charismatic leadership: A self-concept based theory', *Organization Science*, vol. 4, no. 4, pp. 577–94.

Shamir, B. and Howell, J.M. (1999) 'Organizational and contextual influences on the emergence and effectiveness of charismatic leadership', *The Leadership Quarterly*, vol. 10, no. 2, pp. 257–83.

Sigelman, L., Stoker, R.P. and Deering, C.J. (2002) *Post-Traumatic Stress in the White House? An Interrupted Time-Series Analysis of George W. Bush's Rhetoric*, Unpublished manuscript.

Stewart, R. (1967) *Managers and Their Jobs: A Study of the Similarities and Differences in the Way Managers Spend Their Time*, London, Macmillan.

Stewart, R. (1976) *Contrasts in Management*, Berkshire, England, UK, McGraw-Hill.

Waldman, D.A. and Yammarino, F.J. (1999) 'CEO charismatic leadership: Levels-of-management and levels-of-analysis effects', *Academy of Management Review*, vol. 24, no. 2, pp. 266–85.

Willner, A.R. (1984) *The Spellbinders: Charismatic Political Leadership*, New Haven, CT, Yale University Press.

Yukl, G.A. (2002) *Leadership in Organizations* (5th edn), Englewood Cliffs, NJ, Prentice-Hall.

# Can Leadership be Taught? Perspectives from Management Educators

# 15

## Jonathan P. Doh

Leadership is an increasingly ubiquitous subject in business school curricula, a theme of popular business books, and a topic for academic and practitioner research. Leadership research has blossomed: It is now a primary focus of great bodies of scholarly and practitioner research and the domain of more than a dozen journals. Concurrently, undergraduate, graduate, and executive management institutes, programs, and courses directed toward training future leaders and improving leadership skills have proliferated. Historically, there has been debate over whether leadership is a skill, trait, or innate behavior. Although most management educators now agree that leadership is both a skill and a behavior that exhibits that skill, this dual definition has generated additional disagreement over whether leadership can be taught. That question is the primary focus of this forum.

To provide initial observations regarding the question of whether leadership can be taught and to explore the subsidiary issues of the potential effectiveness of leadership education, particularly within U.S. business schools, I interviewed leading management scholars involved in leadership research, education, and development. I chose individuals whose research and pedagogical experience related to leadership (broadly defined), but who also had interests and experiences that would allow them to place leadership within the context of the broader goals of management education. All have had experience in executive education or other contexts that allowed them to critically evaluate the questions posed here. I asked these experts to respond briefly to a series of questions about whether leadership can be learned and if so, whether it can be taught. As a subsidiary focus, I inquired as to what approaches and techniques are likely to be most effective in teaching leadership and developing leadership skills, what

Doh, J.P. (2003) 'Can leadership be taught? Perspectives from management educators', *Academy of Management Learning and Education*, vol. 2, no. 1, pp. 54–67.

individuals and groups are most likely to benefit from leadership education, and what institutions or individuals are best positioned to deliver effective leadership courses.

In the selection of these scholars, I sought to include some of the major living contributors to research at the intersection of leadership and education. I wanted to include educators who had researched and engaged in scholarly exchange about leadership as well as made contributions to practice through their writings, consulting, and executive training.

The panel members are Christopher A. Bartlett, Harvard Business School; Kim S. Cameron, University of Michigan Business School; Jay Conger, London Business School and University of Southern California, Los Angeles: Michael A. Hitt, Arizona State University; Stephen Stumpf, Villanova University; and Michael Useem, Wharton School, University of Pennsylvania.

Three interviews were conducted in person during summer and fall, 2001, and three were conducted by way of e-mail exchange during fall, 2001. The face-to-face interviews were recorded. The respondents were given the opportunity to review the abbreviated written transcripts of the interviews to correct factual errors or clarify meaning, but they were not permitted to alter the transcript or change their responses to the questions posed. To further clarify perspectives related to whether leadership could be taught (versus learned), I conducted a short follow-up interview by way of e-mail during January, 2002.

The small sample is limited in several respects. First, with the exception of Chris Bartlett, it is comprised of U.S. management scholars and educators, and therefore, does not reflect a nationally or culturally diverse population (Bartlett is a native of Australia and divides his time between the United States and Australia). Second, there are no women in the sample, and therefore, the views are not fully representative. Third, the responses may not be fully comparable because those who responded to written inquiries were afforded greater opportunity to contemplate and review their responses prior to making them than were those interviewed in person. Nonetheless, this brief review provides some interesting insights into the individual and collective views of these experts. Such insights may begin to clarify some questions about whether leadership can be taught, and more broadly, may inform discussions regarding the role of management education in developing leadership skills.

## Perspectives on Teaching (and Learning) Leadership

Leadership has long occupied a prominent place in management research and education. Leadership has also become a pervasive subject of management education research and practice. Leadership journals have proliferated and leadership courses are now a part of nearly every major business school's curriculum in the country. More than three fifths of the top 50 U.S. business schools as defined by the 2002 *U.S. News and World Report* rankings publicize that they offer some course-work in leadership. In addition, a wide array of leadership research centers, institutes, and programs within and outside of business schools exists. The existence and proliferation of these initiatives presumes that leadership is (1) an important area for management learning; and (2) that business schools are well equipped to undertake the mission of providing training and education in leadership. [ ... ]

Leadership has also become a pervasive subject of management education research and practice. In 1994, James Bailey, writing in *The Journal of Leadership Studies,* found that

> since the inception of the *Journal of Management Education* in 1991, 10 articles (a little under 10%) have appeared that dealt directly with leadership, with a score of others either indirectly or parenthetically evincing the theme. Such pedagogical attention stands as testimony of the importance of leadership concepts in organizational studies, but more pointedly it underscores the need for innovative methods by which these concepts can be communicated to and understood by the management community (Bailey, 1994, p. 32).

A central question that has not, to date, been satisfactorily answered is whether leadership can be taught, and that is the focus of this discussion.

## Can Leadership be Learned?

All the educators indicated belief that leadership could be learned, although each offered a number of caveats and expressed reservations about how, where, and under what conditions such learning can most usefully take place:

*Steve Stumpf:* 'Can leadership be learned? Of course. Leadership is not like breathing if you don't focus your efforts and work at it, you won't be an effective leader. It may be that every person cannot "learn" how to be an effective leader, but we could say the same about learning chess. Everyone does not have the potential to be a master chess player. There are concepts and practices that can be learned (and taught) that will enhance the leadership effectiveness of many people (but not all).'

*Mike Useem:* 'Some managers have a head start in acquiring leadership capacities, but everyone can improve. It is a learned capacity, albeit one that for many proves very difficult to master.'

*Kim Cameron:* 'Some people have an inclination to learn some competencies faster or better than others, of course, and some people reflect more charismatic or likable characteristics than others. But many great leaders are not those that appear on the covers of *Time* and *Fortune*. They have learned to achieve spectacular results in their own circumstances. Think of parents. Can people learn to become better parents, or are we just born either competent or not? Everyone would agree that effective parenting can be learned and improved. So can effective leadership.'

*Jay Conger*: 'Yes, most definitely. Here work experiences, bosses, special projects, role models, education all play a role in leadership development. Using an analogy with sports, ... not everyone can become an outstanding player despite coaching, yet most will benefit and improve their "game". A few will go on to become stars or outstanding leaders given coaching, extensive experiences, and personal drive.'

*Mike Hitt*: 'I'm not of the view that you are either born with a trait or not. Obviously, some people are more prone to be leaders. For example ... some people are more extroverted and some more introverted. And maybe those who are extroverted would be more comfortable in leadership positions ... but the bottom line is, leadership can be learned.'

## Can Leadership be Taught?

Agreeing that some aspects of leadership can be learned is not the same as saying that they can be taught, at least in the formal sense. Most of the management educators agreed that some aspects of leadership could be taught; although, there were differences in their views regarding how successfully leadership skills can be developed through formal courses and coaching. According to many of the experts, whether leadership can be taught is as contingent on the student as on the teacher.

*Jay Conger*: 'Yes [leadership can be taught], but only certain aspects. Let's say that leadership is made up of three different dimensions: skills, perspectives, and dispositions. Many leadership skills can be taught, and to some extent perspectives may be developed and enhanced through education. For example, we can teach how to present ideas more persuasively and communicate more inspirationally. We can also teach aspects of strategic thinking so one's perspective is broadened. At the same time, there is a critical contextual dimension to strategic thinking which is [the] product of immersion in one's field as well as a mental capacity to think more conceptually. These are difficult to teach. In terms of dispositions, these are a product of life, family, and possibly genes. So the latter cannot be taught. For example, we cannot teach a person to be ambitious or to be more open to risk taking – which would be dispositional characteristics.'

*Kim Cameron*: 'Let's take the assumption that the answer is "no". Leadership can't be taught and leadership can't be learned. That means we should change entirely our research and teaching emphasis in universities. We should begin to focus on finding the genetic code that is associated with leadership. Forget theory. Forget models. Forget correlations and predictors. Forget qualitative investigations of great leaders. Close down *Fortune* and *Business Week* and all the leadership journals. Eliminate training and development departments in most companies. If I can't learn it and I can't help someone else improve it, let's stop wasting resources on all this nonsense we pretend to be doing in higher education. If leaders are born not made – and if no one can teach anyone else to improve – let's start investigating leadership in the biology lab rather than in the business world. So yes, unequivocally [leadership can be taught]. Some people have an inclination to learn some competencies faster or better than others, of course, and some people reflect more charismatic or likable characteristics than others.'

*Steve Stumpf*: 'Can leadership be taught? Of course. But the methods of teaching need to focus on creating meaningful experiences from which the student can learn. Book knowledge is only a small part of effective leadership – just as reading a tennis book is only a small part of being an exceptional tennis player. Leadership is a performance sport. Leadership requires both thinking and doing – to the satisfaction of many others with diverse expectations. Hence, most of what is taught as "best practice" is only best practice for a specific audience – one that the particular learner may not encounter. This is what makes it appear that leadership can be learned, but not taught. If we could stop the world, then the teachings would work next time. With the world changing (i.e., every leadership episode being unique, just like the snow flakes that are falling), what is taught – to be useful – must be learned in a personal, applicable, more intuitive way.'

*Mike Hitt*: 'The basic definitions of *teaching* and *learning* are "to impart knowledge" and "to acquire knowledge", respectively. The short answer to your questions is "yes". Obviously, it is a little more complex, however. The knowledge required to perform what my colleagues and I refer to as strategic leadership has both explicit and tacit components. The explicit components are easier to teach. Some of the explicit components include knowledge of the steps necessary to develop a strategy and vision. There are actions required to "empower" employees to take desired actions. However, there are subtle and tacit actions and processes required to gain commitment to a strategy and vision. There are tacit components of empowering employees (building relationships, demonstrating confidence but with humility). Some of the tacit dimensions may be conveyed through experiential teaching, through case discussions and by "learning by doing" – on the job learning such as an internship. But the bottom line is leadership can be taught.'

*Chris Bartlett*: 'If I define leadership to include knowledge, skills, and attitudes, we can certainly teach the knowledge. Leaders have to know about what it is they are leading. For example, a great political leader has to understand the philosophy, structure, and issues of the country he or she leads. This knowledge is transmittable through either formal training or more often through life experience or development. You can't lead something you don't understand. Acquiring the skills can be accomplished through coaching, mentoring, and those fine-grained skills that include the ability to communicate, to see patterns, and to work effectively through others. These are the sorts of things a good mentor would do. But attitudes are, at best, coachable at the margin. But if you believe that all of this is coachable, then we could simply create leaders with ease. But we don't and we can't.'

## How can Leadership be Taught?

As the scholars considered the caveats and conditions associated with the question of whether leadership can be taught, I asked them to identify what techniques might be more (or less) successful in transmitting some of the skills that they believed could be imparted through formal or informal management education. Common themes were that such programs should be highly practical, include training or coaching from practitioners, that students may learn as much or more from failures in leadership as they would in attempting to replicate successes, and that to effectively teach leadership, programs must be tailored to the particular needs, attitudes and circumstances of the students.

*Mike Useem*: 'Managers can begin by engaging those closest to them in a leadership debate, and asking them to do the same with their associates. They can discuss their moments of both success and setback; ask them to synthesize lessons from their own leadership experiences: provide them with personal coaching and individual mentoring; and change the business culture so they can make decisions without acute fear of failure.'

*Steve Stumpf*: 'Once a foundation of ideas about leadership is internalized (from books, cases, discussions, guest speakers), it must be practiced with feedback in realistic, rich environments. These could be simulation settings, client-consulting settings, internships, role-plays and other experiential exercises.'

*Jay Conger*: 'The dimensions of leadership you wish to teach determine the appropriate pedagogy. For example, case studies and action learning may be most useful for developing strategic thinking. Experiential exercises are most useful for teaching and honing behavioral skills such as communications and persuasion. Feedback questionnaires and coaching can be very helpful in benchmarking one's current capacities in leadership. Personal growth methods can be helpful in focusing individuals on what types of work situations they can be most skillful in and most passionate about and therefore have a higher probability of being an effective leader.'

*Kim Cameron*: 'I would cite David Whetten who advocates a learning model consisting of five distinctive (although sometimes overlapping and integrated) learning activities: (1) skill preassessment, (2) skill learning (concepts and best practices), (3) skill analysis, (4) skill practice (with feedback), and (5) skill application.'

The approaches described above emphasize, in part, the use of modeling techniques that allow students to learn to pattern behavior based on the experiences of successful leaders. Yet, what is relevant to one individual or group may not be valid for others. Further, some educators argued that such patterning efforts could be self-reinforcing and reflect past practice rather than the potential to impart new knowledge or insight.

*Chris Bartlett*: 'Consultants typically go in and interview a bunch of successful people in the company, and they say, "What does it take to succeed in this organization?" Then they document it and look at the common characteristics and say. "Here are the important competencies that you need in this company." What they've just done is capture what it has taken to succeed in the past, embedded it, and locked it in. There is an assumption that all managers are alike and that the challenges of managers are the same – that there is a universal model of management. I think that what we've got to do is decouple this notion of competencies and think about attitudes and knowledge and skills. We can train development of knowledge, of industries, of companies, and of financial tools. We can teach knowledge and develop skills. We can coach people on how to be more effective team players. We can teach them on how to interpret data and think through analysis to recommendation and implementation. But the attitudes part is the harder one.'

*Steve Stumpf*: 'Leadership must go beyond cognitions to actions, communications, inspiring others, and being a role model. There is a difference between a leadership position (a position of power and authority) and leading. If one has no "free will" followers, they are not a "leader" in the sense we mean in management. When a person in a position of authority tells someone subordinate to them to do something – or else – that person is not leading. We should reserve the term *leadership* to something other than directing or coercing.'

*Jay Conger*: 'In terms of "faculty", the ideal leadership development program would include three groups of "instructors". The first would be a small group of faculty who have a depth of knowledge about leadership and possess the capacity to teach using a broad range of pedagogies (plus a keen interest in developing an individual's potential). The second set would be a very small handful of company executives who possess teaching skills, are accepted role models for leadership, and are capable of conveying simple but powerful frameworks about leadership that are derived from their work experiences. The final group would include professional trainers and would include individuals most familiar with using experiential and feedback methods extensively.'

Mike Hitt has found that discussing leadership failures may be more effective than focusing on leadership successes:

*Mike Hitt*: 'Unfortunately, we don't always understand why the success occurs. We think we know why, but we really don't. Often times, we can more easily pinpoint why things didn't go well.'

Useem cites Jon Krakauer's book, *Into Thin Air* as an interesting reference for teaching leadership. The book describes how two climbing groups, simultaneously nearing the summit of Everest, were hit by a violent storm, and how each responded differently to the challenges they faced. His perspective echoes Mike Hitt's comments:

*Mike Useem*: 'It is useful to ask what went right and why so many things went so terribly wrong – for the leaders of the two teams as they desperately sought safety.'

In this particular case, blind ambition to reach the top, and a consistent record of placing individual interests ahead of collective ones, appeared to have caused a lapse in judgment and leadership.

## To Whom can Leadership be Taught?

Not surprisingly, most of the management educators believe that individuals who are motivated to acquire leadership skills and character and who are actively seeking leadership positions are the best subjects for leadership education. However, here again, the educators suggest that not everyone is naturally poised to acquire leadership capability:

*Kim Cameron*: 'Leadership education is most effectively presented to those who are aware that they must be leaders. Often, MBAs or undergraduates do not yet have the experience, nor do they have the perspective that makes leadership a relevant topic. Neither urgency nor importance is attached to leadership development. After these students' first promotion, however – or their first toddler or teenager – leadership becomes a more relevant topic. It is then that leadership education becomes a passionate pursuit. [Hence,] knowing why, and feeling the need, are prerequisites to great leadership development.'

Mike Hitt argues that a broader group might benefit from leadership education;

*Mike Hitt*: 'People who aspire to be in management or leadership roles, and I assume most students in business and other college programs are among these. Even high school students. It would be almost easier to identify those who could not benefit.'

Jay Conger has found that the individuals who can most benefit from leadership education would possess:

*Jay Conger*: '(1) high achievement and ambition needs, (2) a strong capacity for strategic thinking, (3) a strong degree of pragmatism, (4) a baseline of effective communications skills (both in terms of persuasion and inspiration), (5) a measure of emotional intelligence, and (6) a genuine learning orientation and desire to lead.'

*Steve Stumpf*: 'To benefit from leadership education, one must be motivated to be a leader. This suggests a need for both a setting in which one wants to lead (accomplish something with and through others), and some interpersonal maturity (emotional intelligence) based on experience.'

*Mike Useem*: 'Many managers will have known brilliant colleagues who had every answer but no respect. Cognitive intelligence is a prerequisite for most responsible positions, whether a NASA flight director or an investment bank manager. What distinguishes those who move up to those positions is a capacity that writer Daniel Goleman has called *emotional intelligence*. It amounts to the following: If you are self-aware and self-regulating, empathetic and compassionate, and skilled at bringing out the best in people around you, you will hear what you need to know and inspire what they need to do.'

Chris Bartlett argues that there may be a sort of 'creaming' effect, especially in the teaching of executives:

*Chris Bartlett*: 'We take people with records of leadership, and we bring them in, and off they go, and they end up leading great organization[s] and we say "look what we did". We are preselecting to some of that genetic code (for leadership). We give them the trainable and coachable part, and while the skills part may spill over in to the attitude part, the fact is we get highly competitive people in the first instance. And we probably reinforce that, but we aren't changing the world.'

## By Whom can Leadership be Taught?

Many in the group argued that leaders themselves would be among the most effective teachers of leadership. Others cautioned that while the characteristics of individual leaders are interesting to students, they are rarely and not easily imitated. In fact, such behaviors are often idiosyncratic and context dependent, and therefore difficult for students to follow.

*Steve Stumpf*: 'Students of leadership seem to gravitate toward real leaders. They want to hear from them, learn from them, because they have credibility. But they don't necessarily learn a great deal from them. What it takes for the learning to happen is experiences for them to practice what they have heard.'

*Kim Cameron*: 'One would normally say that leaders would be the best teachers of leadership. Jack Welch ought to be the best teacher in the business. He's not, because he describes idiosyncratic events and experiences. I can't do what he does in my role, my organization, and facing my problems. Instead. I need some frameworks, some sense-making devices, and some tools to help me behave effectively in a variety of circumstances. That means the best teachers are those who can provide me with the theoretical frameworks, the models, and the foundation tools that allow me to succeed as a leader.'

Several of the scholars noted that leadership development programs are on the rise, and they predicted a continued expansion and growing demand for such offerings. During the revision of this manuscript, the Economist Intelligence Unit, a division of *The Economist,* published a special supplement on executive education in which several articles evaluated and critiqued various executive education programs based on their effectiveness and value added. Coincidentally, the title of the supplement was 'Can Leadership Be Taught.'

As more corporate universities, training institutes, consultancies (both profit and nonprofit), and nontraditional educational programs continue to enter the management education marketplace, a proliferation of new actors and organizations engaged in leadership training will continue.

*Mike Useem*: 'Abbott Laboratories, a $13 billion U.S. healthcare manufacturer with 57,000 employees, brings groups of 35 high-performing, high-potential directors and vice presidents together for 3 weeks of leadership development over 9 months. Participants examine the leader's role and responsibilities at Abbott, they consider alternative leadership approaches, and they receive feedback on their own leadership style and impact.'

*Mike Hitt*: 'Colleges and universities (but not necessarily colleges of business), businesses themselves, corporate universities, and others [are appropriate organizations for teaching leadership]. You are going to have many players in this game. A lot of organization types can deliver skill training. It is going to be difficult to sort out. And I cannot easily predict what direction it will go.'

# Leadership and Implications for Management Education

In this interview and commentary. I reported on discussions with management scholars about whether leadership can be taught, as well as related questions regarding the potential contribution of management education to leadership development. Although there were distinct perspectives on the basic questions explored in these exchanges, several themes and common perspectives emerged. In the following, I draw from the comments and observations of these educators to derive some broader implications for assessing the contribution of management education to leadership development.

## Implications for Leadership Development

1. The relationship between learning and leading is an important one. As Conger and Benjamin (1999) have argued, an important feature of leaders is their ability to instill a learning mindset throughout the organizations. Mike Useem echoes this view, arguing that effective leaders themselves have a 'teachable' point of view – a message that defines what they want the company to achieve and how it will do so. He suggests both must be conveyed in a form that others can readily learn and transmit. This notion is reflected in Mike Hitt's conception of the importance of vision in realizing 'strategic' leadership and Steve Stumpf's view of leadership as going 'beyond cognitions to actions, communications, inspiring others, and being a role model'.

2. Several of the educators argued that some aspects of leadership are part of innate qualities. Although these characteristics may be enhanced through various learning experiences, there are limits to the contribution of formal teaching to development of such skills. This does not necessarily mean that something cannot still be taught, but like language, it may be much more easily internalized early in life. As Chris Bartlett suggests, 'some people are born as natural competitors or driven achievers or empathetic people. These sorts of attitudes are more deeply embedded and less trainable than other skills and abilities. On the other hand, some of these characteristics, such as good communication, are teachable.'

3. As an extension of the points above, each educator argued that leadership skills are best acquired as part of a practical, experiential educational program, suggesting that traditional classroom teaching methods are best for helping students develop a general familiarity with some attributes or characteristics that have been associated with leadership, but not sufficient for acquiring leadership skills. The group was divided as to whether leaders themselves serve as effective trainers or coaches for developing leadership skills, with several commentators

arguing that the experiences of such figures are inherently idiosyncratic. Hence, modeling or patterning behavior on their experiences is ineffectual.

Again, Chris Bartlett provides a specific example; 'But what is not coachable are the very leadership skills admired by business schools in a figure such as Jack Welch – his ability to engage people personally, the intensity, the incredible competitiveness of the man, his ability to get inside the skin of and empathize [with others], and his ability to challenge and stretch [members of the organization]. There are a lot of those skills that are built in to things that he was born with.'

4. Many of the educators linked leadership character to some aspect of social or ethical responsibility, suggesting that leadership has a moral and ethical dimension beyond the more common definitions that emphasize motivation and power relationships. For example, Steve Stumpf suggested, 'leadership is about what you do to influence others to attain objectives, *ethically,* that they otherwise would not have pursued successfully. To do this, leaders must be ethical, have integrity, be trustworthy, and have credibility to their stakeholders.' Mike Hitt said that 'the value set and integrity is an important part of [leadership]. This is a necessary but insufficient condition to make you an effective leader.'

Kim Cameron made the strongest case for linking leadership to moral and ethical values: 'I ... believe that effective leaders in the 21st century must have a well-developed sense of moral values and possess personal virtues (such as humility, compassion, integrity, and forgiveness). When everything is changing, it is impossible to manage change. Some stable or nonchanging point must be identified in order to understand what is changing. Moral values and virtues provide the solid points that allow effective change (and leadership) to occur.' Chris Bartlett argued: 'With the power of management comes enormous responsibility. We need to focus and draw the students' attention to that. The respect of human dignity and achieving results through others [is essential].'

5. More fundamentally, vigorous debate continues over whether the skills or traits of managers and leaders are distinct, or whether management and leadership are, in fact, part of the same whole. This debate underpinned the varying responses to the questions posed here. Some scholars view leaders' roles as closely associated with the managers' roles and use the terms interchangeably. Others draw sharp distinctions between these two concepts. A classic definition of a leader is 'some-one who occupies a position in a group, influences others in accordance with the role expectation of the position and coordinates and directs the group in maintaining itself and reaching its goal' (Raven and Rubin, 1976, p. 37). A more contemporary perspective shifts the focus to interactions among leaders and groups as a 'process of influence between a leader and his followers to attain group, organizational and societal goals' (Avery and Baker,

1990, p. 453). Among those who *explicitly* distinguish between leadership and management is Abraham Zaleznick. In his classic 1977 *Harvard Business Review* article, Zaleznick argued that managers and leaders differ in terms of motivation, personal history, and in how they think and act. 'Whether his or her energies are directed toward goals, resources, organization structures, or people, a manager is a problem solver.... Leaders have a propensity to influence moods, to shape expectations, and to establish direction. This is clearly seen in their personal attitudes and very active approach toward goals' (Zaleznick, 1992, p. 127). John Kotter echoes this view in distinguishing between what leaders and managers are (and are not) able to accomplish: 'Leadership by itself never keeps an operation on time and on budget year after year. And management by itself never creates significant useful change' (1990, p. 3).

A number of the respondents in this forum accepted these distinctions – explicitly or implicitly – while others argued that they are artificial. As Steve Stumpf argued above, 'When a person in a position of authority tells someone subordinate to them to do something – or else – that person is not leading. We should reserve the term leadership to something other than directing or coercing.' Chris Bartlett, on the other hand, takes issue with the notion that management and leadership are fundamentally different skills:

I think that the literature has created a false dichotomy. I guess it is useful pedagogically, and so people talk about leadership as different from management. They claim management is about administration and control and leadership is about mission and empowerment. I think that is underestimating management. Good management is about achieving results through others and I think that it always encompassed leadership. But if management – like the corporate model – became identified with this hierarchical bureaucracy and managers became administrative controllers, then we shouldn't dispense with the term just as we don't dispense with organization because it became bureaucratic. Leadership is about achieving results through others (and) good management is about achieving results through others. I think that it (the concept of management) always encompassed leadership.

## Implications for Management Education

Management education has undergone extensive efforts to refine, revise, and revisit pedagogical tools and techniques. The emergence of leadership education as a primary activity in business schools and in other educational settings raises serious questions about how such an ambiguous and difficult-to-define concept can be effectively learned and taught. Although some practitioners and researchers routinely detail the characteristics of effective leadership, the effectiveness of leadership training and education remains questioned, particularly by those funding it (Nevins and Stumpf, 1999). Moreover, if leadership skills or capabilities can be developed, whether they can be effectively taught and learned in the context of classroom-based management education is unclear.

At the least, the management educators consulted here generally concurred that leadership – a personal quality more than a professional skill or ability – requires a particular kind of education. Leadership education, like leadership itself, must rely on heuristic approaches such as mentoring, coaching, patterning, and, trial-and-error experience. Jay Conger has argued that while leadership can be taught, not everyone can benefit from such teaching. He suggests that managers and educators need to radically alter conceptions of leadership to view leaders as 'change masters'. As such, Jay Conger suggests, 'leadership training must teach managers and executives how to anticipate what is on their industry horizon and how to mobilize their organization to shape the future.'

Most educators agreed that individual personality traits provide at least part of the basis upon which leadership skills are built, and such characteristics reach stability by adolescence. Hence, a frame is established that drives how future managers view their roles, their style of communicating, and their modes of interaction with others. Clearly, these frames can change, and individuals can learn to view things differently. Managers, like educators, continue to grow socially, physically, and intellectually. However, this early grounding and foundation may strongly influence the choice of career or profession, the style or attitude toward work relationships, and the approach of managerial roles and interactions, including leadership roles.

As educators, we should be skeptical of our ability to mold leaders, and instead should view leadership as one of several characteristics and skill sets that may be further developed by education and practice. Management education is a holistic undertaking, one that does not lend itself to easy compartmentalization or quick fixes. Leadership clearly requires personal commitments on the part of the learner. We as management educators may spur, promote, cultivate, and develop such commitments, but it is unlikely that we can create them from scratch.

--- *References* ---

Avery, G. and Baker, E. (1990) *Psychology at Work*, New York, Prentice Hall.

Bailey, J. 1994. Great individuals and their environments revisited: William James and contemporary leadership theory. *The Journal of Leadership Studies*. 1(4): 28–36.

Conger, J. A. and Benjamin, B. 1999. *Building leaders: How successful companies develop the next generation.* San Francisco: Jossey-Bass.

Kotter, J.P. (1990) *A Force for Change: How Leadership Differs from Management,* New York, The Free Press.

Nevins, M.D. and Stumpf, S.A. (1999) '21st-century leadership: Redefining management education', *Strategy + Business,* Third Quarter, pp. 41–51.

Raven, B.H. and Rubin, J.E. (1976) *Social Psychology: People in Groups*, New York, John Wiley and Sons.

*U.S. News and World Report.* 2002. Best graduate schools. Available at usnews.com/usnews/edu/grad/rankings/mba/mbaindex.

Zaleznik, A. (1992) 'Managers and leaders: Are they different?' *Harvard Business Review,* March/April, pp. 126–35; Reprinted from *Harvard Business Review,* May/June, pp. 67–78.

# Part VI
## Inspiring Others

# Leadership and Influence, Motivation and Inspiration

# 16

*Roger Gill*

[ ... ]

## Inspiration and Charisma

A crisis calls for inspirational leadership. Sir John Egan, as chairman of Inchcape and former head of the UK's Chartered Institute of Management, said, 'It is really inspirational leaders who stand out in a crisis. The Chinese characters for "crisis" are "opportunity" and "danger". That's what it should be seen as – an opportunity' (Simms, 2002).

Inspiring leaders are often regarded as charismatic – a double-edged sword. They are perceived to have a special talent or power to attract followers and inspire them with devotion and enthusiasm. One view is that charismatic leaders are emotionally expressive, self-confident, self-determined and free from internal conflict (Bass, 1992). They also show empathy with followers, they use compelling, emotive language, they display personal competency, they display confidence in their followers, and they provide followers with opportunities to achieve (Behling and McFillen, 1996). However, whether, and to what extent, charisma is essential to effective leadership – or the result of it – is arguable (Drucker, 1992; Sayles, 1993):

> Many of the organisations we know do not have charismatic leaders.... [Their leaders] are usually modest, sometimes even self-effacing, losing no opportunity to stress that real achievement has come from teamwork, not the inspiration of just one individual. (Binney and Williams, 1995)

This raises the question of ego. Maccoby (2000) stimulated a debate about whether effective leaders are egotistical and narcissistic, arguing that because

Gill, R. (2006) 'Leadership and influence, motivation and inspiration', Crafted from Gill, R. *Theory and Practice of Leadership*, London, Sage, pp. 252–64.

of their vision, charisma and energy, they help organizations, which they see as extensions of their egos, become great. But Collins (2001) found in a research programme that the most effective leaders – who have successfully transformed their business organizations – suppress their egos: they are self-effacing, humble and shy, but resolute. Perhaps the real issue is *authenticity:* inspirational leaders inspire others because they communicate *themselves*–their virtues and their flaws (Goffee and Jones, 2000). An example is Mahatma Gandhi, who said, 'My life is its own message' (Lulla, 2002). While charisma is generally viewed as a social process between leader and follower, where the leader might well have some very special gifts, such as oratory, charisma is very much a 'manufactured' phenomenon today (Bryman, 1992, p. 30), especially among politicians.

Leadership is often thought of as a process of *influencing* others in getting them to want to do what needs to be done. One new view of influencing put forward by Eric Knowles concerns removing people's inhibitions, or lowering their resistance (*The Economist,* 2002a). Knowles defines 'alpha' and 'omega' strategies of persuasion. Alpha strategies are concerned with making an offer more attractive, whereas omega strategies focus on minimizing resistance to it. Resistance, of course, is not necessarily logical or rational.

Sir Richard Branson of the Virgin Group – the best business leader in KPMG surveys in 1997 and 1999 (Beckett, 1999) – is an example of a contemporary business leader who inspires loyalty among the Group's employees and is well liked by them and admired among other business leaders. The story is told of how he praised an engineer on board his first transatlantic flight when it ran into difficulties and he solved the problem and how every year the engineer received a handwritten birthday card thanking him for saving the reputation of Virgin Atlantic (Reynolds, 2000). Sidney Harman, chairman of the American top-of-the-line entertainment and hi-fi systems company Harman International, cut costs with 'un-American compassion': he placed surplus workers in spun-off companies, including one that made clocks from waste wood (*The Economist,* 2002b). Harman says workers 'should have a serious emotional connection to the company'. These examples of leadership behaviour illustrate responding positively to the emotional needs of people.

We find many examples of inspirational leadership in the world of sports. For example, a member of the winning yachting team in the 1996–1997 BT Global Challenge round-the-world race, Humphrey Walters, says the team had 'a feeling that they [had] done something they never thought they could do ... [and] ... stretched themselves and reached aspirations and achievement far beyond their thinking' (Walters, 2002).

Inspiration may also come from communicating a clear vision eloquently, confidently and with confidence in it, using appealing language and symbols.

# Inspirational Language and Speech

'Nothing is so akin to our natural feelings as the rhythms and sounds of voices', wrote Cicero (Schama, 2002). The Chinese translation of the word 'speech' is two words that separately mean 'act' and 'talk'. So to make a speech is 'to perform a talking show' (Leung, 2000).

Inspirational speeches contain simple language, imagery and plays on words in a colourful way. They are delivered with sincerity and passion, with confidence and conviction, and often with expansive body language – in particular facial expressions, gestures of the hand, head movements and eye contact. Eye contact gives the audience impressions of spontaneity and being addressed directly (Atkinson, 1984). Inspiring leaders express emotions through their body language. For one CEO, John Robins of Guardian Insurance, 'leadership is about communicating emotions and excitement' (Rajan, 2000).

On two inspirational speakers Bass (1989, p. 56) says

> In the United States, Martin Luther King and Jesse Jackson stirred disadvantaged blacks into believing that by their own personal efforts combined with collective action they could reshape American society to advance their place in it, ultimately for the benefit of all Americans.

Whether you agree with his political ideas or not, 1988 US presidential candidate Jesse Jackson touches hearts in the way he speaks. P.J. O'Rourke (1992, p. 24), the American journalist, says of him:

> He is the only living American politician with a mastery of classical rhetoric. Assonance, alliteration, litotes, pleonasm, parallelism, exclamation, climax and epigram – to listen to Jesse Jackson is to hear everything mankind has learned about public speaking since Demosthenes.

O'Rourke (1992, p. 25) gives an example from his 'A Call to Common Ground' speech:

> So many guided missiles and so much misguided leadership, the stakes are very high. Our choice? Full participation in a democratic government or more abandonment and neglect. So this night, we choose not a false sense of independence.... Tonight we choose interdependency.

Peggy Noonan captures the essence of inspirational public speaking.

> A speech is a soliloquy, one man on a bare stage with a big spotlight. He will tell us who he is and what he wants and how he will get it and what it

means that he wants it and what it will mean when he does or does not get it.... He looks up at us...and clears his throat. 'Ladies and gentlemen ...' We lean forward, hungry to hear. Now it will be said, now we will hear the thing we long for. A speech is part theatre and part political declaration; it is personal communication between a leader and his people; it is an art, and all art is a paradox, being at once a thing of great power and great delicacy. A speech is poetry: cadence, rhythm, imagery, sweep! A speech reminds us that words...have the power to make dance the dullest beanbag of a heart. (MacArthur, 1999, p. xxiv)

Language is one's most powerful tool: without communication skills a leader will fail to have an impact (Goodwin, 1998). Yet most senior executives 'don't make the strong audience connection – visceral, personal, emotional – needed to inspire trust and action', according to Nick Morgan (2001), a communications consultant.

Brian MacArthur (1999, p. xvii), like Simon Schama, laments the lack of oratory in leaders today: 'Where are the visions and where are the words that inspire men and women to greater things and make them vote with enthusiasm, even passion?' Modern egalitarianism may have tended to discourage flights of high rhetoric. Disraeli said of his legendary adversary William Gladstone, 'A sophisticated rhetorician, inebriated with the exuberance of his own verbosity.' Using an esoteric, even if right, quote or allusion may seem pretentious, but politicians today sometimes forget that the common people are actually educated. According to Peggy Noonan, they 'go in for the lowest common denominator – like a newscaster' (MacArthur, 1999, pp. xvi–xvii) – or perhaps a tabloid newspaper. But Morgan (2001) suggests that people in business increasingly expect speakers to connect with them 'viscerally, personally and emotionally'.

Jeremy Paxman, the broadcaster, writer and political commentator, describes how 'the Leader' at party conferences has 'largely discarded the rousing vision, the cloudy imagery and the rhetorical resonance of even twenty years ago' (Paxman, 2002, pp. 151–52). The reason, he says, is that such oratory does not suit television, which is 'a medium of impressions and more intimate tone'. Political conference speeches therefore have become 'an awkward hybrid, part talk, part declamation'. And, he says, it is all 'a sham', for such speeches, and the punctuating and final euphoric hand-clapping and subsequent theatrical departure, are engineered, timed and planned, and the speeches are even not written by the speaker but by teams of speechwriters.

Outstanding leaders do influence and persuade people through inspirational language. This is perhaps the most obvious behavioural characteristic of an outstanding leader. But this poses a problem, even a paradox. If humility is a characteristic of effective leadership, as we find in the teachings of Jesus and Lao Tzu and in the opinion of many successful business leaders, how does this square with the power of oratory, exalted by the Greeks and Romans? 'Silence is of the gods,' says a Chinese proverb; yet 'Silence is the virtue of fools,' said Francis Bacon (1561–1626) (Watts, tr. 1640). Adair (1989, p. 44) suggests the answer is *listening:* humility lies in listening rather than speaking or waiting to speak.

Great leaders, however, have often been elevated to iconic status through their use of language. How do they do it? They inspire people through what they say and how they say it.

> The speeches of Moses, Jesus of Nazareth and Muhammad to their followers are still inspiring men and women to lead lives based on a moral code and still, today, changing the course of history ... the greatest speeches ... move hearts or inspire great deeds [and] uplift spirits. (MacArthur, 1996, p. xv)

The prophet Muhammad 'was noted for superb eloquence and fluency ... [as] an accurate, unpretending straightforward speaker ... [with] the strength and eloquence of bedouin language and the decorated splendid speech of town' (al-Mubarakpuri, 1995, p. 496–97). Inspirational speeches by leaders 'articulate dreams, offer hope, stir hearts and minds, and offer their audiences visions of a better world' (MacArthur, 1999, p. xxiv).

Inspiring leaders communicate a clear vision eloquently and confidently, using appealing language and symbols. They use a 'charismatic tone ... [they] speak with a captivating voice, make direct eye contact, show animated facial expressions, and have a dynamic interaction style' (Kirkpatrick and Locke, 1996).

The ability to communicate a clear, simple vision is a key characteristic: 'The power of language ... [gives] life to vision' (Kouzes and Posner, 1991). David E. Berlew says, 'Leaders must communicate a vision in a way that attracts and excites members of the organization' (Kouzes and Posner, 1991, p. 121). In the words of William Hazlitt (1807):

> The business of the orator is not to convince, but persuade; not to inform, but to rouse the mind; to build upon the habitual prejudices of mankind (for reason of itself will do nothing) and to add feeling to prejudice, and action to feeling.

Table 16.1 shows the famous parts of well-known inspirational speeches by Martin Luther King Jr, Abraham Lincoln, Winston Churchill, John F. Kennedy and Tony Blair.

Martin Luther King Jr delivered his speech before a crowd of 250,000 in Washington, DC. His speech, Kouzes and Posner (1991, p. 125) say, was rooted in fundamental values, cultural traditions and personal conviction, and

---

**Table 16.1** Inspirational speeches

---

**Martin Luther King, Jr**
'I have a dream...'

**Abraham Lincoln**
'...government of the people, by the people, for the people, shall not perish from the earth.'

**Winston Churchill**
'Never in the field of human conflict was so much owed by so many to so few.'
'We shall fight on the beaches...we shall fight in the fields and in the streets, we shall fight in the hills, we shall *never* surrender.'

**John F. Kennedy**
'Ask not what your country can do for you; ask what *you* can do for your country.'
'Let every nation know, whether it wishes us well or ill, that we shall pay any price, bear any burden, meet any hardship, support any friend, oppose any foe, in order to ensure the survival and the success of liberty.'

**Tony Blair**
'Now make the good that is in the heart of each of us serve the good of all of us. Give to our country the gift of our energy, our ideas, our hopes, our talents. Use them to build a country each of whose people will say that "I care about Britain because I know that Britain cares about me." Britain, head and heart, will be unbeatable. That is the Britain I offer you. That is the Britain that together can be ours.'

---

stirred hearts and passions. It is a masterpiece of connecting with an audience and crafting rhetoric. Abraham Lincoln, who 'demonstrated...passionate conviction allied to simple but eloquent words, quietly spoken' (MacArthur, 1996, p. xv) in 270 words spoken in three minutes, gave possibly 'the greatest and noblest speech of modern times' – his famous Gettysburg address. Winston S. Churchill's Battle of Britain speech and his Dunkirk speech inspired the nation. President Kennedy's inaugural presidential address on 20 January 1961 did likewise, rallying the youth of his country in one part of it and displaying its far-reaching influence, on George W. Bush after 9/11, in another part. And Tony Blair's speech to his first Labour Party conference as newly elected prime minister was both triumphal and indicative of radical change in the ideology of Labour:

> [emphasizing] duty over rights, the importance of family life, zero tolerance on crime and a more positive approach to European unity as he appealed for Britain to become a beacon to the world. Even right-wing commentators hailed the speech as a historic statement of intent. (MacArthur, 1999, pp. 511–12)

Following the attacks on the World Trade Center in New York and the Pentagon in Washington, DC, on 11 September 2001, President George W. Bush addressed Congress on 20 September 2001. Extracts appear as a case example below.

## Case Example

### *Extracts from President George W. Bush's Address to a Joint Session of the United States Congress on Thursday night, September 20, 2001*

Mr. Speaker, Mr. President Pro Tempore, members of Congress, and fellow Americans, in the normal course of events, presidents come to this chamber to report on the state of the union. Tonight, no such report is needed; it has already been delivered by the American people.

We have seen it in the courage of passengers who rushed terrorists to save others on the ground. Passengers like an exceptional man named Todd Beamer. And would you please help me welcome his wife Lisa Beamer here tonight?

We have seen the state of our union in the endurance of rescuers working past exhaustion.

We've seen the unfurling of flags, the lighting of candles, the giving of blood, the saying of prayers in English, Hebrew and Arabic.

We have seen the decency of a loving and giving people who have made the grief of strangers their own.

My fellow citizens, for the last nine days, the entire world has seen for itself the state of union, and it is strong.

Tonight, we are a country awakened to danger and called to defend freedom. Our grief has turned to anger and anger to resolution. Whether we bring our enemies to justice or bring justice to our enemies, justice will be done.

All of America was touched on the evening of the tragedy to see Republicans and Democrats joined together on the steps of this Capitol singing 'God Bless America.'

And you did more than sing. You acted, by delivering $40 billion to rebuild our communities and meet the needs of our military. Speaker Hastert, Minority Leader Gephardt, Majority Leader Daschle and Senator Lott, I thank you for your friendship, for your leadership and for your service to our country.

And on behalf of the American people, I thank the world for its outpouring of support.

America will never forget the sounds of our national anthem playing at Buckingham Palace, on the streets of Paris and at Berlin's Brandenburg Gate.

We will not forget South Korean children gathering to pray outside our embassy in Seoul, or the prayers of sympathy offered at a mosque in Cairo.

This is not, however, just America's fight. And what is at stake is not just America's freedom. This is the world's fight. This is civilization's fight. This is the fight of all who believe in progress and pluralism, tolerance and freedom.

We ask every nation to join us…

Our nation, this generation, will lift the dark threat of violence from our people and our future. We will rally the world to this cause by our efforts, by our courage. We will not tire, we will not falter and we will not fail.

Some will remember an image of a fire or story or rescue. Some will carry memories of a face and a voice gone forever.

And I will carry this. It is the police shield of a man named George Howard who died at the World Trade Center trying to save others.

It was given to me by his mom, Arlene, as a proud memorial to her son. It is my reminder of lives that ended and a task that does not end.

I will not forget the wound to our country and those who inflicted it. I will not yield, I will not rest, I will not relent in waging this struggle for freedom and security for the American people. The course of this conflict is not known, yet its outcome is certain. Freedom and fear, justice and cruelty, have always been at war, and we know that God is not neutral between them.

> Fellow citizens, we'll meet violence with patient justice, assured of the rightness of our cause and confident of the victories to come.
>
> In all that lies before us, may God grant us wisdom and may he watch over the United States of America. Thank you.

Dom Anthony Sutch says, 'He came across as "one of us" – he found the mood ... .

He said what the world wanted to hear' (Sutch, 2001). Bush's speech displays the characteristics of inspirational language that are reminiscent of wartime Churchill:

- Vivid imagery of the terrorist enemy, their goal of 'remaking the world', and of life in Afghanistan
- Personalization, by welcoming Lisa Beamer, widow of a passenger on United Airlines flight 93 who died storming the hijackers, and colleagues of the police, firefighters and military who died in the World Trade Center inferno
- His invocation of God
- The symbolism in his display of the police shield of George Howard, who died at the World Trade Center trying to save others
- His stirring language: 'I will not yield, I will not rest, I will not relent in waging this struggle for freedom and security for the American people'; and 'We will not tire, we will not falter, and we will not fail'

While his speech is said to have been written by a speechwriter, and a key feature of inspirational language is authenticity, the speechwriter nevertheless on this occasion seems to have captured his master's voice: simple, direct, natural.

Political leaders may express core values and beliefs in inspirational speech, with potentially productive or dangerous consequences. Examples of those more likely to lead to negative outcomes are a sense of superiority, perceived injustice to oneself or one's group, a sense of vulnerability, distrust and a sense of helplessness (Eidelson and Eidelson, 2003). Effective leaders through their rhetoric may inspire their followers to change the status quo, even violently (Homer-Dixon, 1999), especially when they also communicate innocence and victimization (Stern, 1995). Examples of mutual perceptions of vulnerability and consequential threat are the Israelis and Palestinians in the Middle East and the Protestants and Catholics in Northern Ireland.

We cannot leave this discussion of inspirational speech without a comment on Adolf Hitler. 'Hitler, undoubtedly the greatest speaker of the century ... changed a nation by his oratory,' says MacArthur (1999, p. xvii). He was able to arouse a mass audience and work it up to a frenzy, with a mixture of appeals to idealism, power, hatred and action, the use of symbols, the assertion of a grandiose identity – 'Deutschland über Alles' – and the projection of all evil outside. His moving speeches captured the minds and hearts of a vast number of the German people: he virtually hypnotized his audiences. The inspirational effect of a brilliant speech is illustrated by Hitler's address in 1932 to the Düsseldorf Industry Club. On his arrival:

> his reception ... was cool and reserved. Yet he spoke for two and a half hours without pause and made one of the best speeches of his life, setting out all his stock ideas brilliantly dressed up for his audience of businessmen. At the end they rose and cheered him wildly. Contributions from German industry started flowing into the Nazi treasury. (MacArthur, 1999, pp. xix–xx)

Norman Lebrecht (2000) concurs: 'Hitler was nothing if not a spellbinder ... Mixed with revulsion at the deeds he inspired, one cannot avoid a sneaking admiration for a lone individual who overturned an entire civilization.'

Central to inspirational language are two skills: framing and rhetorical crafting (Georgiades and Macdonnell, 1998). Inspirational language is not the exclusive domain of the speaker's podium or rostrum. The skills of framing and rhetorical crafting apply just as much in any one-to-one conversation between leader and follower, manager and subordinate, or indeed between any two people – where the purpose is to influence, motivate or inspire.

## Framing Language and Speech

Framing is connecting your message with the needs and interests of those whose commitment you need (Conger, 1999). This means first knowing your audience. Framing is the management of meaning, which requires careful thought and forethought (Fairhurst and Sarr, 1996). Meaning is found in the image of the organization, its place in the environment, and its collective purpose, according to Bass (1990, p. 208). Jay Conger (1999) says that

> The most effective leaders study the issues that matter to their colleagues ... in ... conversations ... they collect essential information .... They are good at listening. They test their ideas with trusted confidants, and they ask questions of the people they will later be persuading. These explorations help them think through the arguments, the evidence, and the perspectives they will present.

Framing is about developing a shared sense of destiny through dialogue (Kouzes and Posner, 1991), something both Martin Luther King Jr and Nelson Mandela did so well. Leadership is about building connections with people: effective leaders *make people feel they have a stake in common problems* (Goodwin, 1998). Giving people an identity as stakeholders creates shared ownership and thereby wholehearted commitment to solving problems and building futures together. Framing involves several specific behaviours:

**Catching attention.** First, catching people's attention at the start with something surprising or attention grabbing. Morgan recommends avoiding a joke or rhetorical question and instead telling a carefully crafted 'personal parable' or anecdote that captures your overall theme that the audience can identify with (Morgan, 2001).

**Timing.** Timing is (almost) everything: knowing when to introduce an initiative and when to hold off is a crucial skill (Goodwin, 1998). Hunt (1998) calls this 'exercising theatre'.

**Appealing to common interests.** Your message must be linked to the benefits for everybody involved. This extends to incorporating the values and beliefs of those you are communicating to, appealing to common bonds – noting that 'what is white in one culture may be black in another' (Leung, 2000).

**Avoiding statistics.** Using statistics usually should be avoided. Statistical summaries are regarded by most people as mostly uninformative and unmemorable: 'information is absorbed by listeners in proportion to its vividness' (Conger, 1999). However, as Nick Georgiades and Richard Macdonnell (1998, p. 111) say, telling a group that a project has an 80% chance of success rather than a 20% chance of failure is more likely to win over the group.

**Use of vocabulary.** Framing also entails using vocabulary that matches the listeners' and generally not using a two- or three-syllable word where a one-syllable word will do. Charles Goldie and Richard Pinch (1991) also advocate 'economic representation' in communication: using one word rather than several words to express oneself.

**Showing feelings.** A key element in framing is showing that you are feeling what you are saying, speaking with passion and emotion, and reinforcing the verbal message by using appropriate body language. In the words of Shakespeare's Hamlet's advice to the travelling players – 'Suit the action to the word, the word to the action.' This refers to tone of voice, posture and gestures – what Morgan (2001) calls the 'kines-thetic connection' with the audience.

**Authenticity.** This, of course, requires authenticity in communication. Framing language may be more difficult, however, for a speaker who has strong emotion about a subject, whose authenticity is all too obvious (Rogers and Greenberg, 1952). Inspiring others requires finding out what inspires you and speaking 'from the heart', according to Richard Olivier: 'If the speaker is inspired and moved, it generally follows that the audience will empathise' (Bailey, 2000). MacArthur (1999, pp. xxi–xxii) says:

> However brilliant the words, it is also the manner of delivery, the sincerity of the speaker, that makes a speech great…. Speeches succeed, according to

Lloyd George, by a combination of word, voice and gesture in moving their audiences to the action the orator desires.

Lack of authenticity has become an issue for leaders, particularly those in politics and government. The professional speechwriter has been used for a long time.

Public orators in ancient Greece employed *rhetores* to produce speeches. Simon Schama (2002) notes that former US president Andrew Jackson's best speeches were written by Chief Justice Roger Taney and that Samuel Rosenmann wrote for Franklin D. Roosevelt.

But the rise of the adviser – the 'spin doctor' – has created scepticism among audiences about whether leaders are speaking their own words sincerely or those invented by experts in image management. In fact leaders themselves have been 'invented'. Gardner (1996, p. 60) says, 'even the claim for authenticity can be manufactured ... good actors know how to feign sincerity'. Image management, or impression management, taken to extremes, however, can backfire and have a 'boomerang' effect (Bass, 1988). Authenticity, however, like so many other usually positive leadership characteristics, may have adverse consequences. Saying what you mean may demonize sections of a community, as, for example, it has done in Northern Ireland (de Bono, 1998, p. 55).

**Inclusivity.** In framing your speech, you move from 'I' to 'we' – using words like 'we' and 'our' rather than 'them' and 'they'. This characterizes inclusive language that unifies rather than divides followers (Fiol et al., 1999). This extends to comparing your group and situation with other groups and situations, for example with competitors ('We can do better than ...'), with ideals ('We can achieve our best performance yet), with goals ('We can achieve whatever we set our mind to'), with the past ('We can do better than we've ever done before') with traits ('This is what we could look like if ...') and with stakeholders ('We can make our employees our strongest advocates) (Bass, 1990, p. 208; Conger, 1999).

**Presenting a solution and a challenge.** Finally, framing includes presenting a solution, challenging the audience to implement it (Morgan, 2001), and then 'reading' the audience's reaction – their non-verbal signals – of receptivity, engagement with you, agreement and commitment to your message and adjusting to it accordingly and – better still – involving the audience in some form of physical activity related to your message (Morgan, 2001).

Television has made a difference in public speaking, whether for education, entertainment or to win hearts and minds to a cause. Morgan (2001) says that the 'grand gesture ... sweeping phrases, the grand conceits' and voice projection were *de rigueur* for centuries and, of course, still are so in theatre. But television (and video) has enabled the illusion of people talking to you from a few feet away, more personally, more intimately and therefore more trustworthily. Trust in the speaker – and winning hearts and minds – depends on the connection between the verbal message and the kinesthetic message, in other words, authenticity in communication. Tongue in cheek, Schama (2002) gives a contemporary interpretation of Cicero's five characteristics of oratory:

- *Intentio* – 'the main idea dreamt up and carefully monitored by staff'
- *Dispositio* – 'the arrangement, tailor-made for television and punctuated by gestures to "real life" heroes inserted into the gallery'
- *Memoria* – 'supplied by the invisible teleprompter'
- *Actio* – 'the oxymoronic homely gravitas studded with reassuring simplicities'
- *Elocutio* – 'a delivery finely tuned to reassure that the incumbent can complete sentences but equally finely judged to make them short'

# Rhetorical Crafting of Language and Speech

Inspiring leaders not only frame their language; they also craft their rhetoric. Speaking in West Berlin in 1987, then US President Ronald Reagan said:

> General Secretary Gorbachev, if you seek peace, if you seek prosperity for the Soviet Union and eastern Europe, if you seek liberalization: come here to this gate. Mr Gorbachev, open this gate. Mr Gorbachev, tear down this wall. (Allen-Mills, 2004)

Reagan is widely regarded as having been a great communicator, skilled in both framing his message and in crafting his rhetoric.

Rhetoric is the art of verbal expression. According to Beard (2000), rhetoric was taught in British schools long before English language and literature as we know it came into being. Bass (1988) describes how inspirational leaders substitute simple words, metaphors and slogans for complex ideas, such as glasnost and perestroika representing complex social, economic and political change in the former Soviet Union, and 'Never again!' to convey a response to the Holocaust. Inspiring leaders give examples, tell anecdotes, give quotations and recite slogans. They tell stories.

**Storytelling** Screenwriting coach and award-winning writer and director Robert McKee (2003) believes that 'most executives struggle to communicate, let alone inspire'. He argues for engaging people's emotions not through 'dry' memos, missives, PowerPoint slides or conventional rhetoric, but through storytelling. He says that the former methods are an intellectual exercise whereby one tries to convince or influence people on the basis of facts and logic but that 'people are not inspired to act by reason alone'. A much more powerful way is to unite an idea with feeling – by telling a story. Talula Cartwright (2002) says:

> People naturally gravitate to stories. Nearly everyone can remember stories from childhood that captured the imagination, touched the heart, and helped determine ideals, heroes, religious beliefs.

McKee (2003) suggests that people identify more with a story about struggle against adversity than with rosy pictures because they see it as more truthful. Once again, as has been discussed earlier, self-knowledge is a *sine qua non*. McKee (2003) says:

> A storyteller ... [asks] the question, 'If I were this character in these circumstances, what would I do?' The more you understand your own humanity, the more you can appreciate the humanity of others.

**Use of rhythm, metaphor and symbols**  Inspiring leaders vary their speaking rhythm. They use familiar images, metaphors and analogies to make the message vivid – as did Nelson Mandela with the image of the new South Africa as the 'Rainbow Nation'. They use symbols which capture the imagination – for example, the eagle symbolizes strength, the olive branch peace, the lion courage (Kouzes and Posner, 1991, p. 145). The cross symbolizes suffering, sacrifice and redemption; 'the hammer and sickle signifies the worker and peasant whose proletarian dictatorship would bring forth a communist utopia' (Bass, 1988). Hitler used to great effect symbols such as the swastika, the goose step, the 'Heil Hitler' salute and the 'Horst Wessel' song (Gardner, 1995, p. 261).

Tihamér von Ghyczy (2003) says, 'Metaphors ... [involve] the transfer of images or ideas from one domain of reality to another.' The rhetorical metaphor is well known and heavily used in the business world. It is part of inspirational language, for example 'winning the match', 'star performers', and so on. But linguistics scholars say such metaphors have a 'shelf life', eventually becoming 'dead metaphors'. The 'cognitive metaphor', von Ghyczy points out, serves a different function. He quotes Aristotle's view that good metaphors surprise and puzzle us: while they have familiar elements, their relevance and meaning are not immediately clear. It is in this 'delicately unsettled [state] of mind that we are most open to creative ways of looking at things': 'something relatively unfamiliar (for example, evolutionary biology) [is used] to spark creative thinking about something familiar (business strategy)'.

**Expression of hope**  Inspiring leaders express hope and possibilities. They wax lyrical, as did Martin Luther King Jr, with phrases like 'the jangling discords of our nation' and 'a beautiful symphony of brotherhood'. But, as Adair (1988) says, such leadership is about having the courage to take people forward in a positive way, not about demoralizing them through language filled with threats and fears.

**Repetition** Inspiring leaders also use repetition. This promotes easier recall (Ormrod, 1995). As Churchill said:

> If you have an important point to make, don't try to be subtle or clever. Use a pile-driver. Hit the point once. Then come back and hit it a second time – a tremendous whack! (Fitton, 1997)

Inspiration through language comes not only from magical manipulation and set-piece speeches. The idea of crafting rhetoric underlies the use of poetry by management consultant and poet David Whyte in his leadership development programmes – described in the next chapter – to inspire participants to inspire their people (Hoare, 2001). The idea is that poetry – using words that far better capture the essence of issues that leaders have to deal with – can help them to define a powerful vision and the courage to challenge preconceptions.

Speeches have always had memorable phrases or what today we call 'sound bites' – the invention of their impression managers, the spin doctors, rather than (political) leaders themselves. Examples are: 'With malice towards none ... With charity towards all' (Lincoln); 'He has not a single redeeming defect' (Disraeli on Gladstone); 'The only thing we have to fear is fear itself' (Churchill); and 'Ask not what your country can do for you' (Kennedy) (MacArthur, 1999, p. xvii).

Michael Ignatieff (1985) said, 'We need words to keep us human.' And in the words of Raja Zarith Sofiah Sultan Idris Shah, Crown Princess of Johor (Malaysia), in a speech at the Malaysian Association of Modern Languages:

> To be touched by ... words ... is not a sign of gullibility but of being human. We are not ashamed that we are moved to tears by what someone has written or said .... We should be really proud that we possess such human-ness within us. (Ahmad, 2002)

Aristotle in *The Art of Rhetoric* also recognized the importance in leadership of rhetoric; Socrates, on the other hand, regarded rhetoric as 'sleight of hand' and a 'poor handmaiden to logic' (Wardy, 1996; Grint, 2000). Yet Confucius said, 'He who does not understand the force of words can never know his fellow-men' (Giles, 1976, p. 94). And I say: he who does not know his fellow men cannot inspire them. Outstanding leaders know their followers. They use inspiring language.

Today's world has seen the creation of the World Wide Web and global conglomerates whose influence now exceeds that of any national government. Already we have witnessed the adverse consequences of such creations as well as their benefits. Tomorrow's world consists of many possible futures – scenarios. The scenarios that bring about the greatest good for the greatest number of people depend for their realization on leaders who have the right vision, values and strategies. But leaders will not – and cannot – do this without followers who share the vision, values and strategies and are both empowered and inspired to display them in their everyday behaviour, particularly when times are difficult.

Olivier's analysis of Shakespeare's Henry V as a leader – presented in the following case study – illustrates how he did this, with salutary lessons for our leaders of today and tomorrow (Olivier, 2001). Olivier suggests that inspirational leaders think in terms of the big picture: they go beyond immediate goals, such as making a profit, and they focus on what would serve the community at large. They have, he says, access to 'a muse of fire' (Olivier, 2001, p. 4). The historian Theodore Zeldin (2004) has provided just such access: he established a foundation called 'The Oxford Muse':

> to bring together people who want inspiration to think more imaginatively, to cultivate their emotions through practice of the arts, to understand the past better and to have a clearer vision of the future.

'Inspire others,' Zeldin says, 'and you will feel inspired yourself.'

---

### Case Study

#### *Shakespeare's Henry V and Inspirational Leadership*

The fictional Henry V is Shakespeare's greatest leader – inspired and inspiring, visionary but pragmatic, powerful yet responsible. Richard Olivier, son of Sir Laurence, who introduced him to *Henry V* at an early age, follows the progress of the play and, based on his use of the text in mythodrama seminars and workshops, describes how Henry develops as a paragon of inspirational leadership. In particular, we see how Henry defines, communicates and gathers support for his vision, faces his critics, changes direction without losing support, leads by example and inspires his followers.

Act I in *Henry V* starts with an assessment of the past and depicts visions of the future and Henry building consent around his mission to reclaim the territory of France. He believes this is his right and he visibly commits to it. The Chorus asks for a 'muse of fire' that will exceed the 'brightest heaven of invention'. It is a call to the imagination. Henry's big idea – his mission – is to reunite England and France. He now meets with his nobles to gather support. He starts by ensuring there is proof of his right to do so. And he wants to pick not only the right fight but also the one he knows he has a right to pick.

Henry next marshals and allocates his resources, and he identifies and deals with those who would oppose his mission. Effective leaders identify the forces ranged both for and against them. But they also need to understand their own habits and behaviours that might get in the way of achieving success. Henry disguises his awareness of treachery until an appropriate moment, when he reveals his feeling of betrayal. The culprits are sentenced to death. Dealing with naysayers, critics (both overt and covert) and traitors is important. And objective rather than subjective judgements, even apparently harsh ones at the time, may preserve the trust of others around the leader and save much trouble later.

In Act III, Henry takes the first steps into France, meets the first barriers to success, overcomes them, stages a strategic withdrawal, and ends up being surrounded by a vastly superior force to whom he is asked to surrender – or die. He starts with a plan – to arrive in August with 10,000 troops, take the first foothold in a week, and march on Paris by Christmas. He lands at the coastal town of Harfleur as planned. But three months later is still there, having lost 2,000 men and with another 3,000 ill. He makes his famous rousing speech to his ex-hausted troops:

> Once more unto the breach, dear friends, once more,
> Or close the wall up with our English dead ...
> Then imitate the action of the tiger.
> Stiffen the sinews, conjure up the blood,
> Disguise fair nature with a hard-favoured rage ...
> Now set the teeth and stretch the nostril wide,
> Hold hard the breath, and bend up every spirit
> To his full height. On, on, you noblest English,
> Whose blood is fet from fathers of war-proof ...
> Follow your spirit, and upon this charge
> Cry, 'God for Harry! England and Saint George!'

Olivier comments: however grand the vision or mission, there must be a practical place to start. When things get stuck – especially when it is not the followers' fault – an effective leader will have to speak passionately and imaginatively to motivate them through the blocks. Says Olivier, 'At [this] point the "troops" [would be] about as keen to fight as they would be to jump off a cliff.' Henry's troops have been living in a marsh for three months, watching their mates die, and they *know* what went wrong. What they need is something that will change their energy and create a different result. To do this Henry includes himself in the conversation – 'dear friends'. Olivier comments: 'When was the last time you were three months behind delivery on an important project and your boss called you a dear friend?' What the demotivated troops need is a sense that 'we're in this together'.

The key to re-motivating his troops is Henry's use of imagery. He does not tell them what to do – they already know that – but how they can be successful when they get there. This approach reflects 'active imagination' used in psychology: 'see' the desired result first; next think what energy you need to achieve it; then imagine yourself doing it; finally do it. Framing and rhetoric are key skills in inspirational language, as we have discussed earlier in the chapter. Sparing use of such language and authenticity and careful timing are crucial. Otherwise such language becomes a cliché and leads to cynicism.

Henry appeals to the troops' natural desire to make their parents and ancestors proud of them. And he confirms his hope that they are motivated to move forward, displaying the hallmark of transformational leadership [ ... ] 'You're doing this not just for your parents, or for me, but for our country, and for the great spirit that guides it.' Henry has motivated his troops to go beyond immediate self-interest and serve a greater good. He has transformed their motivation to go beyond what they had previously expected of themselves.

The night before battle, Henry faces up to his fears and duties. He has to inspire his troops to achieve an evidently miraculous victory against all the odds. The Chorus tells us that the English are waiting, like ghosts, to die. At 3 a.m. Henry walks around, visiting all his troops, 'thawing cold fear'. Olivier comments: Henry does what is required of him, not what is easy or comfortable. He displays visible leadership. He is seen by others, and he sees them; he displays confidence. By acting confidently, Henry bolsters his troops' confidence. [...]

Henry tells his brother, 'We are in great danger.' He is asked to meet with his nobles but refuses to do so: 'I and my bosom must debate awhile and then I would no other company.' He takes off his crown, puts on a cloak and walks around unrecognized. He talks to some ordinary soldiers who believe they will die and that if they do not die well 'it will be a black matter for the King that led us to it'.

Leaders need to put on a brave face for their followers. But they also need to face their inner reality, their 'private truth', and reflect on the situation they are in. Henry has the courage to listen (anonymously) to his troops – they, like people in a crisis world over, are blaming the boss. But by practising what we now call MBWA ('Management By Walking Around') and listening carefully to what they are saying he may be able to inspire them later. He feels the weight of responsibility of what people project onto their leaders, the cause of many sleepless nights for leaders. He needs to unload this: failing to do so may lead to decisions based on what others want rather than what he thinks is right. This is what Olivier calls 'appropriate self-ishness'. Finally, in praying he faces his own 'inner demons'. The activities of the 'dark night' have stripped away layers to reveal Henry's core values: why he is doing this. And it is from these core values that he speaks to inspire others. Now he is ready to enter the fray.

Henry returns to his nobles and speaks to them from the heart. He tells them why he believes they are doing the right thing. He says their resources are enough to win honourably or die trying:

No, my fair cousin.
If we are marked to die, we are enough
To do our country loss; and if to live,
The fewer men, the greater share of honour.

He says that those who do not wish to fight may leave, but that any who choose to fight and who survive will remember this day for the rest of their lives. A foolhardy offer, perhaps, but Henry has sown the seeds of inspiration well. He does not talk about the battle to come and what he expects of his troops, but about their retirement! He offers the gift of a future, but without false promises. Now they have something to fight for. He makes an extraordinary offer of equality and turns the outrageous odds against winning into an inspiring challenge:

We few, we happy few, we band of brothers.
For he today that sheds his blood with me
Shall be my brother; be he ne'er so vile,
This day shall gentle his condition.

This speech impressed Winston Churchill so much during the Second World War that he asked Richard's father, Sir Laurence Olivier, to make his film of *Henry V* to enhance morale for the Normandy landings. Churchill himself drew from Henry's image of 'the happy few' in his Battle of Britain speech to the House of Commons on 20 August 1940: 'Never in the field of human conflict was so much owed by so many to so few.'

The battle goes well for the English. The French surrender, Henry thanks God, and he forbids anyone to boast of the victory: he says, 'Boast of this, or take that praise from God, which is His only.' Olivier comments: Henry did not claim credit for the victory: it happened because it was right. Outstanding leaders do not seek credit or applause. Olivier says:

An insecure leader will feel the need to claim the credit for
the victory, to be seen as the superhero who 'made' it happen.
The more secure we are, and the less driven by ego, the more
we will surrender credit to others.

## References

Adair, J. (1988) *The Action Centred Leader*, London, The Industrial Society.

Adair, J. (1989) *Great Leaders*, Guildford, The Talbot Adair Press.

Ahmad, A. (2002) 'The power of language', *New Straits Times,* Malaysia, 17 April, p. 10.

Allen-Mills, T. (2004) 'Deceptive face of the man they always underestimated', *The Sunday Times,* 6 June, p. 1.26.

Al-Mubarakpuri, Safi-ur-Rahman (1995) *Ar-Raheeq Al-Makhtum (The Sealed Nectar): Biography of the Noble Prophet*, Riyadh, Saudi Arabia, Maktaba Dar-us-Salam.

Atkinson, J.M. (1984) *Our Masters' Voices: The Language and Body Language of Politics*, London, Methuen.

Bailey, R. (2000) 'Great expectations', *Management Skills & Development,* vol. 3, no. 1, pp. 58–59.

Bass, B.M. (1988) 'The inspirational processes of leadership', *Journal of Management Development,* vol. 7, no. 5, pp. 21–31.

Bass, B.M. (1989) 'Evolving perspectives on charismatic leadership' in Conger, J.A. and Kanungo, R.N. (eds) *Charismatic Leadership: The Elusive Factor in Organizational Effectiveness*, San Francisco, CA, Jossey-Bass.

Bass, B.M. (1990) *Bass and Stogdill's Handbook of Leadership: Theory, Research and Managerial Applications* (3rd edn), New York, Free Press.

Bass, B.M. (1992) 'Assessing the charismatic leader' in Syrett, M. and Hogg, C. (eds) *Frontiers of Leadership*, Oxford, Blackwell.

Beard, A. (2000) *The Language of Politics*, London, Routledge.

Beckett, M. (1999) 'Tomorrow's leaders filled with self-doubt', *Daily Telegraph,* 26 August.

Behling, O. and McFillen, J.M. (1996) 'A syncretical model of charismatic/transformational leadership', *Group & Organisation Management,* vol. 21, no. 2, pp. 163–85.

Binney, G. and Williams, C. (1995) *Leading into the Future*, London, Nicholas Brealey.

Bryman, A. (1992) *Charisma and Leadership in Organizations*, London, Sage Publications.

Cartwright, T. (2002) 'A question of leadership', *Leadership in Action,* vol. 22, no. 2, May/June, p. 12.

Collins, J.C. (2001) 'Level 5 leadership: the triumph of humility and fierce resolve', *Harvard Business Review,* January–February.

Conger, J.A. (1999) 'The new age of persuasion', *Leader to Leader,* Spring, pp. 37–44.

De Bono, E. (1998) *Simplicity*, Harmondsworth, Penguin.

Drucker, P.F. (1992) *Managing for the Future*, Oxford, Butterworth-Heinemann.

Eidelson, R.J. and Eidelson, J.I. (2003) 'Dangerous ideas: Five beliefs that propel groups towards conflict', *American Psychologist,* vol. 58, no. 3, pp. 182–92.

Fairhurst, G. and Sarr, R. (1996) *The Art of Framing*, San Francisco, CA, Jossey-Bass.

Fitton, R.A. (1997) *Leadership: Quotations from the World's Greatest Motivators*, Oxford, Westview Press.

Gardner, H. (1995) *Leading Minds: An Anatomy of Leadership*, New York, Basic Books.

Georgiades, N. and Macdonnell, R. (1998) *Leadership for Competitive Advantage*, Chichester, John Wiley and Sons.

Giles, L. (1976) *The Analects of Confucius, XII.7*, Translated from the Chinese, Norwalk, CT, The Easton Press.

Goffee, R. and Jones, G. (2000) 'Why should anyone be led by you?' *Harvard Business Review,* September–October, pp. 62–70.

Goldie, C.M. and Pinch, R.G.E. (1991) *Communication Theory*, New York, Press Syndicate of the University of Cambridge.

Goodwin, D.K. (1998) 'Lessons of presidential leadership', *Leader to Leader,* vol. 9, pp. 23–30.

Grint, K. (2000) *The Arts of Leadership*, Oxford, Oxford University Press.

Hazlitt, W. (1807) 'The eloquence of the British senate' in Geoffrey Keynes (ed.) (1946) *Selected Essays of William Hazlitt: 1778–1830*, London, Nonesuch Press.

Hoare, S. (2001) 'Rhymes with leadership. Sunday Business', *Sunday Telegraph,* 4 March.

Homer-Dixon, T.F. (1999) *Environment, Scarcity, and Violence*, Princeton, NJ, Princeton University Press.

Hunt, J.W. (1998) 'A differential equation', *Financial Times,* 25 March.

Ignatieff, M. (1985) *The Needs of Strangers*, New York, Viking.

Kirkpatrick, S.A. and Locke, E.A. (1996) 'Direct and indirect effects of three core charismatic leadership components on performance and attitudes', *Journal of Applied Psychology,* vol. 81, pp. 36–51.

Kouzes, J.M. and Posner, B.Z. (1991) *The Leadership Challenge*, San Francisco, CA, Jossey-Bass.

Lebrecht, N. (2000) 'The humanising of Hitler', *The Spectator,* 28 October, pp. 60–61.

Leung, V. (2000) 'The making of an impressive speech. End-of-millennium Lecture', *The Millennium Journal 2000,* Robert Black College, University of Hong Kong.

Lulla, S. (2002) 'Leadership = character x competence. Indian Management', *Journal of the*

*All-India Management Association,* June.

MacArthur, B. (ed.) (1996) *The Penguin Book of Historic Speeches,* London, Penguin.

MacArthur, B. (ed.) (1999) *The Penguin Book of Twentieth-Century Speeches* (2nd revised edn), London, Penguin.

Maccoby, M. (2000) 'Narcissistic leaders: the incredible pros and inevitable cons', *Harvard Business Review,* January–February.

McKee, R. (2003) 'Storytelling that moves people', *Harvard Business Review,* June, pp. 51–55.

Morgan, N. (2001) 'The kinaesthetic speaker: putting action into words', *Harvard Business Review,* April, pp. 113–20.

O'Rourke, P.J. (1992) *Parliament of Whores,* London, Picador.

Olivier, R. (2001) *Inspirational Leadership: Henry V and the Muse of Fire,* London, The Industrial Society (The Spiro Press).

Ormrod, J.E. (1995) *Human Learning* (2nd edn), Columbus, OH, Merrill.

Paxman, J. (2002) *The Political Animal: An Anatomy,* London, Penguin/Michael Joseph.

Rajan, A. (2000) *Does Management Development Fail to Produce Leaders?* Tonbridge, Kent, Centre for Research in Employment and Technology in Europe.

Reynolds, L. (2000) 'What is leadership?' *Training Journal,* November, pp. 26–27.

Rogers, C.R. and Greenberg, H.M. (1952) 'Barriers and gateways to communication', *Harvard Business Review,* republished 1 November 1991.

Sayles, L.R. (1993) *The Working Leader,* New York, Free Press.

Schama, S. (2002) 'Friends, Romans, Eminem, lend me your ears', *The Sunday Times,* 21 July, p. 4.7.

Simms, J. (2002) 'Is Britain being led astray?' *Director,* January, pp. 48–51.

Stern, P.C. (1995) 'Why do people sacrifice for their nations?' *Political Psychology,* vol. 16, pp. 217–35.

Sutch, A. (2001) 'Case study: Leadership the St Benedictine way', paper presented at the Fourth Annual Conference, 'Leading with Personal Power', The Leadership Trust Foundation, Rosse-on-Wye, 25–26 September.

*The Economist* (2002a) 'Persuasion', 4 May, pp. 95–96.

*The Economist* (2002b) 'Dr Feelgood', 16 March, p. 84.

Von Ghyczy, T. (2003) 'The fruitful flaws of strategy metaphors', *Harvard Business Review,* September, pp. 86–94.

Walters, H. (2002) 'Leadership and teambuilding in a hostile environment', paper presented at a conference on 'The Successful Leader', Institute of Directors, London, 3 May.

Wardy, R. (1996) *The Birth of Rhetoric: Georgias, Plato and Their Successors,* London, Routledge.

Watts, G. (Translator) (1640) *De Dignitate et Augmentis Scientarium* (Of the Advancement and Proficience of Learning, or, The Partitions of Sciences, IX Books), 1, vi, 31, Antiheta, 6, 1, by Francis Bacon, Oxford, Robert Young and Edward Forrest, publishers.

Zeldin, T. (2004) *What is the Good Life? Richer Not Happier: A 21st Century Search for the Good Life.* Debate on 11 February 2004 at the Royal Society of Arts, London. *RSA Journal,* July, 36–39.

# The 'Dark Night of the Soul'

# 17

## Richard Olivier

[ ... ] Act 4 shows Henry going through the long dark night before the battle, facing up to his fears and duties before being able to inspire his troops to an apparently miraculous victory, against the odds.

The Chorus tells us that the English are waiting, like ghosts, to die. At three o'clock in the morning Henry walks around, visiting all his troops, 'thawing cold fear'.

Sometimes the acting makes it real. Henry cannot really want to be out talking to his troops at three o'clock. But he does it because it is required of him. He exercises visible leadership. He is seen by others, and he sees them, thus bolstering confidence.

Henry tells his brother, Gloucester, 'we are in great danger'. He is asked to meet with his nobles but says no; 'I and my bosom must debate awhile and then I would no other company'. He takes off his crown, puts on a cloak and walks about unrecognized. He enters a conversation with some ordinary soldiers who believe they will die, and that if they do not die well 'it will be a black matter for the King that led us to it'. He ends up challenging one of them to a fight, if they both survive the battle. Left alone he unloads some of the burden of leadership that he feels; 'what infinite heartsease must kings neglect that private men enjoy?' He ends with a confessional prayer. Now he feels ready to rejoin his nobles and prepare for battle.

Leaders need to allow themselves to enter the 'dark night of the soul' and face their own innermost fears, doubts and uncertainties, especially in a crisis, and especially before they make decisions that affect the lives of others. If they don't, they may make the wrong decisions for the wrong reasons. There is a point in most meaningful projects when we are forced to ask ourselves: 'Is this the right thing to do?' and 'Am I the right person to do it?' In these times we will have to manage our own fears and the fears of

Olivier, R. (2002) 'The "dark night of the soul" '. Article created from a chapter in his book, *Inspirational Leadership: Henry V and the Muse of Fire*, London, Spiro Press, pp. xxxv–xxxvii and 158–66.

others simultaneously but differently. We need to put on a brave face for the troops, but equally important is our inner reality. Henry finds a brother with whom he can share his private truth. He then takes 'time out' to reflect on the difficult situation they are in.

Henry is courageous enough to listen (in disguise) to what the troops really think. And they, like troops in crisis the world over, are blaming the boss. But if he listens carefully to what they are thinking, he may just be able to inspire them later. However, he also feels the weight of responsibility that many workers project onto their leaders. He needs to unload this or he may make his decision based on what others want, rather than what he thinks is right. Finally, when he prays, he faces his own inner demons. Now he is ready to go back into the fray.

When Henry arrives back at his tent he overhears the nobles wishing for more troops. He speaks to them from the heart, telling them why he, personally, believes they are doing the right thing. He says they are enough to win honourably or die trying. He says those that do not wish to fight can leave, but any who choose to fight and who survive will remember this day for the rest of their lives. He calls them a 'band of brothers' and promises that those who miss the fight will regret it later. The French Herald returns with another offer of surrender which Henry roundly refuses. They go off to start the battle.

The whole process of surviving the 'dark night' has served to strip away layers to reveal Henry's centre, his core values – what he is doing all this for. And it is from this core that he speaks to inspire others.

The battle is going well for the English. They deal with the first wave of French attack and capture many prisoners. Another attack is sounded. Henry orders his men to kill their prisoners. Meanwhile the French have raided the luggage tents and killed all the boys who were guarding them. The Herald enters and tells Henry the day is his. He thanks God and forbids anyone to boast of the victory. They set off for Calais.

Most leaders wish they could get through their career without having to take any of the really tough decisions. Very few get their wish. There is usually a situation in which our innocence dies – in which we are forced to compromise the values on which we prided ourselves when we started our journey into leadership. It is the ability to take these hard decisions and live with the consequences that separates the 'men from the boys' among leaders. Having survived this final initiation, Henry is not naïve enough to claim credit for the victory. It happened because it was right, they did not 'do' it.

[ ... ]

# ACT 4 • Scene 3

## Inspiring the Troops

### The Story

The nobles wait for Henry in his tent:

Gloucester: *Where is the King?*

Bedford: *The King himself is rode to view their battle.*

Exeter: *Of fighting men they have full threescore thousand. There's five to one. Besides, they all are fresh.*

Westmoreland: *'Tis a fearful odds... O that we now had here But one ten thousand of those men in England That do no work today.*

The King has come in unseen and overheard the request; he speaks:

*What's he that wishes so?*
*My cousin, Westmoreland? No, my fair cousin.*
*If we are marked to die, we are enough*
*To do our country loss; and if to live,*
*The fewer men, the greater share of honour.*
*God's will, I pray thee wish not one man more.*
*By Jove, I am not covetous for gold,*
*It yearns me not if men my garments wear;*
*Such outward things dwell not in my desires.*
*But if it be a sin to covet honour*
*I am the most offending soul alive.*
*No, faith, my coz, wish not a man from England.*
*Rather proclaim it presently through my host*
*That he which hath no stomach to this fight,*
*Let him depart. His passport shall be made*
*And crowns for convoy put into his purse.*
*We would not die in that man's company*
*That fears his fellowship to die with us.*
*This day is called the Feast of Crispian.*
*He that outlives this day and comes safe home*
*Will stand a-tiptoe when this day is named*
*And rouse him at the name of Crispian.*
*He that shall see this day and live old age*
*Will yearly on the vigil feast his neighbours*
*And say, 'Tomorrow is Saint Crispian.'*

*Then will he strip his sleeve and show his scars*
*And say, 'These wounds I had on Crispin's day.'*
*Old men forget; yet all shall be forgot,*
*But he'll remember, with advantages,*
*What feats he did that day. Then shall our names,*
*Familiar in his mouth as household words...*
*Be in their flowing cups freshly remembered.*
*This story shall the good man teach his son,*
*And Crispin Crispian shall ne'er go by*
*From this day to the ending of the world*
*But we in it shall be rememberèd,*
*We few, we happy few, we band of brothers.*
*For he today that sheds his blood with me*
*Shall be my brother; be he ne'er so vile,*
*This day shall gentle his condition.*
*And gentlemen in England now abed*
*Shall think themselves accursed they were not here,*
*And hold their manhoods cheap whiles any speaks*
*That fought with us upon Saint Crispin's day.*

The Earl of Salisbury comes in to tell Henry the French are ready to attack:

Henry: *All things are ready if our minds be so.*

Westmoreland: *Perish the man whose mind is backward now.*

Henry: *Thou dost not wish more help from England, coz?*

Westmoreland: *God's will, my liege, would you and I alone, Without more help, could fight this royal battle.*

Henry: *Why now thou hast unwished five thousand men, Which likes me better than to wish us one. – You know your places. God be with you all.*

The French Herald Montjoy enters to ask if Henry will now negotiate his ransom before his 'most assurèd overthrow' and take pity on his soldiers' souls that they may retreat 'From off these fields where, wretches, their poor bodies must lie and fester.'

But Henry has made up his mind:

Henry: *Come thou no more for ransom, gentle herald.*
*They shall have none, I swear, but these my joints –*
*Which if they have as I will leave 'em them,*
*Shall yield them little. Tell the Constable.*

Montjoy: *I shall, King Harry. And so fare thee well.*
*Thou never shalt hear herald any more.*

Henry (aside): *I fear thou wilt once more come for a ransom.*

# What's in It for Me?

While Henry has been on his walkabout the nobles have been busy calculating the odds. Now they publicly wish for more troops. (Funny that, senior managers wanting more resources!) Henry faces a different challenge to the one at Harfleur; at Harfleur they had to achieve the first foothold, now they need to be inspired to fight against the odds. There are defining moments in all our lives and in all the roles we choose to play; this is the moment which sets Henry among the ranks of truly inspirational leaders. He starts, as he will finish, by addressing the request for more troops:

> *No, my fair cousin.*
> *If we are marked to die, we are enough*
> *To do our country loss; and if to live,*
> *The fewer men, the greater share of honour.*

Having survived his 'dark night', he knows why he is here – because he believes it is the right and honourable place to be – and what he is here for:

> *By Jove, I am not covetous for gold,*
> *It yearns me not if men my garments wear;*
> *Such outward things dwell not in my desires.*
> *But if it be a sin to covet honour*
> *I am the most offending soul alive.*

Sometimes, in order to follow you into a seriously tough battle, your people need to know why *you* are doing it. What gets you out of bed in the morning for this fight – besides the gold, the salary or the prospective bonus? Why do you believe this is an honourable cause, the right path to be pursuing? The 'outward things' won't help here; most of your people would be able to get similar 'outward things' from other leaders, other organizations. It is not *what* you can offer them, but *who* is leading them that they need to know. And if you have not gone through the 'dark night' you may not know the answer.

# Less Is More

Henry continues, making what many assume to be a foolhardy offer:

> *No, faith, my coz, wish not a man from England.*
> *Rather proclaim it presently through my host*

*That he which hath no stomach to this fight,*
*Let him depart. His passport shall be made*
*And crowns for convoy put into his purse.*
*We would not die in that man's company*
*That fears his fellowship to die with us.*

If everyone stuck their hand up and said 'Yes please, I'll take the money and run', Henry would, technically speaking, be stuffed. If the majority of people have only followed him because it was a job, something to do, something to bring in a daily crust, he wouldn't have many left. But Henry has sown the seeds of inspiration well. He encouraged others to buy in to the mission before it started, connected the mission to a line of service ('Harry, England and Saint George!'), and has motivated them over all obstacles so far. They'll stay.

There is also a peculiar wisdom in the offer. I can think of several big projects I have been involved in, which some people walked out of, and those remaining achieved twice as much in half the time. By cutting away the dead wood you can sometimes do more with less. Better to have a few inspired 'brothers' than a load of resentful followers.

## The Gift of a Future

Now Henry draws an image from the future, and gives his listeners a glimpse of life beyond the battle. He does not talk about the details of the fight to come and what he expects of them, he talks about their retirement!

*This day is called the Feast of Crispian.*
*He that outlives this day and comes safe home*
*Will stand a-tiptoe when this day is named*
*And rouse him at the name of Crispian.*
*He that shall see this day and live t' old age*
*Will yearly on the vigil feast his neighbours*
*And say, 'Tomorrow is Saint Crispian.'*
*Then will he strip his sleeve and show his scars*
*And say, 'These wounds I had on Crispin's day.'*
*Old men forget; yet all shall be forgot,*
*But he'll remember, with advantages,*
*What feats he did that day. Then shall our names,*
*Familiar in his mouth as household words…*
*Be in their flowing cups freshly remembered.*
*This story shall the good man teach his son,*
*And Crispin Crispian shall ne'er go by*

*From this day to the ending of the world*
*But we in it shall be rememberèd.*

This, to me, is the core of the speech. Henry offers the gift of a future to a group who, up till this moment, has not seen any future; they have been waiting to die. Nor does he make any false promises. He does not say; 'I think most of us will make it', he says that any one who makes it will remember this day and [be] his comrades, forever. When he says *'He* that outlives this day...' everyone listening thinks 'That could be me. I could be the one. I'll have a drink for you lot, promise.'

In the moment Henry paints this picture of the future those listening will start to see it, and when they do, it becomes a possible reality for them. They follow Henry's imagination to see themselves as old men on the anniversary of the battle, in the pub, having a drink and toasting their mates. And then, from the vantage point of this imagined future, Henry gets them all to look back – *on a battle that they have not even fought yet* – as though it were in the past. In their imaginations they have already moved beyond the ugly reality of the present to a happy imagined future from which they can reflect on their glorious struggle. Now they have something to fight for. Survival and honour.

## 'The Few'

Lastly, Henry turns the outrageous odds into an inspiring challenge:

*We few, we happy few, we band of brothers.*
*For he today that sheds his blood with me*
*Shall be my brother; be he ne'er so vile,*
*This day shall gentle his condition.*

He glories in the inequality of numbers, calling out a sense of honour in the underdog. He not only includes himself in the battle with them, he also makes a virtue out of them shedding blood together which, he promises, will bind them together in a bond of brotherhood. This is an extraordinary offer of equality, particularly as in Elizabethan times the monarch was believed to be touched by the divine. Even today a respected leader who transmits the sense that others can be equal to him or her will inspire:

*And gentlemen in England now abed*
*Shall think themselves accursed they were not here,*
*And hold their manhoods cheap whiles any speaks*
*That fought with us upon Saint Crispin's day.*

The final reversal – it will not be us wishing others were here, it will be those others wishing they had been here, to share in the glory of the struggle. It is as if Henry were saying: 'Come on guys, if we had 100,000 here it wouldn't be a real achievement. You'd forget about it in a few years. But if we can win, with 8,000, now that would be one to remember.' He makes a blessing out of their complaint, and reawakens the part in all his listeners that wants to be extraordinary, that yearns to be remembered for a great achievement.

When Henry hears the French are preparing to fight he says 'All things are ready if our minds be so' (sports/performance psychologists would agree). And finally Westmoreland, he who wanted more troops, proves that Henry has indeed 'readied' the minds of others:

> God's will, my liege, would you and I alone,
> Without more help, could fight this royal battle.

As a whole, this is one of the most inspiring speeches in English literature, and it rarely fails to stir up not only the troops on stage, but the audience as well. The impact of this speech was a key factor in Winston Churchill encouraging my father to make his film of *Henry V* during the Second World War, to build morale for the Normandy landings. The story of a successful invasion of France might just ready some more modern minds. Churchill himself memorably drew from Henry's image of 'the happy few' when speaking of the 'Battle of Britain':

> The gratitude of every home in our island, in our Empire, and indeed throughout the world, except in the abodes of the guilty, goes out to the British airmen who, undaunted by odds, unwearied by their constant challenge and mortal danger, are turning the tide of world war by their prowess and by their devotion. *Never in the field of human conflict was so much owed by so many to so few.* (From Churchill's speech to the House of Commons, 20 August 1940)

## Hardening the Resolve

By the time Montjoy arrives with another offer of ransom, it is too late. All the Herald succeeds in doing is giving the King one more chance to answer Williams and any other soldier that doubts his resolve:

> Come thou no more for ransom, gentle herald.
> They shall have none, I swear, but these my joints –
> Which if they have as I will leave 'em them,
> Shall yield them little.

This is not a leader who will risk his people and then look to save himself. People appreciate hearing such loyalty. I recently coached a director in the National

Health Service to risk sharing the private loyalty he felt for his staff with them in public. He told me afterwards he had never received such grateful comments from staff before, nor had he ever thought it necessary to let them know how much he wanted to protect them and how willing he was to fight for them.

## A Sting in the Tail

After all this – Harfleur, the 'dark night', inspiring his troops, publicly refusing to surrender – the private fears remain, just below the surface. As the Herald Montjoy leaves, Shakespeare has Henry mutter under his breath, to himself: 'I fear thou wilt once more come for a ransom'. Which would only happen if the English were near defeat. You can never be sure that any given course of action will succeed, even if you believe it is the right way to go.

[ ... ]

# The Theory Behind the Practice

# 18

*Gareth Morgan*

[ ... ]

## The Importance of Images and Metaphors

In terms of specific background, my interest in this social-constructionist approach to change originated in a study conducted with Gibson Burrell on how different worldviews shape how we understand organization and management (Burrell and Morgan, 1979). One of the main insights emerging from this work was that social scientists, like people in everyday life, tend to get trapped by their perspectives and assumptions. As a result, they construct, understand, and interpret the social world in partial ways, creating interesting sets of insights but obliterating others as ways of seeing become ways of not seeing. [ ... ] Pursuing the insights, I became interested in exploring how different theoretical perspectives could be used to broaden fields of study and to help people generate deeper understandings of the issues addressed.

This eventually led to further investigation of how social scientists working in the field of organization and management construct their theories and perspectives (Morgan 1980, 1983a) and to the role played by images and metaphors in shaping domains of study and in the social construction of reality. As I explored, I came to realize, along with other theorists, that metaphor is not just a literary or linguistic device for embellishing or decorating discourse. It's a primal means through which we forge our relationships with the world (see, for example, Brown 1977; Lakoff and Johnson 1980; Morgan 1980, 1983a, 1983b; Ortony 1979; Schön 1963, 1979; White 1978). Metaphor has a formative impact on language, on the construction and embellishment of meaning, and on the development of theory and knowledge of all kinds.

To illustrate, consider a young child who catches his first sight of the moon and says 'balloon' or who, on seeing a tiger at the zoo, says 'meow'. The child is

Morgan, G. (1993) 'The theory behind the practice', Crafted from Morgan, G. *Imaginization*, Newbury Park, CA, Sage, pp. 271–94.

engaging in metaphor whereby familiar elements of experience (the balloon and cat) are used to understand the unfamiliar (the moon and tiger). This process, it seems, lies at the root of how meaning is forged: from the development of language to how we think and develop formal knowledge.

Language develops as concepts associated with one domain of meaning are extended metaphorically to another. To illustrate, consider the history of the word *organization*. It stems from the ancient Greek word *organon*, meaning a tool or instrument: 'something with which one works'. Gradually, the use of *organon* was extended metaphorically to describe musical instruments, surgical instruments, and body organs of animals and plants – hence the English words *organ, organize,* and *organization. To organize* came to mean putting connected 'organs' into a systematic form, and the word *organization,* a collection of organs used to perform other ends. The idea of describing a group of people as 'an organization' became popular in the wake of the Industrial Revolution and acquired mechanical overtones. Organizations, like machines, came to be viewed as instruments that could be rationally designed and managed, so that their human and technical 'organs' behaved in a rational, predictable way.

The same process can be observed in the development of everyday knowledge and in scientific theory. Knowledge emerges and develops as a domain of extended metaphor. For Newton, the world was seen as a kind of celestial machine. Einstein's breakthrough on relativity came through imagining what it would be like to 'ride on a light wave'. The images thus created allowed reality to be seen in new ways and to be studied in detail through more reductive (metonymical) processes whereby the implications of the guiding image are elaborated in detail (Morgan 1983a, 1983b; White 1978).

Unfortunately, the key role played by metaphor in helping us to understand our world has become obscured. As the word *reality* signifies, people have come to believe that they are living in a domain of meaning that seems much more real and concrete than it actually is. The same is true in science. Scientific knowledge is often seen as searching for, and offering, 'the Truth'. If we take a close look at the process, however, we find that science is just offering an interesting and useful metaphorical perspective, an interesting and useful way of seeing and thinking about the world! This may allow one to act on the world and to produce predictable results, as in scientific experiments, but the broad context of interpretation and meaning is ultimately grounded in the linguistic and other socially constructed frameworks within which the experiments and knowledge are set.

This is a controversial and unpopular view in the scientific community because it undermines the idea that science *should* involve the generation of some kind of literal truth (e.g., Pinder and Bourgeois 1982; Tsoukas 1991). Indeed, metaphorical knowledge is often distinguished from 'literal knowledge'. Metaphor is seen as belonging to the realm of creative imagination. The 'literal' is seen as something that is real and true, as something that has an unambiguous empirical correspondence. Yet, if we examine the very concept of *literal,* we find that it is itself a metaphor. The word plays on the image of a letter or letters and is connected with the notions of literate and literature. The connection would no doubt be much clearer if the word were spelled *letteral!* By *evoking* the idea of a 'literal truth', scientists are in effect *creating* the idea that there is a nonmetaphorical realm of knowledge. But it's no more than a metaphorical idea, one through which we try to create the notion that our understanding of reality is a little more 'real' than it actually may be.

All this may seem to be playing with words. But, at a deeper level, it concerns basic issues relating to the nature of knowledge. In the early eighteenth century, the Irish philosopher George Berkeley (1910a, 1910b) noted that objectivity belongs as much to the realm of the observer as to that of the object observed. This point is central to the issues being discussed here.

Knowledge as objective or literal truth places too much emphasis on the *object* of knowledge and not enough on the paradigms, perspective, assumptions, language games, and frames of reference of the observer. The challenge before us now is to achieve a better balance, by recognizing that all knowledge is the product of an interpretive process. To achieve this, we need fresh metaphors for thinking about the process through which knowledge is generated. Instead of placing emphasis on the need for 'solid', 'literal', 'foundational', 'objective Truth', we need more dynamic modes of understanding that show how knowledge results from some kind of implicit or explicit 'conversation', 'dialogue', 'engagement', or interaction between the interests of people and the world in which they live (Bernstein 1983; Checkland 1981; Checkland and Scholes 1990; Gergen 1982; Morgan 1983a; Rorty 1979, 1985). Instead of seeing knowledge as an objective, known 'thing', we need to see it as a capacity and potential that can be developed in the 'knower'-hence my interest in imaginization as a process through which, metaphorically, we 'read' and 'write' the world of organization and management.

Imaginization, as a way of knowing and as a way of acting, seeks to advance the power of the 'everyday knower' and the power of the 'everyday writer' of social life!

# Images of Organization

My first attempt at exploring this process was presented in my book *Images of Organization* (1986), where I demonstrated the metaphorical basis of organization theory and showed how different perspectives could generate different insights. In essence, the book explored a series of *'what if...?'* questions:

> *What if* we think about organizations as machines?
> *What if* we think about them as organisms?
> ...as brains?
> ...as cultures?
> ...as political systems?

... as psychic prisons?
... as flux and transformation?
... as instruments of domination?

As I developed the implications of each perspective, I showed how they created complementary and competing insights, each of which possesses inherent strengths and limitations. For example, while a 'machine view' of organization focuses on organization as the relationship between structures, roles, and technology, the 'culture view' shows how organization rests in shared meanings. The psychic prison metaphor shows how structures and shared meanings can become conscious and unconscious traps. The political perspective shows how these characteristics are often shaped by clashes of interest and power plays – and so on. I showed how all the different perspectives could be used to 'read' the nature and significance of different aspects of organizational life as well as how the injunctions or implications of each metaphor offered specific ideas for the design and management of organizations in practice. Though the book restricted itself to using eight broad metaphorical frameworks to illustrate its message, it developed the idea that organization ultimately rests in ways of thinking and acting and that, in principle, there are no limits to number of images and metaphors that can be used to enrich this process.

My aim in all this was to show how managers and others interested in the world of organization can become more effective in understanding and shaping the realities with which they have to deal. Throughout, I was at pains to avoid asserting the supremacy of any given metaphor or theoretical perspective, because I wanted to encourage 'the reader' to realize that there is no one theory, metaphor, synthesis, or perspective that is going to provide all the answers. Hence, in using the book, one is left with many insights about the nature of organization but with no single theory saying that 'this is the best way of seeing or thinking about organization'. Instead of trying to offer an authoritative statement on 'the way organizations are', it throws the problem of interpretation right back onto each and every one of us – on 'the knowers' rather than 'the known'. Or, as I put it in earlier chapters of this book, it obliges and encourages us to become 'our own theorists', forging our own understandings and interpretations of the situations we face.

This is what distinguishes *Images of Organization* from the majority of books on organization and management. Most of these offer a specific theory for understanding and managing organizations or try to develop an integrated framework that highlights certain dimensions over others. They reduce our understanding of organization to a particular way of seeing. My approach, on the other hand, was to suggest that, because any *particular* way of seeing is limited (including the one being advocated!), the challenge is to become skilled in the 'art of seeing', in the art of 'understanding', in the art of 'interpreting' and 'reading' the situations we face.

In many respects, the approach fits what is known as a postmodern approach to understanding organizational life. The postmodernist movement has grown in strength and significance over the last few decades, suggesting that the search for universal, authoritative, 'true' explanations of social reality are always problematic and incomplete because they end up elevating the priority of a particular perspective while downplaying others. As it is sometimes put, 'the presence' of the ideas and insights highlighted by a particular theory or perspective always creates 'an absence': the insights, ideas, and perspectives that are pushed from view. This creates a problem for anyone who wishes to interpret and explain something, particularly in science and the humanities, where explanations are expected to carry some weight and authority.

For the most part, postmodernism has only resulted in critiques of modes of writing and social processes that elevate one view over another: to disrupt what is typically viewed as 'normal' and self-evident so that the problematic nature of 'normality' becomes clear. This critical stance has done much to help us understand how biases and blind spots can accompany and sometimes dominate ways of seeing and how all 'explanations' are only forms of rhetoric that seek to persuade people to join or accept a particular point of view (see, for example, Berman 1988; Calas and Smircich 1988; Cooper 1989; Cooper and Burrell 1988; Harvey 1989; Linstead and Grafton-Small 1992; Martin 1990; Reed and Hughes 1992).

But, in my view, there is another way in which the postmodern perspective can be developed: by recognizing that, because partiality, incompleteness, and distortion are ever present in explanations of how we see and understand the world, perhaps we need to develop ways of theorizing and explaining the world that explicitly recognize and deal with the distorting nature of knowledge.

My approach to understanding organization and management discussed in *Images of Organization* began to address this task. It is continued in the current book in my general attempt to develop the process of imaginization, as a mode of theorizing and an approach to social change that seeks to help people mobilize highly relativistic, open-ended, evolving interpretive frameworks for guiding understanding and action. The aim is to help people develop ways of seeing, thinking, and theorizing that can improve their ability to understand and manage the highly relativistic, paradoxical, and changing character of the world with which they have to deal.

The old mechanistic worldview, on which so much organization and management theory – and, indeed, science – has been based, encouraged a search for fixed theories and linear methods and techniques of understanding and practice. The postmodern worldview, which, of interest, is paralleled in aspects of the new science emphasizing the chaotic, paradoxical, and transient nature of order and disorder (see, for example, the work of writers like Gleick 1987; Hampden-Turner 1990; Jantsch 1980; Nonaka 1988; Prigogine and Stengers 1984; Quinn 1990;

Smith and Berg 1987), requires an approach that allows the theory and practice of organization and management to acquire a more fluid form.

This is precisely what my approach to imaginization sets out to achieve. It develops the implications of the basic methodology offered in *Images of Organization* to create a relativistic, self-organizing approach to management and management theory capable of contributing to the challenges of the Einsteinian world in which we now find ourselves.

[ ... ]

## The Interconnection between 'Reading' and 'Writing'

At various points [ ... ], I have used the ideas of 'reading' and 'writing' as metaphors for capturing the challenge of interpreting and shaping organizational life. As noted above, this builds on the underlying metaphor of reality as a kind of living text.

At first glance, the image seems far-fetched. But, if one thinks about it, the language, images, ideas, and actions through which we write daily life parallel how a book uses words to fix and communicate meaning. Readers, whether of books or life, in turn create their own meaning; in effect, they add their own authoring to the text. In this way, the whole of life can be seen as a living 'real time' process of simultaneous reading and writing, producing evolving and diverse patterns of meaning.

This metaphorical frame has provided the basis for a hermeneutic school of social theory specializing in the art of interpretation (see, for example, Boland 1989; Gadamer 1975, 1976; Hollinger 1985; Rorty 1979, 1985; Shotter 1990; Turner 1983). It recognizes that, as readers and authors of our everyday realities, we all have limited horizons, shaped by the values, assumptions, worldviews, interests, and perspectives that we possess as individuals and as members of social groups. Hence our readings and subsequent authorings tend to be partial and one sided, committing us to live realities reflecting all kinds of conscious and unconscious social constructions associated with class, gender, culture, and the daily context in which we live. The hermeneutic perspective focuses on understanding the never-ending circle of relations underlying this social construction of reality.

My theory of reading and writing organizational life builds on these core ideas, but in a loose way. My primary aim has been to develop the metaphor as a *method* for exploring the multidimensional nature of organizations, showing how the horizons generated by different metaphors can be used to create new insights and action possibilities. Richard Boland (1989) has provided an outstanding critique of my approach from this point of view. At its simplest, the approach involves developing a 'diagnostic reading' and 'story line', using different metaphors as frames for highlighting and ordering different aspects of the reality with which we are dealing. [ ... ] I try to remain open to multiple and evolving interpretations of a situation, picking up key cues and signals as I go along, to develop a 'story line' that evaluates and integrates the various insights into an overall understanding of the situation. The evolving story lines [ ... ] are reflected in the progressive development of the 'readings', often captured through new images or metaphors of the moment that helped to make sense of the overall situation. [ ... ]

For any given situation, it's always possible to generate multiple authentic readings and story lines, because readings are just orderings of reality and are always shaped by the horizon of the reader and the interests to be served (Gadamer 1975, 1976; Habermas 1972). The analysis and story lines that emerge are really forms of rhetoric through which the 'author–reader' produces an understanding that serves the interests and agenda that he or she brings to the situation at hand. [ ... ]

This view on the essential relativity of imaginization links back to the point made earlier regarding 'foundational' versus 'conversational' approaches to knowledge. A foundational view leads one to look for authoritative, 'this is the way it is!' interpretations of a situation. Imaginization, on the other hand, builds around the paradox that any given situation may have multiple dimensions and multiple meanings, which acquire significance in the context of interpretation. None of these is necessarily absolute or 'true'. The challenge is to recognize that as interpreters and constructors of reality we face many options and that [ ... ] we can't study all dimensions at the same time. Our challenge is to dialogue and converse with the situations with which we are involved, to 'real-ize' meaningful knowledge, knowledge that will allow us to be edified or to act in a personally significant way. That doesn't necessarily satisfy those who are looking for an absolute meaning or 'truth' in a situation. But it does capture what seems to be the nature of the human condition: that, as humans, we can only ever acquire limited, partial, *personally significant* ways of knowing the world.

Viewed in this way, we are encouraged to see the 'reading' and knowledge generation process in terms of what Donald Schön (1983) has described as 'reflective practice', as the product of a craft shaped by assumptions and perspectives of all kinds. Imaginization is a form of 'reflective practice' encouraging us to become skilled interpreters of the situations with which we have to deal. It encourages us to develop our skills of framing and reframing, so that we can learn to see the same situation in different ways, so that we can remain open and flexible to multiple meanings, so that we can generate new insights and become comfortable with the paradox that the same situation can mean many things at the same time. It encourages us to become reflective, creative, and expansive in understanding the situations with which we have to deal. A reflective practitioner is someone who is aware of how implicit images, ideas, theories, frames, metaphors, and ideas guide and shape his or her practice and how they can be used to create new possibilities.

In this context, and in terms of my own reflective practice, it is appropriate to recognize that the concept of imaginization is itself a metaphor and, as such, has inherent strengths and limitations. In fusing the concepts of imagination and organization, it seeks to open the process of organizing to an expansive, creative mode of thinking, as opposed to the reductive mode that has dominated the development of mechanistic thought. It highlights and stresses creative possibility. But, at the same time, as critics may rush to point out, it can gloss and downplay the importance of existing power relations, a point addressed in the following pages, and may underestimate some of the deep structural rigidities in patterns of both thought and action. It thus suffers the fate of all metaphors, and indeed of all paradigms, concepts, and modes of understanding, in that it elevates the importance of certain aspects of reality over others. [ ... ]

# Images can Provide 'Mirrors' and 'Windows'

At one level, the process of imaginization is about the art of framing and reframing (Schön 1963, 1979; Watzlawick, Weakland, and Fisch 1974). It uses images, metaphors, readings, and story lines to cast situations in new perspective and open possibilities for creative action. But there's another dimension to the process, involving a theory about the relationship between a system's sense of identity and its ability to change. More specifically, imaginization builds on the principle that people and organizations tend to get trapped by the images that they hold of themselves and that genuine change requires an ability to see and challenge these self-images in some way. [ ... I]mages and metaphors can be used as 'mirrors' through which people and groups can see themselves and their situations in fresh light, creating an opportunity for reflection and change.

I like to talk about the process as one involving 'mirrors' and 'windows'. If one can look in the mirror and see oneself in a new way, the mirror can become a 'window', because it allows one to see the rest of the world with a fresh perspective. Or, in terms of the imagery introduced earlier, it opens new 'horizons,' creating opportunities for new actions. [ ... ]

The aim throughout is to disrupt normal ways of seeing so that people can ask constructive questions about what they are seeing and what they should do. I find the use of metaphor particularly powerful in this activity, because it creates distance and space from conventional ways of thinking: space in which people can feel free to think and act creatively. This is vital in trying to unlock

**Exhibit 18.1** The nature of metaphor

Shared features are emphasized

MY MANAGER IS A FOX

Differences are downplayed

*Note:* The 'injunction of the metaphor' is to: *See* the fox-like aspects of the manager: his cunning, guile, craftiness, smooth image.
But: *Ignore* that he doesn't have a black pointed nose, fur, four legs, or tail!

new understandings or a new sense of identity, because one cannot create the new in terms of the old.

Several aspects of the process through which I generate and use metaphorical imagery seem particularly important in this regard.

1. Metaphor always involves a sense of paradox and the absurd, because, as illustrated in Exhibit 18.1, it invites the users to think about themselves or their situations in ways that are patently false. [ ... ] Metaphor works by playing on a pattern of similarity and difference. Its user seeks to evoke the similarities while downplaying the differences. It involves the generation of a 'constructive falsehood' that helps to break the bounds of normal discourse. This plays a crucial role in creating space for change.
2. Metaphor requires its users to *find* and *create* meaning. They have to *find* the similarities between the manager and the fox, to *find* the relevance of the spider plant, to *find* the precise way in which an image can create relevant insights. This helps to create distance and space from conventional understandings and also helps to create *ownership* of the insights. There is nothing self-evident in the meaning of metaphor; meaning has to be created by those involved. Meaning is thus immediate and personal, not distant or abstract.
3. Metaphors only have an impact when they 'ring true', 'hit a chord', and 'resonate' around fundamental insights. One cannot force a metaphor to work, because the process soon becomes an empty ritual where everyone realizes there is little substance. The process thus has a self-regulating quality;

there has to be a resonance and authenticity to create energy and involvement. When different people generate different metaphors that have a great deal in common [ ... ] one knows that one is dealing with highly resonant insights.

4. Metaphors that are generated by the participants in a change project are often more powerful than those generated from outside, because they are directly owned and have immediate meaning. The facilitator of a process can, however, play a powerful role in finding resonant metaphors for capturing insights that others may not see or for recovering and synthesizing key insights that have gotten lost from view. In either case, resonance is key. The metaphor must energize and 'take hold'.

5. When metaphors are introduced from the outside, it's crucial that people be encouraged to find and elaborate meaning for themselves. When the implications of a metaphor are laid out in detail, its evocative power is often lost. Metaphors invite a conversational style where meaning and significance emerge through dialogue; resonant meaning cannot be imposed, it has to be evoked.

6. The tentative nature of metaphorical insights means that they cannot be taken too seriously or made too concrete. This has the advantage of helping to create open modes of understanding that have a capacity to self-organize and evolve as one goes along.

When used with these principles in mind, metaphorical images can provide powerful tools for helping people look at themselves and their situations in new ways and, as a result, see and act in the world somewhat differently. The process operates by creating a tension between existing and potential understandings, creating space for the new to emerge. [ ... ] However, new images do not result in new actions, unless there is an appropriate degree of shared understanding and a will to act on the insights thus generated.

This, I believe, defines an important frontier for development. People writing on the theory of change (e.g., Argyris and Schön 1974; Watzlawick et al. 1974) have made important distinctions between superficial change where the context remains invariant (called single-loop learning or first order change) and change where the context is also transformed (called double-loop learning or second order change). This has important implications for the practice of imaginization, because it highlights how one may be able to generate hundreds of new insights without substantial impact. The challenge of imaginization is to create insights that allow one to reframe contexts substantially rather than superficially. It's the old problem of rearranging the deck chairs on the Titanic! Superficially, one can create the impression of making a lot of changes; but, at base level, nothing of significance may have really changed.

This issue brings us back to the point made earlier about the role of imaginization in transforming horizons. Horizons define contexts. The challenge of imaginization is to help people see and understand the horizons that shape their context, to appreciate their limits, and to open up other horizons when necessary. Or, to change the metaphor, again, the challenge is to open new windows on the world, to create new ways of seeing that can lay the basis for new ways of acting.

[ ... ]

## References

Argyris C. and Schön, D. (1974) *Theory in Practice*, Reading, MA, Addison-Wesley.

Berkeley, G. (1910a) *A Treatise Concerning the Principles of Human Knowledge*, New York, Everyman (reprint).

Berkeley, G. (1910b) *A New Theory of Vision*, New York, Everyman (reprint).

Berman, A. (1988) *From the New Criticism to Deconstruction*, Urbana, IL, University of Illinois Press.

Bernstein, R.J. (1983) *Beyond Objectivism and Relativism: Science, Hermeneutics and Praxis*, Philadelphia, PA, University of Pennsylvania Press.

Boland, R.J. (1989) 'Beyond the objectivist and the subjectivist: Learning to read accounting as text', *Accounting, Organizations and Society*, vol. 14, pp. 591–604.

Brown, R.H. (1977) *A Poetic for Society*, New York, Cambridge University Press.

Calas, M. and Smircich, L. (1988) 'Reading leadership as a form of cultural analysis' in Hunt, J.G., Belliga, R.D., Dachler, H.P. and Schriesheim, C.A. (eds) *Emerging Leadership Vistas*, Lexington, MA, Lexington, pp. 201–26.

Checkland, P. (1981) *Systems Thinking, Systems Practice*, Chichester, UK, John Wiley.

Checkland, P. and Scholes, J. (1990) *Soft Systems Methodology in Action*, Chichester, UK, John Wiley.

Cooper, R. (1989) 'Modernism, postmodernism, and organizational analysis 3: The Contribution of Jacques Derrida', *Organization Studies*, vol. 10, no. 4, pp. 479–502.

Cooper, R. and Burrell, G. (1988) 'Modernism, postmodernism and organizational analysis: An introduction', *Organization Studies*, vol. 9, pp. 91–112.

Gadamer, H.G. (1975) *Truth and Method*, New York, Seabury.

Gadamer, H.G. (1976) *Philosophical Hermeneutics*, Berkeley, CA, University of California Press.

Gergen, K.J. (1982) *Toward Transformation in Social Knowledge*, New York, Springer-Verlag.

Gleick, J. (1987) *Chaos*, New York, Viking.

Habermas, J. (1972) *Knowledge and Human Interests*, London, Heinemann.

Hampden-Turner, C. (1990) *Charting the Corporate Mind*, New York, Free Press.

Harvey, D. (1989) *The Condition of Postmodernity*, Oxford, UK, Basil Blackwell.

Hollinger, R. (ed.) (1985) *Hermeneutics and Practice*, Notre Dame, University of Notre Dame Press.

Jantsch, E. (1980) *The Self Organizing Universe*, Oxford, UK, Pergamon, 1980.

Lakoff, G. and Johnson, M. (1980) *Metaphors We Live By*, Chicago, IL, University of Chicago Press.

Linstead, S. and Grafton-Small, R. (1992) 'On reading organizational culture', *Organization Studies*, vol. 13, pp. 331–56.

Martin, J. (1990) 'Deconstructing organizational taboos: The suppression of gender conflict in organizations', *Organization Science*, vol. 1, pp. 339–59.

Morgan, G. (1980) 'Paradigms, metaphors and puzzle-solving in organization theory', *Administrative Science Quarterly*, vol. 25, pp. 605–22.

Morgan, G. (ed.) (1983a) *Beyond Method: Strategies for Social Research*, Beverly Hills, CA, Sage.

Morgan, G. (1983b) 'More on metaphor: Why we cannot control tropes in administrative science', *Administrative Science Quarterly*, vol. 28, pp. 601–07.

Morgan, G. (1986) *Images of Organization*, Newbury Park, CA, Sage.

Nonaka, I. (1988) 'Creating organizational order out of chaos: self renewal in Japanese firms', *California Management Review,* Spring, pp. 57–73.

Ortony, A. (ed.) (1979) *Metaphor and Thought*, Cambridge, MA, Cambridge University Press, 1979.

Pinder, C.C. and Bourgeois, V. W. (1982) 'Controlling tropes in administrative science', *Administrative Science Quarterly,* vol. 27, pp. 641–52.

Prigogine, I. and Stengers, I. (1984) *Order Out of Chaos*, New York, Bantam.

Quinn, R.E. (1990) *Beyond Rational Management: Mastering the Paradoxes and Competing Demands of High Performance*, San Francisco, CA, Jossey-Bass.

Reed, M. and Hughes, M. (eds) (1992) *Rethinking Organization*, London, Sage.

Rorty, R. (1979) *Philosophy and the Mirror of Nature*, Princeton, NJ, Princeton University Press.

Rorty, R. (1985) *Consequences of Pragmatism*, Minneapolis, MN, University of Minneapolis Press.

Schön, D.A. (1963) *Invention and the Evolution of Ideas*, London, Tavistock.

Schön, D.A. (1979) 'Generative metaphor: A perspective on problem setting in social policy' in Ortony, A. (ed.) *Metaphor and Thought,* Cambridge, MA, Cambridge University Press, pp. 254–83.

Schön, D.A. (1983) *The Reflective Practitioner*, New York, Basic Books.

Shotter, J. (1990) 'The manager as author', a paper prepared for the Conference on Social-Organizational Theory, St. Gallen, Switzerland, August.

Smith, K.K. and Berg, D.N. (1987) *Paradoxes of Group Life*, San Francisco, CA, Jossey-Bass.

Tsoukas, H. (1991) 'The missing link: A transformational view of metaphors in organizational science', *Academy of Management Review,* vol. 16, pp. 566–85.

Turner, S. (1983) 'Studying organization through Levi-Strauss's structuralism' in Morgan, G. (ed.) *Beyond Method*, Beverly Hills, CA, Sage.

Watzlawick, P., Weakland, J. and Fisch, R. (1974) *Change: Principles of Problem Formation and Problem Resolution*, New York, Norton.

White, H. (1978) *The Tropics of Discourse*, Baltimore, MD, Johns Hopkins University Press.

# Part VII

## Gender Issues in Leadership

# Female Leadership Advantage and Disadvantage: Resolving the Contradictions

19

*Alice H. Eagly*

A good introduction to the complexities of women's current status as leaders can follow from contemplating journalists' discussions of this topic. The most striking aspect of some recent statements in newspapers and magazines is that they are favorable to women's abilities as leaders. Some journalists seem to be saying that women have arrived or are arriving at their rightful position as leaders. Consider the following statement, from *Business Week:* 'After years of analyzing what makes leaders most effective and figuring out who got the Right Stuff, management gurus now know how to boost the odds of getting a great executive: Hire a female (Sharpe, 2000, p. 74). Not only did *Business Week* announce that women have the 'Right Stuff'. But also *Fast Company* maintained that '[t]he future of business depends on women' (Heffeman, 2002, p. 9). *Business Week* followed with a cover story on the new gender gap, stating, 'Men could become losers in a global economy that values mental power over might' (Conlin, 2003, p. 78). Readers of these articles might conclude that contemporary women are well prepared for leadership and have some advantages that men do not possess.

Now examine statements of a different sort. Consider, for example, a *New York Times* editorial clearly stating that being a woman is a decided disadvantage for leadership:

> When the crunch comes, the toughest issue for Clinton may be the one that so far has been talked about least. If she runs, she' II be handicapped by her gender. Anyone who thinks it won't be difficult for a woman to get elected

Eagly, A.H. (2007) 'Female leadership advantage and disadvantage: Resolving the contradictions', *Psychology of Women Quarterly*, vol. 31, pp. 1–12.

president of the United States should go home, take a nap, wake up refreshed and think again. (Herbert, 2006, p. A29)

Concerning corporate leadership, a *Wall Street Journal* editorial conveyed a lack of confidence in women in the statement that '[m]ale directors are simply afraid to take an unnecessary risk by selecting a woman' (Dobryznyski, 2006, p. A16). In addition, consider editorial writer Maureen Dowd's *New York Times* commentary on Katie Courie's ascension as the first female network evening news anchor: 'The sad truth is, women only get to the top of places like the network evening news and Hollywood after those places are devalued' (Dowd, 2006, p. A21).

In contemporary culture of the United States, women on the one hand are lauded as having the right combination of skills for leadership, yielding superior leadership styles and outstanding effectiveness. On the other hand, there appears to be widespread recognition that women often come in second to men in competitions to attain leadership positions. Women are still portrayed as suffering disadvantage in access to leadership positions as well as prejudice and resistance when they occupy these roles.

How can women enjoy a leadership advantage but still suffer from disadvantage? To answer this question, the first step for social scientists should be to figure out if these female advantage and disadvantage themes have any validity. If both themes are to some extent accurate, a second challenge is to determine how these seemingly contradictory views can be reconciled with one another. I will show that these opinions put forth by journalists do have some validity. In addition, I argue that the paradoxical phenomena that they note reflect the particular conditions in the United States (and some other nations) in this period of history – an era marked by considerable change in women's roles, combined with the persistence of many traditional expectations and patterns of behavior.

To address these important issues, I first consider cultural and scholarly definitions of what good leadership is and compare women and men in terms of this contemporary model of leadership. Then I present research pertaining to the actual effectiveness of female and male leaders as well as prejudice directed toward female leaders. Finally, I draw conclusions about the likely future of women's representation as leaders.

# How is Good Leadership Defined?

Are women excellent leaders, perhaps even better than men, on average or in some circumstances? To address these issues, researchers first have to answer the question of what good leadership is – what behaviors characterize effective leaders? Does effective leadership consist of the resolute execution of authority, the ability to support and inspire others, or skill in motivating teams to engage in collaborative efforts? All such characterizations of good leadership probably have some validity. As situational theorists of leadership contend (see Ayman, 2004), the appropriateness of particular types of leader behaviors depends on the context – features such as societal values, the culture of organizations, the nature of the task, and the characteristics of followers. Yet, despite this situational variability, leadership has historically been depicted primarily in masculine terms, and many theories of leadership have focused mainly on stereotypically masculine qualities (e.g., Miner, 1993). However, given that leaders' effectiveness depends on context, it is reasonable to think that stereotypically feminine qualities of co-operation, mentoring, and collaboration are important to leadership, certainly in some contexts and perhaps increasingly in contemporary organizations. As I show in this article, these issues are critical to understanding women's participation and success as leaders.

To answer the question of what constitutes good leadership, let us consider the very substantial knowledge that researchers have amassed concerning leadership style. Styles are relatively consistent patterns of social interaction that typify leaders as individuals. Leadership styles are not fixed behaviors but encompass a range of behaviors that have a particular meaning or that serve a particular function. Depending on the situation, leaders vary their behaviors within the boundaries of their style. For example, a leader with a typically participative style might display the collaborative behaviors of consulting, discussing, agreeing, cooperating, or negotiating, depending on the circumstances. Moreover, leaders may sometimes abandon their characteristic style in an unusual situation. In a crisis, for example, a leader who is typically participative may become highly directive because emergency situations can demand quick, decisive action.

In recent decades, leadership researchers have attempted to identify the types of leadership that are most appropriate under the conditions that are common in contemporary organizations. These conditions include greatly accelerated technological growth and the increased complexity of organizations' missions that follows from globalization of business and other endeavors. Accompanying these changes are increasing workforce diversity and, for many organizations, intense competitive pressures. As more complex relationships of interdependency have emerged, many of the traditional ways of managing have come under pressure to change (Kanter, 1997).

Leadership researchers responded to this changing environment by defining good leadership as future-oriented rather than present-oriented and as fostering followers' commitment and ability to contribute creatively to organizations. An early statement of this approach appeared in a book by political scientist James McGregor Burns (1978), who delineated a type of leadership that he labeled *transformational*. Researchers then developed these ideas about leadership style by designing instruments to assess transformational leadership and studying its effects (e.g., Avolio, 1999; Bass, 1998). In this tradition, transformational leadership involves establishing oneself as a role model by gaining followers' trust and confidence. Such leaders delineate organizations' goals, develop plans to achieve those goals, and creatively innovate, even in organizations that are already successful. Transformational leaders mentor and empower their subordinates and encourage them to develop their potential and thus to contribute more effectively to their organization. Other researchers have incorporated some of these same qualities under other labels, such as *charismatic leadership* (e.g., Conger and Kanungo, 1998).

These researchers also portrayed a more conventional type of leadership that they labeled *transactional*. Such leaders appeal to subordinates' self-interest by establishing exchange relationships with them. Transactional leaders clarify subordinates' responsibilities, reward them for meeting objectives, and correct them for failing to meet objectives. Finally, transformational and transactional leadership are both contrasted with a *laissez-faire* style that is defined by an overall failure to take responsibility for managing. [ ... ]

Is transformational leadership actually effective? Research based primarily on subordinates', peers', and superiors' evaluative ratings of leaders has shown that the answer to this question is yes. In a meta-analysis of 87 studies testing the relationships between these styles and measures of leaders' effectiveness (Judge and Piccolo, 2004; see also Lowe, Kroeck, and Sivasubramaniam, 1996), transformational leadership was associated with greater effectiveness. As for transactional leadership, its 'contingent reward' component, which features rewarding subordinates for appropriate behavior, also predicted effectiveness, and it appeared to be almost as effective as transformational leadership. Rewarding subordinates for good performance especially predicted followers' satisfaction with their leaders. In contrast, drawing followers' flaws to their attention and otherwise using punishment to shape their behavior (the style aspect known as 'active management by exception') showed only a weak positive relation to leaders' effectiveness. As expected, intervening only when situations become extreme (the passive aspect of management by exception) was ineffective, as was the uninvolved laissez-faire leadership style.

Researchers' attention to transformational leadership reflects the cultural shift that has occurred in norms about leadership: In many contexts, the Powerful Great Man model of leadership no longer holds. Good leadership is increasingly defined in terms of the qualities of a good coach or teacher rather than a highly authoritative person who merely tells others what to do. As a demonstration of this shift, Mike Krzyzewski, the coach of the highly successful Duke University basketball team, has become not only a famous sports figure, but also a leadership guru who is in great demand for giving lectures to business executives (Sokolove, 2006). Krzyzewski's prominence as a model of good leadership is a sign of the times. The leadership styles that are most valued in contemporary organizations are modeled by an outstanding coach's ability to mentor athletes and foster effective teams.

The collaborative and participative aspects of leadership style, which are the major emphasis in feminist writing on good leadership (e.g., Chin, 2004), are inherent in this culturally approved style of transformational leadership. However, effective leadership is not defined merely by collaboration. Among other important qualities of this coach/teacher model of leadership is inspiring others to be creative and to go beyond the confines of their roles. It is also critical to serve as a role model who elicits pride and respect and to present a vision that delineates the values and goals of an organization. Rose Marie Bravo, CEO of Burberry Group, described her leadership style in terms that epitomize many of these features of transformational leadership:

> We have teams of people, creative people, and it is about keeping them motivated, keeping them on track, making sure that they are following the vision. I am observing, watching and encouraging and motivating.... We try to set an agenda throughout the company where everyone's opinion counts, and it's nice to be asked (Beatty, 2004, p. B8).

Business journalists have echoed some of these themes with statements such as 'Boards are increasingly looking for CEOs who can demonstrate superb people skills in dealing with employees or other stakeholders while delivering consistent results' (Tischler, 2005).

# Do Women have an Advantage in Leadership Style?

If women have a leadership advantage, it might show up in effective leadership styles that diverge somewhat from those that are typical of their male colleagues. Yet, traditionally, researchers resisted any claims that women and men have different leadership styles. They argued that particular leader roles demand certain types of leadership, essentially confining men and women in the same role to behave in the same ways (e.g., Kanter, 1977; Nieva and Gutek, 1981; van Engen, van der Leeden, and Willemsen, 2001). This argument surely has some validity because women and men have to meet similar requirements to gain leadership roles in the first place. Once a leader occupies such a role, the expectations associated with it shape behavior in particular directions. These pressures toward similarity of male and female leaders make it likely that any differences in the leadership styles of women and men are relatively small.

Despite these similarity pressures, leaders have some freedom to choose the particular ways that they fulfill their roles. Good illustrations of opportunities for choice come from research on *organizational citizenship behavior*, which consists of behaviors that go beyond the requirements of organizational roles (Borman, 2004; Podsakoff, MacKenzie, Paine, and Bachrach, 2000). For example, leaders may help others with their work and may volunteer for tasks that go beyond their job description. Most leadership roles afford considerable discretion in certain directions – for example, to be friendly or more remote, to mentor or pay little attention to subordinates, and so forth. Female–male differences in leadership behavior are most likely to occur in these discretionary aspects of leadership that are not closely regulated by leader roles.

Why might women and men display somewhat different leadership styles within the limits set by their leader roles? Women are faced with accommodating the sometimes conflicting demands of their roles as women and their roles as leaders. In general, people expect and prefer that women be communal, manifesting traits such as kindness, concern for others, warmth, and gentleness and that men be agentic, manifesting traits such as kindness, concern for others, warmth, and gentleness and that men be agentic, manifesting traits such as confidence, aggressiveness, and self-direction (e.g., Newport, 2001; Williams and Best, 1990). Because leaders are thought to have more agentic than communal qualities (Powell, Butterfield, and Parent, 2002; Schem, 2001), stereotypes about leaders generally resemble stereotypes of men more than stereotypes of women. As a result, men can seem usual or natural in most leadership roles, thereby placing women at a disadvantage (Eagly and Karau, 2002; Heilman, 2001). Although this dissimilarity between women and leaders appears to be decreasing over time, it has not disappeared (Duehr and Bono, 2006; Sczesny, Bosak, Neff, and Schyns, 2004). As a result, people more easily credit men with leadership ability and more readily accept them as leaders.

Because of these cultural stereotypes, female leaders face a double bind (Eagly and Carli, 2004, in press). They are expected to be communal because of the expectations inherent in the female gender role, and they are also expected to be agentic because of the expectations inherent in most leader roles. However, because agentic displays of confidence and assertion can appear incompatible with being communal, women are vulnerable to becoming targets of prejudice. Sometimes people view women as lacking the stereotypical directive and assertive qualities of good leaders – that is, as not being tough enough or not taking charge. Sometimes people dislike female leaders who display these very directive and assertive qualities because such women seem unfeminine – that is, just like a man or like an iron lady. Carly Fiorina, former CEO of Hewlett-Packard, complained, 'In the chat rooms around Silicon Valley ... I was routinely referred to as either a "bimbo" or a "bitch" – too soft or too hard, and presumptuous, besides' (Fiorina, 2006, p. 173).

Tension between the communal qualities that people prefer in women and the predominantly agentic qualities they expect in leaders produces cross-pressures on female leaders. They often experience disapproval for their more masculine behaviors, such as asserting clear-cut authority over others, as well as for their more feminine behaviors, such as being especially supportive of others. Given such cross-pressures, finding an appropriate and effective leadership style is challenging, as many female leaders acknowledge. In fact, a study of *Fortune* 1000 female executives found that 96% rated as *critical* or *fairly important* 'developing a style with which male managers are comfortable' (Catalyst, 2001).

How do female leaders resolve these cross-pressures? It would seem reasonable that these women might split the difference between the masculine and feminine demands that they face. Perhaps female leaders seek and often find a middle way that is effective yet neither unacceptably masculine nor unacceptably feminine (Yoder, 2001). The contemporary coach/teacher style, as epitomized by transformational leadership, might approximate this middle way because it has culturally feminine aspects, especially in its 'individualized consideration' behaviors (Hackman, Furniss, Hills, and Patterson, 1992), and is otherwise quite androgynous. Is there evidence to support this supposition that women differ from men in leader behaviors, especially in the transformational aspects of style?

Empirical research for addressing this question about female and male styles of leading is extensive. The most recent meta-analysis comparing the leadership styles of men and women examined the contemporary distinctions between transformational, transactional, and laissez-faire styles (Eagly, Johannesen-Schmidt, and van Engen, 2003). This review integrated the findings of 45 studies. Although many types of organizational managers were represented in the studies that were included, the majority were from either business or educational organizations. The managers' median age was 44 years; 53% of the studies examined managers in the United States and 47% examined managers in other nations or mixed, global samples. The measures of managers' typical leadership styles elicited estimates of the frequencies of the differing types of leader behaviors, which were provided by leaders' subordinates, peers, or superiors, or by the leaders themselves.

[Eagly et al., 2003] revealed that female leaders were more transformational than male leaders. Among the five aspects of transformational leadership women most exceeded men on individualized consideration, which encompasses supportive, encouraging treatment of subordinates. Female leaders were also more transactional than male leaders in their contingent reward behaviors, whereas male leaders were more likely than female leaders to manifest the two other aspects of transactional leadership (active and passive management by exception) as well as laissez-faire leadership. All of these differences between male and female leaders were small, consistent with substantially overlapping distributions of women and men (Hyde, 2005).

Given the findings on the effectiveness of these leadership styles noted earlier (Judge and Piccolo, 2004), this project shows that women, somewhat more than men, manifest leadership styles that relate positively to effectiveness, and men, more than women, manifest styles that relate only weakly to effectiveness or that hinder effectiveness. Replicating these findings, a large-scale study primarily of business managers, which was not available when the meta-analysis was conducted, produced very similar results (Antonakis et al., 2003).

Although revealing relatively small differences, findings indicate an advantage for women leaders. Women, more than men, appear to lead in styles that recommend them for leadership. In contrast, men, more than women, appear to lead in less advantageous styles by (a) attending to subordinates failures to meet standards, (b) displaying behaviors that entail avoiding solving problems until they become acute, and (c) being absent or uninvolved at critical times.

What accounts for these findings? As I have already suggested, the transformational repertoire of leadership behaviors (and contingent reward behaviors) may help women to resolve some of the typical incongruity between leadership roles and the female gender role because these styles are not distinctively masculine and some aspects, especially individualized consideration, are relatively feminine. Because transformational and contingent reward leadership are more compatible with the female gender role than were most older models of leadership, women may adopt these behaviors and thereby become more effective. Another possibility is that double standards, in which men have greater access than women to leadership roles, require that women be more highly qualified than men to obtain leadership roles in the first place (e.g., Biernat and Kobrynowicz, 1997; Foschi, 2000). In fact, research shows that women face some disadvantage in obtaining promotions at all levels in organizations, not just at the highest levels (e.g., Baxter and Wright, 2000; Elliott and Smith, 2004). To the extent that women must overcome barriers to attain leadership roles and therefore are more stringently selected than men, women leaders may manifest a more effective set of leader behaviors mainly because they are more qualified. Both of these explanations, the one based on gendered expectations and the one based on double standards, may well underlie the observed differences in the leadership styles of women and men. Because this issue could not be resolved within Eagly et al.'s (2003) meta-analysis on leadership styles, it remains a critical issue for additional research. What is clear from the meta-analysis is that women leaders, on average, exert leadership through behaviors considered appropriate for effective leadership under contemporary conditions.

# Do Women have an Advantage in Leader Effectiveness?

The research that I have described so far pertains to leadership style, which researchers have in turn linked to leaders' effectiveness. Based on these sources, the argument that women are more effective leaders than men is indirect – that is, women, somewhat more than men, manifest leadership styles that have been associated with effectiveness. Although this research is informative, it is important to examine research that has assessed effectiveness with more direct measures. There are two traditions of such research: (a) studies that relate organizations' effectiveness to the percentages of women among their executives and (b) studies that assess the effectiveness of individual male and female leaders.

Business organizations produce financial data that can serve as one measure of effectiveness. Thus, the studies relating the gender diversity of management groups to effectiveness are from the business sector. One such study, conducted by Catalyst, which is a research and advisory organization dedicated to advancing women's careers, analyzed data from the *Fortune* 500, which are the largest corporations in the United States as defined by their revenues. Using appropriate measures of financial performance for the period 1996 to 2000, Catalyst (2004) found that the companies in the top quartile of representing women among their executives had substantially better financial performance than the companies in the bottom quartile.

A more sophisticated study related the percentage of women in the top management teams of the companies in the *Fortune* 1000 to their financial performance from 1998 to 2000 (Krishnan and Park, 2005). These researchers took into account numerous control variables such as company size and industry performance. The findings showed that companies with larger percentages of women in their top management groups had better financial performance. Similar studies on large U.S. companies have revealed positive relationships between the percentage of women on boards of directors and financial performance in the 1990s (Carter, Simkins, and Simpson, 2003; Erhardt, Werbel, and Shrader, 2003). Yet, earlier U.S. studies produced more ambiguous outcomes (e.g., Shrader, Blackburn, and Iles, 1997), and a British study found no relation between board gender diversity and financial performance in the FTSE 100, the largest corporations in the United Kingdom (Cranfield University School of Management, 2005).

These studies present the usual ambiguities of correlational data, and there is a clear need for larger-scale analyses that include a wider span of years and data from more nations. Nonetheless, recent U.S. studies show that women's participation as business leaders can coincide with economic gains for corporations. The good performance of business organizations that have more women among their executives provides an argument for nondiscrimination that complements the more fundamental arguments that discrimination flouts laws and violates the American value of equal opportunity.

The second approach to examining the effectiveness of female and male leaders entails assessments of the effectiveness of individual leaders, followed by comparisons of the male and female leaders. Given the wide range of leader roles examined in past studies of leaders' effectiveness, this research should reveal context effects by which leaders' effectiveness depends on the contours of leadership roles. Although leader roles are traditionally masculine in their cultural definition and male-dominated numerically, they vary widely in these, respects. Some leader roles are less culturally masculine and in recent years are occupied by more women than men (e.g., human resources manager, medical and health services manager; U.S. Bureau of Labor Statistics, 2006, Table 11). Given the importance of the fit between gender roles and the requirements of leader roles (Eagly and Karau, 2002), the relative success of male and female leaders should depend on the particular demands of these roles. Leader roles that are highly male dominated or culturally masculine in their demands present particular challenges to women because of their incompatibility with people's expectations about women. This incompatibility not only restricts women's access to such leadership roles but also can compromise their effectiveness. When leader roles are extremely masculine, people may suspect that women are not qualified for them, and they may resist women's authority (Carli, 1999; Eagly and Karau, 2002; Heilman, 2001).

Empirical support for the principle that the effectiveness of male and female leaders depends on the context emerged in another meta-analysis (Eagly, Karau, and Makhijani, 1995). This project integrated the results of 96 studies that had examined how well male and female leaders performed as leaders. The majority of these projects had studied managers in organizations, and a few had studied leaders in laboratory groups. The male and female leaders who were compared held the same or generally comparable roles. Most of the studies had evaluated leaders' effectiveness by having people (i.e., subordinates, peers, superiors, or leaders themselves) evaluate how well the leaders performed, and a few studies had objective performance-based outcome measures. Subjective performance evaluations can be biased – they could in particular be contaminated by prejudice against women, especially in male-dominated organizational settings. Nonetheless, a leader cannot be effective unless others accept his or her leadership. Therefore, subjective performance evaluations, even if biased, serve as one relevant measure of how well a person leads.

As anticipated, this meta-analysis found that men's effectiveness as leaders surpassed women's in roles that were male dominated or masculine in other ways. However, women's effectiveness surpassed men's in less male dominated or less masculine roles. Specifically, women were judged to be less effective than men in leadership positions occupied by more men or associated with a higher proportion of male subordinates (or when effectiveness was assessed by ratings performed by a higher proportion of men; see also Bowen, Swim, and Jacobs, 2000, for similar findings). Consistent with these results, women were judged substantially less effective than men in the military, one of the most traditionally masculine environments. However, women were somewhat more effective than men in educational, governmental, and social service organizations, which have more women in managerial roles.

This meta-analysis also showed that female managers fared particularly well in effectiveness, relative to male managers, in middle-level leadership positions. This finding is sensible, given middle management's usual demands for complex interpersonal skills (e.g., Paolillo, 1981), most of which are encompassed in the communal repertoire of behaviors. Additional data on characteristics of the leadership roles was derived from a panel of judges assembled to give ratings of the roles. These data showed that women exceeded men in effectiveness in leader roles perceived as attractive to women and as requiring such stereotypical female characteristics as cooperativeness and the ability to get along well with others. Men exceeded women in effectiveness in roles perceived as attractive to men and as requiring such male stereotypical characteristics as directiveness and the ability to control others. Overall, effectiveness tracked gender stereotyping quite closely. These findings likely reflect a conflux of causes, including women's generally effective leadership styles, gender stereotypes about abilities and personality traits, and the prejudicial reactions that female leaders encounter, especially in more masculine settings.

It is hardly surprising that female leaders encounter difficulties in masculine settings. In such environments, leaders often confront the challenges of

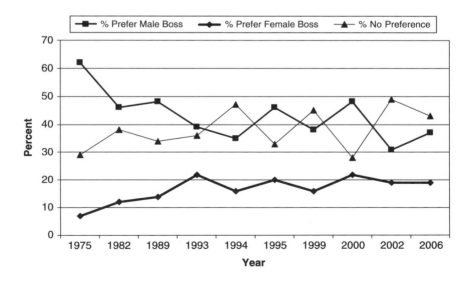

**Figure 19.1**   Preferences for male or female boss in Gallup polls from 1953 through 2006 (Carroll, 2006)

masculine organizational culture that may make it difficult for women to feel comfortable and to gain authority (e.g., Alvesson and Billing, 1992; Lyness and Thompson, 2000; Silvestri, 2003; Wajeman, 1998). Further, women in highly masculine domains often have to contend with expectations and criticisms that they lack the toughness and competitiveness needed to succeed. In such settings, it is difficult for women to build helpful relationships and to gain acceptance in influential networks (Timberlake, 2005). Given these hurdles, advancing up a highly male-dominated hierarchy requires an especially strong, skillful, and persistent woman. She has to avoid the threats to her confidence that other people's doubts and criticisms can elicit. Such a woman is also vulnerable because her gender, which is so highly salient to others, can be quickly blamed for any failings.

# Where is the Female Disadvantage?

Our meta-analytic demonstration that women fare less well than men in male-dominated and masculine leadership roles identifies context-specific disadvantage (e.g., Eagly et al., 1995) – that is, in some leadership roles, women face obstacles that men do not face. If women who are in fact equal to their male counterparts are treated differently either in their access to male-dominated leader roles or in evaluations of their performance once they are in such roles, women would indeed face disadvantage as leaders. Such disadvantage would be prejudicial, as defined by less favorable treatment of women than men, despite their objective equality (Eagly and Diekman, 2005).

One place to look for evidence of prejudicial disadvantage is in studies of attitudes toward female and male leaders. Especially informative are national polls that have asked representative samples of respondents for evaluations of men and women as leaders. Such polls have consistently shown favoritism toward male over female leaders. For example, for many years, pollsters have asked people what they think about personally having a job in which a woman or a man has authority over them. The specific Gallup Poll question is 'If you were taking a new job and had your choice of a boss, would you prefer to work for a man or woman?' The responses obtained from Americans in selected years ranging from 1953 to 2006 appear in Figure 19.1. These data show a preference for male bosses over female bosses, although this differential in favor of men has decreased substantially through the years. In particular, a sharp drop occurred from 2000 to 2002, albeit followed by a modest increase in favor of men from 2002 to 2006 (Carroll, 2006). Despite this marked erosion of the huge advantage that male bosses had in the middle of the twentieth century,

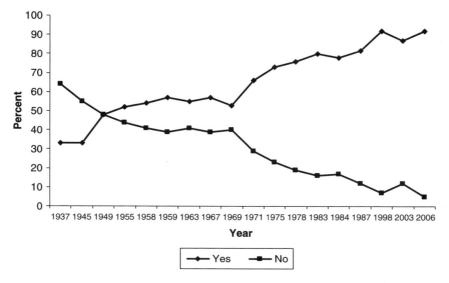

**Figure 19.2**   Willingness to vote for a woman candidate for president in Gallup polls from 1937 through 2006 (CBS News/New York Times, 2006; Moore, 2003)

men still retain a clear advantage in 2006, with 37% of respondents preferring a male boss compared with 19% preferring a female boss. However, the most popular response in recent polls, given by 43% of the respondents in 2006, is the egalitarian 'no preference' or 'it doesn't matter' response, which requires that the respondent spontaneously break away from the man versus woman response format of the question.

Another poll question appearing over many decades has addressed political leadership. Since 1937, polls have asked whether respondents could vote for a well-qualified woman nominated for president by their own party. As shown in Figure 19.2, approval has increased from only 33% of respondents in 1937 to 92% in 2006 (CBS News/New York Times, 2006; Moore, 2003). However, in response to the question about whether America is 'ready for a woman president', only 55% agreed in 2006, up from 40% in 1996 when this question first appeared (CBS News/New York Times, 2006). Despite these apparent reservations about a female president, the results of elections give some evidence of support for office holding by women. Once women achieve nomination (and women are far less likely than men to become candidates; Fox and Lawless, 2004), women are as successful as men in winning primary and general elections for state legislatures, governorships, and the U.S. House and Senate (Seltzer, Newman, and Leighton, 1997). There is even evidence that in recent years women are slightly preferred in some elections, although this type of female advantage emerges only among female voters (Smith and Fox, 2001).

The favorable changes that have taken place in attitudes about female leaders reflect more general changes in attitudes about gender (Brooks and Bolzendahl, 2004; Inglehart and Norris, 2003). Those who support women's leadership opportunities also endorse less traditional gender roles and approve of women's paid employment. All of these attitudes have changed greatly over the years, often with very pronounced changes toward greater endorsement of equality in the 1970s and 1980s, generally with some leveling off or even small reversals of change in quite recent years. Of course, gender prejudice can be compounded by prejudice based on other types of group membership such as race, ethnicity, and sexual orientation (Ferdman, 1999; Ragins, Cornwell, and Miller, 2003). [ ... ]

## Consequences of Prejudice toward Female Leaders

Although prejudicial attitudes do not invariably produce discriminatory behavior, such attitudes can limit women's access to leadership roles and foster discriminatory evaluations when they occupy such roles. Social scientists have evaluated women's access to leadership roles through a large number of studies that implement regression methods.

To explain gender disparities in leadership, such studies have determined whether variables that may differ between the sexes, such as hours worked per year and type of occupation, account for gender gaps in wages or promotions (see Blau and Kahn, 2000; Maume, 2004; U.S. General Accounting Office, 2003). These studies examine whether sex still predicts wages or promotions even after the effects of the other variables are controlled – thus making men and women statistically as equivalent as possible except for their sex. Sometimes researchers control not only for differences between women and men in characteristics such as years of education and work experience, but also for differences in the wage returns associated with such characteristics. The gender gap that remains after instituting such controls provides an estimate of sex discrimination. Such methods have almost always shown that women have a discriminatory wage and promotion disadvantage compared with men. This generalization holds for studies with nationally representative samples as well as for studies with more specialized or limited samples (see Eagly and Carli, in press).

To address the question of discrimination in hiring, some psychologists and researchers in organizational behavior have used a different research method – specifically, experiments in which research participants evaluate individual male or female managers or job candidates. In such experiments, all characteristics of these individuals are held constant except for their sex. The participants evaluate how suitable these individuals are for hiring or promotion or how competent they are in their jobs. These experiments have also demonstrated bias against women.

One type of experiment has presented application materials such as résumés to research participants, with either a male name or a female name attached to the materials. Different participants receive the otherwise identical male and female versions of the information. Davison and Burke (2000) conducted the most recent review of these experiments, integrating the findings of 49 reports. This meta-analysis found that men were preferred over women for masculine jobs such as auto salesperson and sales manager for heavy industry (mean $d = 0.34$), and women over men for feminine jobs such as secretary and home economics teacher (mean $d = -0.26$). For gender-neutral jobs such as psychologist and motel desk clerk, men were also preferred over women, although to a somewhat lesser extent than for masculine jobs (mean $d = 0.24$; Davison, 2005, personal communication). Thus, men had an advantage over equivalent women, except in culturally feminine settings. These biases are not trivially small. For example, the bias against women in masculine jobs roughly corresponds to rates of success of 59% for men and 42% for women, when success is a favorable recommendation for a job.

Other experiments have examined evaluations of leaders, usually by presenting written descriptions of managerial behavior that differ only in the sex of the leader. A related type of experiment examined subordinates' evaluations of male and female leaders who had been trained to lead laboratory groups in the same style. A meta-analysis of 61 of these two types of experiments assessing the evaluation of equivalent male and female leaders yielded a very small overall tendency for participants to evaluate female leaders less favorably than male leaders, but this devaluation increased for male-dominated leadership roles and especially for leaders with more autocratic and directive styles (mean $d = 0.05$ for overall bias, 0.09 for male-dominated roles, 0.30 in autocratic style; Eagly, Makhijani, and Klonsky, 1992).

In summary, correlational and experimental studies of gender bias show female disadvantage that is concentrated in male-dominated roles. Although this bias reverses to favor women in feminine settings such as applying for a secretarial job, it is not clear that the attitudinal bias systematically favors women for any leader roles. [ ... ]

## Advantage Plus Disadvantage

Research has established a mixed picture for contemporary female leadership. Women leaders on average manifest valued, effective leadership styles, even somewhat more than men do, and are often associated with successful business organizations. Attitudinal prejudice against women leaders appears to have lessened substantially, although even now there are more Americans who prefer male than female bosses. People say that they would vote for a woman for president; however, only slightly more than half of Americans indicate that the country is ready to have a female president. Because of the remaining prejudicial barriers, women face challenges as leaders that men do not face, especially in settings where female leaders are nontraditional. Such signs of advantage mixed with disadvantage and trust mixed with distrust are contradictory only on the surface. They are manifestations of gender relations that have changed dramatically yet have not arrived at equality between the sexes.

Many women have contended successfully with barriers to their leadership, as shown by the fact that women now have far more access to leadership roles than at any other period in history. This access is especially great in the United States, where women constitute 24% of the chief executives of organizations, 37% of all managers, and 43% of individuals in management, financial, and financial operations occupations (U. S. Bureau of Labor Statistics, 2006, Table 11). Although no one would argue that gender equality has arrived or is even near at hand, such statistics reflect massive social change in women's roles and opportunities.

The inroads of women into positions of power and authority reflect many underlying changes (Eagly and Carli, 2003, in press) – above all, women's high level of paid employment (U.S. Census Bureau, 2007) and a lessening of the time demands of women's housework, accompanied by greater sharing of childcare and housework with husbands and partners (Bianchi, Robinson, and Milkie, 2006; U.S. Bureau of Labor Statistics, 2005). Associated with these shifts in roles is a large increase in women's education, whereby young women have become more educated than young men (U. S. National Center for Education Statistics, 2005). Because these changes in employment and education are accompanied by psychological changes in the form of increasing agency in women (e.g., Twenge, 1997, 2001) and greater career ambition (e.g., Astin, Oseguera, Sax, and Korn, 2002), women have achieved many more leadership positions than in the past. Women continue to encounter impediments to leadership within organizations, but many of these impediments can be removed or weakened by organizational changes designed to improve women's (and minorities') access to and success in leadership roles (e.g., Kalev, Dobbin, and Kelly, 2006; Rapoport, Bailyn, Fletcher, and Pruitt, 2002; Yoder, Schleicher, and McDonald, 1998).

Given the profound changes taking place in women's roles and in the cultural construal of good leadership, it is clear that women will continue their ascent toward greater power and authority. The twentieth-century shift toward gender equality has not ceased but is continuing (Jackson, 1998). The presence of more women in leadership positions is one of the clearest indicators of this transformation.

## References

Alvesson, M. and Billing, Y.D. (1992) 'Gender and organization: Towards a differentiated understanding', *Organization Studies*, vol. 13, pp. 73–103.

Antonakis, J., Avolio, B.J. and Sivasubramaniam, N. (2003) 'Context and leadership: An examination of the nine-factor full-range leadership theory using the Multifactor Leadership Questionnaire', *Leadership Quarterly*, vol. 14, pp. 261–95.

Astin, A.W., Oseguera, L., Sax, L.J. and Korn, W.S. (2002) *The American Freshman: Thirty-Five Year Trends, 1966–2001*, Los Angeles, Higher Education Research Institute, UCLA.

Avolio, B.J. (1999) *Full Leadership Development: Building the Vital Forces in Organizations*, Thousand Oaks, CA, Sage.

Ayman, R. (2004) 'Situational and contingency approaches to leadership' in Antonakis, J., Cianciolo, A.T. and Sternberg, R.J. (eds) *The Nature of Leadership*, Thousand Oaks, CA, Sage, pp. 148–70.

Bass, B.M. (1998) *Transformational Leadership: Industrial, Military, and Educational Impact*, Mahwah, NJ, Erlbaum.

Baxter, J. and Wright, E.O. (2000) 'The glass ceiling hypothesis: A comparative study of the United States, Sweden, and Australia', *Gender & Society*, vol. 14, pp. 275–94.

Beatty, S. (9 September 2004) 'Boss talk: Plotting plaid's future: Burberry's Rose Marie Bravo designs ways to keep brand growing and still exclusive', *Wall Street Journal*, p. B1, 8.

Bianchi, S.M., Robinson, J.P. and Milkie, M.A. (2006) *Changing Rhythms of American Family Life*, New York, Russell Sage Foundation.

Biernat, M. and Kobrynowicz, D. (1997). Gender- and race-based standards of competence: Lower minimum standards but higher ability standards for devalued groups. *Journal of Personality and Social Psychology, 72*, 544–557.

Blau, F.D. and Kahn, L.M. (2000) 'Gender differences in pay', *Journal of Economic Perspectives*, vol. 14, pp. 75–99.

Borman, W.C. (2004) 'The concept of organizational citizenship', *Current Directions in Psychological Science*, vol. 13, pp. 238–41.

Bowen, C., Swim, J.K. and Jacobs, R.R. (2000) 'Evaluating gender biases on actual job performance of real people: A meta-analysis', *Journal of Applied Social Psychology*, vol. 30, pp. 2194–215.

Brooks, C. and Bolzendahl, C. (2004) 'The transformation of U.S. gender role attitudes: Cohort replacement, social-structural change, and ideological learning', *Social Science Research*, vol. 33, 106–33.

Burns, J.M. (1978) *Leadership*, New York, Harper and Row.

Carli, L.L. (1999) 'Gender, interpersonal power, and social influence', *Journal of Social Issues*, vol. 55, 81–99.

Carroll, J. (1 September 2006) *Americans Prefer Male Boss to a Female Boss*, Retrieved 10 September 2006 from Gallup Brain Web site: http://brain.gallup.com

Carter, D.A., Simkins, B.J. and Simpson, W.G. (2003) 'Corporate governance, board diversity, and firm value', *Financial Review*, vol. 38, pp. 33–53.

Catalyst. (2001) *Women in Corporate Leadership: Comparisons among the US, the UK, and Canada*, Retrieved 27 September 2006 from http://www.catalyst.org/files/fact/US,%20UK,%20Canada%20WICL%20Comparisons.pdf

Catalyst. (2004) *The Bottom Line: Connecting Corporate Performance and Gender Diversity*, Retrieved 27 September 2006 from https://www.catalyst.org/files/full/financialperformancereport.pdf

CBS News/New York Times. (5 February 2006) *A Woman for President*, Retrieved 10 September 2006 from http://www. cbsnews.com/htdocs/pdf/020306woman.pdf#search=% 22a%20woman%20for%20president%20CBS%20News% 2FNew%20York%20Times%20Poll%22

Chin, J.L. (2004) 'Feminist leadership: Feminist visions and diverse voices', *Psychology of Women Quarterly*, vol. 28, pp. 1–8.

Conger, J.A. and Kanungo, R.N. (1998) *Charismatic Leadership in Organizations*, Thousand Oaks, CA, Sage.

Conlin, M. (26 May 2003) 'The new gender gap: From kindergarten to grad school, boys are becoming the second sex', *Business Week*. Retrieved 18 September 2006 from http://www.businessweek.com/magazine/content/03_21/_b3834001mz001.htm?chan=search

Cranfield University School of Management (2005) *The female FTSE Report: 2005*, Cranfield, Bedford, UK, Author. Retrieved December 18, 2006 from http://www.som. cranfield.ac.uk/som/research/centres/cdwbl/downloads/FTSE2005full.pdf

Davison, H.K. and Burke, M.J. (2000) 'Sex discrimination in simulated employment contexts: A meta-analytic investigation', *Journal of Vocational Behavior*, vol. 56, pp. 225–48.

Dobryznyski, J.H. (4 August 2006) 'Cherchez la femme', *Wall Street Journal*, p. A16.

Dowd, M. (6 September 2006) 'New themes for the same old songs', *New York Times,* p. A21.

Duehr, E.E. and Bono, J.E. (2006) 'Men, women, and managers: Are stereotypes finally changing?' *Personnel Psychology*.

Eagly, A.H. and Carli, L.L. (2003) 'The female leadership advantage: An evaluation of the evidence', *Leadership Quarterly*, vol. 14, pp. 807–34.

Eagly, A.H. and Carli, L.L. (2004) 'Women and men as leaders' in Antonakis, J., Cianciolo, A.T. and Sternberg, R.J. (eds) *The Nature of Leadership*, Thousand Oaks, CA, Sage, pp. 279–301.

Eagly, A.H. and Carli, L.L. (in press) *Through the Labrinth: The Truth about How Women Become Leaders*, Boston, MA, Harvard Business School Press.

Eagly, A.H. and Diekman, A.B. (2005) 'What is the problem? Prejudice as an attitude-in-context' in Dovidio, J. F., Glick, P. and Rudman, L. (eds) *On the Nature of Prejudice: Fifty Years after Allport*, Malden, MA, Blackwell, pp. 19–35.

Eagly, A.H., Johannesen-Schmidt, M.C. and van Engen, M.L. (2003) 'Transformational, transactional, and laissez-faire leadership styles: A meta-analysis comparing women and men', *Psychological Bulletin*, vol. 129, pp. 569–91.

Eagly, A.H. and Karau, S.J. (2002) 'Role congruity theory of prejudice toward female leaders', *Psychological Review*, vol. 109, pp. 573–98.

Eagly, A.H., Karau, S.J. and Makhijani, M.G. (1995) 'Gender and the effectiveness of leaders: A meta-analysis', *Psychological Bulletin*, vol. 117, pp. 125–45.

Eagly, A.H., Makhijani, M.G. and Klonsky, B.G. (1992) 'Gender and the evaluation of leaders: A meta-analysis', *Psychological Bulletin*, vol. 111, pp. 3–22.

Elliott, J.R. and Smith, R.A. (2004) 'Race, gender, and workplace power', *American Sociological Review*, vol. 69, pp. 365–86.

Erhardt, M.L., Werbel, J.D. and Shrader, C.B. (2003) 'Board of director diversity and firm financial performance', *Corporate Governance*, vol. 11, pp. 102–11.

Ferdman, B.M. (1999) 'The color and culture of gender in organizations: Attending to race and ethnicity' in Powell, G. (ed.) *Handbook of Gender & Work*, Thousand Oaks, CA, Sage, pp. 17–34.

Fiorina, C. (2006) *Tough Choices: A Memoir*, New York, Penguin.

Foschi, M. (2000) 'Double standards for competence: Theory and research', *Annual Review of Sociology*, vol. 26, pp. 21–42.

Fox, R.L. and Lawless, J.L. (2004) 'Entering the arena? Gender and the decision to run for office', *American Journal of Political Science*, vol. 48, pp. 264–80.

Hackman, M.Z., Furniss, A.H., Hills, M.J. and Patterson, T.J. (1992) 'Perceptions of gender-role characteristics and transformational and transactional leadership behaviours', *Perceptual and Motor Skills*, vol. 75, pp. 311–19.

Heffernan, M. (August 2002) 'The female CEO ca. 2002', *Fast Company*, vol. 61, pp. 9, 58, 60, 62, 64, 66.

Heilman, M.E. (2001) 'Description and prescription: How gender stereotypes prevent women's ascent up the organizational ladder', *Journal of Social Issues*, vol. 57, pp. 657–74.

Herbert, B. (19 May 2006) 'Hillary can run, but can she win?' *New York Times*, p. A29.

Hyde, J.S. (2005) 'The gender similarities hypothesis', *American Psychologist*, vol. 60, pp. 581–92.

Inglehart, R. and Norris, P. (2003) *Rising Tide: Gender Equality and Cultural Change around the World*, New York, Cambridge University Press.

Jackson, R.M. (1998) *Destined for Equality: The Inevitable Rise of Women's Status*, Cambridge, MA, Harvard University Press.

Judge, T.A. and Piccolo, R.F. (2004) 'Transformational and transactional leadership: A meta-analytic test of their relative validity', *Journal of Applied Psychology*, vol. 89, pp. 901–10.

Kalev, A., Dobbin, F. and Kelly, E. (2006) 'Best practices or best guesses? Assessing the efficacy of corporate affirmative action and diversity policies', *American Sociological Review*, vol. 71, pp. 589–617.

Kanter, R.M. (1977) *Men and Women of the Corporation*, New York, Basic Books.

Krishnan, H.A. and Park, D. (2005) 'A few good women – on top management teams', *Journal of Business Research*, vol. 58, pp. 1712–20.

Lowe, K.B., Kroeck, K.G. and Sivasubramaniam, N. (1996) 'Effectiveness correlates of transformational and transactional leadership: A meta-analytic review of the MLQ literature', *Leadership Quarterly*, vol. 7, pp. 385–425.

Lyness, K.S. and Thompson, D.E. (2000) 'Climbing the corporate ladder: Do female and male executives follow the same route?' *Journal of Applied Psychology*, vol. 85, pp. 86–101.

Maume, D.J., Jr (2004) 'Is the glass ceiling a unique form of inequality? Evidence from a random-effects model of managerial attainment', *Work and Occupations*, vol. 31, pp. 250–74.

Miner, J.B. (1993) *Role Motivation Theories*, New York, Routledge.

Moore, D.W. (10 June 2003) *Little Prejudice against a Woman, Jewish, Black, or Catholic Presidential Candidate*, Retrieved 10 September 2006 from Gallup Brain Web site: http://brain.gallup.com

Newport, F. (21 February 2001). *Americans See Women as Emotional and Affectionate, Men as More Aggressive: Gender Specific Stereotypes Persist in Recent Gallup Poll*, Retrieved 10 September 2006 from Gallup Brain Web site: http://brain.gallup.com

Nieva, V.G. and Gutek, B.A. (1981) *Women and Work: A Psychological Perspective*, New York, Praeger.

Paolillo, J.G.P. (1981) 'Manager's self assessments of managerial roles: The influence of hierarchical level', *Journal of Management*, vol. 7, pp. 43–52.

Podsakoff, P.M., MacKenzie, S.B., Paine, J.B. and Bachrach, D.G. (2000) 'Organizational citizenship behaviors: A critical review of the theoretical and empirical literature and suggestions for future research', *Journal of Management*, vol. 26, pp. 513–63.

Powell, G.N., Butterfield, D.A. and Parent, J.D. (2002) 'Gender and managerial stereotypes: Have the times changed?' *Journal of Management*, vol. 28, pp. 177–93.

Ragins, B.R., Cornwell, J.M. and Miller, J.S. (2003) 'Heterosexism in the workplace: Do race and gender matter?' *Group & Organization Management*, vol. 28, pp. 45–74.

Rapoport, R., Bailyn, L., Fletcher, J.K. and Pruitt, B.H. (2002) *Beyond Work-Family Balance: Advancing Gender Equity and Workplace Performance*, San Francisco, CA, Jossey-Bass.

Schein, V.E. (2001) 'A global look at psychological barriers to women's progress in management', *Journal of Social Issues*, vol. 57, pp. 675–88.

Sczesny, S., Bosak, J., Neff, D. and Schyns, B. (2004) 'Gender stereotypes and the attribution of leadership traits: A cross-cultural comparison', *Sex Roles*, vol. 51, pp. 631–45.

Seltzer, R.A., Newman, J. and Leighton, M.V. (1997) *Sex as a Political Variable: Women as Candidates and Voters in U.S. Elections*, Boulder, CO, Lynne Reinner.

Sharpe, R. (20 November 2000). 'As leaders, women rule: New studies find that female managers outshine their male counterparts in almost every measure', *Business Week*, p. 74. Retrieved 15 December 2000, from *Business Week Online*, http://www.businessweek.com/common_frames/ca.htm?/2000/00_47/b3708145.htm

Shrader, C.B., Blackburn, V.B. and Iles, P. (1997) 'Women in management and firm financial performance: An exploratory study', *Journal of Management Issues*, vol. 9, pp. 355–72.

Silvestri, M. (2003) *Women in Charge: Policing, Gender and Leadership*, Portland, OR, Willan Publishing.

Smith, E.R.A.N. and Fox, R.L. (2001) 'The electoral fortunes of women candidates for Congress', *Political Research Quarterly*, vol. 54, pp. 205–21.

Sokolove, M. (February 2006) 'Follow me', *New York Times Sports Magazine*, pp. 96–101, 116–17.

Timberlake, S. (2005) 'Social capital and gender in the work-place', *Journal of Management Development*, vol. 24, pp. 34–44.

Tischler, L. (September 2005) 'The CEO's new clothes', *Fast Company*, pp. 27–28.

Twenge, J.M. (1997) 'Changes in masculine and feminine traits over time: A meta-analysis', *Sex Roles*, vol. 36, pp. 305–25.

Twenge, J.M. (2001) 'Changes in women's assertiveness in response to status and roles: A cross-temporal meta-analysis, 1931–1993', *Journal of Personality and Social Psychology*, vol. 81, pp. 133–45.

U.S. Bureau of Labor Statistics (September 2005) *News: American Time-Use Survey – 2004 Results Announced by BLS.* Retrieved 10 June 2006 from http://www.bls.gov/news.release/pdf/atus.pdf

U.S. Bureau of Labor Statistics (2006) *Women in the Labor Force: A Databook.* Report 996. Retrieved 18 December 2006 from http://www.bls.gov/cps/wlf-databook2006.htm

U.S. Census Bureau (2007) *Statistical Abstract of the United States: 2007*, Washington, DC, U.S. Government Printing Office. Retrieved 18 December 2006 from http://www.census.gov/prod/www/statistical-abstract.html

U.S. General Accounting Office (2003). *Women's Earnings: Work Patterns Partially Explain Difference between Men's and Women's Earnings* (Gao-04–35), Washington, DC, Author. Retrieved July 30, 2004 from http://www.gao.gov/new.items/d0435.pdf

U.S. National Center for Education Statistics (2005) *Digest of Education Statistics, 2005*, Washington, DC, Author. Retrieved 3 June 2006 from http://nces.ed.gov/programs/digest/d05_tf.asp

van Engen, M.L., van der Leeden, R. and Willemsen, T.M. (2001) 'Gender, context and leadership styles: A field study', *Journal of Occupational and Organizational Psychology*, vol. 74, pp. 581–98.

Wajcman, J. (1998) *Managing like a Man: Women and Men in Corporate Management*, University Park, PA, Pennsylvania State University Press.

Williams, J.E. and Best, D.L. (1990) *Measuring Sex Stereotypes: A Multination Study*, Newbury Park, CA, Sage.

Yoder, J.D. (2001) 'Making leadership work more effectively for women', *Journal of Social Issues*, vol. 57, pp. 815–28.

Yoder, J.D., Schleicher, T.L. and McDonald, T.W. (1998) 'Empowering token women leaders: The importance of organizationally legitimated credibility', *Psychology of Women Quarterly*, vol. 22, pp. 209–22.

# Effects of Sex and Gender Role on Leader Emergence

# 20

## Russell L. Kent and Sherry E. Moss

[ ... ] Past research has consistently shown that men more often emerge as leaders than women (Carbonnell, 1984; Megargee, 1969). This phenomenon has been attributed to internal (Terborg, 1977; Wentworth and Anderson, 1984; White, DeSanctis, and Crino, 1981) and external (Ahrons, 1976; Bowman, Worthy, and Greyson, 1965; Goodale and Hall, 1976; Powell, 1993; Weisman, Morlock, Sack, and Levine, 1976) barriers limiting women's leader emergence. However, recent evidence suggests that there have been shifts in societal acceptance of women as leaders (Sutton and Moore, 1985) and that some of the barriers that prevented women from emerging as leaders may be coming down (Brenner, Tomkiewicz, and Schein, 1989; Chusmir and Koberg, 1991).

Changes also appear to be occurring in perceptions of the importance of stereotypically masculine and feminine characteristics for leaders. Past research has overwhelmingly associated masculine characteristics with leader emergence (Fagenson, 1990; Goktepe and Schneier, 1989), but recent studies present somewhat different views. For example, Brenner and colleagues (1989) found that female managers described the 'successful middle manager' as possessing both stereotypically masculine and feminine characteristics. Other studies suggest that an androgynous leadership style may help women overcome stereotypes that have prevented them from being viewed as leaders in the past (e.g., Korabik, 1990).

Given what appear to be changing perceptions of leaders, a reexamination of the characteristics of emergent leaders is appropriate. Thus, the purpose of this study was to reexamine the relationships between leader emergence and the characteristics of sex and gender role. Specifically, this study had three objectives: (1) to determine whether men are still more likely to emerge as leaders in group situations, (2) to further investigate the effects of gender role on leader

Kent, R.L. and Moss, S.E. (1994) 'Effects of sex and gender role on leader emergence', *Academy of Management Journal*, vol. 37, no. 5, pp. 1335–46.

emergence, and (3) to determine whether sex or gender role better predicts leader emergence.

## Sex Effects

Over the past three decades, many studies of sex and leader emergence have been conducted. A classic study by Megargee (1969) examined the effects of dominance and sex on leader emergence. In what Megargee intended to be a gender-neutral task, subjects rated high on dominance, as measured by the dominance scale on the California Personality Inventory, (Gough, 1957), and working in same-sex dyads emerged as leaders 69 percent of the time. In mixed-sex dyads with high-dominance men and low-dominance women, the men emerged as leaders 88 percent of the time. However, in mixed-sex dyads with high-dominance women and low-dominance men, the women emerged as leaders only 25 percent of the time. A similar pattern of results was produced when a masculine task was used.

There have been several replications of the original Megargee (1969) study. Anticipating that shifts in societal gender-role expectations would affect the frequency of women's leader emergence, Nyquist and Spence (1986) used what they thought to be a more gender-neutral task and found similar results. In Carbonell's (1984) replication study, only 30 percent of the high-dominance women in mixed-sex pairs became leaders when a masculine task was used. Women were somewhat more likely to emerge as leaders when a feminine task was used, but not more likely than men.

A study by Wentworth and Anderson (1984) included masculine, neutral, and feminine tasks. Using only low-dominance subjects, they found that men emerged as leaders in the masculine and neutral tasks and women emerged in the feminine tasks. Interestingly, those authors attributed women's leader emergence in the feminine tasks to task expertise but attributed men's emergence in the masculine and neutral tasks to role expectations. Thus, the researchers concluded that women must be seen as experts to be perceived as leaders, whereas men become leaders when there are no female experts because it is expected.

Fleisher and Chertkoff (1986) conducted the most recent replication of the Megargee study, using a gender-neutral task. In the critical groups pairing high-dominance women and low-dominance men, women emerged as leaders 50 percent of the time. An additional feature in this study was that half the subjects in the high-dominance female–low-dominance male dyads received feedback that the women had performed better than the men on a task-related pretest. Results indicated that the men who received this information were significantly more willing to have a female leader than those who did not receive the information. The results of Fleischer and Chertkoff (1986), Wentworth and

Anderson (1984), and Carbonell (1984) suggest that women may have been slightly more likely to emerge as leaders in the 1980s than in the 1960s, but their chances of doing so were best when they were perceived as experts.

Finally, Dobbins, Long, Dedrick, and Clemons (1990), using a different research method, asked groups consisting of four subjects to work on a task that allowed them to interact for longer than was allowed in the Megargee paradigm. Upon task completion, subjects were asked to (1) choose one leader and (2) to rate each group member on the extent to which they would like him or her to be leader. Men were rated higher and chosen more often as leaders than women. Thus, even though recent research shows that barriers to female leader emergence are being lowered (Brenner et al., 1989; Chusmir and Koberg, 1991), most research supports the notion that men are still more likely to emerge as leaders than women.

# Gender-Role Effects

Because of traditional gender stereotypes, it appears that the possession of feminine characteristics is detrimental to leader emergence, and the possession of masculine characteristics is beneficial (Fagenson, 1990). However, with the women's movement of recent decades, the mass entrance of women into the work force, the increasing number of female managers (Powell, Posner, and Schmidt, 1984), and societal shifts in gender-role perceptions (Helmreich, Spence, and Gibson, 1982), the formerly clear, unambiguous roles of the sexes have been blurred. In principle, the concepts of masculinity and femininity are not necessarily precise correlates of biological sex (Bem, 1974). Thus, a man or a woman may possess either masculine or feminine characteristics, or both. Given the changes in societal perceptions of the role of women and the advancement of some women into leadership positions, it is possible that women today possess more masculine characteristics than they have at any time in the past. Several studies support this contention. For example, Powell and Butterfield (1979) found that female master's in business administration (M.B.A.) students rated themselves higher in masculinity than in femininity. Additionally, women who have chosen traditionally masculine or managerial careers have very likely rejected customary gender stereotypes (Brenner et al., 1989), are more likely to have been raised in families with full-time working mothers (Almquist, 1974), and possess attitudes uncorrelated with interest in traditional feminine professions (Tipton, 1976).

Several studies have shown masculinity to be associated with leader emergence. In a study by Goktepe and Schneier (1989), college students performed gender-neutral tasks over the course of a semester. The effects of both sex and gender role on leader emergence were assessed. The results indicated that sex had no effect on leader emergence, but gender role did. Specifically, regardless of sex, masculine subjects were more likely to emerge as leaders than feminine, androgynous, and undifferentiated individuals.

A field study by Fagenson (1990) produced similar results. Men and women in this study who were high in an organizational hierarchy were significantly higher on measures of masculinity than were lower-level workers. These significant findings emerged after the researcher had controlled for several important demographic variables.

In view of these findings, we predicted that gender identity would better explain leader emergence than sex.

> *Hypothesis 1: Men will more often emerge as leaders in group situations than women.*
>
> *Hypothesis 2: Group members high in masculinity will emerge as leaders more frequently than those low in masculinity.*
>
> *Hypothesis 3: Gender identity will account for more variance in leader emergence than biological sex.*

An additional feature of our study was an attempt to further assess the relationship between gender role and leader emergence. To do this, we followed Bem's (1974) method of classifying individuals on the basis of their levels of both masculinity and femininity, since these are considered to be independent dimensions. Thus, individuals were classified as (1) masculine when they rated high on items assessing masculinity and low on those assessing femininity; (2) feminine, low masculinity and high femininity; (3) androgynous, high masculinity and high femininity, or (4) undifferentiated, low masculinity and low femininity. In view of the research overwhelmingly concluding that masculinity is related to leader emergence, we hypothesized:

> *Hypothesis 4: Individuals classified as masculine or androgynous will emerge as leaders more frequently than individuals classified as feminine or undifferentiated.*

However, it was not clear whether having feminine characteristics would strengthen or weaken the prospects of leader emergence for those high in masculinity. Thus, an exploratory aspect of this study was to identify potential differences in leader emergence between masculine and androgynous subjects.

# Methods

## Participants

Participants in this study were 122 undergraduate, mostly nonworking, business students enrolled in one of three upper-division courses in business policy or organizational behavior at a large southeastern university [in the USA]. Students in each class were asked to complete questionnaires near the end of the semester, and all agreed. Seven students were eliminated from the study because they did not fully complete all necessary measures, making the final number of participants 115 (67 men and 48 women).

At the beginning of the semester, the students formed 23 groups, each of which had four to seven members. Students selected their own groups under no constraints imposed by the instructors. Proximity was the primary basis of group formation. Twenty-one of the 23 groups (91%) had five or six members, 1 had four members, and 1 had seven members. Group size was not expected to influence leader emergence (Goktepe and Schneier, 1989). However, because there were more men than women overall, the sex composition of the groups was noteworthy. Sixteen of the groups (70%) had at least two women, 6 groups had one woman, and 1 group had no women.

## Procedures

Throughout the semester, group members worked together on several required case presentations or written case analyses, depending on the class. These tasks were considered to be gender-neutral (Goktepe and Schneier, 1989) compared to a masculine task such as repairing machinery (Carbonell, 1984) or a feminine task such as planning a wedding budget (Wentworth and Anderson, 1984), both of which have been used in other studies. Preparing the assignments required a significant amount of interaction outside of class. The students' frequent interactions provided the opportunity for them to develop relatively strong perceptions about their group members' leader-related behaviors as well as their own.

Immediately following completion of the final group project, all participants responded to the Bern Sex-Role Inventory (BSRI; Bem, 1974) and to three items designed to measure their perceptions of their own leader behaviors as well as those of their group members.

## Measures

**Gender role.** By comparing individuals' scores on the BSRI to the medians for the entire study group on masculinity and femininity, we assigned each individual to one of the four gender-role categories, masculine, androgynous, feminine, and undifferentiated. In these data, the median cutoffs for masculinity and femininity were scores of 5.3 and 4.7, respectively. Individuals categorized as androgynous had mean masculinity and femininity scores of 5.84 and 5.18, and those categorized as masculine had mean masculinity and femininity scores of 5.73 and 4.03. Feminine individuals had mean masculinity and femininity scores of 4.57 and 5.38. Undifferentiated individuals had mean masculinity and femininity scores of 4.59 and 4.09.

**Leader emergence.** Leader emergence was assessed using a three-item scale [ ... ] (Kent and Moss, 1990). These items are based on research summarized in Bass (1981) that suggests that the emergent leaders in groups talk more than others, participate more actively, and make more attempts to influence the group. An interesting feature of this instrument is that it allows for the assessment of both self-perceptions of leader emergence and group perceptions, thus providing information about the roles of both internal (self) and external (group) barriers to leader emergence. We used the following measure: 'Please rate the extent to which *you* and *each member of your group* (1) assumed a leadership role, (2) led the conversation, and (3) influenced group goals and decisions' (1, never, 7, always).

[ ... ] This measure [ ... ] has an important advantage. [ ...It] allows for the possible emergence of more than one leader by not forcing subjects to choose between two or more group members who each played significant roles in leading the group. [ ... ]

Self-perceptions of leader emergence were obtained by averaging self-ratings on the three items. Leader emergence scores based on the perceptions of group members were obtained by combining the average rating on the three items into a composite based on the responses of all other group members. The reliabilities for self-reported and group-reported leader emergence were 0.90 and 0.94, respectively.

# Results

Initial inspection of Table 20.1 reveals that masculinity was positively and significantly correlated with both self-perceived leader emergence and group-perceived leader emergence, supporting Hypothesis 2. Femininity was not significantly related to either measure of leader emergence. No significant correlation was found between sex and either measure of leader emergence.

Table 20.2 contains a cross-tabulation of sex and gender role for participants in this study. Approximately the same number of men and women were categorized as androgynous. However, more men were masculine and more women, feminine, and nearly twice as many men as women were undifferentiated.

Because there were fewer women than men in the study and because groups varied with respect to sex composition, all analyses controlled for the percentages of women in the groups. Percentage of women rather than number of women was used because percentage allows for variation in group size. We

**Table 20.1** Pearson Correlations[a]

| Variables | Means | s.d. | 1 | 2 | 3 | 4 |
|---|---|---|---|---|---|---|
| 1. Self-perceived leader emergence | 5.25 | 1.83 | (.90) | | | |
| 2. Group-perceived leader emergence | 4.81 | 1.04 | .49** | (.94) | | |
| 3. Sex | | | .06 | −.09 | | |
| 4. Masculinity | 5.25 | 0.73 | .37** | .22* | .31** | |
| 5. Femininity | 4.69 | 0.75 | .08 | −.06 | −.33** | −.10 |

*Note*: a Reliabilities of leader emergence scales are in parentheses. $N = 115$.
* $p < .05$
** $p < .01$

conducted a two-by-four multivariate analysis of covariance [ ... ] controlling for the percentage of women in each group with sex and gender role as the independent variables and self- and group perceptions of leadership emergence as the two dependent variables. The results revealed a marginally significant effect for sex ($F = 2.50$, $df = 2$, $105$, $p = 0.087$) and a significant effect for gender role ($F = 3.12$, $df = 6$, $210$, p = 0.006).

[In further analysis,] sex was not related to self-perceptions of leader emergence (F = 0.061, $df = 1$, $106$, n.s.), but there was a significant relationship between sex and group perceptions of leader emergence ($F = 4.264$, $df = 1$, $106$, $p = 0.041$). It appears that women (andxmacr; = 4.94) were slightly more likely to be perceived as leaders by group members than men (andxmacr; = 4.77) when means were adjusted to account for the percentage of women in a group. [ ... The] results support Hypothesis 3 but do not support Hypothesis 1.

Table 20.2 reports means and standard deviations for each of the four gender-role classifications. To further explore the relationships between specific gender classifications and leader emergence, we performed pairwise *t*-tests. These tests revealed that androgynous and masculine participants scored higher on both self- and group perceptions of leader emergence than feminine and undifferentiated individuals.

Specifically, for self-perceptions of leadership, androgynous individuals scored significantly higher than feminine ($t = 3.60$, $p = 0.001$) and undifferentiated individuals ($t = 2.92$, $p = 0.005$). Masculine participants also scored higher on self-reports of leader emergence than feminine ($t = 2.94$, $p = 0.005$) and undifferentiated ($t = 2.49$, $p = 0.016$) people. There were no significant differences in the self-perceptions of leadership held by feminine and undifferentiated participants ($t = 0.11$, n.s.). On group perceptions of leader emergence, androgynous individuals scored higher than either feminine ($t = 1.87$, $p = 0.067$) or undifferentiated individuals ($t = 1.94$, $p = 0.058$). Similarly, masculine participants

**Table 20.2** Cross-tabulation of sex and gender and leader emergence ratings

| Gender-Role Class | Number of Men | Percent of Men | Number of Women | Percent of Women | Self-Perceived Leader Emergence | | Group-Perceived Leader Emergence | |
| --- | --- | --- | --- | --- | --- | --- | --- | --- |
| | | | | | Means | s.d. | Means | s.d. |
| Androgynous | 15 | 22.4 | 13 | 27.1 | 5.702 | 0.803 | 5.059 | 0.916 |
| Masculine | 26 | 38.8 | 5 | 10.4 | 5.613 | 1.026 | 5.269 | 0.904 |
| Feminine | 9 | 13.4 | 21 | 43.8 | 4.867 | 0.953 | 4.611 | 0.910 |
| Undifferentiated | 17 | 25.4 | 9 | 18.7 | 4.833 | 1.334 | 4.500 | 1.197 |
| Totals | 67 | | 48 | | | | | |

scored higher on group perceptions of leadership than individuals classified as feminine ($t = 2.83$, $p = 0.006$) or undifferentiated ($t = 2.76$, $p = 0.008$). There was no significant difference in group perceptions for feminine and undifferentiated individuals. These results support Hypothesis 4.

To address the exploratory component of our study, we conducted a paired comparison between androgynous and masculine individuals. There were no significant differences between these two groups for either self-perceptions ($t = 0.37$, n.s.) or group perceptions ($t = -0.88$, n.s.) of leader emergence.

# Discussion

The most significant result of this study, that androgynous individuals have the same chances of emerging as leader as masculine individuals, has three important implications. First, consistent with previous studies and in support of Hypothesis 2, it is clear that masculinity is still an important predictor of leader emergence. In the correlational analysis, participants' masculinity scores were the only variables significantly associated with either measure of leader emergence. Second, contrary to previous findings, the emergence of androgynous leaders suggests that the possession of feminine characteristics does not decrease an individual's chances of emerging as a leader as long as the individual also possesses masculine characteristics. Third, as an extension, if women in other contexts are more likely to be androgynous than masculine, as they were in our study, they may have better chances of rising to leadership status. Of course, verification of this finding depends upon whether future studies find androgyny to be related to leader emergence in other settings.

The second important finding of the study, contrary to Hypothesis 1, was that women were slightly more likely than men to be perceived as leaders by group members when the percentage of women per group was controlled statistically. This finding is significantly different from the results of all other studies linking sex to leader emergence. Although some recent studies have found maleness to be less predictive of leader emergence than it has been in the past (e.g., Goktepe and Schneier, 1989), no study has found women more likely to emerge as leaders than men. However, we feel that this finding should be regarded with some caution because of the unequal distribution of women in the student groups studied here and the small amount of variance explained by sex. [ ... ] Even though the current finding is tentative, we should consider alternatives explaining why group members were slightly more likely to perceived women than men as leaders. It is possible that female participants were perceived as leaders because they tended to be more grade conscious than men (Hornaday, Wheatley, and Hunt, 1989) and may have pushed for higher levels of group performance. Alternatively, Eagly's (1987) gender-role theory may provide some insight. Eagly suggested, and a subsequent meta-analysis confirmed, that men are more likely to emerge as leaders in task-oriented groups, but women are more likely to emerge as leaders in socially oriented groups (Eagly and Karau, 1991). Though the groups in this study were initially task-oriented, they may have developed a social component because this study allowed for extensive interaction time between group members, unlike previous studies in which group members only interacted for a few minutes. As a result, group members may have perceived the women as having considerable influence over the social components of the group. Finally, another possible explanation for this nonconvergent finding is that women are exerting their leadership abilities more today than ever before and group members are becoming more accepting of female leaders.

A third important finding was that gender role is a better predictor of leader emergence than sex. Though women were slightly more likely to be perceived by the groups as leaders, gender role explained more variance in leader emergence. [ ... ]

Finally, the results on self-perceptions of leadership emergence are interesting. Comparing the effects of gender role on the self- and group perceptions makes it clear that those classified as masculine and androgynous were not only more likely than feminine and undifferentiated subjects to be perceived by their groups as leaders, but were also more likely to perceive themselves as leaders. Also notable was the nonsignificant effect of sex on self-perceptions of leadership emergence, which suggests that women were as likely as men to perceive themselves as leaders. In general, it appears that those whom others perceive as leaders also perceive themselves as leaders.

[ ... ] In summary, the results of this study suggest that androgynous individuals and women may be more likely than they were in the past to emerge as leaders in business school settings, where becoming a leader is fairly important. Although we must be cautious in generalizing our results to present business people, we feel that these changes in a college setting mean that future business people may be more accepting of female and androgynous leaders than their counterparts have been in the past. This acceptance could affect the probabilities of emergent leadership for future female and androgynous business people.

--------------------------- *References* ---------------------------

Ahrons, C.R. (1976) 'Counselor's perceptions of career images of women', *Journal of Vocational Behavior*, vol. 8, pp. 197–207.

Almquist, E.M. (1974) 'Sex stereotypes in occupational choice: The case for college women', *Journal of Vocational Behavior*, vol. 5, pp. 13–21.

Bem, S.L. (1974) 'The measurement of psychological androgyny', *Journal of Consulting and Clinical Psychology*, vol. 42, pp. 155–62.

Bowman, G.W., Worthy, N.B. and Greyson, S.A. (1965) 'Problems in review: Are women executives people?' *Harvard Business Review*, vol. 43, no. 4, pp. 52–67.

Brenner. O.C., Tomkiewicz, J. and Schein, V. (1989) 'The relationship between sex-role stereotypes and requisite management characteristics revisited', *Academy of Management Journal*, vol. 32, pp. 662–69.

Carbonell, J.L. (1984) 'Sex roles and leadership revisited', *Journal of Applied Psychology*, vol. 69, pp. 44–49.

Chusmir, L.H. and Koberg, C.S. (1991) 'Relationship between self-confidence and sex role identity among managerial women and men', *Journal of Social Psychology*, vol. 161, pp. 781–90.

Dobbins, G.H., Long, W.S., Dedrick, E.J. and Clemons, T.C. (1990) 'The role of self-monitoring and gender on leader emergence: A laboratory and field study', *Journal of Management*, vol. 16, pp. 609–18.

Eagly, A.H. (1987) *Sex Differences in Social Behavior: A Social-Role Interpretation*, Hillsdale, NJ, Erlbaum.

Eagly, A. H., and Karau, S. J. 1991. Gender and the emergence of leaders: A meta-analysis. *Journal of Personality and Social Psychology*, 60: 685–710.

Fagenson, E.A. (1990) 'Perceived masculine and feminine attributes examined as a function of individuals' sex and level in the organizational power hierarchy: A test of four theoretical perspectives', *Journal of Applied Psychology*, vol. 75, pp. 204–11.

Fleischer, R.A. and Chertkoff, J.M. (1986) 'Effects of dominance and sex on leader selection in dyadic work groups', *Journal of Personality and Social Psychology*, vol. 50, pp. 94–99.

Goktepe, J.R. and Schneier, C.E. (1989) 'Role of sex, gender roles, and attraction in predicting emergent leaders', *Journal of Applied Psychology*, vol. 74, pp. 165–67.

Goodale, J.G. and Hall, D.T. (1976) 'Inheriting a career: The influence of sex, values, and parents', *Journal of Vocational Behavior*, vol. 8, pp. 19–30.

Gough, H.G. (1957) *Manual for the California Psychological Inventory*, Palo Alto, CA, Consulting Psychologists Press.

Helmreich, R.L., Spence, J.T. and Gibson, R.H. (1982) 'Sex role attitudes: 1972–1980', *Personality and Social Psychology Bulletin*, vol. 8, 656–63.

Hornaday, R.W., Wheatley, W.J. and Hunt, T.G. (1989) 'Differences in performance between male and female business students', *Journal of Education for Business*, vol. 64, no. 6, pp. 259–64.

Kent, R.L. and Moss, S.E. (1990) 'Self-monitoring as a predictor of leader emergence', *Psychological Reports*, vol. 66, pp. 875–81.

Korabik, K. (1990) 'Androgyny and leadership style', *Journal of Business Ethics*, vol. 9, pp. 283–292.

Megargee, E.I. (1969) 'Influence of sex roles on the manifestation of leadership', *Journal of Applied Psychology*, vol. 53, pp. 377–82.

Nyquist, L.V. and Spence, J.T. (1986) 'Effects of dispositional dominance and sex role expectations on leadership behaviors', *Journal of Personality and Social Psychology*, vol. 50, pp. 87–93.

Powell, G.N. (1993) *Women and Men in Management* (2nd edn), Newbury Park, CA, Sage.

Powell, G.N. and Butterfield, D.A. (1979) 'The "good manager": Masculine or androgynous?' *Academy of Management Journal,* vol. 22, pp. 395–403.

Powell, G.N., Posner, B.Z. and Schmidt, W.H. (1984) 'Sex effects on managerial value systems', *Human Relations,* vol. 37, pp. 909–21.

Sutton, C.D. and Moore, K.K. (1985) 'Executive women – 20 years later', *Harvard Business Review,* vol. 63, no. 5, pp. 43–66.

Terborg, J.R. (1977) 'Women in management: A research review', *Journal of Applied Psychology,* vol. 62, pp. 647–64.

Tipton, R.M. (1976) 'Attitudes towards women's roles in society and vocational interests', *Journal of Vocational Behavior,* vol. 8, pp. 155–65.

Weisman, C.S., Morlock, L.L., Sack, D.G. and Levine, D.M. (1976) 'Sex differences in response to a blocked career pathway among unaccepted medical school applicants', *Sociology of Work and Occupations,* vol. 3, pp. 187–208.

Wentworth, D.K. and Anderson, L.R. (1984) 'Emergent leadership as a function of sex and task type', *Sex Roles,* vol. 11, pp. 513–23.

White, M.C., DeSanctis, G. and Crino, M.D. (1981) 'Achievement, self-confidence, personality traits, and leadership ability: A review of literature on sex differences', *Psychological Reports,* vol. 48, pp. 547–69.

# Female First, Leader Second? Gender Bias in the Encoding of Leadership Behavior

21

## Kristyn A. Scott and Douglas J. Brown

In recent years, a substantial amount of attention has been paid to the progress of females in the work-force, especially females in leadership positions. As a whole, this work suggests that a considerable amount of bias exists against females. For example, despite holding 37% of all management positions (US Bureau of Labor Statistics, 2005), women hold only 7.9% of the highest corporate officer titles and make up only 5.2% of the top earners in Fortune 500 companies (Catalyst, 2002). Similarly, Canadian statistics indicate that women are better represented at lower managerial levels (36%) compared to more senior managerial positions (24%; Statistics Canada, 2004). Recent European data, which show that women hold only 30% of managerial positions and make up only 3% of CEOs in the top 50 publicly quoted companies (European Commission, 2005), suggest that gender bias may not be isolated to North America. Supporting these statistics, a series of recent meta-analyses has demonstrated that gender differences do exist, do exist, to varying degrees, in leadership emergence, effectiveness, evaluation, and style, most notably when the leadership position is defined to be clearly masculine (Eagly and Johnson, 1990; Eagly and Karau, 1991; Eagly, Karau, and Makhijani, 1995; Eagly, Makhijani, and Klonsky, 1992), and that females are preferred less by decision makers for male sex-typed positions (e.g., leadership roles; Davison and Burke, 2000).

Previous leadership research into gender bias has focused on perceivers' biased memory (e.g., Martell, [ ... ] 1996), the process of making judgments about females in leadership roles (e.g., Heilman, Block, Martell, and Simon, 1989), and the incongruity between expected gender-role behavior and the

Scott, K.A. and Brown, D.J. (2006) 'Female first, leader second? Gender bias in the encoding of leadership behavior', *Organizational Behavior and Human Decision Processes*, vol. 101, pp. 230–42.

definition of the leadership role (e.g., Eagly and Karau, 2002). Despite such varied approaches, little is known about whether gender bias may emerge earlier, when leadership behaviors are initially encountered and encoded by observers. Encoding is a basic stage of information processing in which environmental stimuli are translated (or encoded) into mental representations that can be operated upon and utilized by other components of the human cognitive architecture (Von Hippel, Sekaquaptewa, and Vargas, 1995). Hence, how behavior is encoded can significantly impact subsequent judgments, thoughts, and decisions about a target. Although some leadership scholars have proposed that gender information may bias the encoding of leadership behaviors (Lord and Maher, 1991), this possibility has not been empirically tested. In the present paper, we redress this gap and examine whether gender biases arise when leadership behaviors are initially encountered and encoded into their underlying traits by observers. We focus on traits not only because they are central to basic person perception processes, but also because they are the foundation upon which leadership perceptions are the foundation upon which leadership perceptions are formed and decisions regarding managerial potential are made by observers (Lord and Maher, 1991).

To situate our research, we first review previous theoretical work on leadership perceptions, focusing on leadership categorization theory. Second, we review literature on gender bias in leadership, focusing on how gender-role expectations and stereotypes may color reactions to female leaders. Third, we discuss how preexisting gender stereotypes can interfere with a perceiver's ability to encode leadership behavior. Finally, we present three studies that examine whether gender stereotypes undermine the extent to which perceivers encode leadership behaviors into their underlying trait concepts.

# Leader Categorization Theory

Categorization theory posits that perceivers rely upon symbolic knowledge structures, called prototypes, to make sense of their environments (Rosch, 1978). Conceptually, prototyes are cognitive schemas that are stored in memory and that consist of the most representative features of a given category. As with other knowledge structures, prototypes assist perceivers to make sense of their surroundings (Weick, 1995) and generate adaptive behavioral responses (Johnson-Laird, 1989; Newell, Rosenbloom, and Laird, 1989). [ ... ]

According to Lord and his colleagues, each individual holds within long-term memory a large and well-elaborated belief system, consisting of the features that distinguish leaders from non leaders (Lord, Foti, and Phillips, 1982; Phillips and Lord, 1981). This belief system is often referred to as an implicit leadership theory or leader prototype (Lord et al., 1984). Leadership prototypes allow individuals to both understand and respond to managerial behaviors (Epitropaki and Martin, 2004; Lord and Maher, 1991). Previous work has demonstrated that the leader prototype is a multidimensional, widely shared, trait-based knowledge structure that is formed very early in life (Epitropaki and Martin, 2004; Lord and Maher, 1991; Offermann, Kennedy, and Wirtz, 1994). Thus, from the perspective of categorization theory, leadership can be viewed as a social-cognitive category that organizes our memories of leadership, guides how leadership information is processed, and mediates our leadership perceptions (Lord et al., 1984; Lord and Maher, 1991).

Lord and Maher (1991) suggest that one of the ways in which leadership perceptions emerge is through recognition-based processing, which depends both upon exposure to a target's behavior and preexisting knowledge structures regarding the traits that underlie that behavior (i.e., leader prototype). Although recognition-based leadership perception processes can result from either controlled or automatic information processing, automatic recognition-based processing appears to be more typical. That is, during the normal flow of interpersonal activities behavior is automatically encoded, without intent, effort, or awareness, into preexisting knowledge structures (Lord and Maher, 1991). As such, automatic recognition-based leadership processes simplify the processing of incoming leader behavior by allowing perceivers to utilize the leader prototype.

Implicitly, the recognition process outlined by Lord and his colleagues (Lord and Maher, 1991) follows two-stages. Initially, observers process and encode a target's behaviors into their relevant traits and, following this, the traits associated with a target are compared to an observer's preexisting leader prototype (Lord et al., 1984; Rush and Russell, 1998). For example, after observing a manager staying late in the evening to finish a presentation, a perceiver must first encode the behavior into its underlying trait (i.e., dedicated) and subsequently, when a leadership judgment is needed, compare the encoded traits with those contained in his/her leader prototype. Thus, Lord's discussion of recognition-based processes suggests that an individual could fail to be perceived as 'leader-like' either because his/her behavior is not mapped into prototypical leadership traits (Stage 1: trait encoding and activation) or because the traits associated with a target do not match the perceiver's leadership prototype (Stage 2: recall and prototype matching). To date, most research into recognition processes has focused on the matching stage while relatively little attention has been paid to the encoding stage (Lord and Brown, 2004; for two exceptions see Phillips and Lord, 1981; Cronshaw and Lord, 1987).

Although behavioral encoding processes have largely been ignored by leadership categorization theorists, these processes have received extensive attention in the person perception literature. This work not only suggests that traits are a critical component of person perception and memory, but that behavior is rapidly and automatically, encoded into its underlying traits when observers encounter trait-related behaviors (Uleman, Newman, and Moskowitz, 1996). Encoding a target's behavior in terms of traits is so natural that it occurs even when an observer is otherwise preoccupied (Gilbert, 1989) or has no intention to form an impression of a target (Winter and Uleman, 1984). As a result of this process, exposure to behavior activates relevant trait concepts, increasing their accessibility in the perceiver's mind (Van Overwalle, Drenth, and Marsman, 1999; Winter and Uleman, 1984). Simultaneously, activated traits are generalized to the actor and subsequently used to describe him/her (Van Overwalle et al., 1999). In the present paper, we utilize the automatic activation of traits during behavioral encoding (Uleman, Hon, Roman, and Moskowitz, 1996; Uleman, Newman et al., 1996) to investigate whether any gender bias arises against female leaders when observers initially encounter leadership behaviors. To understand how gender information may bias behavioral encoding processes we next discuss work on gender stereotypes and the leader prototype.

## Gender Stereotypes, Leader Prototypes, and Behavioral Encoding

An extensive amount of literature has investigated sex trait stereotypes, which refer to the psychological characteristics or behavioral traits that are believed to characterize men with much greater (or lesser) frequency than they characterize women (Williams and Best, 1990). Unlike investigations of actual gender differences in psychological traits (e.g., Feingold, 1994), gender trait stereotypes refer to beliefs regarding the traits that are thought to characterize men and women. Stereotypical beliefs about the attributes of men and women are pervasive, and widely shared by men and women (Broverman, Vogel, Broverman, Clarkson, and Rosenkrantz, 1972; Williams and Best, 1990). Although numerous dimensions have been proposed to differentiate male and female stereotypes (Deaux and Lewis, 1984), from a trait perspective women are typically thought to be communal and expressive in nature while men are typically thought to be agentic and instrumental in nature (Williams and Best, 1990). Generally, the female communal/expressive stereotype refers to an interpersonally sensitive orientation in which the individual is both concerned with the welfare of others and their connection to others. In line with this idea, women are typically assumed to be helpful, kind, and sympathetic as well as motivated by stronger needs for nurturance, affiliation, and succorance (Williams and Best, 1990). In contrast, the male agentic/instrumental stereotype reflects a self-interested, task focused orientation in which men are believed to strive to master, dominate, and control the self and the environment. In line with this position, men are stereotypically believed to be independent, ambitious, competent, and competitive as well as motivated by stronger needs for dominance, autonomy, aggression, achievement, and endurance (Williams and Best, 1990). In the current paper we utilize the labels agentic and communal to reflect male and female stereotypical characteristics, respectively.

During the past 30 years, a considerable amount of research has documented the dissimilarity that exists between perceivers' stereotypes of females and their prototypes of leaders (Eagly and Karau, 2002). For instance, cross-cultural research has demonstrated that although people generally perceive that substantial overlap exists between the traits associated with 'male' and 'manager', they see little overlap between the social categories 'female' and 'manager' (Brenner, Tomkiewicz, and Schein, 1989; Schein, 1975, 2001). Other work has shown that labeling a female manager as 'successful' serves to mitigate some of the bias demonstrated in past research. However, despite the increased congruence afforded by this label, females are still perceived to lack leadership and business acumen (Heilman et al., 1989). In part, it has been suggested that such biased judgments arise because while the female stereotype is communal (e.g., helpful, sensitive), the leader prototype primarily contains characteristics that are more closely aligned with the male stereotype (e.g., aggressive, dominant; Eagly and Karau, 2002; Heilman, 2001). Thus, because masculine views of leadership and leadership roles are widely held, a bias emerges against females because they are seen as a poor fit for such positions by observers (Eagly and Karau, 2002; Lord and Maher, 1991; Powell, Butterfield, and Parent, 2002).

Although the dissimilarity between female gender stereotypes and the leader prototype does appear to bias perceivers' judgments of a female's ability to assume a leadership position (Eagly and Karau, 2002; Heilman, 2001), what remains less evident is whether gender stereotypes can bias leadership perceptions prior to judgment during encoding. Because incoming information is processed in terms of a single underlying cognitive structure (Malt, Ross, and Murphy, 1995) and gender stereotypes are easily and automatically activated by gender-related cues (Blair and Banaji, 1996; Brewer, 1998) it seems plausible that gender stereotypes may bias behavioral encoding. Further, given that the traits encompassed by the female gender stereotype are largely inconsistent with those associated with the leader prototype (Eagly and Karau, 2002; Lord and Maher, 1991) it seems reasonable that a bias against females will emerge. In fact, Lord and Maher (1991) suggest that when female gender stereotypes guide a perceiver's information processing, relevant leadership behaviors may not be encoded into prototypical leadership traits or may be done so more weakly by perceivers. Consistent with this view, recent work indicates that stereotypic beliefs can bias behavioral encoding (Dijksterhuis and van Knippenberg, 1996; Von Hippel et al., 1995; Wigboldus, Dijksterhuis, and van Knippenberg, 2003).

Previous research has shown that stereotypes both facilitate the encoding and subsequent activation of stereotype consistent traits (Devine, 1989; Stangor and Lange, 1994), as well as render inconsistent traits *less* accessible (Dijksterhuis and van Knippenberg, 1996). For instance, Dijksterhuis and van Knippenberg found that exposing participants to the image of a 'soccer hooligan' increased the ease with which stereotype-consistent trait words (e.g., aggressive) were activated, but inhibited the activation of words inconsistent with the stereotype (e.g., intelligent). Wigboldus et al. (2003) extended the idea of trait inhibition, incorporating theory on behavioral encoding processes (Winter and Uleman, 1984) to determine whether basic information processing could be impeded by stereotype activation. Generally, their results demonstrated that behavioral encoding was disrupted by stereotype-inconsistent information such that participants encoded information in a manner that was consistent with their pre-existing stereotypical beliefs.

## The Current Research

The literature reviewed above leads us to propose that a leader's gender can bias the manner in which leadership behaviors are encoded by observers. Because behavior is automatically encoded into traits during behavioral encoding, and behavioral encoding increases the accessibility of behavior implying traits during encoding (e.g., Uleman et al., 1996; Uleman, Newman et al., 1996; Wigboldus et al., 2003), in each of the studies reported below we assess encoding bias in terms of trait activation. That is, following current conceptualizations, we assessed encoding in terms of the extent to which leadership behaviors primed or increased the accessibility of relevant traits. Moreover, because increased accessibility can be operationalized in alternative ways, such as facilitated reaction times and judgments, we attempted to triangulate our findings by using alternative operationalizations of trait activation in each of our studies. Prior to discussing the methods and results of each study, we first present the focal hypotheses to be tested.

## Study 1

Considering the prior literature, it seems plausible that a target's gender will influence the encoding of leadership behaviors into their underlying prototypical trait concepts. In this regard, the literature reviewed previously indicates that (a) behaviors are automatically encoded into relevant traits by perceivers (Van Overwalle et al., 1999; Wigboldus et al., 2003), (b) social category cues, such as gender, facilitate access to stereotype-consistent trait terms and inhibit access to stereotype-inconsistent trait terms (Von Hippel et al., 1995), (c) stereotypes can color behavioral encoding into traits (Wigboldus et al., 2003), and (d) the female gender stereotype, which is communal, is largely inconsistent with the leader prototype, which is agentic, but that the male stereotype is largely consistent with the leader prototype (Eagly and Karau, 2002; Heilman, 2001). Together, these findings lead us to propose that during encoding, perceivers will demonstrate a distinct processing disadvantage towards female targets, relative to male targets.

In large part, the proposed processing bias against female leaders should arise because the content of the female gender stereotype, which is communal, is inconsistent with the leadership prototype, which is largely agentic. This suggests that the behavioral encoding disadvantage for female targets will be isolated to only agentic leadership behaviors (i.e., behaviors that imply agentic traits). Although there is little doubt that the leader prototype primarily consists of agentic traits (Lord and Maher, 1991) previous research has revealed that there are a limited number of communal traits in the leader prototype. Research that has examined the structure of the leader prototype suggests that eight overarching dimensions underlie the prototype (Offermann et al., 1994). A close inspection of these dimensions, and their associated traits, reveals that while seven of the eight dimensions are consistent with agentic characteristics (i.e., masculine), one of the eight is quite clearly communal (i.e., sensitivity). Based on the logic outlined above, we anticipated that evidence for gender encoding biases in leadership would depend upon the match between the gender of the leader and the dimension under consideration (i.e., communal versus agentic). Based on this, we hypothesized:

> **Hypothesis 1.** *Encoding will depend upon the match between the leadership behavior and the gender of the leader. Participants will have more difficulty encoding leadership trait words when there is incongruence between the leadership behavior (agentic vs. communal) and the gender of the leader (male vs. female).*

## Method

### Participants

One hundred and thirty-nine undergraduate students from a large Canadian university participated in this study in exchange for extra credit towards their introductory psychology course grade. Fifty-eight percent of participants were female and the mean age was 19.57 ($SD$ = 2.96).

### Procedure

[ ... ] In this task, participants were presented with behavioral sentences paired with a letter string which was either a word or a nonword (each behavior letter string combination is labeled a trial). [ ... ] A behavioral sentence appeared on the computer screen for three seconds. At the end of the three seconds the sentence disappeared and was replaced by a letter string (either a trait-implying word or a nonword), which remained on the computer screen until participants registered a response. Participants were instructed to indicate whether the letter string was a word or nonword by pressing '1' on the computer keyboard if the letter string was a word, and '3' on the computer keyboard if the letter string was a non-world. The more strongly that a behavior has been encoded into its underlying trait, the faster should be a participant's reaction time to the trait (Bassili, 2003). That is, the extent to which the trait has been encoded can be assessed by the degree to which the behavior primes the trait.

[ ... ] Participants completed 96 experimental trials. On 48 of these trials participants were presented with one of the leadership behavior sentences followed by the matched prototypical leadership trait. For half of these 48 trials (i.e., 24 trials) the target of the behavior was male while on the remaining half of these 48 trials the target of the behavior was female. Thus, participants were presented with each of the 24 leadership behavior–trait combinations twice, once with a female target and once with a male target for a total of 48 trials. For example, each participant would read the sentence 'Suzanne works relentlessly to solve difficult problems' and they would also read 'William works relentlessly to solve difficult problems', in each case the trait determination (i.e., agentic trait) would serve as the letter string. Similarly, each participant would also read, 'Jill encourages employees to approach her if a problem arises' and, 'Russell encourages employees to approach him if a problem arises', in each case the trait understanding (i.e., communal trait) would serve as the letter string. On the remaining 48 trials, participants were presented with 24 neutral behavioral sentences twice, once with a male target and once with a female target. Each of these neutral behavioral sentences was paired with a nonword. The order in which the sentences and their corresponding letter strings were presented was randomly generated by the computer program such that the order of presentation was unique for each participant. The amount of time participants took to make the word decision served as the dependent variable in the current study.

[ ... ]

## Results

[ ... ]
Data were analyzed using a 2 (leadership behavior: agentic vs. communal) × 2 (target gender: male vs. female) within-subjects ANOVA. Significant main effects were found for target gender ($F(1, 137) = 8.25$, $p < 0.01$, $\eta^2 = 0.06$) and for behavior ($F(1, 137) = 8.34$, $p < 0.01$, $\eta^2 = 0.06$). These results indicated that response times were significantly faster when the leader target was male

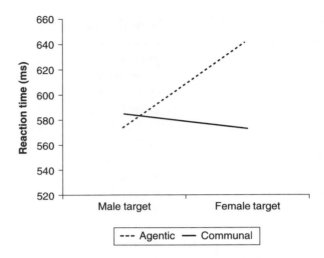

**Figure 21.1** Two-way interaction between leadership behavior (agentic vs. communal) and leader gender (male vs. female).

(vs. female) and when the behavior was communal (vs. agentic). However these results were qualified by the hypothesized two-way interaction between target gender and behavior ($F(1, 137) = 13.53$, $p < 0.01$, $\eta^2 = 0.09$) (see Figure 21.1). An examination of the means [ ... ] shows that, following the presentation of an agentic behavior, participants were slower to recognize the corresponding trait when the target was a female compared to a male ($t(137) = -3.60$, $p < 0.01$), providing partial support for Hypothesis 1.

## Study 2a and Study 2b

The results of Study 1 suggest that perceivers may not encode agentic leadership behaviors into their underlying traits as strongly or as easily when they are presented with a female target. Specifically, our results demonstrated that although the encoding of communal traits may not vary as a function of leader gender, the encoding of agentic leadership behavior appeared to be dependent upon leader gender such that agentic leadership traits were less accessible when the leader was female (vs. male). The fact that there was no significant difference in the encoding of communal traits was somewhat surprising, although perhaps not entirely unexpected. A [ ... ] meta-analysis of gender differences in leadership revealed that males and females were evaluated similarly when they led in a feminine, communal style (Eagly et al., 1992). Moreover, other findings suggest that males and leaders are not perceived to differ in the extent to which they possess person-oriented (i.e., communal) and task-oriented (i.e., agentic) skills (Sczesny, 2003). In line with these findings, our results suggest that any gender bias during automatic behavioral encoding may be isolated to agentic leadership behaviors.

In Studies 2a and b we attempted to replicate the biased encoding of agentic leadership behaviors using an alternative dependent variable, self-perceptions. Prior research has demonstrated that trait activation increases the likelihood that a trait will be used in subsequent judgments (e.g., Srull and Wyer, 1979, 1980). Extending this principle, Wheeler and Petty (2001) have suggested that trait activation can bias self-perceptions, leading individuals to assimilate their self-descriptions towards the activated trait. Based on this research, in Studies 2a and b, we had participants read the agentic leadership behaviors from Study 1, manipulating target gender, and examined the extent to which our participants' self-descriptions shifted as a function of the agent's gender. Given that Study 1 indicated that agentic leadership traits were more readily encoded, and thus more strongly activated, when enacted by a male vs. female, and the fact that prior work has suggested that activated traits influence self-judgments (e.g., Wheeler and Petty, 2001) we hypothesized:

> **Hypothesis 2.** *Participants asked to form an impression of a female leader who has displayed agentic leadership behaviors, relative to a male leader, will display evidence of weaker encoding of relevant agentic traits in their self-judgments.*

## Study 2a and 2b: Method

### Participants and Procedure

Forty-seven students from a large Canadian university were recruited to participate in Study 2a and 82 students were recruited to participate in Study 2b. All participants in Study 2a were recruited from the student center and received a candy bar in exchange for their participation, while all participants in Study 2b volunteered to complete the study as part of an in class exercise.

In both Study 2a and 2b, participants were randomly assigned to read about and form an impression of either a male or a female who had engaged in agentic managerial behaviors. Participants were asked to read the managerial description and spend a few minutes writing down their general impressions of the individual. Following the impression formation task, each participant completed a self-report trait questionnaire that was designed to assess the extent to which he/she felt that a series of 38 personality traits were self-descriptive. Finally, participants were fully debriefed regarding the purpose of the study.

[ ... ]

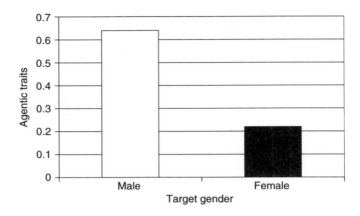

**Figure 21.2**  Self-described agentic traits for participants exposed to agentic male leaders compared to those exposed to agentic female leaders in Study 2a

## Study 2a: Results

The data were analyzed using a one-way ANOVA, with the total number of agentic traits selected serving as the dependent variable. A significant difference was found between conditions, $F(1, 45) = 5.09$, $p<.05$, $\eta^2 = 0.10$. An examination of the means [ ... ] revealed that participants who had read and formed an impression of the male manager, on average, selected significantly more of the agentic traits as self-descriptive compared to participants who had read about the female manager (see Figure 21.2). When the analysis was repeated using the number of communal traits endorsed, no significant differences emerged, $F(1, 45) = 0.81$, *ns*. Finally, we examined whether the effect on the number of agentic traits endorsed remained significant once the number of communal traits selected was controlled. This analysis indicated that the difference in agentic traits remained, $F(1, 44) = 4.93$, $p< 0.05$, $\eta^2 = 0.10$.

## Study 2b: Results

As in Study 2a, the data were analyzed using a one-way ANOVA, with the total number of agentic leadership traits selected serving as the dependent variable. A significant difference was found between conditions, $F(1, 80) = 4.50$, $p< 0.05$, $\eta^2 = 0.053$. An examination of the means [ ... ] revealed that participants who had read and formed an impression of the male manager, on average, selected significantly more of the agentic leadership traits as self-descriptive compared to participants who had read about the female manager (see Figure 21.3). When the analysis was repeated using the number of communal traits endorsed,

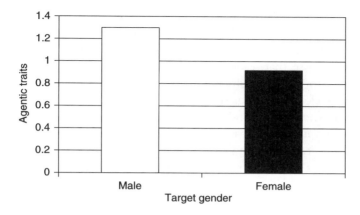

**Figure 21.3**  Self-described agentic traits for participants exposed to agentic male leaders compared to those exposed to agentic female leaders in Study 2b

no significant differences emerged, $F(1, 80)= 0.37$, *ns.* Finally, we examined whether the effect on the number of agentic traits endorsed remained significant once the number of communal traits selected was controlled. This analysis indicated that the difference in agentic traits remained, $F(1, 79) = 4.40$, $p< 0.05$, $\eta^2 = 0.053$.

# Discussion

[ ... ]

In Study 1, we demonstrated that the extent to which agentic leadership traits are spontaneously encoded from trait-implying leader behaviors was dependent upon the gender of the target under consideration. Our findings suggested that participants more readily encoded agentic behaviors into prototypical leadership traits when the target was male, versus female. Study 2a and b replicated this effect, demonstrating that, on average, participants who had read about a male manager were more likely to endorse agentic traits as self-descriptive relative to those participants who had read about a female manager. Taken together, our studies are the first to suggest that gender bias in leadership may emerge quite early on during information processing.

At a general level, our findings extend the [ ... ] research that has examined behavioral encoding. Unlike previous work into the encoding process, which has largely focused on determining whether leadership behaviors are noticed and processed by observers (e.g., Cronshaw and Lord, 1987), our work focused on understanding the nature of the cognitive structures that perceivers use when encoding leadership behavior, traits. Theoretically, our findings represent an important test of the automatic recognition-based processes outlined by Lord and Maher (1991). In their model of leadership perceptions, Lord and Maher propose that leadership behavior is automatically encoded, without intent or effort, into an observer's preexisting leader prototype. Consistent with their model, our findings suggested that relevant traits may be automatically encoded when corresponding behaviors are processed by an observer and that this occurs unbeknownst to the observer. Beyond supporting Lord and Maher's model, our work suggests that it may be necessary to expand it to include aspects of the context and the target that can influence automatic recognition based leadership perceptions. [ ... ]

The findings of Study 2a and b may have rather grim implications for female leadership in organizations. As Lord and Brown (2004) suggest, leadership is a process of influence in which one individual, typically labeled a leader, attempts to change the attitudes, behaviors, or reactions of a second individual or group of individuals, typically labeled a follower or subordinate. Critically, these authors suggest that a leader's influence flows through a subordinate's conceptualization of the self, which in turn serves to regulate a subordinate's current action, thought, and behavior. As such, Study 2a and b may suggest that because of perceiver biases, female leaders will experience substantially more difficulty in getting subordinates to conceptualize themselves as possessing agentic characteristics (e.g., ambitious) through, for example, role modeling behaviors. Given the important relationship between agentic characteristics and relevant work behaviors such a perceptual bias may undermine the effectiveness of female leaders. [ ... ]

## References

Blair, I.V. and Banaji, M.R. (1996) 'Automatic and controlled processes in stereotype priming', *Journal of Personality and Social Psychology,* vol. 70, pp. 1142–63.

Brenner, O.C., Tomkiewicz, J. and Schein, V.E. (1989) 'The relationship between sex role stereotypes and requisite management characteristics revisited', *Academy of Management Journal,* vol. 32, pp. 662–69.

Brewer, M.B. (1998) 'A dual process model of impression formation' in Srull, T.K. and Wyer, R.S. (eds) *Advances in Social Cognition* (Vol. 1), Hillsdale, NJ, Erlbaum.

Broverman, I.K., Vogel, S.R., Broverman, D.M., Clarkson, F.E. and Rosenkrantz, P.S. (1972) 'Sex-role stereotypes: a current appraisal', *Journal of Social Issues,* vol. 28, pp. 59–78.

Catalyst (2002) 'Census of women corporate officers and top earners', Retrieved 6 January 2006 from http://www.catalyst.org/knowledge/titles/title.php?page = cen_WOTE02.

Cronshaw, S.F. and Lord, R.G. (1987) 'Effects of categorization, attribution, and encoding processes on leadership perceptions', *Journal of Applied Psychology,* vol. 72, pp. 97–106.

Davison, H.K. and Burke, M.J. (2000) 'Sex discrimination in simulated employment contexts: a meta-analytic investigation', *Journal of Vocational Behavior,* vol. 56, pp. 225–48.

Deaux, K. and Lewis, L. (1984) 'Structure of gender stereotypes: interrelationships among components and gender label', *Journal of Personality and Social Psychology,* vol. 46, pp. 991–1004.

Devine, P.G. (1989) 'Stereotypes and prejudice: their automatic and controlled components', *Journal of Personality and Social Psychology*, vol. 56, pp. 5–18.

Dijksterhuis, A. and van Knippenberg, A. (1996) 'The knife that cuts both ways: facilitated and inhibited access to traits as a result of stereotype activation', *Journal of Experimental Social Psychology*, vol. 32, pp. 271–88.

Eagly, A.H. and Johnson, B.T. (1990) 'Gender and leadership style: A meta-analysis', *Psychological Bulletin*, vol. 108, pp. 233–56.

Eagly, A.H. and Karau, S.J. (1991) 'Gender and the emergence of leaders: a meta-analysis', *Journal of Personality and Social Psychology*, vol. 60, pp. 685–710.

Eagly, A.H. and Karau, S.J. (2002) 'Role congruity theory of prejudice toward female leaders', *Psychological Review*, vol. 109, pp. 573–98.

Eagly, A.H., Karau, S.J. and Makhijani, M.G. (1995) 'Gender and the effectiveness of leaders: a meta-analysis', *Psychological Bulletin*, vol. 117, pp. 125–45.

Eagly, A.H., Makhijani, M.G. and Klonsky, B.G. (1992) 'Gender and the evaluation of leaders: a meta-analysis', *Psychological Bulletin*, vol. 111, no. 1, pp. 3–22.

Epitropaki, O. and Martin, R. (2004) 'Implicit leadership theories in applied settings: factor structure, generalizability and stability over time', *Journal of Applied Psychology*, vol. 89, pp. 293–310.

European Commission (31 March 2005) 'Decision making in the top 50 publicly quoted companies', Retrieved 18 January 2006 from: http://europa.eu.int/comm/employment_social/women_men_stats/ out/measures_out438_en.htm.

Feingold, A. (1994) 'Gender differences in personality: a meta-analysis', *Psychological Bulletin*, vol. 116, pp. 429–56.

Gilbert, D.T. (1989) 'Thinking lightly about others: Automatic components of the social inference process' in Bargh, J.A. and Uleman, J.S. (eds) *Unintended Thought*, New York, Guilford, pp. 189–211.

Heilman, M.E. (2001) 'Description and prescription: how gender stereotypes prevent women's ascent up the organizational ladder', *Journal of Social Issues*, vol. 57, pp. 657–74.

Heilman, M.E., Block, C.J., Martell, R.F. and Simon, M.C. (1989) 'Has anything changed? Current characterizations of men, women, and managers', *Journal of Applied Psychology*, vol. 74, no. 6, pp. 935–42.

Johnson-Laird, P.N. (1989) 'Mental Models' in Posner, M.I. (ed.) *Foundations of Cognitive Science*, Cambridge, MA, MIT Press, pp. 469–99.

Lord, R.G. and Brown, D.J. (2004) *Leadership Processes and Self-Identity: A Follower-Centered Approach to Leadership*, Mahwah, NJ, Lawrence Erlbaum and Associates.

Lord, R.G., Foti, R.J. and DeVader, C.L. (1984) 'A test of leadership categorization theory: internal structure, information processing, and leadership perceptions', *Organizational Behavior and Human Performance*, vol. 34, pp. 343–78.

Lord, R.G., Foti, R.J., and Phillips, J.S. (1982) 'A theory of leader categorization' in Hunt, J.G., Sekaran, U. and Schriesheim, C. (eds) *Leadership: Beyond Establishment Views*, Carbondale, IL, Southern Illinois University Press, pp. 104–21.

Lord, R.G. and Maher, K.J. (1991) *Leadership and Information Processing*, Boston, MA, Routledge.

Malt, B.C., Ross, B.H. and Murphy, G.L. (1995) 'Predicting features for members of natural categories when categorization is uncertain', *Journal of Experimental Psychology: Learning, Memory, and Cognition*, vol. 21, pp. 646–61.

Martell, R.F. (1996) 'What mediates gender bias in work behavior ratings?' *Sex Roles,* vol. 35, pp. 153–69.

Newell, A., Rosenbloom, P.S. and Laird, J.E. (1989) 'Symbolic Architecture for Cognition' in Posner, M.I. (ed.) *Foundations of Cognitive Science*, Cambridge, MA, MIT Press, pp. 93–131.

Offermann, L.R., Kennedy, J.K. and Wirtz, P.W. (1994) 'Implicit leadership theories: content, structure and generalizability', *Leadership Quarterly*, vol. 5, pp. 43–58.

Phillips, J.S. and Lord, R.G. (1981) 'Causal attributions and perceptions of leadership', *Organizational Behavior and Human Decision Processes*, vol. 28, pp. 143–63.

Powell, G.N., Butterfield, D.A. and Parent, J.D. (2002) 'Gender and managerial stereotypes: have the times changed?' *Journal of Management*, vol. 28, pp. 177–93.

Rosch, E. (1978) 'Principles of categorization' in Rosch, E. and Lloyd, B.B. (eds) *Cognition and Categorization*, Hillsdale, NJ, Erlbaum.

Rush, M.C. and Russell, J.E.A. (1998) 'Leader prototypes and prototype-contingent consensus in leader behavior descriptions', *Journal of Experimental Social Psychology*, vol. 24, pp. 88–104.

Schein, V.E. (1975) 'Relationships between sex role stereotypes and requisite management characteristics among female managers', *Journal of Applied Psychology*, vol. 60, pp. 340–44.

Schein, V.E. (2001) 'A global look at psychological barriers to women's progress in management', *Journal of Social Issues*, vol. 57, pp. 675–88.

Sczesny, S. (2003) 'A closer look beneath the surface: various facets of the think-manager-think-male stereotype', *Sex Roles*, vol. 49, pp. 353–63.

Srull, T.K. and Wyer, R.S. (1979) 'The role of category accessibility in the interpretation of information about persons: some determinants and implications', *Journal of Personality and Social Psychology*, vol. 37, pp. 1660–72.

Srull, T.K. and Wyer, R.S. (1980) 'Category accessibility and social perception: some implications for the study of person memory and interpersonal judgments', *Journal of Personality and Social Psychology*, vol. 38, pp. 841–56.

Stangor, C. and Lange, J.E. (1994) 'Mental representations of social groups: Advances in understanding stereotypes and stereotyping' in Zanna, M. (ed.) *Advances in Experimental Social Psychology* (Vol. 27), New York, Academic Press.

Statistics Canada (2004) 'Women in Canada: Work chapter updates 2003', Retrieved 10 January 2006 from http://www.statcan.ca/ english/freepub/89F0133XIE/89F0133XIE2003000.pdf.

Uleman, J.S., Hon, A., Roman, R.J. and Moskowitz, G.B. (1996) 'Online evidence for spontaneous trait inferences at encoding', *Personality and Social Psychology Bulletin*, vol. 22, pp. 377–94.

Uleman, J.S., Newman, L.S. and Moskowitz, G.B. (1996) 'People as flexible interpreters: Evidence and issues from spontaneous trait inference' in Zanna, M. (ed.) *Advances in Experimental Social Psychology* (Vol. 28), San Diego, CA, Academic Press.

US Bureau of Labor Statistics (2005) 'Women in the labor force: A databook', Retrieved 5 January 2006 from http://www.bls.gov/cps/wlf-databook-2005.pdf.

Van Overwalle, F., Drenth, T. and Marsman, G. (1999) 'Spontaneous trait inferences: are they linked to the actor or the action?' *Personality and Social Psychology Bulletin*, vol. 25, pp. 450–62.

Von Hippel, W., Sekaquaptewa, D. and Vargas, P. (1995) 'On the role of encoding processes in stereotype maintenance' in Zanna, M. (ed.) *Advances in Experimental Social Psychology* (Vol. 27), New York, Academic Press.

Weick, K.E. (1995) *Sensemaking in Organizations*, London, Sage.

Wheeler, S.C. and Petty, R.E. (2001) 'The effects of stereotype activation on behavior: a review of possible mechanisms', *Psychological Bulletin*, vol. 127, pp. 797–826.

Wigboldus, D.H.J., Dijksterhuis, A. and van Knippenberg, A. (2003) 'When stereotypes get in the way: stereotypes obstruct stereotype-inconsistent trait inferences', *Journal of Personality and Social Psychology*, vol. 84, pp. 470–84.

Williams, J.E. and Best, D.L. (1990) '*Measuring Sex Stereotypes: A Multination Study*, Newbury Park, CA, Sage Publications.

Winter, L. and Uleman, J.S. (1984) 'When are social judgments made? Evidence for the spontaneousness of trait inferences', *Journal of Personality and Social Psychology*, vol. 47, pp. 237–52.

# Part VIII
## Ethical Issues in Leadership

# Ethics and Leadership Effectiveness

## 22

*Joanne B. Ciulla*

The moral triumphs and failures of leaders carry a greater weight and volume than those of nonleaders (Ciulla, 2003b). In leadership we see morality magnified, and that is why the study of ethics is fundamental to our understanding of leadership. The study of ethics is about human relationships. It is about what we should do and what we should be like as human beings, as members of a group or society, and in the different roles that we play in life. It is about right and wrong and good and evil. Leadership is a particular type of human relationship. Some hallmarks of this relationship are power and/or influence, vision, obligation, and responsibility. By understanding the ethics of this relationship, we gain a better understanding of leadership, because some of the central issues in ethics are also the central issues of leadership. They include the personal challenges of authenticity, self-interest, and self-discipline, and moral obligations related to justice, duty, competence, and the greatest good.

Some of the most perceptive work on leadership and ethics comes from old texts and is out there waiting to be rediscovered and reapplied. History is filled with wisdom and case studies on the morality of leaders and leadership. Ancient scholars from the East and West offer insights that enable us to understand leadership and formulate contemporary research questions in new ways. History and philosophy provide perspective on the subject and reveal certain patterns of leadership behavior and themes about leadership and morality that have existed over time. They remind us that some of the basic issues concerning the nature of leadership are inextricably tied to the human condition.

The study of ethics and the history of ideas help us understand two overarching and overlapping questions that drive most leadership research. They are: What is leadership? And what is good leadership? One is about what leadership *is,* or a descriptive question. The other is about what leadership *ought to be,* or a normative question. These two questions are sometimes confused in the

Ciulla, J.B. (2004) 'Ethics and leadership effectiveness' in Antonakis, J., Cianciolo, A.T. and Sternberg, R.J. (eds) *The Nature of Leadership*, Newbury Park, CA, Sage, pp. 302–27.

literature. Progress in leadership studies rests on the ability of scholars in the field to integrate the answers to these questions. [ ... ]

# The Normative Aspects of Definitions

Leadership scholars often concern themselves with the problem of defining leadership. Some believe that if they could only agree on a common definition of leadership, they would be better able to understand it. This really does not make sense, because scholars in history, biology, and other subjects do not all agree on the definition of their subject, and, even if they did, it would not help them to understand it better. Furthermore, scholars do not determine the meaning of a word for the general public. Would it make sense to have an academic definition that did not agree with the way ordinary people understood the word? Social scientists sometimes limit the definition of a term so that they can use it in a study. Generally, the way people in a culture use a word and think about it determines the meaning of a word (Wittgenstein, 1968). The denotation of the word *leadership* stays basically the same in English. Even though people apply the term differently, all English-speaking leadership scholars know what the word means. Slight variations in its meaning tell us about the values, practices, and paradigms of leadership in a certain place and at a certain time.

Rost (1991) is among those who think that there has been little progress in leadership studies. He believed that there will be no progress in leadership studies until scholars agree on a common definition of leadership. He collected 221 definitions of leadership, ranging from the 1920s to the 1990s. All of these definitions generally say the same thing – leadership is about a person or persons somehow moving other people to do something. Where the definitions differ is in how leaders motivate their followers, their relationship to followers, who has a say in the goals of the group or organization, and what abilities the leader needs to have to get things done. I chose definitions that were representative of definitions from other sources from the same era. Even today one can find a strong family resemblance in the ways various leadership scholars define leadership.

Consider the following definitions (all from American sources), and think about the history of the time and the prominent leaders of that era. What were they like? What were their followers like? What events and values shaped the ideas behind these definitions?

> 1920s [Leadership is] the ability to impress the will of the leader on those led and induce obedience, respect, loyalty, and cooperation.
>
> 1930s Leadership is a process in which the activities of many are organized

to move in a specific direction by one.

1940s Leadership is the result of an ability to persuade or direct men, apart from the prestige or power that comes from office or external circumstance.

1950s [Leadership is what leaders do in groups.] The leader's authority is spontaneously accorded him by his fellow group members.

1960s [Leadership is] acts by a person which influence other persons in a shared direction.

1970s Leadership is defined in terms of discretionary influence. Discretionary influence refers to those leader behaviors under control of the leader which he may vary from individual to individual.

1980s Regardless of the complexities involved in the study of leadership, its meaning is relatively simple. Leadership means to inspire others to undertake some form of purposeful action as determined by the leader.

1990s Leadership is an influence relationship between leaders and followers who intend real changes that reflect their mutual purposes.

Notice that in the 1920s leaders 'impressed' their will on those led. In the 1940s they 'persuaded' followers, in the 1960s they 'influenced' them, whereas in the 1990s leaders and followers influenced each other. All of these definitions are about the nature of the leader/follower relationship. The difference between the definitions rests on normative questions: 'How *should* leaders treat followers? And how *should* followers treat leaders?' Who decides what goals to pursue? What *is* and what *ought* to be the nature of their relationship to each other? One thing the definition debate demonstrates is the extent to which the concept of leadership is a social and historical construction. Definitions reflect not only the opinions of researchers but the conditions of life at a particular time in a particular society and the values that are important to either the public or the leaders. The definition of leadership is a social and normative construction.

For contemporary scholars, the most morally attractive definitions of leadership hail from the 1940s, 1950s, 1960s, and Rost's (1991) own definition of the 1990s. They imply a noncoercive, participatory, and democratic relationship between leaders and followers. There are two appealing elements of these theories. First, rather than *induce,* these leaders *influence,* which in moral terms implies that leaders recognize the autonomy of their followers. Rost's definition used the word *influence,* which carries an implication that there is some degree of voluntary compliance on the part of followers. In Rost's (1991) chapter on ethics he stated, 'The leadership process is ethical if the people in the relationship (the leaders and followers) *freely* agree that the intended changes fairly reflect their mutual purposes' (p. 161). Followers are the leader's partner in shaping the goals and purposes of a group or organization. For Rost, consensus is an important part of what makes leadership ethical and what makes leadership *leadership*. Free choice is morally pleasing because it shows respect for persons. But the fact that people consent to make changes does not mean that those changes are ethical or that their mutual purposes are ethical. An ethical process may not always yield ethical results. The second morally attractive part of these definitions is that they imply recognition of the beliefs, values, and needs of the followers. Today, we may not agree with the 1920s characterization of leadership, not because leadership is incorrectly defined, but because we do not think that is the best way to lead. Nonetheless, there are plenty of leaders around today that fit that description of command-and-control leadership. If we all accepted Rost's definition of leadership, we would not be able to use the term to talk about a number of leaders whose leadership does not fit the bill.

# The Hitler Problem

The morally attractive definitions also speak to a distinction frequently made between leadership and headship (or positional leadership). Holding a formal leadership position or position of power does not necessarily mean that a person exercises leadership. Furthermore, you do not have to hold a formal position to exercise leadership. People in leadership positions may wield force or authority using only their position and the resources and power that come with it. Some scholars would argue that bullies and tyrants are not leaders, which takes us to what I have called 'the Hitler problem' (Ciulla, 1995). The Hitler problem is based on how you answer the question, 'Was Hitler a leader?' According to the morally unattractive definitions, he was a leader, perhaps even a great leader, albeit an immoral one. Heifetz (1994) argued that, under the 'great man' and trait theories of leadership, you can put Hitler, Lincoln, and Gandhi in the same category because the underlying idea of the theory is that leadership is influence over history. However, under the morally attractive or normative theories, Hitler was not a leader at all. He was a bully or tyrant or simply the head of Germany.

To muddy the waters even further, according to one of Bennis and Nanus's (1985) characterization of leadership – 'Managers are people who do things right and leaders are people who do right things' (p. 21) – one could argue that Hitler was neither unethical nor a leader. Bennis and Nanus are among those scholars who sometimes slip into using the term *leader* to mean a morally good leader. However, what appears to be behind this in Bennis and Nanus's comment is the idea that leaders *are* or *should be* a head above everyone else morally. This normative strand exists throughout the leadership literature, most noticeably in the popular literature. Writers will say leaders *are* participatory, supportive, and so forth, when what they really mean is that leaders *should* have these qualities. Yet it may not even be clear that we really want leaders with these qualities. As former presidential spokesman Gergen (2002) pointed out, leadership scholars all preach and teach that participatory, empowering leadership is best. A president like George W. Bush, however, exercises a top-down style of leadership that is closer to the 1920s definition than the 1990s one. Few leadership scholars would prescribe such leadership in their work. Nonetheless, President Bush scored some of the highest approval ratings for his leadership in recent history (Gergen, 2002).

# Moral Luck

Leadership scholars who worry about constructing the ultimate definition of leadership are asking the wrong question but trying to answer the right one. The ultimate question about leadership is not, 'What is the definition of leadership?' We are not confused about what leaders do, but we would like to know the best way to do it. The whole point of studying leadership is to answer the question, 'What is good leadership?' The use of the word *good* here has two senses, morally good leadership and technically good leadership (i.e., effective at getting the job-at-hand done). The problem with this view is that when we look at history and the leaders around us, we find some leaders who meet both criteria and some who only meet one. History only confuses the matter further. Historians do not write about the leader who was very ethical but did not do anything of significance. They rarely write about a general who was a great human being but never won a battle. Most historians write about leaders who were winners or who change history for better or for worse.

The historian's assessment of leaders also depends on what philosophers call moral luck. Moral luck is another way of thinking about the free will/determinism problem in ethics. People are responsible for the free choices they make. We are generally not responsible for things over which we have no control. The most difficult ethical decisions leaders make are those where they cannot fully determine the outcome. Philosopher Bernard Williams (1998) described moral luck as intrinsic to an action based on how well a person thinks through a decision and whether his or her inferences are sound and turn out to be right. He stated that moral luck is also extrinsic to a decision. Things like bad weather, accidents, terrorists, malfunctioning machines, and so forth can sabotage the best-laid plans (B.A.O. Williams, 1981). Moral luck is an important aspect of ethics and leadership, because it helps us think about ethical decision-making and risk assessment.

Consider the following two examples. First, imagine the case of a leader who is confronted with situation where terrorists are threatening to blow up a plane full of people. The plane is sitting on a runway. The leader gets a variety of opinions from her staff and entertains several options. Her military advisers tell her that they have a plan. They are fairly certain they will be able to free the hostages safely. The leader is morally opposed to giving in to terrorists but also morally opposed to killing the terrorists if it is not necessary. She has duties to a variety of stakeholders and long- and short-term moral obligations to consider. She weighs the moral and technical arguments carefully and chooses to attack, but she is unlucky. Things go wrong and the hostages get killed. Consider the case of another leader in the same situation. In this case, the negotiations are moving forward slowly, and his advisers tell him that an attack is highly risky. The leader is impatient with the hostages and his cautious advisers. He does not play out the moral arguments. For him it is simple: 'I don't give a damn who gets killed; these terrorists are not going to get the best of me!' He chooses to attack. This leader is lucky. The attack goes better than expected and the hostages are freed without harm.

Some leaders are ethical but unlucky, whereas others are not as ethical but very lucky. Most really difficult moral decisions made by leaders are risky, because they have imperfect or incomplete information and lack control over all of the variables that will affect outcomes. Leaders who fail at something are worthy of forgiveness when they act with deliberate care and for the right moral reasons, even though followers do not always forgive them or lose confidence in their leadership. Americans did not blame President Jimmy Carter for the botched attempt to free the hostages in Iran, but it was one more thing that shook their faith in his leadership. He was unlucky because if the mission had been successful, it might have strengthened people's faith in him as a leader and improved his chances of retaining the presidency.

The irony of moral luck is that leaders who are reckless and do not base their actions on sound moral and practical arguments are usually condemned when they fail *and* celebrated as heroes when they succeed. That is why Immanuel Kant (1993) argued that because we cannot always know the results of our actions, moral judgments should be based on the right moral principles and not contingent on outcomes. The reckless, lucky leader does not demonstrate moral or technical competency, yet because of the outcome often gets credit for having both. Because history usually focuses on outcomes, it is not always clear how much luck, skill, and morality figured in the success or failure of a leader. This is why we need to devote more study to the ethics of leaders' decision-making processes in addition to their actions and behavior.

# The Relationship between Ethics and Effectiveness

History defines successful leaders largely in terms of their ability to bring about change for better or worse. As a result, great leaders in history include everyone from Gandhi to Hitler. Machiavelli was disgusted by Cesare Borgia the man, but impressed by Borgia as the resolute, ferocious, and cunning prince (Prezzolini, 1928, p. 11). Whereas leaders usually bring about change or are successful at doing something, the ethical questions waiting in the wings are the ones found in the various definitions mentioned earlier. What were the leader's intentions? How did the leader go about bringing change? And was the change itself good?

In my own work, I have argued that a good leader is an ethical and an effective leader (Ciulla, 1995). Whereas this may seem like stating the obvious, the problem we face is that we do not always find ethics and effectiveness in the same leader. Some leaders are highly ethical but not very effective. Others are very effective at serving the needs of their constituents or organizations but not very ethical. U.S. Senator Trent Lott, who was forced to step from his position as Senate Majority leader because of his insensitive racial comments, is a compelling example of the latter. Some of his African American constituents said that they would vote for him again, regardless of his racist beliefs, because Lott had used his power and influence in Washington to bring jobs and money to the state. In politics, the old saying 'He may be a son-of-a-bitch, but he's *our* son of a bitch', captures the trade-off between ethics and effectiveness. In other words, as long as Lott gets the job done, we do not care about his ethics.

This distinction between ethics and effectiveness is not always a crisp one. Sometimes being ethical *is* being effective and sometimes being effective *is* being ethical. In other words, ethics *is* effectiveness in certain instances. There are times when simply being regarded as ethical and trustworthy makes a leader effective and other times when being highly effective makes a leader ethical. Given the limited power and resources of the secretary-general of the United Nations, it would be very difficult for someone in this position to be effective in the job if he or she did not behave ethically. The same is true for organizations. In the famous Tylenol case, Johnson & Johnson actually increased sales of Tylenol by pulling Tylenol bottles off their shelves after someone poisoned some of them. The leaders at Johnson & Johnson were effective *because* they were ethical.

The criteria that we use to judge the effectiveness of a leader are also not morally neutral. For a while, Wall Street and the business press lionized Al Dunlap ('Chainsaw Al') as a great business leader. Their admiration was based on his ability to downsize a company and raise the price of its stock. Dunlop apparently knew little about the nuts and bolts of running a business. When he failed to deliver profits at Sunbeam, he tried to cover-up his losses and was fired. In this case and in many business cases, the criteria for effectiveness are practically and morally limited. It does not take great skill to get rid of employees, and taking away a person's livelihood requires a moral and a practical argument. Also, one of the most striking aspects of professional ethics is that often what seems right in the short run is not right in the long run or what seems right for a group or organization is not right when placed in a broader context. For example, Mafia families may have very strong internal ethical systems, but they are highly unethical in any larger context of society.

There are also cases when the sheer competence of a leader has a moral impact. For example, there were many examples of heroism in the aftermath of the September 2001 terrorist attack on the World Trade Center. The most inspiring and frequently cited were the altruistic acts of rescue workers. Yet consider the case of Alan S. Weil, whose law firm Sidley, Austin, Brown, and Wood occupied five floors of the World Trade Center. Immediately after watching the Trade Center towers fall to the ground and checking to see if his employees got out safely, Weil got on the phone and within 3 hours had rented four floors of another building for his employees. By the end of the day he had arranged for an immediate delivery of 800 desks and 300 computers. The next day the firm was open for business with desks for almost every employee (Schwartz, 2001). We do not know if Mr. Weil's motives were altruistic or avaricious, but his focus on doing his job allowed the firm to fulfill its obligations to all of its stakeholders, from clients to employees.

On the flip side of the ethics effectiveness continuum are situations where it is difficult to tell whether a leader is unethical, incompetent, or stupid. As Price (2000) has argued, the moral failures of leaders are not always intentional. Sometimes moral failures are cognitive and sometimes they are normative (Price, 2000). Leaders may get their facts wrong and think that they are acting ethically when, in fact, they are not. For example, in 2000 South African president Thabo Mbeki issued a statement saying that it was not clear that HIV caused AIDS. He thought the pharmaceutical industry was just trying to scare people so that it could increase its profits (Garrett, 2000). Coming from the leader of a country where about one in five people test positive for HIV, this was a shocking statement. His stance caused outrage among public health experts and other citizens. It was irresponsible and certainly undercut the efforts to stop the AIDS epidemic. Mbeki understood the scientific literature, but chose to put political and philosophical reasons ahead of scientific knowledge. (He has since backed away from this position.) When leaders do things like this, we want to know if they are unethical, misinformed, incompetent, or just stupid. Mbeki's actions seemed unethical, but he may have thought he was taking an ethical stand. His narrow mindset about this issue made him recklessly disregard his more pressing obligations to stop the AIDS epidemic (Moldoveanu and Langer, 2002).

In some situations, leaders act with moral intentions, but because they are incompetent they create unethical outcomes. Take, for instance, the unfortunate case of the Swiss charity Christian Solidarity International. Its goal was to free an estimated 200,000 Dinka children who were enslaved in Sudan. The charity paid between $35 and $75 a head to free enslaved children. The unintended consequence of the charity's actions was that it actually encouraged enslavement by creating a market for it. The price of slaves and the demand for them went up. Also, some cunning Sudanese found that it paid to pretend that they were slaves so that they could make money by being liberated. This deception made it difficult for the charity to identify those who really needed help from those who were faking it.

Here the charity's intent and the means it used to achieve its goals were not unethical in relation to alleviating suffering in the short run; however, in the long run, the charity inadvertently created more suffering. A similar, but more understandable, mistake was made by some American schoolchildren who, out of compassion and a desire to help, collected money to buy the slaves' freedom. [ ... ]

# Moral Standards

People often say that leaders should be held to 'a higher moral standard', but does that make sense? If true, would it then be acceptable for everyone else to live by lower moral standards? The curious thing about morality is that if you set the moral standards for leaders too high, requiring something close to moral perfection, then few people will be qualified to be leaders or will want to be leaders. For example, how many of us could live up to the standard of having never lied, said an unkind word, or reneged on a promise? Ironically, when we set moral standards for leaders too high, we become even more dissatisfied with our leaders because few are able to live up to our expectations. We set moral standards for leaders too low, however, when we reduce them to nothing more than following the law or, worse, simply not being as unethical as their predecessors. A business leader may follow all laws and yet be highly immoral in the way he or she runs a business. Laws are moral minimums that do not and cannot capture the scope and complexity of morality. For example, an elected official may be law abiding and, unlike his or her predecessor, live by 'strong family values'. The official may also have little concern for the disadvantaged. Not caring about the poor and the sick is not against the law, but is such a leader ethical?

So where does this leave us? On the one hand, it is admirable to aspire to high moral standards, but on the other hand, if the standards are unreachable, then people give up trying to reach them (Ciulla, 1994, pp. 167–83). If the standards are too high, we may become more disillusioned with our leaders for failing to reach them. We might also end up with a shortage of competent people who are willing to take on leadership positions because we expect too much from them ethically. Some highly qualified people stay out of politics because they do not want their private lives aired in public. If the standards are too low, we become cynical about our leaders because we have lost faith in their ability to rise above the moral minimum.

History is littered with leaders who did not think they were subject to the same moral standards of honesty, propriety, and so forth, as the rest of society. One explanation for this is so obvious that it has become a cliché – power corrupts. Winter's (2002) and McClellend's (1975) works on power motives and on socialized and personalized charisma offer psychological accounts of this kind of leader behavior. Maccoby (2000) and a host of others have talked about narcissistic leaders who, on the bright side, are exceptional, and, on the dark side, consider themselves exceptions to the rules.

Hollander's (1964) work on social exchange demonstrates how emerging leaders who are loyal to and competent at attaining group goals gain 'idiosyncrasy credits' that allow them to deviate from the groups' norms to suit common goals. As Price (2000) has argued, given the fact that we often grant leaders permission to deviate or be an exception to the rules, it is not difficult to see why leaders sometimes make themselves exceptions to moral constraints. This is why I do not think we should hold leaders to higher moral standards than ourselves. If anything, we have to make sure that we hold them to the same standards as the rest of society. What we should expect and hope is that our leaders will fail less than most people at meeting ethical standards, while pursuing and achieving the goals of their constituents. The really interesting question for leadership development, organizational, and political theory is, What can we do to keep leaders from the moral failures that stem from being in a leadership role? Too many models of leadership characterize the leader as a saint or 'father-knows-best' archetype who posses all the right values.

# Altruism

Some leadership scholars use altruism as the moral standard for ethical leadership. In their book *Ethical Dimensions of Leadership,* Kanungo and Mendonca (1996) wrote, 'Our thesis is that organizational leaders are truly effective only when they are motivated by a concern for others, when their actions are invariably guided primarily by the criteria of the benefit to others even if it results in some cost to oneself' (p. 35). When people talk about altruism, they usually contrast altruism with selfishness, or behavior that benefits oneself at a cost to others (Ozinga, 1999). Altruism is a very high personal standard and, as such, is problematic for a number of reasons. Both selfishness and altruism refer to extreme types of motivation and behavior. Locke brings out this extreme side of altruism in a dialogue with Avolio (Avolio and Locke, 2002). Locke argued that if altruism is about self-sacrifice, then leaders who want to be truly altruistic will pick a job that they do not like or value, expect no rewards or pleasure from their job or achievements, and give themselves over totally to serving the wants of others. He then asked, 'Would anyone want to be a leader under such circumstances?' (Avolio and Locke, 2002, pp. 169–71). One might also ask, Would we even want such a person as a leader? Whereas I do not agree with Locke's argument that leaders should act according to their self-interest, he does articulate the practical problem of using altruism as a standard of moral behavior for leaders.

Avolio's argument against Locke is based on equally extreme cases. He drew on his work at West Point, where a central moral principle in the military is the willingness to make the ultimate sacrifice for the good of the group. Avolio also used Mother Teresa as one of his examples. In these cases, self-sacrifice may be less about the ethics of leaders in general and more about the jobs of military leaders and missionaries. Locke's and Avolio's debate pits the extreme aspects of altruism against its heroic side. Here, as in the extensive philosophic literature on self-interest and altruism, the debate spins round and round and does not get us very far. Ethics is about the relationship of individuals to others, so in a sense both sides are right and wrong.

Altruism is a motive for acting, but it is not in and of itself a normative principle (Nagel, 1970). Requiring leaders to act altruistically is not only a tall order, but it does not guarantee that the leader or his or her actions will be moral. For example, stealing from the rich to give to the poor, or Robinhoodism, is morally problematic (Ciulla, 2003a). A terrorist leader who becomes a suicide bomber might have purely altruistic intentions, but the means that he uses to carry out his mission – killing innocent people – is not considered ethical even if his cause is a just one. One might also argue, as one does against suicide, that it is unethical for a person to sacrifice his or her life for any reason because of the impact that it has on loved ones. Great leaders such as Martin Luther King, Jr., and Gandhi behaved altruistically, but what made their leadership ethical was the means that they used to achieve their ends and the morality of their causes. We have a particular respect for leaders who are martyred for a cause, but the morality of King and Gandhi goes beyond their motives. Achieving their objectives for social justice while empowering and disciplining followers to use nonviolent resistance is morally good leadership.

Altruism is also described as a way of assessing an act or behavior, regardless of the agent's intention. For example, Worchel, Cooper, and Goethals (1988) defined altruism as acts that 'render help to another person' (p. 394). If altruism is nothing more than helping people, then it is a more manageable standard, but simply helping people is not necessarily ethical. It depends on how you help them and what you help them do. It is true that people often help each other without making great sacrifices. If altruism is nothing more than helping people, then we have radically redefined the concept by eliminating the self-sacrificing requirement. Mendonca (2001) offered a further modification of altruism in what he called 'mutual altruism'. Mutual altruism boils down to utilitarianism and enlightened self-interest. If we follow this line of thought, we should also add other moral principles, such as the golden rule, to this category of altruism.

It is interesting to note that Confucius explicitly called the golden rule altruism. When asked by Tzu-Kung what the guiding principle of life is, Confucius answered, 'It is the word altruism (shu). Do not do unto others what you do not want them to do to you' (Confucius, 1963, p. 44). The golden rule crops up as a fundamental moral principle in most major cultures because it demonstrates how to transform self-interest into concern for the interests of others. In other words, it provides the bridge between altruism and self-interest (others and the self) and allows for enlightened self-interest. This highlights another reason why altruism is not a useful standard for the moral behavior of leaders. The minute we start to modify altruism, it not only loses its initial meaning, it starts to sound like a wide variety of other ethical terms, which makes it very confusing.

## Why being Leader is Not in a Just Person's Self-Interest

Plato believed that leadership required a person to sacrifice his or her immediate self-interests, but this did not amount to altruism. In Book II of the *Republic*, Plato (1992) wrote,

> In a city of good men, if it came into being, the citizens would fight in order *not to rule*...There it would be clear that anyone who is really a true ruler doesn't by nature seek his own advantage but that of his subjects. And everyone, knowing this, would rather be benefited by others than take the trouble to benefit them. (p. 347d)

Rather than requiring altruistic motives, Plato was referring to the stress, hard work, and the sometimes thankless task of being a morally good leader. He implied that if you are a just person, leadership will take a toll on you and your life. The only reason a just person will take on a leadership role is out of fear of punishment. He stated further, 'Now the greatest punishment, if one isn't willing to rule, is to be ruled by someone worse than oneself. And I think it is fear of this that makes decent people rule when they do' (Plato, 1992, p. 347c). Plato's comment sheds light on why we sometimes feel more comfortable with people who are reluctant to lead than with those who are eager to do so. Today, as in the past, we worry that people who are too eager to lead want the power and position for themselves or that they do not fully understand the enormous responsibilities of leadership. Plato also tells us that whereas leadership is not in the just person's immediate self-interest, it is in their long-term interest. He argued that it is in our best interest to be just, because just people are happier and lead better lives than do unjust people (Plato, 1992, p. 353e).

Whereas we admire self-sacrifice, morality sometimes calls upon leaders to do things that are against their self-interest. This is less about altruism than it is about the nature of both morality and leadership. We want leaders to put the interests of followers first, but most leaders do not pay a price for doing that on a daily basis, nor do most circumstances require them to calculate their interests in relation to the interests of their followers. The practice of leadership is to guide and look after the goals, missions, and aspirations of groups, organizations, countries, or causes. When leaders do this, they are doing their job; when they do not do this, they are not doing their job. Ample research demonstrates that self-interested people who are unwilling to put the interests of others first are often not successful as leaders (Avolio and Locke, 2002, pp. 186–88).

Looking after the interests of others is as much about what leaders *do* in their role as leaders as it is about the moral quality of leadership. Implicit in the idea of leadership effectiveness is the notion that leaders do their job. When a mayor does not look after the interests of a city, she is not only ineffective, she is unethical for not keeping the promise that she made when sworn in as mayor. When she does look after the interests of the city, it is not because she is altruistic, but because she is doing her job. In this way, altruism is built into how we describe what leaders do. Whereas altruism is not the best concept for characterizing the ethics of leadership, scholars' interest in altruism reflects a desire to capture, either implicitly or explicitly, the ethics-and-effectiveness notion of good leadership. [ ... ]

# The Bathsheba Syndrome

The moral foible that people fear most in their leaders is personal immorality accompanied by abuse of power. Usually, it is the most successful leaders who suffer the worst ethical failures. Ludwig and Longenecker (1993) called the moral failure of successful leaders the 'Bathsheba syndrome', based on the biblical story of King David and Bathsheba. Ancient texts such as the Bible provide us with wonderful case studies on the moral pitfalls of leaders. King David is portrayed as a successful leader in the Bible. We first meet him as a young shepherd in the story of David and Goliath. This story offers an interesting leadership lesson. In it, God selects the small shepherd David over his brother, a strong soldier, because David 'has a good heart'. Then as God's hand-picked leader, David goes on to become a great leader, until we come to the story of David and Bathsheba (2 Samuel 11–12).

The story begins with David taking an evening stroll around his palace. From his vantage point on the palace roof, he sees the beautiful Bathsheba bathing. He asks his servants to bring Bathsheba to him. The king beds Bathsheba and she gets pregnant. Bathsheba's husband, Uriah, is one of David's best generals. King David tries to cover-up his immoral behavior by calling Uriah home. When Uriah arrives, David attempts to get him drunk so that he will sleep with Bathsheba. Uriah refuses to cooperate, because he feels it would be unfair to enjoy himself while his men are on the front. (This is a wonderful sidebar about the moral obligations of leaders to followers.) David then escalates his attempt to cover things up by ordering Uriah to the front of a battle where he gets killed. In the end, the prophet Nathan blows the whistle on David and God punishes David.

The Bathsheba story has repeated itself again and again in history. Scandals ranging from Watergate to the President Clinton and Monica Lewinsky affair to Enron all follow the general pattern of this story (Winter, 2002, gives an interesting psychological account of the Clinton case). First, we see what happens when successful leaders lose sight of what their job is. David should have been focusing on running the war, not watching Bathsheba bathe. He was literally and figuratively looking in the wrong place. This is why we worry about men leaders who are womanizers getting distracted from their jobs. Second, because power leads to privileged access, leaders have more opportunities to indulge themselves and, hence, need more willpower to resist indulging themselves. David could have had Bathsheba brought to him by his servants with no questions asked. Third, successful leaders sometimes develop an inflated belief in their ability to control outcomes. David became involved in escalating cover-ups.

The most striking thing about leaders who get themselves in these situations is that the cover-ups are usually worse than the crime. In David's case, adultery was not as bad as murder. Also, it is during the cover-up that leaders abuse their power as leaders the most. In Clinton's case, a majority of Americans found his lying to the public far more immoral than his adultery. Last, leaders learn that their power falls short of the ring of Gyges. It will not keep their actions invisible forever. Whistleblowers such as Nathan in King David's case or Sharon Watkins in the Enron case call their bluff and demand that their leaders be held to the same moral standards as everyone else. When this happens, in Bible stories and everywhere else, all hell breaks loose. The impact of a leader's moral lapses causes great harm to their constituents.

Read as a leadership case study, the story of David and Bathsheba is about pride and the moral fragility of people when they hold leadership positions. It is also a cautionary tale about success and the lengths to which people will go to keep from losing it. What is most interesting about the Bathsheba syndrome is that it is difficult to predict which leaders will fall prey to it, because people get it after they have become successful. [ ... ]

# Conclusion

[ ... ] A richer understanding of the moral challenges that are distinctive to leaders and leadership is particularly important for leadership development.

Whereas case studies of ethical leadership are inspiring and case studies of evil leaders are cautionary, we need a practical understanding of why it is morally difficult to be a good leader and a good follower. Leaders do not have to be power-hungry psychopaths to do unethical things, nor do they have to be altruistic saints to be ethical. Most leaders are not charismatic or transformational leaders. They are ordinary men and women in business, government, nonprofits, and communities who sometimes make volitional, emotional, moral, and cognitive mistakes. More work needs to be done on ordinary leaders and followers and how they can help each other be ethical and make better moral decisions.

Aristotle (1984) said that happiness is the end to which we aim in life. The Greek word that Aristotle uses for happiness is *eudaimonea*. It means happiness, not in terms of pleasure or contentment, but as flourishing. A happy life is one where we flourish as human beings, both in terms of our material and personal development and our moral development. The concept of *eudaimonea* gives us two umbrella questions that can be used to assess the overall ethics and effectiveness of leadership. Does a leader or a particular kind of leadership contribute to and/or allow people to flourish in terms of their lives as a whole? Does a leader or a particular kind of leadership interfere with the ability of other groups of people or other living things to flourish? Leaders do not always have to transform people for them to flourish. Their greater responsibility is to create the social and material conditions under which people can and do flourish (Ciulla, 2000). Change is part of leadership, but so is sustainability. Ethical leadership entails the ability of leaders to sustain fundamental notions of morality such as care and respect for persons, justice, and honesty, in changing organizational, social, and global contexts. [ ... ]

## References

Aristotle (1984) 'Nichomachean ethics (trans. W.D. Ross)' in Barnes, J. (ed.) *The Complete Works of Aristotle: The Revised Oxford Translation* (Vol. 2), Princeton, NJ, Princeton University Press.

Avolio, B.J. and Locke, E.E. (2002) 'Contrasting different philosophies of leader motivation: Altruism versus egoistic', *Leadership Quarterly,* vol. 13, pp. 169–71.

Bennis, W. and Nanus, B. (1985) *Leaders: The Strategies for Taking Charge*, New York, HarperCollins.

Ciulla, J.B. (1994) 'Casuistry and the case for business ethics' in Donaldson, T. and Freeman, R.E. (eds) *Business as a Humanity*, Oxford, UK, Oxford University Press.

Ciulla, J.B. (1995) 'Leadership ethics: Mapping the territory', *Business Ethics Quarterly,* vol. 5, pp. 5–24.

Ciulla, J.B. (2000) *The Working Life: The Promise and Betrayal of Modern Work*, New York, Crown Books.

Ciulla, J.B. (2003a) 'The ethical challenges of non-profit leaders' in Riggio, R. (ed.) *Improving Leadership in Non-Profit Organizations*, San Francisco, CA, Jossey-Bass.

Ciulla, J.B. (2003b) *The Ethics of Leadership*, Belmont, CA, Wadsworth.

Confucius (1963) 'Selections from the *Analects*' in W. Chan (trans. and ed.) *A source book in Chinese philosophy*, Princeton, NJ, Princeton University Press.

Garrett, L. (29 March 2000) 'Added foe in AIDS war: Skeptics', *Newsday*, p. A6.

Gergen, D. (November 2002) *Keynote Address*. Delivered at the meeting of the International Leadership Association, Seattle, WA.

Heifetz, R.A. (1994) *Leadership without Easy Answers*, Cambridge, MA, Belknap Press.

Hollander, E.P. (1964) *Leaders, Groups, and Influence*, New York, Oxford University Press.

Kant, I. (1993) *Foundations of the Metaphysics of Morals* (trans. J.W. Ellington), Indianapolis, IN, Hackett.

Kanungo, R.N. and Mendonca, M. (1996) *Ethical Dimensions of Leadership*, Thousand Oaks, CA, Sage.

Ludwig, D. and Longenecker, C. (1993) 'The Bathsheba syndrome: The ethical failure of successful leaders', *Journal of Business Ethics*, vol. 12, pp. 265–73.

Maccoby, M. (2000) 'Narcissistic leaders', *The Harvard Business Review*, vol. 78, pp. 69–75.

McClelland, D.C. (1975) *Power: The Inner Experience*, New York, Halsted.

Mendonca, M. (2001) 'Preparing for ethical leadership in organizations', *Canadian Journal of Administrative Sciences*, vol. 18, pp. 266–76.

Moldoveanu, M. and Langer, E. (2002) 'When "stupid" is smarter than we are' in Sternberg, R. (ed.) *Why Smart People Can Be So Stupid*, New Haven, CT, Yale University Press.

Nagel, T. (1970) *The Possibility of Altruism*, Oxford, UK, Clarendon.

Ozinga, J.R. (1999) *Altruism*, Westport, CT, Praeger.

Plato (1992) *The Republic* (trans. G.M.A. Grube), Indianapolis, IN, Hackett.

Prezzolini, G. (1928) *Nicolo Machiavelli, the Florentine* (trans. R. Roeder), New York, Brentano's.

Price, T. (2000) 'Explaining ethical failures of leadership', *The Leadership and Organizational Development Journal*, vol. 21, pp. 177–84.

Rost, J. (1991) *Leadership for the Twenty-First Century*, New York, Praeger.

Schwartz, J. (16 September 2001) 'Up from the ashes, one firm rebuilds', *New York Times*, Sec. 3, p. 1.

Williams, B.A.O. (1981) *Moral Luck*, Cambridge, UK, Cambridge University Press.

Winter, D.G. (2002) 'The motivational dimensions of leadership: Power, achievement and affiliation' in Riggio, R.E., Murphy, S.E. and Pirozzolo, F.J. (eds) *Multiple Intelligences and Leadership*, Mahwah, NJ, Lawrence Erlbaum, pp. 119–38.

Wittgenstein, L. (1968) *Philosophical Investigations* (trans. G.E.M. Anscombe), New York, Macmillan.

Worchel, S., Cooper, J. and Goethals, G. (1988) *Understanding Social Psychology*, Chicago, IL, Dorsey.

# Leadership Research in an International and Cross-Cultural Context

## 23

*Terri Scandura and Peter Dorfman*

## Introduction

In this exchange of theoretical letters, Terri Scandura and Peter Dorfman discuss leadership research in an international and cross-cultural context. In particular, they focus on leadership cultural-specifics and leadership cultural-universals in a post-Global Leadership and Organizational Behavior Effectiveness (GLOBE) project world. The exchange covers theoretical, methodological, and practical issues in cross-cultural leadership research.

## Letter #1 – Leadership Research in a Post-GLOBE World

[ ... ]

Dear Peter

In light of the recent events occurring in our country and around the world, we are once again reminded of the significance of understanding perceptions and interpretations of leadership in a global context. I recall how *Time* magazine struggled with their decision regarding who would be the 'Man of the Year'. If they used the usual criterion of the person who had the most impact on history that year, they might likely have named Osama Bin Laden as the Man of the Year. However, they shied away from such a cover story, deeming it perhaps too disrespectful to those closely touched by the events that took place on September 11, 2001. Instead they choose Rudolph Guiliani, the leader who seemed to be everywhere

Scandura, T. and Dorfman, P. (2004) 'Leadership research in an international and cross-cultural context', *Leadership Quarterly*, vol. 15, pp. 277–307.

at the time of the crisis: at ground zero, in newsrooms, with the president, with the victims, and at the funeral services.

Guiliani's emergence as a charismatic leader once again reminded us of the powerful effect that context has on perceptions of leadership. Not that Guiliani had not already made sweeping changes in New York City, but the crisis created a need – a need for people to have a leader to look up to for guidance, reassurance, and sense-making during utter chaos. From the Western perspective on leadership, Guiliani certainly fit the role of transformational leader, as the steward of the vision of a healed New York City, and, perhaps, the entire country.

But, from another perspective, who would the Man of the Year be? We can only speculate that the interpretation of these events might be very different from another cultural perspective, and who the heroes and villains are might be seen differently. In some other leadership reality, the events of September 11 make perfect sense and are seen as a fair way to engage in war. In some other cultural context, all American citizens are targets, and there was sufficient justification to do the unthinkable. In such a world-view turned inside out, insanity is sanity, and wrong is right. As I watched the news coverage unfold, I felt as helpless as any other American, and I wondered why we know so little about the manner in which leadership interacts with national culture. After thousands of studies of leadership (Bass, 1990), we have learned some important things about the emergence of charismatic leaders, and yet, some of most important questions about leadership in an international context have not been addressed.

I am writing in the hope that we might reflect on some of what we know about the international context of leadership and begin to forge some ways of thinking about leadership that might move the field forward, even if it is just a small step or two. I reread your 1996 article from the *Handbook of International Leadership* and was struck by some of the insights you had then regarding some of the key issues for international and cross-cultural leadership research. You raised several important questions, and I wondered if research on international and cross-cultural leadership has addressed them, and if so, how? In 1996, the Global Leadership and Organizational Behavior Effectiveness (GLOBE) Research Project was just beginning and I am wondering if that has moved the field forward. The GLOBE research program has investigated culture-specific attributes of leadership compared with culturally generalizable leadership in over 60 countries (Den Hartog, House, Hanges, Ruiz-Quintanilla and Dorfman, 1999). I see the GLOBE project as a landmark study in the development of cross-cultural leadership research. Since you have been a member of the GLOBE coordinating team, I thought that perhaps you might reflect on the project and whether you believe that this is a useful model for future research on international leadership. What are the costs and benefits of this approach? What lessons have been learned and how might some of the problems with this be avoided in future research endeavors. In short, what will leadership research look like in a post-GLOBE world?

I would like to highlight five issues for you to think about in terms of how much progress we have really made in each of these areas. You wrote about these in your 1996 handbook article, of course, but I would like to know what your current thoughts are, given the research that has been done in the past several years on international leadership research. We are clearly seeing more international research being conducted, submitted to journals, and published. But is this body of research addressing any of the critical issues you identified?

First and, perhaps, the most global question, is that of whether or not there are universally endorsed prototypes of leadership. It seems that there would be culturally contingent aspects of leadership and what is effective in one culture may not be effective in others. As noted by Adler (2002): 'Prudent leaders assume that current American-based theories apply to the United States, not, as is so tempting, the world at large' (p. 165). This appears to be wise advice, since the classic research of Hofstede (1980) on cultural contingencies suggested that Western management theories might not apply abroad. But is this really the case? Research summarized by Bass (1990) and the GLOBE project suggests that some aspects of leadership may be universal. If this is the case, what are the explanatory variables? Is a convergence of leadership styles occurring, led by the West, via increased dissemination of leadership theory via television, the Internet, and MBA programs abroad? Or are they inherent leadership behaviors that cut across cultures and address basic human perception and/or needs? If convergence is occurring, is this a desirable state? What might be lost by individuals suppressing their unique cultural identities at the workplace in favor of a U.S.-derived prototype of leader behavior? Chinese history, for example, is replete with leadership prototypes from the teachings of Confucius to Sunzi's *Art of War*. My question goes beyond the matter of whether there are universal prototypes, I suppose. An additional question on my mind is, 'If there are universal leadership prototypes, is this really what we want?' [ ... ]

The identification of cultural contingencies and how they may impact leadership were a trend in the late 1980s and early 1990s. In this approach, culture variables (e.g., collectivism) would be tested as moderators of the relationship of leader behavior and outcomes of work attitudes and performance. Has this trend continued? Is this the dominant approach to the study of culture and leadership? Have any other models emerged and been tested (e.g., culture as independent variable, culture as mediating variable, or culture and leadership as reciprocal influences)? Are researchers exploring different types of models? [ ... ]

I guess there is just no escaping the 'so what' question. What have we learned about the role of international leadership and outcomes of performance, job satisfaction, stress, turnover, and other outcome criterion typically employed in leadership research? Are there different outcomes in the international context that you think we should be looking at? Any thoughts on what they are? Many studies, in their conclusion sections, discuss the implications of their finding for training and development of expatriate managers. By now, I would expect that research is being conducted evaluating the effectiveness of expatriate leadership training and various outcomes such as effectiveness in the international assignment. Yet, I do not recall seeing too many of these studies published in our major journals. [ ... ]

I do not expect you to have all the answers to this myriad of questions. It seems we always have more questions than answers in the area of international and cross-cultural leadership research. Yet, the need to discern how perceptions of leadership may vary from one culture to another and the implications for understanding seem more pressing than ever in the context of leader emergence today. My hope is that I have identified some key issues in international leadership research and that we can begin a dialogue regarding where international leadership research has been and where it should go in the future. Improved research will lead to more answers and, hopefully, better understandings across cultures.

With regards,
Terri A. Scandura

## References

Adler, N.J. (2002) *International Dimensions of Organizational Behavior* (4th edn), Cincinnati, OH, South-Western.

Bass, B.M. (1990) *Bass and Stogdill's Handbook of Leadership: Theory, Research and Managerial Applications* (3rd edn), New York, Free Press.

Bass, B.M. (1997) 'Does the transactional-transformational paradigm transcent organizational and national boundaries?' *The American Psychologist*, vol. 52, no. 2, pp. 130–39.

Den Hartog, D.N., House, R.J., Hanges, P.J., Ruiz-Quintanilla, S.A. and Dorfman, P.W. (1999) 'Culture specific and cross-culturally generalizable implicit leadership theories: Are attributes of charismatic/transformational leadership universally endorsed?' *The Leadership Quarterly*, vol. 10, no. 2, pp. 219–56.

Dorfman, P.W. (1996) 'International and cross-cultural leadership research' in Bunnett, B.J. and Shenkar, O. (eds) *Handbook For International Management Research*, Oxford, Blackwell, pp. 267–349.

Hofstede, G. (1980) *Culture's Consequences: International Differences in Work-Related Values*, Beverly Hills, Sage Publications.

# Letter #2

[ ... ]
Dear Terri
The anniversary of September 11, 2001, has passed, yet, we can surmise that this event will remain a focal point for Americans, as did the bombing of Pearl Harbor and the Cuban missile crisis for past generations. This terrorist act

provides a horrific, but useful, vehicle to discuss the interconnected topics of leaders, leadership, and culture. You introduced the discussion of leadership and culture by asking an interesting question as to whether *Time* magazine in December 2001 would name Osama bin Laden as the 'Man of the Year'. At the time, my friends and I freely debated this question, and I suspect many others were also intrigued about this decision. We were not sure, but we predicted that *Time* magazine would not select bin Laden, and we speculated that Rudolph Giuliani might be a viable candidate among several others. Is not hindsight great!

Even if our predictions turned out not to be true, however, 'we' Americans clearly knew the villains and heroes of this terrorist event. Your letter, however, asked the somewhat rhetorical question as to whether the interpretation of the events of 9/11 would be viewed differently from other cultural perspectives and whether 'our' villains and heroes would be perceived very differently by people in other cultures. I assume your choice of words about other cultures was an allusion to radical religious fundamentalists in Islamic cultures. We should not be surprised that our villains and heroes are reversed in the eyes of Islamic militants who have a visceral hatred of America. For instance, media reports indicate that Osama bin Laden is revered by Ilich Ramirez Sanchez, aka Carlos the Jackal (Nationmaster.com). But villain or hero, Osama bin Laden personifies the characteristics of a charismatic leader.

Let me follow up with a discussion of charismatic leadership because it relates to leadership in general, results from the GLOBE leadership project, and events of 9/11. As leadership researchers are well aware, the meaning of *charisma* and *charismatic leadership* is derived from the Greek word meaning *divinely inspired gift*. The meaning has metamorphosed to indicate a leader who possesses extraordinary qualities. Terri, in a previous article of yours, you pointed out that in Arabic, the word for leadership is *al kiyada* and refers to officers in the military or high-ranking members of the government. You spoke about how, historically, a leader in the Arab world refers to a great hero who leads warriors into battle and, therefore, not unexpectedly, their concept of leadership is rooted in traditional military concepts of leadership (Scandura, Von Glinow, and Lowe, 1999).

We can surmise that to Osama bin Laden's followers, he is an extraordinary leader, endowed with exceptional qualities. His videotaped speeches after 9/11 provide a glimpse of impression management techniques often used by charismatic leaders; he was clearly aware of his self-image as a highly self-confident and optimistic leader. Like other charismatic leaders, his future vision of the world is effectively communicated to followers because it stems from deeply held personal values. Clearly, he is a strong motivating force that inspires followers to accomplish his, and now their, vision of Islamic Jihad. The failed U.S. mission to neutralize Osama bin Laden after the destruction of the American embassies in Kenya and Tanzania in 1998 solidified his stature in the Arab world. As Wright (2002), in *The New Yorker,* states, '...the popular response to this man whose defiance of America now seemed blessed by divine favor'.

Interesting how the concept of a charismatic leader in the Arab culture returns to the original notion of a divinely inspired gift. While he did find Al Qaeda (meaning 'the base'), the reality of Osama's accomplishments is far more complex. The brains behind Al Qaeda, along with the accomplishments attributed to him, must certainly be shared with Dr. Ayman al-Zawahiri. In addition, a radical Islamist, the CIA and FBI credit Dr. Zawahiri for planning most of the terrorist operations against the United States. Nevertheless, Osama represents to (most?) Americans what social scientists describe as the 'dark side of charisma' in that the consequences of these leaders' actions are negative, rather than positive. Freely admitting my bias of viewing Osama as a negative rather than positive charismatic, I take solace that this type of charismatic leader often falls from power due to a propensity for risk taking coupled with the likelihood of making determined enemies because of their polarizing decisions.

## Leadership in an International Context

Returning to a central point in your letter, I certainly agree with your statement '...some of the most important questions about leadership in an international context have not been addressed'. Your letter includes questions that I have thought about for some time, as well as many new ones. Certainly, there is the metaquestion 'if the phenomenon of leadership is universal and found in all societies (Bass, 1990; Murdoch, 1967), to what extent is leadership culturally contingent?' Do we know anything for sure about the mix of leadership and culture? It has become almost axiomatic for researchers to argue that the kind of leadership attempted and the level of leadership success will depend on the congruence between the cultural values and leadership processes. Does the evidence support this assertion? The answer is both yes and no. It should be of no surprise that there appears to be a wide divergence of beliefs in the world about what behaviors or styles constitute effective leadership. Consider that charismatic leadership may be enacted in a highly assertive manner, as in the case of John F. Kennedy and Martin Luther King, Jr., or in a quiet, nonassertive manner, as in the case of Mahatma Gandhi, Nelson Mandela, and Mother Teresa (House, Wright, and Aditya, 1997). Or that leadership styles emphasizing participation, commonly accepted in the individualistic West, are of questionable desirability and, perhaps, effectiveness in other cultures, such as in the collectivistic East (Dorfman, 2003). Nevertheless, without denying the important role of culture, there are substantive issues regarding the magnitude of the impact on leadership processes. There is also the strong possibility of cultural universals regarding effective leadership. More about this later.

You asked what lessons may be gleaned from the GLOBE project, to which I have contributed for some eight years. Some of the hypotheses developed by

GLOBE researchers allude to the concept of universality. Actually, despite what one might suspect, the meaning of this term is quite complex. Researchers across many disciplines have created a host of terms, including simple universals, variform universals, systematic behavioral universals, etc., to describe the levels of similarity across cultures. In addition, variables are discussed in terms of conceptual, functional, and metric equivalence; each term relates to a kind of universal.

We can safely assert that one leadership universal is that leaders have existed in all cultures throughout history. Nonetheless, perhaps surprisingly, even the concept of leadership has not always had, and, perhaps, does not continue to have, a universally positive connotation around the world. How can that be? Clearly, Americans think of leadership in a somewhat revered sense – as one *Time* magazine article once queried on its cover, 'Where are the leaders?' One local newspaper used the headline 'City Suffers Leadership Drought'. Meindl, Ehrlich, and Dukerich (1985) refer to this heroic nature of leadership as 'the romance of leadership'. Individuals are often viewed as the sole causal agent for organizational success or failure. Americans frequently attribute positive and negative organizational outcomes to single individuals, even when it should be clear that many factors contribute to success and failure.

I am not suggesting that leaders are inconsequential. Clearly, leaders matter. The recent fiasco of Enron and WorldCom has the mark of impoverished (criminal?) leadership, but even here, controversial accounting principles, a closed corporate culture, the general Zeitgeist of corporate greed, and incompetent oversight by the board of directors and investment bankers have contributed to these debacles. Maybe surprisingly, anecdotal evidence exists that people in other cultures do not view the concept of leadership with the same glowing reverence that we do. Consider the statement 'everything seems to indicate that leadership is an unintended and undesirable consequence of democracy, or a "perverse" effect, as we say in France' (Graumann and Moscovici, 1986). This statement is quite a slam against our most revered concepts – democracy and leadership. While this cultural view is likely not the European norm, the fact is, the terms *leaders* and *leadership* are not as universally revered as we in America think. In addition, while empirical evidence is scant, I suspect that there are fairly significant differences about leadership *attributions* from a cross-cultural perspective. In contrast, some GLOBE results support a universalistic interpretation of many desirable leadership characteristics – more about this in a moment.

## Cultural Dimensions and Prototypes of Ideal Leaders

I would like to discuss two issues together: the possibility of identifying a universal leadership prototype and the specification of cultural dimensions as a way of characterizing cultural similarities and differences. First, is there even a remote possibility that an ideal leader prototype exists – one universally accepted by all cultures? If not, to what extent do prototypes of ideal leaders vary across cultures? Second, does there continue to be a trend in studying the influence of culture by conceptualizing and measuring cultural dimensions? If so, which dimensions of cultural variation and theoretical frameworks are most useful? Furthermore, how do these mechanisms operate such that cultural variation affects individuals, groups, organizations, industries, and societies?

Let me comment on the second question first. If the GLOBE project and other large-scale studies are indicative (Peterson, Smith, et al., 1995), the simple answer is that the researchers continue to use cultural dimensions as a framework for understanding cultural effects on organizational behavior. There should be no doubt that the seminal research by Hofstede (1980, 2001) has had an enduring legacy and contributes to this trend. In fact, Yukl (2002) argues that the quality of cross-cultural leadership research is dependent on the adequacy of the conceptual framework used to identify cultural dimensions.

Without denigrating the importance of 'values and cultural dimensions', an alternative perspective is that culture limits the repertoire of acceptable strategies of action rather than being the end *value* toward which the action is directed (Swidler, 1986). That is, while people are socialized culturally to naturally know 'how to act' in certain situations, they do not necessarily have to be able to espouse the 'value' consistent with the action nor cognitively realize that a particular behavior is directed toward a specific value. The medieval archer may have been exceedingly accurate in hitting a target, but cognitively unaware of the physics of an arrow in flight. Likewise, supervisors may practice a particular form of managerial leadership but be unaware of the underlying rationale as to why employees expect specific behaviors from them.

The 'event management' research by Smith and Peterson (1994) is consistent with the behavioral repertoire perspective. They studied how managers interpret and use information to solve common everyday events in organizations (e.g., how much reliance should be placed on subordinates as sources of guidance when selecting a new employee). Even this line of research, however, links behavioral consistencies to various culture dimensions. My perspective is that both the 'cultural dimensions/values' and 'behavioral repertoire/routines' explanations are valid causal mechanisms by which organizational behaviors become culturally contingent; however, the former are more established in the leadership literature.

You asked if we know which cultural dimensions are most important, and how these dimensions are linked to leadership processes. Other questions arise as to whether these cultural variables should be thought of as antecedent and mediating variables, along with the more prevalent view of culture as a moderating variable. A dozen or so cultural dimensions have been discussed as those most likely to influence leadership processes. All of us are aware of the four culture dimensions of Hofstede (power distance, individualism/collectivism, uncertainty avoidance, and masculinity/femininity) and, more recently, a fifth dimension (long- vs. short-term orientation). Researchers have conceived of these dimensions as having the multiple kinds of effects you mention: antecedent, mediating, and/or moderating effects. Unfortunately, more anecdotal than empirical evidence exists as to the impact of each of these dimensions on leadership. This is probably inevitable given the difficulty of conducting large-scale research studies.

While the dimensions of Hofstede are often cited, and researchers frequently use his country rankings for each dimension as part of their research design, there are significant questions as to the meaning, measurement, and validity of these cultural dimensions. The GLOBE project builds on the initial research of Hofstede but had the advantage of knowing the strengths and weaknesses of his previous work. In addition to the four original Hofstede dimensions, GLOBE researchers conceptualized, operationalized, and used the cultural dimensions labeled performance orientation, future orientation, and humane orientation [based on theories by McClelland (1961, 1985) and others]. GLOBE researchers also separated two of Hofstede's original four dimensions on the basis of empirical data. Hofstede's masculinity/femininity dimension was divided into assertiveness and gender egalitarianism dimensions.

Furthermore, GLOBE researchers determined that the individualism/ collectivism dimension should be conceived as two distinct aspects of collectivism – one reflecting the construct for in-groups and organizations, the other reflecting societal values and practices. Project GLOBE's nine cultural dimensions are by no means exhaustive. Trompenaars (1993), for instance, suggests the importance of an 'achievement versus ascription' dimension. This concerns the importance placed on accomplishment and record (i.e., achievement) with that of your status that is attributed to you on the basis of birth, kinship, and who you know (i.e., ascription). It would be presumptuous to suggest that *all important* cultural dimensions have been identified, but clearly, we know several. Let us consider the question as to which cultural dimensions are the *most* important for leadership.

Triandis (1993), based on years of cross-cultural research, believes that individualism/collectivism is perhaps the most important dimension of cultural variation. After all, leadership, by definition, is a collective process. The leader interacts with one individual as a dyad, is responsible in leading and supervising team members, and engages in boundary spanning actions with other organizational members and other organizations. Triandis suggests that leadership processes may differ in individualist and collectivist cultures in the following manner. For collectivist cultures, successful leaders should be supportive and paternalistic (i.e., maintaining the harmony of the workgroup, solving workers' personal problems, being generally helpful and considerate). For individualist cultures, support might be valued when needed, but *achievement-oriented* and *participative* leadership would be key leader behaviors.

A strong case can also be made for the importance of the cultural dimension labeled as Power Distance by Hofstede (1980) and GLOBE (House et al., 1999). It is relatively easy to envision why power stratification should be important. In cultures characterized by low power distance, subordinates expect superiors to consult them and use their suggestions, whereas in cultures characterized by high power distances, subordinates expect supervisors to act more directively and, perhaps, in an autocratic manner. Again, careful theorizing should help determine which cultural factors are most important in any given situation. As a second example, in cultures characterized by high uncertainty avoidance, leaders are more likely to provide direction in tasks to be accomplished and specify methods to accomplish these tasks. The GLOBE research found a clear link between the endorsement of leadership prototypes and several cultural dimensions. Following from the example above, high power distance and uncertainty avoidance cultures are less inclined to endorse *participative* leadership (House et al., 2004). Empirical research of this sort should help determine which dimensions are most important for leadership.

## Project GLOBE: Leadership and Cultural Variation

Let me respond in a somewhat roundabout way to your question about whether there are universally endorsed prototypes of leadership. It is an important question. Given the evidence that culture matters a great deal in leadership, why would we expect universals? The GLOBE research program has hypothesized that charismatic leadership, or at least, significant elements of charismatic or transformational leadership, will find universal endorsement (Den Hartog et al., 1999). Previously, Bass (1991, 1997) argued that it may be possible for a single transformational and transactional leadership theory to explain leadership and its consequences across differing cultures. According to Bass, leaders who engage in transformational behaviors will be more effective than those who do not, regardless of culture. House (1991) and House et al. (1997) have a similar belief in the robustness of charismatic leadership across cultures.

However, does not this assertion about universality fly in the face of overwhelming evidence that cultural values influence leadership? Yes, but a closer look at the respective positions reveals a more complex understanding of possible cultural influences. As noted by Chemers and Ayman (1993), the Bass transformational theory (Bass and Avolio, 1993) focuses on the transformational characteristics of outstanding leaders across different cultures, whereas the charismatic leadership theory developed by House and Shamir (1993) addresses how differences in cultures will make followers more susceptible to a particular charismatic leader. Bass speculates that transformational leaders will be more participative in India and Japan than in Pakistan and Taiwan because worker participation is viewed more favorably in the former countries. House and Shamir also suggest that the strategies employed by the charismatic leader may be culturally contingent. For instance, Gandhi's exhortations for love and acceptance of others aroused the need for affiliation, whereas General George Patton evoked the negative image of the enemy, which aroused the power motive essential for combat.

Because the title of your letter pointedly asked about leadership research post-GLOBE, let me briefly describe the GLOBE project. Bob House, from the Wharton School of Management, and approximately 170 colleagues from more than 62 nations have been engaged in this long-term programmatic series of cross-cultural leadership studies. Field data were collected from more than 17,000 managers, in 900 organizations, across three industries, and in 62 countries. The initial results of the first two phases of the study were published by House (1999) and Den Hartog (1999). A complete discussion of the findings can be found in the forthcoming book titled, *Leadership, Culture and Organizations: The GLOBE Study of 62 Societies* (House et al., 2004).

What is particularly noteworthy about this project is the use of a combination of quantitative and qualitative methods. Quantitative aspects include scales that measure societal culture, organizational culture, and leadership attributes believed to be important in contributing to outstanding leadership. That is, an initial goal of the study was to develop and validate the societal and organizational measures of culture. This was accomplished in the first phase of research. Nine psychometrically sound culture dimension scales were developed. They are (1) uncertainty avoidance, (2) power distance, (3) institutional collectivism, (4) in-group collectivism, (5) gender egalitarianism, (6) assertiveness, (7) future orientation, (8) performance orientation, and (9) humane orientation. Qualitative interpretations of culture and leadership were developed through interviews, focus groups, and the use of unobtrusive measures. GLOBE researchers are currently writing in-depth descriptions of leaders and leadership for each nation/societal culture to be published soon in a second GLOBE book (Chhokar, Brodbeck, and House, in progress).

## Leadership Universals: Do They Exist?

Common sense would lead us to expect at least some variation among countries as to desirable leadership characteristics. GLOBE researchers found this to be the case. But results from the GLOBE project can be used to support culture-universal, as well as culture-specific, positions. The following leadership attributes found within leadership dimensions were universally believed to contribute to effective leadership: being trustworthy, just, and honest (integrity); having foresight and planning ahead (charismatic/visionary); and being positive, dynamic, encouraging, motivating, and building confidence (charismatic/inspirational). Other attributes were universally rejected, such as being irritable or dictatorial. Most intriguing were those that were endorsed in some countries but rejected in others. Examples include cautious, independent, and sensitive.

One of the more controversial hypotheses in the GLOBE project postulated that charismatic leadership would be universally endorsed as contributing to outstanding leadership. We can summarize our findings for GLOBE'S metadimension, labeled charismatic/value-based leadership, as 'Yes, but....' The charismatic/value-based leadership dimension contains the most number of attributes universally perceived as contributors to effective leadership. However, one aspect of charismatic leadership, *self-sacrifice* (which includes the item 'risk taking') was not universally endorsed, although other critical leadership aspects, *visionary* and *inspirational,* were. Returning to your opening comment regarding the interpretation of 9/11, how can people in widely differing cultures identify and endorse the same leadership characteristics? Simple. Consider the visionary aspect of charismatic leadership. We did not study *what vision (i.e., the content), how, where, when or why that vision is enacted.*

# Culturally Endorsed Implicit Leadership Theory (CLT)

As part of the GLOBE project, we expanded the concept of individualized implicit leadership theories (ILT) into a cultural level theory that we labeled 'culturally endorsed implicit leadership theory' (CLT). A leadership CLT profile was developed for each of 10 culture clusters (i.e., groupings of countries) using six global leadership CLT dimensions. The six global leadership dimensions were charismatic/value-based, team oriented, participatory, humane oriented, autonomous, and self-protective. We hypothesized and effectively demonstrated that individuals within countries share a common frame of reference regarding effective leadership. In addition, not only is there agreement within each country (e.g., the United States), but there is also agreement within each societal cluster of countries (e.g., the Anglo cluster). Most importantly, we were also able to identify specific differences among the countries as well as among the clusters.

Thus, we found that these culturally endorsed leadership profiles highlight elements of leadership perceived to be culturally common, as well as those which are culturally unique. When examining the content of the leadership profiles for the 10 culture clusters, an interesting worldwide view of leadership emerges. In many instances, the single country and cluster rankings for the CLT leadership dimensions present an enigma. They highlight commonalities among cultures by illustrating their universal endorsement of some leadership attributes and global CLT leadership dimensions (e.g., charismatic/value-based) while simultaneously highlighting meaningful differences, indicated in the findings of cultural specificity for other leadership attributes and CLT dimensions (e.g., participative leadership).

The 10 country clusters demonstrated differences in their endorsement of each of the six leadership dimensions. Let us look at the differences between two country clusters, obviously of interest since 9/11. Results regarding the Anglo cluster can be compared with results from the Middle East cluster. The Anglo cluster includes the United States, Australia, England, Ireland, New Zealand, Canada (English speaking), and South Africa (White sample). This cluster is characterized by its high mean scores (both raw and response bias-corrected scores) and rank (compared with those of other clusters) for charismatic/value-based, participative, and humane leadership. The Anglo cluster is ranked very low on the self-protective leadership dimension, indicating that leader attributes such as *status conscious, face saving,* and *self-centered* are believed to strongly inhibit effective leadership.

The Middle East cluster includes Egypt, Qatar, Turkey, Kuwait, and Morocco. There are a number of striking differences for the Middle East cluster and other clusters. The mean scores for the charismatic/value-based and team-oriented leadership were the lowest scores (both raw and response bias-corrected scores), considering all other clusters. Thus, the rankings for these dimensions were also the lowest of all country clusters. While *participative* leadership was viewed positively, scores were low compared with other clusters' scores and ranks. The self-protective leadership dimension was viewed almost neutrally for this cluster (i.e., neither contributes to nor inhibits effective leadership), but the mean score and ranking were higher than all of the other clusters.

Two explanations, although speculative, come to mind as to why the Middle East cluster is the most unusual of all country clusters (Robert House, personal communication). First, Middle Easterners may not require the same amount of leadership from their leaders as do other clusters. However, this is unlikely which leads to an alternative explanation – that critical leadership attributes for this cluster were not part of the GLOBE attribute list and, hence, were not captured as part of the GLOBE leadership dimensions. This alternative explanation gains credence from the findings of GLOBE researchers who administered a version of the research instrument in Iran (an Islamic Persian country that is not Arabic). This instrument contained additional leadership attributes not found in the final GLOBE-administered questionnaire (Dastmalchian, Javidan, and Alam, 2001). Somewhat fortuitously, factor analyses of their data indicated the presence of leadership dimensions similar with the six GLOBE dimensions (e.g., charismatic/value-based, team oriented, etc.), but, in addition, there were several more that may help explain the enigma of the Middle Eastern leadership profile. These additional leadership dimensions were labeled 'familial', 'humble', and 'faithful' (faithful in a religious sense). It is likely that the pervasive influence of the Islamic religion is a key to understanding the Arab world and, presumably, leadership in the Arab world (Hagan, 1995). I am not suggesting that the GLOBE results speak directly to the specifics of 9/11, but only that we need to know more, not less, about leadership in Middle Eastern countries, and that GLOBE is a start in this direction. [ ... ]

To summarize, for many years, the academic literature barely touched on the influence of culture on leadership processes. Managers working in multinational companies, however, instinctively knew its importance. They hardly need to be reminded of the wide variety of management practices found around the world. Laurent (1983) and, more recently, Trompenaars (1993) and Hofstede (2001), document the astonishing diversity of organizational practices worldwide, of which many are acceptable and considered effective in one country but ineffective in a neighboring country. The multicultural reality is even more complex when considering real people in such companies. Titus Lokananta, for example, is an Indonesian Cantonese holding a German passport, managing a Mexican multinational corporation (MNC) producing Gummi bears in the Czech Republic (*Wall Street Journal*, 9 May 2000). What management practices will he use, and for which subordinates, colleagues, and supervisors? [ ... ]

Cordially,
Peter W. Dorfman

[Editor's note: A Further exchange of letters on this subject has been omitted.]

---

## *References*

Bass, B.M. (1990) *Bass and Stogdill's handbook of leadership: Theory, research, and managerial applications*, (3rd edn), New York, Free Press.

Bass, B.M. (1991) 'Is there universality in the Full Range Model of leadership?' Paper presented at the National Academy of Management Annual Meeting, Miami.

Bass, B.M. (1997) 'Does the transactional–transformational leadership paradigm transcend organizational and national boundaries?' *American Psychologist*, vol. 52, no. 2, pp. 130–39.

Bass, B.M. and Avolio, B.J. (1993) 'Transformational leadership: A response to critiques' in Chemers, M.M. and Ayman, R. (eds) *Leadership Theory and Research*, San Diego, CA, Academic Press, pp. 49–80.

Chemers, M.M. and Ayman, R. (1993) 'Directions for leadership research' in Chemers, M. and Ayman, R. (eds) *Leadership Theory and Research*, San Diego, CA, Academic Press, pp. 321–32.

Chhokar, J.S., Brodbeck, F. and House, R.J. (in progress) *Managerial cultures of the world: GLOBE in-depth studies of the cultures of 25 countries, vol. 2*, Thousand Oaks, CA, Sage.

Dastmalchian, A., Javidan, M. and Alam, K. (2001) 'Effective leadership and culture in Iran: An empirical study', *International Review of Applied Psychology*, vol. 50, no. 4, pp. 532–51.

Den Hartog, D., House, R.J., Hanges, P.J., Ruiz-Quintanilla, S.A., Dorfman, P.W. (1999) 'Culture specific and cross culturally generalizable implicit leadership theories: Are attributes of charismatic/transformational leadership universally endorsed?' *The Leadership Quarterly*, vol. 10, pp. 219–56.

Dorfman, P. (2003) 'International and cross-cultural leadership research' in Punnett, B.J. and Shenkar, O. (eds) *Handbook for International Management Research* (2nd edn), Ann Arbor, MI, University of Michigan.

Graumann, C.F. and Moscovici, S. (1986) *Changing Conceptions of Leadership*, New York, Springer-Verlag.

Hagan, C.M. (1995) 'Comparative management: Africa, the Middle East, and India', (Working Paper), Boca Raton, FL, Florida Atlantic University.

Hofstede, G. (1980) *Culture's Consequences: International Differences in Work-Related Values*, London, Sage.

Hofstede, G. (2001) *Culture's Consequences: Comparing Values, Behaviors, Institutions, and Organizations across Nations*, Thousand Oaks, CA, Sage.

House, R.J. (1991) 'The universality of charismatic leadership', paper presented at the National Academy of Management Annual Meeting, Miami.

House, R.J., Hanges, P.J., Javidan, M., Dorfman, P.W., Gupta, V. and GLOBE Associates (2004) *Leadership, Culture and Organizations: The GLOBE Study of 62 Societies*, Thousand Oaks, CA, Sage.

House, R.J., Hanges, P.J., Ruiz-Quintanilla, S.A., Dorfman, P.W., Javidan, M., Dickson, M., Gupta, V., et al. (1999) 'Cultural influences on leadership and organizations: Project GLOBE' in Mobley, W.F., Gessner, M.J. and Arnold, V. (eds) *Advances in Global Leadership*, vol. 1, Stamford, CT, JAI Press, pp. 171–233.

House, R.J. and Shamir, B. (1993) 'Toward the integration of transformational, charismatic and visionary theories' in Chemers, M.M. and Ayman, R. (eds) *Leadership Theory and Research: Perspectives and Directions*, San Diego, CA, Academic Press, pp. 81–107.

House, R.J., Wright, N.S. and Aditya, R.N. (1997) 'Cross-cultural research on organizational leadership: A critical analysis and a proposed theory' in Earley, P.C. and Erez, M. (eds) *New Perspectives in International Industrial/Organizational Psychology*, San Francisco, CA, The New Lexington Press, pp. 535–625.

McClelland, D.C. (1961) *The Achieving Society*, Princeton, NJ, Van Nostrand-Reinhold.

McClelland, D.C. (1985) *Human Motivation*, Glenview, IL, Scott-Foresman.

Meindl, J.R., Ehrlich, S.B. and Dukerich, J.M. (1985) 'The romance of leadership', *Administrative Science Quarterly*, vol. 30, pp. 78–102.

Murdoch, G. (1967) *Ethnographic Atlas*, Pittsburgh, PA, University of Pittsburgh Press.

Nationmaster.com (n.d.) 'Encyclopedia: Ilich Ramirez Sanchez', Retrieved 22 September 2003, from http://www.nationmaster.com/encyclopedia/Ilich-Ramirez-Sanchez.

Peterson, M.F., Smith, P.B., et al. (1995) 'Role conflict, ambiguity and overload: A 21 nation study', *Academy of Management Journal*, vol. 38, no. 2, pp. 429–53.

Scandura, T.A., Von Glinow, M.A. and Lowe, K.B. (1999) 'When East meets West: Leadership "best practices" in the United States and the Middle East' in Mobley, M. J. Gessner, W. and Arnold, V. (eds) *Advances in Global Leadership*, vol. 1,Stamford, CT, JAI Press, pp. 235–48.

Smith, P.B. and Peterson, M.K. (1994) 'Leadership as event-management: A cross-cultural survey based upon middle managers from 25 nations', paper presented at the Cross-cultural Studies of Event Management at the International Congress of Applied Psychology, Madrid, Spain.

Swidler, A. (1986) 'Culture in action: Symbols and strategies', *American Sociological Review*, vol. 51, pp. 273–86.

Triandis, H.C. (1993) *The Contingency Model in Cross-Cultural Perspective*, San Diego, CA, Academic Press.

Trompenaars, F. (1993) *Riding the Waves of Culture: Understanding Cultural Diversity in Business*, London, Breatley.

van de Vijver, F. and Leung, K. (1997) *Methods and Data Analysis for Cross-Cultural Research*, Thousand Oaks, CA, Sage.

Wright, L. (2002) 'The Man behind Bin Laden', *The New Yorker*, pp. 56–85.

Yukl, G.A. (2002) *Leadership in Organizations* (5th edn), Upper Saddle River, NJ, Prentice-Hall.

# Firing Back: How Great Leaders Rebound After Career Disasters

24

## Jeffrey Sonnenfeld and Andrew Ward

Whether it is movie or media stars, artists, politicians, business leaders, or even academics, there is a fascination with those who fall from grace, who get knocked off their pedestals either through their own slipups or by external overthrow. For many, the derailment of a career of high accomplishment compounds adversity, because their path has been so all consuming that much has been sacrificed in its pursuit. Private dreams became public possessions, which were then cavalierly tossed away by an unappreciative, fickle society. F. Scott Fitzgerald's famous admonition that there are no second acts in American lives casts an especially dark shadow over the derailed careers of leaders and those focused on creative expression.

For leaders, life's adversity can turn hard-earned assets into monumental barriers to recovery. Leaders can enjoy such resources as great popular recognition, vast networks of supporters, and gushing pools of finances. Yet celebrity, popularity, and wealth do not insulate them from fate. Indeed, fortunes can change in an instant – one moment we can be on top of the world, and the next, trodden underfoot. While prominent leaders may be presumed to have the resources to rebound from any disaster, those very presumed advantages can easily turn into great obstacles to recovery.

Nonetheless, some do recover with their careers brighter than ever, while others flame out into obscurity. Consider the resilience of John Irving, Mike Nichols, Robert Altman, Carlos Santana, and John Travolta against the retreats of Kurt Vonnegut, J. D. Salinger, Alan Jay Lerner, Judy Garland, and Orson Welles. Some were energized by their losses, while others were forever haunted by the specter of their own early careers. What distinguishes those who stare down setback, determined to rebuild, from those who stare despondently into a

Sonnenfeld, J. and Ward, A. (2008) 'Firing Back: How Great Leaders Rebound After Career Disasters', *Organizational Dynamics*, vol. 37, no. 1, pp. 1–20.

void, never able to recapture the spark that ignited the flames of past glory? And what are the lessons for all who suffer career setbacks, at whatever level?

Former president Jimmy Carter challenged a group of chief executive officers (CEOs) at one of our conferences to consider how they would recover if the American public had fired them. Despite failing to be reelected, Carter continued tirelessly in his humanitarian, public health, and diplomacy missions, heavily promoting democratic reform around the world. Carter has become revered by virtually all as the United States' greatest *former* president and recognized as a Nobel Laureate for Peace. Leaders should not be measured by how they bask in the gratification of their accomplishments. Rather, they should be measured by how they respond when fate deflates the joys of hard-earned triumphs.

# Firing Back

This quality of resilience is critical in the lives of creative figures such as leaders and artists. The rise, the fall, and the recovery of both leaders and artists face common stages. Back in the 1930s, Otto Rank was one of the first to link these extraordinary contributors. He suggested that their accomplishments were the consequence of a shared, superhuman urge to create, fueled by a heightened quest for immortality.

Artists and leaders were similarly considered in Howard Gardner's book *Extraordinary Minds*. He proposed a set of traits shared by 'influencers' – those truly great historic figures across professions. After studying such creative figures as Wolfgang Mozart, Virginia Woolf, Sigmund Freud, and Mahatma Gandhi, Gardner concluded that rather than raw intellect, lucky circumstances, or even indefatigable energies, these figures possessed powerful skills at (1) candid self-assessment of their strengths and weaknesses, (2) keen situational analysis, and (3) the capacity to reframe past setbacks into future successes. A defeat merely energized them to rejoin the fray with greater ardor. It is not the proportion of their losses that differentiates these influencers from the rest of us, but how they construed their losses.

It is in fact, wrong to consider adversity a diversion from the path toward greatness. Resilience from calamities has been revealed as vital to the character formation and differentiation of heroic figures. Anthropologist Joseph Campbell studied, across cultures and eras, religious and folk heroes such as Jesus, Moses, Mohammed, Buddha, Cuchulain, Odysseus, Aeneas, and the Aztecs' Tezcatlipoca, and discerned a universal 'monomyth' of the life stages of these heroes. One stage involved a call to greatness, which led to a separation from one's past to realize superhuman talent. This was followed by a series of continual trials and ultimately profound setbacks that were met with eventual triumph and reintegration back into society.

The apparent losses were reconstructed into assets. These visionary leaders were able to inspire others to join them though their own sagas of redemption. They gained the confidence for transformational leadership, in part, through their stunning transcendence over life's adversity.

[ ... ]

# Fight, Not Flight: Facing up to the Issue

We have long known that career distress can be one of the greatest sources of life stress. Being fired, for example, has been ranked as number eight among the most stressful events in life – just after death of family members, jail, and personal injury or illness. Loss of title and social role ambiguity are powerful workplace stressors as well. While the psychological and physiological symptoms of chronic stress can have a profoundly corrosive effect, many of the bromides of our therapeutic society are not appropriate stress responses for creative individuals and leaders. Stress is the perception of helplessness in dealing with serious demands. There is no such thing as objective stress existing on its own. We only stressfully respond to people, places, and events, our response dependent upon our perceptions of the adequacy of resources to deal with the stressor(s).

Thus, since stress is an interpreted phenomenon based on one's feeling of competence and strength, it is unlikely that vacations and retreats so often prescribed will yield creative individuals the sense of potency and connectedness they require to feel back in control. Research on psychological hardiness in responding to stress suggests that victims must regain control, make commitments to external events, respond to challenges, be willing to take a radical approach, and essentially become blind to their fears. Coping with stress does not mean accommodating and accepting the stress. Often victims are encouraged to reduce the *importance* of stress, through denial, avoidance, projection, and withdrawal, or else to reduce the *effects* of stress, through exercise, diet, meditation, and support groups; but it is also worth examining ways of reducing the *source* of the stress, perhaps through direct confrontation. [ ... ]

The first decision that faces the person responding to a significant career setback is the question of whether to fight or take flight – to fight against allegations, or to retreat and weather the storm. The main principle here is that the key determinant in the fight or flight question is the damage incurred or potential damage to the leader's reputation. While allegations, or the fallout from a public downfall, can be damaging in and of themselves, fighting them can exacerbate the damage by extending the accusations and making them more public. Particularly if the battles extend to the court of law as well as the court of public opinion, the collateral damage of the fight may itself prove insurmountable. Therefore it is only when the allegations themselves are sufficient to cause – or have already caused – a catastrophic career setback, *and* would block a career comeback, that they certainly need to be fought. If they are less damaging, then careful consideration needs to be taken as to their potential collateral damage and the risk that entails, versus the potential benefits of a successful fight. As Pyrrhus, king of Epirus from 319 to 272 bc found out too late in battling the Romans in 279 bc, battles, even if won, are not always worth the cost. Fights that will only result in at best a 'pyrrhic victory' are to be avoided.

However, there are times when battle is a necessity. The foundation of recovery from catastrophic career setback rests on the rock of reputation. When a person's reputation is at stake, and can be restored or preserved through battle with those who seek to destroy it, then the battle is well fought. For leaders without intact reputations, reaching the upper echelons of their field again is difficult, if not impossible. Therefore, protecting reputation with every means available becomes the first step on the road to rebuilding a tattered career, and the first lesson we can learn from leaders who have accomplished this feat. [ ... ]

# Rebuild Heroic Stature: Spread the True Nature of the Adversity

[ ... ] Great leaders acquire a heroic persona that gives them a larger than life presence. When that is removed, and the trappings, status and positional power of office are taken away, leaders risk the loss of their identities, which, in their minds and the minds of others, had become intertwined with the organizations they led. Such personalities are not comfortable merely being one of the crowd, but have a need to lead others. Great leaders achieve this by developing a personal dream that they offer as a public possession. If it is accepted, they become renowned, but if it is discarded, they suffer the loss of both a private dream and a public identity. [ ... ] When a hero stumbles, the constituents have to reconcile two images of the person – the larger-than-life presence the hero held, and his or her new fallen state. It is essential for the leader to maintain faith in his or her prior heroic status, and eliminate the confusion of current images by ensuring that others know what really happened, externalizing or isolating the reason for the downfall, providing a rationale for others to believe in his or her new mission, and building on the support of those loyal backers to reach a wider audience.

[ ... ] John Eyler, who became the chief executive of Toys 'R' Us Inc. and previously was CEO of FAO Schwarz Inc., was terminated at a large clothing retailer on Christmas Eve. He feels what was critical to his resilience was that he did not let the situation define him to others, because if it had, he says, 'I might have started to doubt myself as well.' Scholars of reputation management have long recognized the value of reputation as a corporate and a personal asset. It is built through experience, performance, and affiliations. When that reputation comes under attack, however, two conditions are necessary for the attack to pose a substantial risk to the person's reputation: the act is undesirable and has serious repercussions; and the person can be held accountable or responsible for the action that led to the attack – i.e., that the accusation is valid. While any attack is undesirable, some are not directly threatening to the person's position, and thus do not have the serious repercussions that could result in damaging the person's reputation. Certainly a reputation can be damaged through an accumulation of small hits, but most of the reputational attacks which result in downfall are of a serious nature and can be distinguished as such.

Given a serious attack on the person's reputation, and particularly one that leads to downfall, the accountability question comes into play. The occurrence of the downfall itself indicates that the person has been held accountable by the organization, but that is not necessarily the end of the story, particularly in terms of the person's ability to rebound from the setback. By virtue of the leadership position, leaders are often held to account for the misdeeds or performance of the organization, even if they were not directly responsible. Additionally, the story portrayed publicly through the media may not tell the whole story, but serve to cover-up the true reason for dismissal for the benefit of the organization or board. In such cases, it is vital for the leader to be able to make his or her own side of the story known to the wider audiences beyond friends and acquaintances, who may play gatekeeper roles in providing access to future opportunities – communities such as executive search firms or sources of funding for a new venture. The leader must be able to spread the true nature of the adversity, maintaining the confidence held by others in his or her ability to perform. New accounts that one circulates must embrace several critical elements for successful image restoration:

- Clearly denying culpability.
- Shifting responsibility for the mishap.
- Reducing the offensiveness of the act.
- Giving the appearance of reasonable behavior.
- Offering acceptable motives.

[ ... ] These principles of rebuilding reputation are just as applicable even when the downfall comes about through self-inflicted errors or misjudgments. True, there is often a sense of schadenfreude – or delight in the humiliation of those we envy – when high profile people fall from grace, the American public also has a great capacity to forgive if the individual takes an attitude of humility and apology for the mistakes he has made, and is able to provide a credible assurance that these mistakes won't reoccur. For instance, actor Hugh Grant, best known for his roles as a blundering Englishman with an awkward, goofy politeness, seemed to have secured a breakthrough with his role in the 1994 film *Four Weddings and a Funeral*. Unfortunately, he blundered his way into a reputational disaster when, in 1995, he was caught with a prostitute just before a high-profile celebrity marriage to actress Elizabeth Hurley. Rather than retreat, he signed up for the late-night talk show circuit; with self-ridicule he charmingly apologized his way back into the public's sympathy, and secured starring roles in a long string of successful films. Similarly in politics, Bill Clinton's mea culpa following the Monica Lewinsky affair reignited his presidency from the brink of disaster.

While it may have been embarrassing for Grant and Clinton to talk about their failings, this at least helped them begin the rebuilding process. In our interviews with fired CEOs, we found the greatest frustration derived from not being able to rebuild their heroic stature by telling their side of the story. [ ... ]

We have interviewed several people who had seven-figure separation agreements that were contingent on them toeing the party line on their exit. One fired CEO told us:

> The agreement that we reached was that basically I'm going to get what works out to a million dollars to put on a public face that [this is a smooth transition for the company]. You know, don't go public with the true reasons as to why I'm leaving. And since I've still got a half-million shares in the company myself, I don't want to see the stock drop, so I've got no interest in going public with the true reasons as to why I'm leaving.

In this instance, the organization placed the blame for the exit on the CEO, and restricted the CEO from coming out with his side of the story to rebuild his reputation. While in many instances this type of cover-up can harm the individual reputation of the departing CEO, especially when he or she takes the blame for things beyond his or her control or responsibility, these cover-ups may not always be detrimental to the departing leader. Indeed, the fact that the organization tries to minimize the damage to itself, can potentially have positive benefits for the CEO if it portrays the succession as a smooth, voluntary one, such that the CEO's reputation is not damaged. The damage comes, however, if the CEO is publicly sacrificed regardless of his or her culpability in the accusations leading to the ouster. In such cases, the CEO's lack of ability to challenge and set straight false accusations can lead to damaging speculation in the press that can spread the reputation damage, making it all but impossible to recover. The perception portrayed by the media can be a far stronger force than the reality behind the story, and the power of the media to mold the perceptions of the public and important gatekeepers can prove highly damaging and make recovery exponentially more difficult. As noted lawyer Alan Dershowitz wrote in his introduction to Fenton Bailey's book, *Fall From Grace: The Untold*

*Story of Michael Milken:*

> The sad truth is that today, the media has more power than ever before to create, out of whole cloth, ersatz individuals to replace the real people whose names they bear, and who make far less 'interesting' copy. This unprecedented power to malign can destroy innocent people so quickly, so thoroughly and so pervasively, that it may take an individual the better part of a lifetime to restore a savaged reputation – if at all.

# Proving Your Mettle: Regaining Trust and Credibility

Regaining the trust of others through fighting unjust accusations, bringing trusted others on board and restoring reputation are all important precursors to re-launching a career in the aftermath of catastrophic setback. Ultimately though, the stature of the leader is only fully regained when he or she takes steps towards re-launching that career – taking that next role or starting that new organization. It is when concrete action is taken to set out on a new path, that final proof of the leader's heroic stature is restored in her own mind and that of others. It is not easy. As we have discussed, there are numerous barriers facing the fallen leader on the path to recovery, not least of which are self-doubts in his or her ability to get back on top. As one fired CEO told us, 'I'd never sit here and say, "Geez, all I have to do is just replicate and do it again." The chances of doing it again are pretty small.' However, those who are successful get over this doubt about their ability to 'do it again' and set out to take action in their new roles. Even when forced from familiar arenas to totally new pastures, by industry norms or other restrictions placed upon them, some leaders remain unafraid of trying new ventures. William Shakespeare penned the immortal words, 'Some men are born great, some men achieve greatness, and some men have greatness thrust upon them.' But perhaps what marks greatness above all else is the ability to be great again – to re-achieve greatness when greatness, however initially gained, is torn from one's possession. It is the ability to bounce back from adversity – to prove your mettle once more by getting back into the game – that separates the lasting greats from the fleeting greats.

Artists and performers need their work to be shown, but others often control the display and access to their viewers. Regularly, actors hear that they are too old, musicians that they are passé, and artists that galleries will no longer present their work. Similarly, even chief executives face gatekeepers when it comes to showcasing their skills.

Tarred with the brush of controversy and competing with the ready pool of rising stars, a leader may easily be cast aside as last year's model. After setbacks, leaders have had to demonstrate that they still have the skills that have made them great. [ ... ]

The name Trump could easily have gone the way of other real estate titans of the 1980s, such as the Reichmann brothers and Robert Campeau. Donald Trump joined the family real estate business after graduating from Wharton in 1968. In his 20s he was already considered New York's paramount developer, his name whispered in the same breath as the legendary William Zeckendorf. At the age of 36, he put up his Trump Tower, the tallest, most expensive reinforced concrete structure in the city. Trump's name appeared brazenly on his building projects, but by 1990, he was caught in a real estate crunch, with a crushing $975 million debt.

A dozen years later, his net worth was reportedly back to $3.5 billion, his casinos were booming, and he was wheeling and dealing in real estate development just as before. Both he and financial analysts consider the resurgence of his Atlantic City casinos, Trump Plaza, the Taj Mahal, and Trump's Castle as the source of his comeback. In addition to the disposal of personal assets, however, he made his much-derided ego and celebrity a bankable asset. His book *Trump: The Art of the Comeback, in 1997,* was a proud follow-up to his brazen book *Trump: The Art of the Deal,* of a decade earlier. His celebrity, though, was cemented with his hit television show, *The Apprentice,* which, as NBC's blockbuster series season after season, portrayed him as the mentor for a nation of aspiring business leaders. With $11 billion in sales, his empire has continued to grow. He has acquired the GM Building and half of the Empire State Building, and built the world's tallest residential building, the 90-story Trump World Tower.

While Trump may have made a mistake in taking on so much debt in the late 1980s before the real-estate crunch, leading to pressure from his bankers, there were no accusations of breaking the law. Such self-inflicted mistakes may seem to put a person in a position from which comeback is impossible. But consider the seemingly unlikely comeback of the 1980s iconic financier, Michael Milken. Many have seen Milken's life as the essence of American myth. He was born on the Fourth of July, 1946, to a modest California family. By the mid-1980s, he was a billionaire and one of the most influential investment bankers in the world. He bypassed Wall Street snobs by building the moderate-sized, stodgy Drexel Burnham Lambert into the capital of high-yield (junk bond) debt. By 1987, the value of junk bond debt rose from almost nothing to about $200 billion. However, investigations by the Justice Department, led by Rudolph Giuliani as U.S. Attorney, led to Milken's plea of guilty to six breaches of securities law. He was fined over $1 billion and sent to prison for two years, his reputation shattered – a lifetime ban prevents his return to the securities business. [ ... ] To make matters worse, soon after leaving prison, Milken was told he had prostate cancer and had eighteen months to live.

Nonetheless, Milken is alive and well. His cancer is in remission, and he has written several cookbooks for fighting cancer through diet. He is growing a cradleto-grave learning company he founded in 1997 with his brother and with Oracle chief executive Larry Ellison. He has a consulting firm called Nextera and funds an economic institute called the Milken Institute. His CaP CURE charity, renamed the Prostrate Cancer Foundation, has raised more than $260 million and provided funding to more than 1,200 researchers around the world to develop vaccines and treatments to fight prostrate cancer as well as create genetic therapies.

Milken was unwilling to wallow in grief, to accept any of the externally imposed constraints on his desire to create and regain prominence. As he returned to demonstrate his business acumen, so did the rush of old and new partners to join him.

## Rediscovering the Heroic Mission: Clearing the Past and Charting the Future

The renowned playwright Arthur Miller once noted, 'One of the central elements in life is the driving need of people to define themselves, not merely as individuals, but also in terms of a function they can respect.' For leaders, often the only function they can respect is a place in history, endowing them with a sense of immortality – to have achieved a sense of accomplishment in obtaining a lasting legacy that will continue beyond their mortal existence. This legacy is not having their names etched on an ivy-clad university building, but most often in effecting change in society through building and leading an organization to fulfill their heroic mission. Even more challenging than the externally imposed barriers that confront exceptional people after setbacks are the self-imposed barriers due to shattered confidence or a lack of replenishment of their ideas and their energy. In many of the cases discussed earlier, this meant lowering their image of the place they left off. [ ... ] Milken had to start over from scratch. [ ... ] Trump had to rebuild [his] own wrecked empire. [ ... ]

Most leaders we came across in our research have been engaged in their quest for immortality through their pursuit of a heroic mission before they suffer their catastrophic career setback. Accordingly, it is the loss of this mission that makes the setback of catastrophic proportions in the leader's own mind, as it puts at risk their lifetime of achievement. Those who have gone through such catastrophic setback, or know well those that have, also are aware how devastating such a loss can be. On the day Steve Jobs was fired from Apple Computer Inc. In 1985, he called a couple of close friends, including Mike Murray to tell them the news. Murray's wife was on the phone when an emergency interrupt came through. She told the operator that it had better be important and then heard Jobs' voice saying simply, 'It is.' Once Murray was on the phone, Steve simply stated, 'It's all over. John [Sculley] and the board have voted me out of Apple. Goodbye Mike', and hung up the phone. Murray, aware of the significance of this loss to Jobs, was afraid of what Jobs might do to himself. Unable to get him on the phone, Murray went over to his house and sat with him for hours until he was convinced Jobs would not commit suicide that night. Later, describing how it felt to be separated from the organization he created, Jobs said, 'You've probably had somebody punch you in the stomach. It knocks the wind out of you and you can't breathe. If you relax, you can start breathing again. That's how I felt. The thing I had to do was try to relax. It was hard. But I went for a lot of long walks in the woods and didn't really talk to a lot of people.'

Once separated from their organizations – their vehicles for the journey to immortality – the biggest barrier to career recovery for leaders is often in re-conceptualizing or redirecting their heroic mission to be achieved without the benefit of their organization. While, as we have described, support systems such as friends and family play an important role in helping the victim through such times, it is the individuals themselves who need to be able to think through their future objectives.

A week after his ouster from Apple, Jobs flew to Europe, and after a few days in Paris, headed for the Tuscan hills of northern Italy. He bought a bicycle and a sleeping bag and camped out under the stars thinking through the events that led to his departure and contemplating what he would do next. From Italy, he went to Sweden and then to Russia before returning home.

He contemplated a few ideas, including hiring a political consulting firm to decide whether he had a future as a politician, but was persuaded that this was not for him. He even tried to be selected as the first civilian to fly on the Space Shuttle, but was passed over in favor of elementary schoolteacher, Christa McAuliffe, who was on the mission that resulted in the tragic Columbia disaster.

Within a few months though, Jobs was beginning to clarify what his heroic mission had been at Apple and how he could take that forward once again with a new organization. He spent a lot of time wandering around the Stanford University campus, reading in the library, immersing himself in new topics, such as biochemistry, the Bay Area's other big growth industry, including a key meeting with Nobel Prize winning biochemist, Paul Berg. This time allowed him to put together the important pieces of the puzzle of his heroic mission. As he described what thinking led to crystallizing his core mission:

I think what I'm best at is creating new, innovative products. That's what I enjoy doing. I enjoy, and I'm best working with, a small team of talented people. That's what I did with the Apple II, and that's what I did with Macintosh.

I had a piece of paper one day, and I was writing down the things that I cared the most about, that I was most proud of personally at my ten years at Apple. There's obviously the creation of the Apple II and the Macintosh. But other than that, the thing I really cared about was helping to set up the

Apple Education Foundation. I came up with this crazy idea that turned into a program called 'The Kids Can't Wait,' in which we tried to give a computer to every school in America and ended up giving one to every school in California, about 10,000 computers.

I put those two together, working with small teams of talented people to create breakthrough products and education.

As a result, Jobs gathered together a few of the people he had worked with at Apple on the Macintosh project, and convinced them of his new vision of returning to the metaphorical garage to create the next great computer, designed specifically for the higher education market. He named the company NeXT, and set off with renewed passion to create a new product and regain his stature as a visionary in the computer industry.

The resulting NeXT computer was typically Steve Jobs. It was elegantly designed, technically advanced, and ahead of any competitor in terms of performance – but incompatible with the industry standard and premium priced. So while it found a small niche in some university laboratories, it was out of reach of most students and was a commercial flop. Jobs however, was vindicated when in the ironic twist that brought Jobs back full circle, Apple purchased NeXT in 1996 for $400 million, and Jobs returned to Apple, twenty years after founding the company, becoming, a few months later, the CEO once again, free to pursue his original heroic mission at his original organization. Once there, he revived and reenergized the company with breakthrough, typically Jobs high-design products, such as the iMac, iBook, and iPod, and took the company into new emerging businesses, such as creating the world's largest music download store, iTunes.

Steve job's new mission was born out of the opportunity to step back and reflect on what was important to him from his original mission – creating 'insanely great' innovative products, working with a small team, and a passion for education. Often this opportunity to take a step back and reflect on the underlying dimensions of the past achievements and contributions leads to the creation of the revitalized mission.

In the world of communications, Michael Bloomberg has become a near overnight legend. He was fired as a Wall Street broker and went on to build one of the fastest-growing media empires in the world. His TV stations broadcast 24 hours a day to 40 countries in seven languages. His radio networks, publishing empire, on-line businesses, and wire service approach a $2 billion empire with 4,000 workers. He calls himself the David who challenged the Goliath of financial news. In 1981, Bloomberg was fired by Salomon Brothers, the elite investment bank where he had flourished for 15 years. The night he was fired, he bought his wife a sable jacket, saying, 'Job or no job, we are still players.' The next morning, he settled down to work at his customary 7 a.m. to launch Bloomberg with his $10 million of severance.

Not every accomplished creative person can drop back and start anew. In his late 20s and 30s, Alan Jay Lerner wrote or co-wrote great Broadway classics like *Brigadoon, Paint Your Wagon, Gigi, My Fair Lady,* and *Camelot.* By his 50s and 60s, he felt his creative genius suffocated by his own creations. 'The older a writer gets, the harder it is for him to write. This is not because his brain slows down; it is because his critical faculties grow more acute. If you're young, you have a sense of omnipotence. You're sure you're brilliant. Even if youth is secretly frightened, it assumes an outer assurance, and plows through whatever it is.'

It was not his public that held Lerner to punishing standards, it was he, himself. In contrast, many we have profiled take a more optimistic view, adhering to Nietzsche's maxim: 'What does not destroy me, makes me stronger.' Through heavy life demands, these exceptional people are strengthened rather than weakened by fighting back from their adversity. The ability to triumph over tragedy rests on these five foundation stones we have just outlined.

## When Bad Things Happen to Good Leaders: Thoughts for Future Heroes

It has been observed that if you want to be successful in life, you should first select great parents. Much of life is out of our control. Rising leaders, however, can anticipate that they will experience a wide array of life's adversity. The nature and timing of setbacks will never be convenient. The costs may include derailed career momentum, personal humiliation, the draining of finances, strained personal health, the shattering of personal dreams, and the suffering of innocent family and associates.

At the same time, these occasions of distress are potentially clouds with silver linings. It is through such loss that we often discover what we truly value. It is through such loss that we discover whom we can really trust. It is through such loss that we reveal new dimensions of our own character. The heroic persona is one that emerges only through triumphant battle over sadness and adversity. While many of these leaders had plenty of resources available to them when they were on top, when they fell from grace, many of those resources were also stripped from them. They had to dig deep inside themselves to find the wherewithal to rebound. Indeed, the contrast between where they were and where they fell to makes the old adage, 'the bigger they are, the harder they fall' fit perfectly to these downfalls. Consequently, their path to rebound provides a great template for those suffering setbacks across many career settings.

As new leaders see that their success spiral has just smacked into a wall, they should step back, catch their breath, and then embrace the obstacle itself as a fresh opportunity to meet unfamiliar challenges. At the same time, they must realize that their mission cannot be accomplished alone. They will need to draw upon the full reservoir of their early career experiences and relationships. Once a devastating crisis hits, it is too late to make friends, too late to establish professional credibility, and too late to build a reputation for integrity. As French field-based scientist Louis Pasteur observed, 'Chance favors the mind that's prepared.' By learning and applying the lessons of fight not flight; recruiting others into battle; rebuilding heroic stature; proving your mettle; and rediscovering heroic mission, successful career rebound is possible in almost any circumstance.

When players walk onto the most hallowed ground in the world of tennis, Centre Court, Wimbledon – the site where careers are made or broken – they are admonished by Rudyard Kipling's words, carved above the doorway leading to that manicured court:

> If you can meet with Triumph and Disaster
> And treat these two impostors just the same...

As Kipling hints, resilience is born from being able to contend with both triumph and disaster, neither succumbing to the mythological Icarus' temptation of hubris in success, nor being forever in despair when life's inevitable failures strike.

# Index